Pitied But Not Entitled

Pitied But Not Entitled

Single Mothers and the History of Welfare
1890–1935

LINDA GORDON

HARVARD UNIVERSITY PRESS
Cambridge, Massachusetts

Printed in the United States of America

This Harvard University Press paperback edition published by arrangement with The Free Press, a division of Macmillan, Inc.

First Harvard University Press paperback edition, 1995

Library of Congress Cataloging-in-Publication Data

Gordon, Linda.
   Pitied but not entitled: single mothers and the history of welfare, 1890–1935 / Linda Gordon.
      p. cm.
   Includes bibliographical references and index.
   ISBN 0-674-66982-7 (pbk.)
      1. Single mothers—Services for—United States—History.   2. Aid to families with dependent children programs—United States—History.   3. Public welfare—United States—History.   I. Title.
HV699.G67   1994
362.82'948'0973—dc20   94-18800
                                                                                         CIP

Some material in chapters 4 and 5 appeared originally in Linda Gordon, "Black and White Visions of Welfare: Women's Welfare Activisms, 1890–1945," *Journal of American History*, 788 (Sept. 1991), 559–90. Copyright Organization of American Historians, 1991.

For Allen and Rosie

Contents

Acknowledgments

Scores of historians have remarked that the new women's history, indeed the whole new social history, has been an extraordinarily collective process in which ideas are shared and developed so quickly that it is hard to say who originated them. By the time I was writing this book, that process was moving at a velocity I could not have anticipated when I began in this field twenty years ago. I experienced it sometimes as a pressure when I was completing this book, because new work which I wanted to incorporate appeared so constantly and plentifully that it threatened my ability to finish; I had to call an arbitrary halt to revising. Several just-published or forthcoming books are not in my footnotes and if I had waited a few months there would no doubt have been several more.

So my highest level of gratitude goes to a large community of social historians, social scientist, humanists, and activists working on issues related to welfare. There is no way to list those that I have learned from and there is likely to be work that has influenced me that I have mistakenly omitted from my footnotes, due to my imprecise bibliographical records.

Some colleagues and friends gave me more than their ideas—their time and specific help as well. A few to whom I am deeply grateful read and criticized all or substantial portions of this manuscript for me: Rosalyn Fraad Baxandall, Nancy Cott, Susan Friedman, Joel Handler, Allen Hunter, Alice Kessler-Harris, Judith Walzer Leavitt,

Kathryn Sklar, Landon Storrs, and Susan Traverso. Some of my graduate students worked for me as research assistants and I would be publishing this book at least two years later if not for their intelligent and forgiving labor: Ellen Baker, Lisa Brush, Jennifer Frost, Kelly Eilis Harris, Bethel Saler, and Susan Traverso. An article I wrote with Sara McLanahan provided material for chapter 2 as well as an education in demographic analysis. Scholars Mimi Abramovitz, Edward Berkowitz, Blanche Coll, John Cooper, Alan Dawley, Nancy Folbre, Nancy Fraser, Dirk Hartog, Evelyn Brooks Higginbotham, Cheryl Johnson-Odim, Molly Ladd-Taylor, Gerda Lerner, Ann Orloff, Frances Fox Piven, Anthony Platt, Theda Skocpol, Anne Firor Scott, Deborah Gray White, and Ann Withorn read and offered trenchant comments on particular chapters or related articles. Edward Berkowitz, Randall Burkett, Kenneth Casebeer, Clarke Chambers, Stan Cohen, Lela Costin, Ellen DuBois, Maureen Fitzgerald, James Grossman, Molly Ladd-Taylor, Kathryn Sklar, Vivien Hart, and Susan Ware shared valuable materials and/or ideas with me. All the contributors to my 1990 anthology, *Women, the State and Welfare*, taught me, but particularly Nancy Fraser, and I benefited from collaborating with her on several articles. Conversations of a truly midwestern sort with Jeanne Boydston, Sara Evans, Linda Kerber, Judith Walzer Leavitt, and Elaine Tyler May helped keep my perspective balanced. Jennifer Frost's unusual kindness and intelligence in the last year helped me keep errors to a minimum and precision to a maximum. Rosie Hunter spared some energy from an intense and demanding life to offer me love, support, and encouragement.

The research for this book was made possible because of generous financial help, mainly in the form of release from some teaching responsibilities. For that I am grateful to the University of Wisconsin Graduate School; the ASPE program of the Department of HHS, through the University's Institute for Research on Poverty; the Rockefeller Foundation for a residency at Bellagio; the Vilas Associates Fund of the University of Wisconsin; and most recently the Vilas Research Trust.

Joyce Seltzer was a wonderful, challenging editor and Bob Harrington, my production editor, a pleasure to work with.

Pitied But Not Entitled

Pro-welfare Cartoon, 1916

1

What Is "Welfare"?

In two generations the meaning of "welfare" has reversed itself. What once meant well-being now means ill-being. What once meant prosperity, good health, and good spirits now implies poverty, bad health, and fatalism. A word that once evoked images of pastoral contentment now connotes slums, depressed single mothers and neglected children, even crime. Today "welfare" means grudging aid to the poor, when once it referred to a vision of a good life.

This historical transformation in meaning is the theme of this book. Centuries of social and economic change contributed to the transmutation, but the definitive shifts in meaning occurred between 1890 and 1935. In that period the United States evolved a set of programs of public provision that ultimately made "welfare" a pejorative term, although the word itself did not come into common use in its current meaning until the 1960s. Its negative charge rests on a popular definition of government provision that labels only some programs "welfare" and understands others to be in a different category. "Welfare" today refers almost exclusively to a few programs of assistance to the very poor, particularly Aid to Families with Dependent Children (AFDC)* and "general relief," the last-resort program for the destitute

---

*The original program was named Aid to Dependent Children (ADC); in 1962 it was renamed Aid to Families with Dependent Children (AFDC). In this book the program is referred to by its historical name when speaking of the past, by its current name only when speaking of the present.

and desperate. "Welfare" could as accurately refer to all of a government's contributions to its citizens' well-being. These include paved streets and sidewalks; highways; public transportation systems; schools; parks; tree maintenance; policing; firefighting; public water, sewerage, and sewage treatment; garbage collection; food and drug regulation; pollution regulation; building inspection; and driver testing and licensing. In some countries many of these functions are considered to be part of the welfare state. But even if we label as welfare only those programs that provide cash to citizens, we could include home mortgage tax deductions, business expense deductions, medical expense deductions, farm subsidies, corporate subsidies, government college scholarships and loans, capital gains tax limits, Social Security old-age pensions, and Medicare. In this book the term welfare refers to the entire social service system, and "welfare" to contemporary usage.

AFDC is the best-known public assistance program, and most people who speak of welfare are referring to it, almost always with hostility. The hostility is remarkably democratic, however: "Welfare" is hated by the prosperous and the poor, by the women who receive it and by those who feel they are paying for it. It stigmatizes its recipients, not least because they are so often suspected of cheating, claiming "welfare" when they could be working or paying their own way. It humiliates its recipients by subjecting them to demeaning supervision and invasions of privacy. Yet it does nothing to move poor women and their children out of poverty and often places obstacles in the paths of women's own attempts to do so.

The modern pejorative meaning of "welfare" results from the debasing conditions of receiving public assistance, but it also causes them. The cultural meanings of the welfare system have been a powerful force in shaping it. Values and ideas about how, how much, when, and by whom the needy should be helped influence our welfare system as much as do the federal budget, eligibility criteria, and unemployment rates. Indeed, these values are in a mutually influencing relation to the federal budget: They influence it directly, while the budget, in setting national priorities, influences popular sensibility about what is important and urgent. Moreover, welfare values and ideas are not timeless or universal. They were created in recent centuries, and they are changeable. Yet the shape they acquired in the first third of this century has been extremely resistant to change. To understand why, one must know that history.

In this book I examine the history of welfare in the twentieth century with more attention to those values—to visions of what welfare should be like—than to administrative arrangements and costs. Many previous historians have discussed these well, and I am able to stand on their shoulders, so to speak.[1] Less has been written about how ideas of charity or government aid expressed fundamental social, political, and ethical values—visions of a good society.

Uncovering those past visions requires examining not only what happened but also what did not. Too often history is written in a determinist way, as if the alternatives chosen had been the only possible ones. History has long been the legitimator of kings, and the stories of losers have often been lost, erased, or distorted. Modern social historians often define their task as the search for the origins of contemporary structures, and that search for evidence is more likely to roll along the well-trod trail of the victors than the overgrown path of the losers.[2] Defeated alternatives illuminate the choices historical actors made—in this case the choices among welfare designs—and the way their options looked to them then, rather than in hindsight. Losing proposals illuminate victorious ones. Just as one needs to back up to look at most large paintings, so one needs some distance to recognize what is being taken for granted. For example, assumptions that virtually all women would marry, remain domestic, and be supported by their husbands imbued virtually all our welfare programs; yet some welfare advocates knew even in the 1930s that these assumptions were wrong and offered different proposals. Although there was little political possibility that they could have been enacted, they reveal the assumptions embedded in what was.

The Social Security Act of 1935, the central legislation of the U.S. welfare state, was formed through a process of rejecting some alternatives and compromising over others. At the beginning of Franklin Roosevelt's administration in 1933, most welfare advocates expected to get federal health insurance and an integrated, centrally controlled system of public assistance. We can understand the contributions and limitations of the Social Security Act much better by regarding it as a proposal among others, seeing how it was shaped within a field of options, and noticing what and whom it excluded as well as what and whom it included.

Thinking about past alternatives reminds us not only that the particular shape of our welfare state was not inevitable but may expand our sense of today's range of possibilities. The historical record shows that the choices are not simply more or less welfare spending, but rather that the shape and spirit of public provision matter very much to its impact. The constriction of possibility in this time of conservatism and economic depression blocks our creative vision and chokes off hope.

=

Although today AFDC is the essence of the so-called welfare system, it was originally regarded as an insignificant small program within the Social Security Act, the 1935 law that is the source of virtually all federal social provision. Social Security was a major achievement in itself and a historic transformation in the role of the federal government. One historian has called the New Deal expansion of the federal government a "third American revolution;"[3] another described its shift in economic philosophy as "a general attack upon the doctrines of laissez-faire individualism. . . . No longer were poverty and unemployment to be condoned as the fruits of improvidence."[4] Reformers fought an arduous and protracted campaign for this legislation and, even during the depression, had to mobilize against substantial conservative opposition to get it through Congress. Millions of Americans were protected from impoverishment through its provisions, and millions more, while they remained in poverty, were at least kept alive. AFDC in particular rendered critical support to women, support that contributed to safety and self-respect for millions.

Social Security is an omnibus act, and rather than choose among the various welfare models available, it incorporated them all. Its eleven titles created nine different programs. The one today called "Social Security" is Old-Age Insurance (OAI), which provides pensions to many but not all workers. This plus unemployment compensation are generically social insurance programs, so-called mainly because they are funded by special earmarked taxes on employees and employers. Titles V and VI of Social Security provided grants to the states for certain public health, today prominently including aid to the disabled. The Social Security public assistance programs, the only ones today called "welfare," are Title I (Old-Age Assistance, OAA, aid to the indigent elderly who cannot get OAI), Title IV (AFDC, the largest Social Security program), and Title X (Aid to the Blind). The Social Security Act created the contemporary meaning of "welfare" by setting up a stratified system of provision in which the social insurance programs were superior both in payments and in reputation, while public assistance was inferior—not just comparatively second-rate but deeply stigmatized. Public assistance is what Americans today call "welfare"; recipients of the good programs are never said to be "on welfare." And while most people hate "welfare," they pay the utmost respect to Old-Age Insurance.

There were three stages in the stratification of the welfare system. First, in 1935, Social Security excluded the most needy groups from all its programs, even the inferior ones. These exclusions were deliberate and mainly racially motivated, as Congress was then controlled by wealthy southern Democrats who were determined to block the possibility of a welfare system allowing blacks freedom to reject extremely low-wage and exploitive jobs as agricultural laborers and domestic servants. Then some of these groups—minorities, the very poor, out-of-wedlock mothers, for example—won inclusion, by a series of amendments and court cases stretching from 1939 through the 1970s. They were included, however, not in social insurance but mainly in public assistance programs, which by then had become even stingier and more dishonorable than they had been originally. Finally, in 1974, OAA and Aid to the Blind and the Disabled were folded into the social insurance system under the Supplemental Security Income program. This left *only* AFDC as a maligned "welfare" program. Historians seem to share in this perspective: Most studies of Social Security concentrate almost entirely on its old-age and unemployment insurance sections and neglect AFDC.

The stratification within Social Security programs has become so naturalized that many think of it as somehow inevitable. The superior programs, such as Old-Age Insurance, are regarded as contributory because beneficiaries pay taxes earmarked for them. But the "contributions" to old-age and unemployment insurance do not really fund those programs. What people get back is not proportional to what they put in, and the money paid in is used as a part of general revenues. Also, many workers are not allowed to pay these honorable, earmarked taxes. And there are no free rides: Everyone contributes to all social services through taxes, sales and gas and real estate as well as income. When we do not pay these taxes directly, we pay them indirectly, through the higher prices charged by manufacturers and landlords and other businessmen to make up for the taxes they pay.

In general Social Security helped most those who needed help least. And the very same people who got public pensions and unemployment compensation were most likely also to obtain private pensions, sick leave, and health insurance during the ensuing decades. Meanwhile the very poor sank relatively lower. Often able to improve their living conditions and income during good economic times, they rarely attained security and steadily lost ground in relation to those who received more. One can evaluate Social Security as half full or half empty: It helped many working- and middle-class men and their families rise to a more stable and prosperous standard of living; it aggravated the relative poverty and deprivation of many women and agricultural workers, minorities in particular. Certainly it deepened inequality among working people and their families, which in turn worsened the stigmatization and despair of some of the very poor. Those who received "nonwelfare" did well; those who received "welfare" did badly. Today the "welfare" class is what many call the "underclass."

The perverse tendency of our welfare system to deepen inequality has been particularly pronounced in the case of AFDC. The stigmas of "welfare" and of single motherhood intersect; hostility to the poor and hostility to deviant family forms reinforce each other. The resentment undercuts political support for the program, and benefits fall farther and farther behind inflation. The resulting immiseration makes poor single mothers even more needy and less politically attractive. The economic downturn of the last decade has deepened both the poverty and the resentment, and created the impression that we are experiencing a new, unprecedented, and primarily minority social problem.

But single motherhood is not new, although it has grown. Single mothers—by which I mean all mothers alone with children, whether divorced, separated, widowed, or never married—have long been over-represented among the poor. There were always widows, absconding husbands, unmarried mothers. Poverty has long been "feminized," particularly because women alone with children have been exceptionally poor. But in many traditional agricultural societies, single mothers had kinship and community support. Patriarchal communities controlled not only women but men too, and husbands were less likely to get away with desertion, although marriages were more often dissolved by death. Since most families were economic enterprises in which all members participated, and in which workplace and home were usually the same, women had access to productive labor while they raised children. The loss of a husband might lead to a widow's taking over his work. The modern problem of single motherhood was defined within the last one hundred years, in the context of the decline of this patriarchal family and community system. Instead, as more men earned their living through wage labor, the loss of a husband's income left a wife without support. Wage-laboring men more often worked outside their homes, alienating them from domestic life and attenuating father-child bonds. Large cities and geographical mobility made it easier for fathers to leave their children and wives, boyfriends to refuse to marry, while migration left single mothers more often distant from kinfolk on whom they previously depended. As a result single motherhood has been a central concern for welfare designers since the 1880s.

Worry about single mothers and their children was a major influence on the development of modern welfare policy. Reformers designed programs intended not only to help lone mothers raise their children but also to prevent single motherhood by providing incentives for proper and stable families. The norms used in evaluating families involved, of course, deeply held values regarding appropriate male and female responsibilities. In the last century, the dominant family standard included a breadwinner husband/father and an economically dependent, domestic wife/mother. Although this standard was never an accurate description of most American families, it nevertheless guided most welfare designs. Aid to unemployed men, for example, aimed to preserve the male breadwinner status and to keep wives and children at home. Aid to single mothers aimed to prevent its recipients from being too comfortable on their own.

These family norms contributed to the stratification of welfare and to making programs for women inferior to programs for men. Provisions for men, such as workers' compensation, unemployment compensation, and retirement pensions, were more generous and dignified in design than ADC, the quintessential program for women. One might ask why women didn't get a program like Old-Age Insurance—respectable, reliable, nonstigmatizing, and financially adequate. Many feminists have understandably assumed that women were slotted into inferior programs because of "patriarchy" and men's monopoly on state power. But the fact is that ADC was designed by women and indeed by feminist women, champions of child welfare. One of the ironies of welfare state development is that in the United States, where women exerted more influence on domestic social policy than in most other countries, female welfare clients (and children) were treated worse than in most other countries.

To explain this apparent paradox we need to consider the legacy of feminism. The feminists who dreamed up and promoted welfare programs in the early twentieth century were neither like contemporary feminists nor identical among themselves. In fact, in labeling them feminists I am making a historical claim with which some disagree. Some would circumscribe the term to refer only to those who struggled primarily for sex equality.[5] I have been more comfortable with a broader definition: Feminism is a political perspective that considers women unjustly subordinated, finds that oppression to be humanly changeable, and strategizes for women's advancement. This definition takes in, for example, women and men who did not believe in total sex equality, believed women better off in a secondary role in politics and the market, but who agitated for greater respect and power for women in their proper sphere. This definition, in fact, recognizes feminism as a historically and contextually changing impulse with a core of continuity and expects nineteenth-century feminists to think differently than late-twentieth-century ones, urban working-class feminists to think differently than prosperous clubwomen. The breadth of this definition allows us to understand a wide variety of advocacy for women as part of a feminist legacy and heads off unproductive debates about "true" or "real" feminism.[6] The definition thus includes many who did not call themselves feminists and who may never have heard the term, which was invented only in this century. But this is how language works—we frequently use neologisms to illuminate the past. With a historical understanding of feminism as a living, changing legacy, we will be able to see that the design of AFDC is not so much a paradox as a legacy of historical change and complexity.

=

Historian Michael Ignatieff has characterized welfare policy in modern states in terms of the "needs of strangers."[7] This phrase can remind us that aid and mutual aid are harder to organize and justify among strangers than among intimates. Calamities (earthquakes, riots, toxic spills) may stimulate some to offer shelter, food, or even

money to perfect strangers. But these acts of kindness are more likely when the strangers are tangible, visible, or in some way vividly
represented. When they are distant, and above all when their misfortune is long-term or chronic, individual charity is inadequate. This
was a major lesson of the Great Depression. And in modern society
almost everyone is a distant stranger and by far their greater needs
are chronic, yet mutual aid is not less necessary. An African proverb
tells us that it takes a village to raise a child. We no longer have many
villages in the United States, but parents cannot manage to raise children in modern societies without substantial help from others. In villages and families the bases for giving or asking for help seem transparent, "natural," explanations unneeded. We help because family
members and neighbors are part of our responsibility and equally because we ourselves may need help from them. Part of the very definition of a stranger is that we have no responsibility for this person.

The welfare state arises as a means of organizing mutual aid among
strangers. It is based on a division of labor. I am employed full-time
and have no leisure to volunteer, say, in a homeless shelter, yet I would
like the homeless to receive homes, steady incomes, health, and counseling if they need it. I write checks to charities and "causes." But I
could never give to everything I think worthwhile, and charitable
fund-raising is inefficient. So it is fine that a portion of my income is
taxed and used for such purposes. For this reason mutual aid among
strangers must be somewhat redistributive. When I give money to my
daughter I do not feel that I am really giving it away, alienating it. It
stays or will return. When I give money through taxes I imagine that it
leaves me forever. This is not exactly true, because I might become
homeless or, more likely, will need help in old age, when my money
may come back to me. And like most middle-class Americans I probably get back from the government more than I pay to the poor. But the
structure of the system disguises this, as I don't get checks from the
government, only tax exemptions and services. And my vote only marginally influences what my tax money will be used for. These are the
experiences of helping strangers in today's welfare system.

And yet that very welfare system constructs our sense of a unidi-
rectional transfer of resources. Ironically, in a more generous welfare
system, those who are not poor and pay high taxes would get more.[8]
Suppose that public work programs drastically reduced unemployment, with a resulting big decline in the despair that creates violence

and drug taking. Suppose that adequate support for poor parents and their children allowed them to move out of segregated slums into neighborhoods where their children grew up with safety and stability, their parents with economic security and the better mood it produces. Suppose that federal funding for education lowered public-school class size to levels at which all children could learn enough to compete for good jobs. In such a situation the middle class would get safety from violence and robbery, a decline in AIDS and other contagious diseases, and the beautification of inner cities. The fact is that a puny welfare system gives no one what they want and thus makes itself universally unpopular.

Even those who might see the argument for a big welfare system in principle will run into major obstacles in imagining how to achieve it. Since its fundamental premise is that we must aid strangers, the question arises: Who is to determine what are the needs of strangers? They need food, but how much and of what quality? They need shelter and transportation and education, but at what expense? And do they need medical care or therapy, not to mention love and friendship? Can it work to let the needy define what they need? Probably not, but who is to say what another person needs? In families or small villages it may be possible to see needs or to negotiate them; not so in large cities.

What, then, is the justification for welfare claims in a complex society with an impersonal state? Historically activists and policy makers have advanced three types of claims: needs, earnings, and rights.[9] Each type has thrived in a different arena. Within families, for example, needs claims dominate. Asked why they care for children or aged parents, most people might have no simple answer, since the obligation just is, but the basis on which they decide to offer help is need. Family obligations often appear "natural," although they have actually shifted rather rapidly over time as needs have changed. For example, today adults in the United States may, if they choose, accept no responsibility for grown siblings or parents. Aged parents are cared for when they need it, and care for children is withdrawn when they no longer need it. In the economic arena, by contrast, need is rarely an important principle; for example, workers do not get higher wages because of greater need. Here the rationale is earning, return for service. Earning wages has also come to seem natural, inevitable, self-evident, although just a few centuries ago it appeared as illegitimate to the majority. Here too ideas have shifted radically: A century ago men were expected to work ten to twelve hours, six days a week, to "earn" a living wage; today in the United States more of them expect to "earn" it in forty hours a week. When citizens seek to make claims on government, they often speak of rights, appealing to existing law or to what they argue should be law; some of these claims become rights by consensus even without statute or constitutional law. This is quite a different sort of claim from those customary in family or market. One has neither "earned" nor "needed" the right to vote; one is not supposed to have more votes than others because of greater need or greater contribution. We look upon some rights as owed to all citizens, others as owed to all human beings.

Claims to welfare have been justified on all three bases, and the choice of different claims has had a great deal of historical consequence. Not all the claims are equal—rights have usually been stronger than earnings, while earnings are stronger than needs. Workers have been denied earned pensions because their employers moved elsewhere or could not afford the pension while maintaining profitability—ultimately because property ownership as a right trumps earnings or contributions as a claim. And in the structure of welfare in the United States, rights-based provision is usually superior—more generous, less intrusive, more respected. Moreover, these varying justifications have gendered histories: Needs have often been feminine, while earnings and rights, speaking of power in the economy and state, have more often been masculine.

The stratification of the U.S. welfare system can be described in terms of these varying types of claims: The better welfare strata, like old-age and unemployment insurance, are rights- and earnings- or contribution-based; the worse, like AFDC, are only needs-based. Then all sorts of other distinctions can be mapped onto this stratification: The better welfare programs are federal, just as the federal Constitution and courts are the guarantors of rights, while the inferior programs are state (or even local). The better programs disproportionately serve whites, the inferior programs disproportionately minorities. The better programs benefit men more than women, adults more than children. The better programs respect a recipient's privacy, while the inferior ones bring with them supervision. Since these inequalities are translated into different justifications, it no longer appears unfair that, say, poor single mothers and their children receive less, and receive it less securely, than well-to-do elderly women, or that young men who have never been able to get a job don't get unemployment compensation while laid-off professionals with money in the bank and a better chance at another job do. Nor does it appear discriminatory that old-age insurance recipients take their pensions as rights while AFDC recipients are expected to be grateful and to accept conditions on their stipends humbly. Indeed the stratification steadily increases, setting up a spiral: The worse the inferior programs are, the more they stigmatize their recipients. The better welfare programs appear as entitlements; the worse appear as charity.

While there are many causes for these distinctions, this book concentrates on their gendered roots. That focus does not mean that it is a study of women and the welfare system. Even in programs aimed at men, ideas and visions about proper family life and gender relations were salient. It is a commonplace that a key function of a welfare state is to replace *wages* lost through illness, disability, unemployment, or death. A more inclusive generalization is that welfare programs were intended to replace and defend the *family wage,* by which is meant the wage that should (theoretically) allow a husband to earn enough to support a nonemployed wife and children. Without a family wage, it seemed to welfare advocates of the 1930s, several essential principles of the social order would come unraveled; for example, men might lose their authority in families and households—and possibly, as a result, in the nation; women would be drawn into public employment and, as a result, greater public activity and independence; women's time and energy for domestic labor would diminish; women would have an incentive to lower their fertility and some of the constraints on their sexual activity would be lost.

These unwanted developments are, of course, exactly what transpired in this century. Few figures symbolize these changes as vividly as do single mothers. Their place in any modern society tells us about the status of women—their access to jobs and education, their vulnerability to violence, for example—about the degree of community, and about the actual (as opposed to rhetorical) commitment of a welfare state to children.

Why did the welfare system fail to support the family wage? The major reason was dramatic change in the economy and society that drew masses of women, including mothers, into the paid labor force, undercut the bases of women's subordination, and threw relations between the sexes into a period of contestation and transformation. Like most legislation, that of 1935 was backward looking—it defined the problems it hoped to solve on the basis of experience—and failed to predict new circumstances. But the failure of Social Security to achieve its family-stabilizing goals also derived from internal contradictions in the legislation, which are explicable from an examination of its gendered history. This requires looking at male as well as female interests, feminist as well as antifeminist perspectives, on welfare. It does not imply that relations between the sexes were necessarily more influential on welfare than on class or race relations. It is, rather, a way of scouting an unexplored trail in welfare history.

Moreover, when we ask gendered questions of welfare history we also see another perspective on the difficulties of helping strangers. It was easier to help and, perhaps, to claim help in small villages, but the defining of needs was usually extremely rigid and intolerant of individual freedom. In most of the world the standards were patriarchal. Fathers, male heads of families, controlled not only wives and daughters but junior men in their families. Patriarchs also exercised power in social units larger than families. Not only were women subordinated but so were children and even grown sons. For better or worse, few people in the United States could tolerate a return to that kind of unfree, nosy, rigid and hierarchical community. Few young people would want their parents to arrange their marriages or to dictate their occupations. Few women will accept a husband's right to "chastise" them, and most men agree. While old people had certain privileges in patriarchal systems, it is doubtful that a majority of them would elect to try to exercise that kind of control over a younger generation. Everyone wants individual freedom. The price of that is that we must help strangers as well as friends. Welfare is the only name we have yet developed for that process, and we need to know its history.

Single Mother, Early Twentieth Century

2

Single Mothers

The Facts and the Social Problem

In the last four decades the numbers of single mothers have increased so much that many incorrectly assume they represent a
new phenomenon. In fact, single motherhood has been defined as a
social problem for at least a century. Both actual single mothers and
reformers' perceptions of them influenced our welfare system.

Who were the single mothers? Here are some glimpses, in the
words of contemporary social workers:

> You live in three rooms in Essex street [on New York City's Lower East
> Side, 1909]. . . . There is a boarder who helps out with the rent. . . . You
> only have one bed. The boarder must have it. The three older children
> slept on a mattress on the floor after she brought them in from the street
> at eleven o'clock. The baby who is only eight months old, slept with you
> on the fire escape, and you stayed awake half the night for fear you
> might lose your hold on him and he might fall. Widowhood is a matter
> of some months with you. . . . Nellie [an older daughter, relied on for
> help] is not as tractable as she used to be when you were working at
> home. . . . Willie has a running nose and they tell you at the day nursery
> that if it is not better to-day you will have to keep him home. . . . That
> means that Nellie will have to stay away from school and take care of
> him. You are only thirty-six years old, but you look forty-nine.[1]
>
> The mother was sixteen and the father twenty-two at marriage [in
> Chicago, 1910]. . . . The father died three years ago, and the mother is a

miserable, incompetent, degraded woman, ill most of the time, without any moral standards, who, although she has been a widow for three years, has a child thirteen months old. She is now living with five children in two rooms in an old shed which an uncle owns and in which he keeps vegetables. The whole place is squalid and wretched. During one illness the boy begged. He had one leg cut off by a train several years ago.[2]

A woman was at service [as a maid], with her baby in a kind family twenty miles out of Boston [1901], when one of the woman's friends arranged a marriage with the father of her child, and she went to live with him. Soon after the marriage the man lost his work . . . he drank, and twice the wife fled to a temporary home to escape starvation and his beatings. Once she went back of her own accord; the second time he came for her. . . . After this he did fairly well for a while, then deserted, sailing for Ireland, where he has remained, leaving the wife with a boy of three and a girl one year old. [Boston's Associated Charities approached the former employer,] who replied she would employ the woman again with one child but not with two. [But] the mother would not be separated from either of her little ones.[3]

Rather than asking for agency help [in Minneapolis, 1920s], Mrs. Pernet turned to those who lived nearby when her husband, not yet fifty, lay dying of heart trouble. . . . She had written a letter explaining her dilemma and carried it door-to-door [asking for donations]. . . . [Agency investigation revealed that] The landlord dismissed the woman as a careless mother, a liar, and a thief; the husband was no good either—a dishonest "boozer" . . . [He was] quarrelsome and had refused to go to the hospital at the same time he protested that he had "lost interest in his home" because his wife failed to prepare meals and neglected the children. Mrs. Pernet furthermore showed "no motherly affection." . . . the Humane Society called [Associated Charities] saying that Mrs. Pernet had given the infant away . . . medical examination . . . revealed the child had syphilis.[4]

These vignettes were written about single mothers by observers from another class and with particular interests—charity workers, social workers, those who felt responsible to help, to reform, to discipline. They did not hesitate to make moral—or often glaringly moralistic[5]—judgments based on inadequate information and knowledge of the context.

"Moralistic" has a variety of meanings: Preachy, rigid, inflexible, ignoring the actual universe of choice available to the one who is criticized. In actual usage "moralistic" is often applied, of course, to moral views to which the speaker is opposed. Indeed the very question of what discourse is moral and what moralistic is at issue in the current politicized discussion of single motherhood. Few would deny that ethical judgments may be appropriate, but the moralistic register has often produced a discourse that reverberates with victim blaming.

The facts about single motherhood in the early twentieth century often differ from its highly moralistic interpretations by reformers. This distinction is sometimes merely one between present and past: The "facts" are what contemporary scholars say, while the moralistic discourse is what those of the past said. Changing consciousness about social problems influences what "facts" are collected. Just what the "facts" are is much contested; even statistical information is structured by the questions we ask, which in turn are shaped by values and anxieties. For example: Most factual accounts of single motherhood in the past few decades have prominently featured race differences; these reflect the contemporary consciousness that black single motherhood is a particularly acute problem. In studies of single motherhood before about 1930, experts did not examine black-white differences. So today, when scholars produce racially differentiated facts about, say, 1900, they are applying a contemporary consciousness that black family patterns are particularly problematic that did not exist then.

Everything about single motherhood is charged with the emotional and moral intensities that saturate social phenomena concerned with sex, reproduction, and family. Everything we learn about single mothers reaches us through the filter of the contemporary understanding of the problem, defined variably as teenage pregnancy, out-of-wedlock childbirth, female-headed households, and the "underclass." Still we can resist and compensate for it. We can try to avoid sliding into the interpretative ruts created by today's discourse by paying close attention to the historical context.

Raising Children Alone

While single motherhood increased substantially in the last few decades, there is no evidence of similar change between 1890 and 1960.[6] Looking at the situation from the point of view of children, in 1900, 9 percent of children lived with just one parent; in 1960 this figure was 9.1 percent—not a great deal of change.[7] To express this another way, in 1900, 86 percent of children lived with two parents, in 1960, 87 percent. The great majority of single-parent children lived with mothers.[8] In 1930, 8.4 percent of families with children under twenty one were headed by single mothers. Figured in terms of individuals, the numbers were almost the same: 8.5 percent of the population, or 10.5 million people, lived in female-headed households.

These estimates are probably low because they tell us only about single mothers at the moment when the census was taken. The proportion of women who were single mothers for some period during their lives was much higher. Moreover the 1930 and 1940 figures only include households headed by women, and many single mothers lived in other people's households—as, for example, with their parents, siblings, or with nonrelatives who took in boarders.[9] In 1900, 20 percent of single parents lived as subfamilies in households headed by others.[10]

Unfortunately many commentators confuse single motherhood with female-headed households. This is a serious mistake not only because it results in underestimates of single motherhood but also because it leads to misunderstandings of the living conditions and experience of single mothers. The term "female-headed household" first became popular in the 1970s. The notion that households had "heads," normatively male, had of course been a basic organizing principle of all censuses from the first in 1790, and of income tax from its beginnings in 1913.[11] As women gained in equality the general phrase "head of household" was used less frequently, and the census abandoned it in 1980. Thus today "female-headed household" is used without a common opposite phrase; we do not normally call a two-parent household either male-headed (or "double headed"!).

Today's reliance on the term "female-headed household" calls our attention to a gradual increase, starting in the late nineteenth century, not of single motherhood per se but of female-headed households in particular, and to another starting in the 1960s. This increase is important to social policy because single mothers who live in other people's families are less visible and possibly less economically and socially needy than those who head their own households. The multiplication of female-headed households derived from several new social and economic factors in industrial cities. Many women were far from relatives who might have taken them in, because they were immigrants from abroad or migrants from the countryside. Many urban families lived in extremely crowded conditions and on bare subsistence budgets, making it impossible for them to take in single-mother subfamilies. In addition the new aspirations nurtured in industrial society, including hopes of mobility and greater female independence, and the decline of patriarchal family power stimulated more women to want to head their own households. The result may have been greater impoverishment and neglect of children; it surely made poverty and child neglect more evident in the central-city slums.

Single motherhood was not, of course, evenly distributed among all groups in all regions. In the early twentieth century, cities seemed to produce more single motherhood, and the cities were growing rapidly. By 1930 only 22 percent of Americans lived on farms. Single mothers gravitated to cities, where there was more work for women. While black Americans had higher overall rates of single motherhood—in 1900, 14 percent of black children lived with single mothers[12]—city living had a particularly strong tendency to increase black single motherhood. Among whites the urban-rural difference was 1.4 percent, but among blacks it was nearly 20 percent: That is, 14 percent of rural black children lived with single mothers, and 23 percent of urban black children did so.

"Single" or "lone" or "solo" mother is itself a recent aggregate term.[13] In the early twentieth century, women alone with children were referred to more specifically as widows, deserted women, unmarried, "illegitimate" mothers, and, very occasionally, divorced women. These categories have the advantage that they tell us something about the histories of these women; if we look at each group separately we can learn something about the causes of single motherhood.

From the late nineteenth century until the 1930s, in all classes, races, and ethnic groups, most single mothers were widows.[14] In 1900, 77 percent of single mothers heading households were widows.[15] There were more widows with young children then because mortality rates among the young were much higher. There were many more (male) widowers too, but they were much less likely to become single parents because they rarely cared for their children when their wives died; usually widowers either remarried quickly or found a female relative to take charge of the children. By the 1930s the proportion of widows among single mothers had fallen to 55 percent or less.[16]

The next largest group of single mothers were married women whose husbands were absent—16 percent of the single mothers in 1900. Today we would call these "separated" women; at the turn of the century they were more likely to be labeled "deserted." To understand this then-common notion of desertion, we must recall the nineteenth-century family and gender norms dominant in the United States, which considered marriage as eternal and women as inevitably the weaker sex. Very few Americans at that time approved of breaking a marriage covenant: To do so was to commit a sin. In such sinful behavior there was a sinner and a sinned against; marital separation was rarely conceived of as mutual, a concept that expresses a greater acceptance, characteristic of the late twentieth century, of separation as an honorable alternative and of marriage as a human, not a divine, institution.[17] Moreover, most people agreed that women, because of their economic dependence on men and their social and political subordination, were usually the victims of marital breakup. Thus the term "desertion" might describe either the particular circumstances of a marital separation—that is, a man's unilateral decision to walk out—or it might describe the cultural understanding of the mother's helplessness, particularly in relation to the difficult task of simultaneously earning and caring for her children. Occasionally women left their husbands, but since mothers virtually always took their children with them if they left, these actions were not called desertions.

There was a considerable increase in "desertion" in the large cities of the United States at the turn of the century, for reasons of both opportunity and incentive.[18] The combination of urban anonymity and geographical mobility meant that men could "disappear" in a way that was impossible in small-town and agrarian communities. The situation of the working class was new, and most cities were overwhelmingly populated by some kind of migrants, either foreign or domestic. These migrants were mainly former farmers or peasants, accustomed to a family economy and taken aback by the wage-labor system that placed the responsibility for supporting an entire family exclusively on the male head.[19] A new set of norms concerning the responsibilities of men and women meant that in addition to creating deprivation for whole families, unemployment, underemployment, and low wages, appeared as male failure. Since in fact the industrial economy often rendered individuals helpless in the face of economic recessions and resultant unemployment, men often found their family responsibilities extremely stressful. In an agricultural economy a large family was an economic advantage; in an industrial economy "dependents," as their label implies, were economically disadvantageous. In addition, the decline of patriarchal work patterns, in which production was done at home and children worked alongside their parents, weakened father-child attachments. Mother-child bonds, by contrast, intensified, in response not only to men's defection from active parenting but also to the cultural romanticization of motherhood. All these influences conditioned men's desertions.

Very few of the deserted wives of the early twentieth century got legal divorces. Many did not approve of divorce, and even if they had they would have had a hard time getting one, because the legal grounds were limited and the financial costs substantial. As late as 1930 only 1.3 percent of single mothers were divorced.[20] The fact that most separated women could not legally remarry meant that they had to do without male support, which deepened their poverty.

Unmarried single motherhood, while growing slightly, remained infrequent in the early twentieth century. In 1900, 4.6 percent of children in female-headed households were "illegitimate," to use the parlance of the day; in 1938 it was 3.8 percent.[21] (Unwed motherhood was higher in rural areas—5.8 percent.) The biggest race difference appeared here: 11 percent of black children had unmarried mothers compared to 3 percent of white. Although we know that whites were extremely embarrassed about "illegitimate" children and regularly lied to cover up their existence, while blacks were evidently more accepting, this distortion is insufficient to eliminate the entire race difference, which points to a distinct family pattern among African Americans.

Two fundamentally different conditions were merged in the early-twentieth-century concept of illegitimacy. One was that of never-married women, often girls, who had become pregnant and had neither an abortion nor a marriage. An entirely different situation involved older women, often married and separated, who often had some legitimate children. Because divorce was unattainable and/or unacceptable for most, their subsequent relationships with men were "illicit," outside marriage. Yet these relationships were common, especially among poor women who desperately needed male economic help to get by and support their children. Many such unmarried couples lived together as husband and wife. Their offspring were technically illegitimate, although they might well live with both parents. These "illegitimate" mothers were not actually single mothers. Such couples often lied about their marital status to census takers and other surveyors because of the moral stigma attached to their situations.[22]

Single mothers were more likely than mothers in two-parent families to be employed outside their homes.[23] In Philadelphia in 1918–19, 22 percent of working mothers were widows, 13 percent were deserted, 11 percent were not supported by their husbands, 14 percent had husbands who were ill, and 29 percent had husbands who simply couldn't earn enough to support the family; only 11 percent were married with supporting husbands.[24] In 1930 nationally, an estimated 11.7 percent of all married women were employed and 34 percent of widows.[25]

From both women's and children's perspectives, the economics of single motherhood created terrible paradoxes: Those women with the heaviest domestic workloads were those most likely to be employed. Those with the youngest children were most likely to be employed. Those who needed money the most tended to earn the least. In the first decade of this century, when eight dollars a week was considered a living wage for one, most employed single mothers earned from two to four dollars a week. Single mothers tended to earn less because they were more restricted in the kinds of jobs they could take. One study of nine large cities found that 48 percent took low-wage night jobs, most often cleaning office buildings, in order to have time for their children during the day, with the result that they got little sleep and were in poor health.[26] Others took homework jobs, earning piece rates for hand sewing, the lowest wages available. These women not only had the worst working conditions, grinding themselves through night and day, depriving themselves of sleep, but also frequently pressured their own children into long hours of work to ensure the food and rent money. Most single mothers worked either in agriculture or as domestic servants. Between 1900 and 1930 there was some upward job mobility for white single mothers but virtually none for blacks; in 1900, 97 percent of black single mothers worked on the land or in domestic service, and by 1930 this proportion remained at 93 percent.[27]

Single mothers' employment created paradoxical effects. Those who were most successful at earning to support themselves and their children might be least successful at parenting, because the best jobs required leaving one's children during the day; those whose employment would least damage their children—for example, mothers with child care help from relatives—were least likely to take employment because they often got economic help. Indeed the essence of single motherhood was a vicious circle from the perspective of children's needs: Those who most needed parenting were most likely to be left alone.

One reason single mothers did so much night and homework was the absence of child care facilities. While there had been some development of day nurseries in the late nineteenth century, it was followed by an early-twentieth-century retreat, even an attack on such institutions as undermining proper family life. There were exceptions, particularly among Catholics and African Americans.[28] But day care did not gain popularity among the white Protestant charity and social work establishment.[29] In 1905 only 206 day nurseries were counted throughout the United States. Poor mothers used them only as a last resort. The fact that the providers of this care emphasized moral uplift toward the children no doubt seemed insulting and possibly threatening to poor mothers.[30] In addition, this kind of impersonal child care seemed strange to most mothers.

The organized child care option most used by single mothers was long-term placement in institutions or foster care. Only these arrangements provided the long hours of care that working mothers required for their children. Because orphanages and foster care had existed in traditional societies, they seemed less alien than day nurseries. Many single mothers were separated from their children because poverty and long working hours persuaded them to arrange voluntary placements in what they considered to be their children's interest; others had their children forcibly removed because of allegations of neglect; many others lived in fear of these outcomes.[31] A 1912 Massachusetts study found that 57 percent of children not living with their widowed mothers had been separated only because of the mothers' inability to support them.[32] The majority of children in "orphanages" were actually not orphans, but children whose mothers could not support them.[33]

These long-term placements created dangers. Once having given up their children, many parents—precisely because they were poor and often foreign-born or nonwhite—found that they could have trouble getting their children returned. Through the "placing out" system, as foster care was then called, institutions often literally "lost" children. Especially in New York City, reformers in the late ninetieth century operated a system of placing out poor and neglected children in the West, expecting these to be permanent placements, and many poor parents claimed that their children were literally kidnapped by the zealous "child savers." Moreover, unsupported children might be placed into terrible conditions. Institutions were usually cold, rigid, punitive, and unhealthy; placements in individual homes were often exploitative, as many foster "parents" took children because they were seeking household, farm, or small-business labor power. Asylums were also physically dangerous: Infectious diseases would sweep through an institution, killing many of the youngest. In 1890 a death rate of 97 percent per year for children under three was not uncommon, partly because many children were in very poor health when they arrived.[34]

As children grew older, they were less often placed out and more often sent to work; for this reason the discussion of single motherhood engaged those concerned about child labor as well. Single mothers relied on older children's earnings if they could. One study estimated that 7 percent of daughters and 18 percent of sons aged six to fourteen worked, but this greatly underestimated the girls' contribution because the figures did not include girls who took live-in domestic positions or did the housework so that their mothers could take employment. The rate of employment for the children of single mothers was two to three times higher than that for children living with two parents. Above age fourteen, child labor escalated dramatically.[35]

Creating the Single Mother Problem

While single mothers had been the objects of charity and moral reform for centuries, in the first two decades of this century reformers created an alarm that single motherhood was a major social problem. In an agitation that continued for three decades, subsiding somewhat in the 1920s, they convinced many that single mothers represented both a symptom and a cause of threatening social breakdown.

The concept of the problem that ADC was to remedy derived from this discourse. The discussion was nurtured by several contemporary concerns: anxiety about how immigration and industrialism was changing the country, "child-saving"—the campaign against child labor and child abuse, ambivalent attitudes towards women's increasing rights, and the growth of public welfare advocacy—the idea that government must take responsibility for the poor. From its beginning, the social problem of single motherhood was a welfare problem, created by welfare reformers and always framed by the question, what should be done? The debate rested on some erroneous assumptions, which contributed to making ADC, in its very design, ill fitted for the task it was supposed to accomplish.

Deserted wives were the initial focus in discussion of single mothers between about 1890 and 1910, and their situation produced an almost feverish spate of study and publication.[36] While most commentators believed that there was a drastic increase in desertion, charity leader Zilpha Smith suggested astutely that the new visibility of desertion was also due to wives' increasing assertiveness in seeking help from organized charity.[37] In Boston in the 1890s, 9.3 percent of families asking for relief contained deserted wives;[38] by 1910 several urban charity organizations found 10 to 13 percent of their requests for help coming from deserted women.[39] Social workers labeled desertion a "great evil" requiring "heroic treatment"[40]—an early demand for public policy to prevent deterioration of family values.

Most reformers considered desertion to be fundamentally a moral problem,[41] in two dimensions: allocating fault and determining worthiness with respect to relief. Thus their discussion featured methods of identifying who was blameworthy. Some writers were more sympathetic to the wives. Ada Eliot and many others, influenced by consciousness of women's subordination, emphasized male irresponsibility: "The bread-winner shifts his burdens for bachelor freedom. . . . If he is at all clever, he can in most cases escape punishment."[42] A variety of groups in many cities set up desertion bureaus to track down the absconders and, just as today, urged punitive action to get nonsupporting fathers to provide child support.[43] MAKING THE DESERTER PAY THE PIPER, headlined one editorial.[44] One concerned social worker proposed requiring prospective husbands to make a security deposit for their future wives and children; another demanded sterilization for deserters.[45] These were extremes, but the consensus demanded some deterrent policy. Other writers, such as Walter Weyl, imagined the husband's point of view: "Esther was no longer the wife he had married . . . sick and irritable. . . . For a whole month Simon had not had a pleasant word from Esther."[46] The woman blamers were by no means only men, however. Zilpha Smith described deserted wives as often untidy, lazy, shiftless, neglectful of housework; Lilian Brandt cited women's intemperance, slovenliness, trying disposition, extravagance and sexual immorality.[47] The search for blame produced sharp disagreements. One family court judge branded desertion the "poor man's divorce."[48] Social work leader Joanna Colcord answered him sharply: it was more like a poor man's vacation, she insisted, hostile to any semblance of excusing this behavior.[49] Many commentators blamed both parties. But in practice the varied gender analyses did not seem to make much of a difference for policy, because, even in the cases of the wives deemed most blameless, charity workers were extremely reluctant to offer them financial support for fear of encouraging desertion. They presumed that men who knew their families could receive support if they fled would lose any remaining sense of responsibility.[50] (This fear of welfare as an incentive to family breakdown continues today.) The result was that deserted wives themselves were made suspect by the stigma of the family form in which they functioned—single-mother families—no matter what their contribution to the situation.

Talk about desertion incorporated environmental factors into causal analyses: ease of travel, urban anonymity, both unemployment *and* work opportunities in new communities, women's employment.[51] A 1925 social work textbook insisted that poverty was not an important factor and that desertion was not correlated to income level—an assertion that contradicted existing evidence.[52] And there was contention between those who treated desertion as a sin and sought deterrence and punishment as answers, and those who considered it a pathology requiring treatment. But even environmental explanations of desertion retained an essentially moralistic tone, condemning permissiveness and restlessness in the culture, the "vastly increase [d] . . . opportunity for sexual adventure" in large cities.[53]

Widows, who actually formed the majority of single mothers, only came to dominate the discussion later, between 1910 and 1920. This shift did not result from belief that widowhood was increasing. Rather welfare reformers redrew the image of the single mother, from deserted wives to widows, for reasons of welfare-state-building strategies. By now they had stirred up enough public concern for unsupported mothers and children to have a political chance to win programs of public aid. But in order to do so, they believed, they needed to defang those who condemned aid to immoral women. The chorus of sympathetic studies of the plight of widows emerged mainly from among those who were campaigning for state and local "mothers' aid" laws.[54]

By focusing on quintessentially blameless widows, reformers planned to avoid the stigma attached to deserted wives, but their discursive strategy had contradictory consequences. Mothers' aid advocates praised widows as models of true womanhood, commenting on their forbearance, hard work, and good housekeeping.[55] When widows lacked these virtues, experts often explained that poverty and overwork prevented them from meeting their own domestic standards. "Again and again in these cases we find the children straying into bad company because the [widowed] mother, herself respectable, cannot give them her mothering while she is forced to work for their living. . . . we lock them up as incorrigibles or charge the honest, slaving mother with neglect."[56] Of course the same might have been said of deserted mothers and their children; the widow had become not so much an individual but a synonym for "virtuous mother," while any woman whose marriage had come unstuck, whatever the circumstances, was suspect. Thus the widow discourse worked to intensify the stigmatization of other single mothers; the emphasis on the widow's innocence insinuated the noninnocence of others. At the same time, however, the fervent sympathy engendered for widows constituted a critique of existing, punitive social policy, and above all an argument for public obligation. The widow not only had a "unique claim on the community," but was also "uniquely open to constructive educational endeavors."[57] She thus served also as raw material on which the social work and reform projects could work.

Indeed the "widow" appellation lost some of its specificity in this campaign and occasionally served to cover and legitimate other single mothers. Studies of single mothers were titled as if they were only about widows to maximize reader sympathy, as in that of the New York State Commission on Relief for Widowed Mothers, which reported in 1914 that the "incapacity" of the breadwinner was a greater problem than was widowhood.[58] "Widow" became to some extent a generic term for single mothers, occasionally blocking the awareness that other kinds of single mothers existed. The mothers' aid programs passed in most of the states after 1910 were interchangeably called "mothers' pensions" and "widows' pensions." Social insurance advocates Abraham Epstein and Isaac Rubinow classified the entire problem of "dependent" mothers as one of widows until well into the New Deal. (And they accordingly believed that the problem could be handled through adequate life insurance for men.[59])

But widows were not entirely immune from the stigmas attached to single-mother families. They were somewhat less liable to be considered ipso facto immoral than other types of single mothers, but they were suspect and closely watched nonetheless. Even the staunchest supporters of public aid insisted on scrutinizing widows' domestic standards closely, examining their housekeeping, their children's cleanliness, whether they drank or had objectionable companions, and making sure they did not consort with men.

Unmarried mothers did not figure importantly in this discussion until the 1920s. Many Progressive Era reformers were intensely concerned about sexual immorality and women's sexual victimization; feminists conducted a substantial crusade against prostitution, for example. But those concerned with single mothers and public aid did not at first generate an alarm about out-of-wedlock motherhood, probably because they did not want to call attention to these examples of unchastity among potential beneficiaries of aid. Widespread discussion of unmarried mothers began only after the wave of mother's aid laws was well under way.

When an illegitimacy discussion did begin, it had two streams, one focused on the mothers and another on the children. The first was, of course, a moralistic discourse. Out-of-wedlock pregnancy had been a popular issue in the nineteenth-century, when it was defined as the fate of "fallen women." Progressive Era feminists tried to make this moralistic discourse more sympathetic to the women: emphasizing their youth, positioning them as victims. Conservatives were more likely to treat them as problem girls, delinquents.[60] Both sides engaged in biologistic explanations, immediately looking for "feeble-mindedness:" "Every unmarried mother [should] be given a mental test as the first step."[61] Experts of all political orientations equally searched for environmental causes of sexual delinquency in bad companions, lack of healthy recreational opportunities, or mental deficiency; but despite environmentalism, 1920s illegitimacy discourse remained moralistic, if somewhat less punitive toward the mothers. Starting in the 1940s illegitimate mothers were rewritten as neurotics, in the terms of the new psychiatric and then psychoanalytic social work.[62] But this discussion centered on the motives of the girls and the best treatment for their moral rehabilitation; it did not concern itself in a major way with their lives as single mothers raising children, or with their economic welfare. Moreover, even the most sympathetic explanations of illegitimate motherhood were often wide of the mark because at the turn of the century so many out-of-wedlock mothers were formerly married women now living in out-of-wedlock partnerships.

A second discourse, more directly connected to welfare issues, spotlighted infant and child welfare. By focusing on the children and avoiding their mothers' morals, reformers hoped to sidestep the stigma of illegitimacy. This child welfare reform campaign, launched by the U.S. Children's Bureau, had in it something of "strategic amoralization,"[63] but it was also principled and feminist: a campaign against the victimization of women and children by a double standard of sexual morality. Reform-oriented research demonstrated higher rates of infant mortality among "illegitimate" children (in one study double that of legitimate children).[64] The Children's Bureau drafted and distributed a recommended state Uniform Illegitimacy Act in 1921, aimed at undoing the old "unscientific viewpoint . . . inspired by moral indignation" and enforcing paternity and child support (particularly by expediting cooperation between the states in enforcement). Its goals were to remove the stigma of illegitimacy from the child altogether and to reduce the stigma on unmarried mothers by positioning them as victims rather than sinners and by affording them opportunities for reform—a new start.[65]

Early-twentieth-century observers of single motherhood wrongly believed that single mothers—particularly deserted wives and illegitimate mothers—were disproportionately composed of immigrants. Immigrants were for several reasons the prime objects of social work and charity in the early twentieth century: because the immigrant population in the cities was growing so fast; because this second wave of immigrants came mainly from different places and different religions (eastern and southern Europe, primarily Catholics, Jews, and Eastern Orthodox) than had the first wave of immigrants; because the immigrants were more ghettoized and therefore more visible than the nonmigrant poor, who were more scattered and more rural; and, not least, because the very foreignness of these unfortunates justified the charity workers' sense of mission and superiority in ministering to them. "In the foreigner's struggle with the new conditions of American life we may find one reason for the increase of illegitimacy. . . . The younger generation quickly learns our language, our customs. . . . The girls go into shops and factories rather than into domestic service, because of the greater freedom. . . . They soon look down on their parents . . . find their pleasures away from home."[66] Progressive Era reports on single motherhood frequently made ethnic generalizations and distinctions. From a 1904 report on desertion: "With all our . . . Catholics, the wide open door of our immense institutional system makes it easy for a man to lay down his obligations. . . . [Despite] the dogged perseverance of the Hebrew race [there is] no more flagrant offender than the Jew. If the rent is over-due he disappears."[67] Some scholarly studies as late as the 1920s seem today saturated with such racist and misogynist insults; for example: "The most outstanding feature of our Slavic desertion cases seems to be the extreme undesirability of the women as wives . . . immorality, more or less intemperance, dirtiness, wretched housekeeping, quarreling, and defiance of their husbands' wishes."[68] Such observations were explained by less racist scholars in terms of the disintegrating and centrifugal effect of the immigration experience on family life.

Closely related was the belief that single motherhood was uniquely urban. This too was false. But the assumption that urban life produced social breakdown reverberated with a American tradition of romanticizing rural life. There was a major overlap between blaming immigrants and city life, since by the early twentieth century the two went together, while the declining rural population appeared to be "American." Child welfare workers imagined the rural life as the healthiest one and sent children there for foster care; when early Children's Bureau reports, such as the infant mortality study, showed that rural health indicators were worse than urban ones, this came as a surprise even to many sophisticated social workers.

The single-mother discourse was particularly contradictory with respect to mothers' employment. Even those who knew that existing aid was inadequate insisted that somehow mothers had to stay home. Several serious concerns—child abuse and neglect, delinquency and truancy, for example—were blamed on mothers' employment.[69] While many reformers understood perfectly the difficulties of the double burden for poor single mothers—having to earn and to raise children without help—their proposals for releasing women from this double bind were never adequate. No locality ever provided aid that was adequate to keep widows out of the labor force. Indeed reformers contributed to the double bind: They used arguments against mothers' employment to win support for mothers' aid, but the stigmatization of mothers who worked then made those women seem less deserving of support.[70]

The early-twentieth-century discourse about single mothers was strongly influenced by the women's rights movement, which, unlike its late-twentieth-century counterpart, accepted the strong and exclusive identification of women with children. Women's rights sentiment literally saturated the child welfare and moral reform campaigns that created the single-mother discourse. In the Progressive Era many charity and social workers, and especially leaders in this field, were "social feminists,"[71] women who considered themselves part of a larger "woman movement" and understood their own work as helping poor women in particular and as an expression of the essential female. Women were disproportionally numerous in organized child welfare activity. Not only the campaign against child abuse, born in the 1870s, but also the growth of services for dependent children were owing in large part to women's activism. The discourse about helpless, tender, "innocent" children was often covertly an antimale discourse, criticizing men's irresponsibility and brutality. In this discourse children figured to some extent as a surrogate for women as victims of men. Not only was women's responsibility for child mistreatment deemphasized at the turn of the century, but child abuse and wife beating were often regarded, along with excessive drinking, as virtually interchangeable.[72]

In representing single mothers exclusively as victims, feminists were of course trying to rescue them from blame and moral condemnation. One important ideological division in the discussion of single mothers resembled that in the debate about the welfare poor today: liberals tended to present them as victims of structural forces, like unemployment, while conservatives positioned them as responsible agents, their poverty due to lack of character. The resulting crude dichotomy makes the historian long for some evidence of the women's own perspective, some letters, diaries, or reliable interviews. Did some of these early-twentieth-century women, like those of today, choose to be single mothers? Did some choose it secondarily, having been so mistreated or embittered by men that they thought they were better off on their own? We cannot know, but we must be aware that it is dangerous and often misleading to treat any group of people solely as helpless, for most people in most situations have some leverage with which to affect their fate.

The desire to exculpate single mothers from all responsibility may have made it harder for the reformers to ask what these single mothers really wanted. Certainly their wishes must have varied greatly, but if some felt themselves better off without men and wanted support in developing stable female-headed households, the reformers were unlikely to have been able to hear this. Committed to women's exclusive mothering and domesticity, they imagined proper family life only with a male breadwinner and a full-time housewife; thus single-mother families, however formed, were defective. In this view they expressed a distinctly elite and white perspective. Many black and/or poor women had different attitudes, experiences, and aspirations regarding married women's economic position. Researcher Gwendolyn Hughes, writing in 1925 and fairly typical of the women's reform network views of that time, condemned the "feminist"* advocacy of employment outside the home for wives and mothers. She noted that nine-tenths of the working mothers she studied took jobs because of economic necessity rather than because they preferred them to housework, but she did not emphasize that both preferences were constricted ones: Mothers' employment necessarily meant a "double day," and their choices might have been quite different had they had access to better jobs, higher pay, housework assistance, and child care; nor did she emphasize the advantages to women of having their own wages in terms of self-esteem and, for married women, domestic power.[73]

---

*Hughes used the word "feminist" not as a generic for women's rights advocacy, as I do, but as it was primarily used in the early twentieth century—referring to the tendency that supported the Equal Rights Amendment and insisted on identical treatment of women and men.

The social concern with single mothers dwindled after the Progressive Era. No significant welfare activities in the 1920s were directed toward them, and the social work debate about how to treat them declined as well. By the 1930s single mothers appeared less often in policy discussions, although their numbers had not decreased.[74] Most social problems have a short public life, of course, but the major reason for the decline in interest in this problem was the decline in energy of the women's rights movement.

The decline of feminist thinking and gender analysis can be seen in the diagnoses of 1930s caseworkers who continued to have to deal with family problems involving single mothers. The dominant social work view of single mothers in the 1930s was at once more accepting and less sympathetic. Marital breakup was treated less moralistically. Wife beating, which social workers had discussed and condemned energetically two decades before, was now an unmentionable, and, if its presence could not be ignored, it was disguised as mutual conflict. What had once been called "desertion" and blamed exclusively on men was now more and more often labeled neutrally "marital separation" (divorce was still very rare), with an assumption of mutual responsibility for the failure of the marriage. Yet failure it was, with the end result that single mothers (other than widows) were usually considered guilty of something. A similar change in attitude took place toward never-married mothers: In the Progressive Era an unmarried mother might be construed as the victim of a seduction and therefore a fallen innocent; changes in sexual norms by the 1930s no longer made men into sexual villains and more often blamed women for their sexual immorality. Without a feminist consciousness in the air, rape was not an important issue, and the economic inequality inherent in out-of-wedlock birth or marital separation was not acknowledged. Concern with "deserted" wives or "fallen" girls was increasingly considered old-fashioned, unsophisticated, prudish.

Today's common misperception that single motherhood is a new phenomenon results, then, in part from the repression of the issue during the 1930s, 1940s, and 1950s. Without a continuous history, we may treat as abnormal social phenomena that have, in fact, been typical.

At the same time, to rediscover a history does not mean to project contemporary politics onto the past. Despite some similarities, the present alarm about single motherhood and out-of-wedlock childbirth does not carry quite the same meanings as that of the early twentieth century. Nonetheless, there is some continuity in the gendered content of today's discussion of welfare and that of eighty years ago. Then and now one dominating concern is a fear that "proper" families would be destabilized by the provision of incentives to single motherhood—whether through marital breakup or out-of-wedlock births—a fear which reveals not far below the surface a view that proper families must be enforced precisely because they do not always come "naturally" and are not always inherently desirable. Fear of single women's immorality has escalated, due to the prominence today of never-married mothers. In the earlier wave of concern about single mothers, widows occupied a large share of the attention; today widows with young children are very few and "deserted" wives fewer still. The availability of contraception and abortion, particularly to those with medical insurance and/or good incomes, contributes to the fact that unmarried motherhood occurs more often among the poor. Overall a higher proportion of single mothers today enter that situation with some degree of volition—through ending a marriage or bearing a child without marriage. Thus today's discourse is both new and old, repeating the anxiety about the decline of male-headed families that was apparent ninety years ago but blaming single mothers more.

But perhaps the most important difference in the meaning of single motherhood today has to do with race. In the late nineteeth and early twentieth centuries, social problems were often cast in images of immigrant residents of large cities, workers in a new industrial economy. African Americans were not at the center of attention for the elite reformers who defined the problem. Many scholars, particularly black sociologists, understood that single motherhood was quite common among poor working-class and rural blacks.[75] But southern blacks in the 1930s seemed a world apart to the northern elite whites who dominated the national welfare discourse. The meanings of "single mother" in the depression and of "dependent children" in the Social Security Act were shaped by the white experience.

By contrast, when single motherhood was rediscovered in the 1960s, blacks were represented in substantial numbers in northern cities. Black single motherhood then became more noticed, if not necessarily understood, by white welfare experts. Even today there remain many misunderstandings. African American family patterns

were somewhat different from those of whites, immigrants or otherwise: more likely to share child raising among extended networks of
kin, more likely to respect women's and mothers' employment and
other activity outside the home—and more likely to suffer from discrimination and poverty. (The fact that these patterns derive both
from choice—from preferences constructed by autonomous cultural
legacies—and from poverty and discrimination is often missing from
the discussion.[76]) In short, at the turn of the century the rural and
southern concentration of blacks rendered these patterns invisible to
the influential experts, while from the beginning of its second life in
the 1960s, the single-mother problem was defined in racial terms.

Thus, during the first third of the twentieth century, when reformers envisioned and agitated for programs of public aid to single
mothers, their understanding of the problem was not identical to
that of the late twentieth century. Many though not all of them believed they were primarily dealing with widows. Many believed that
female-headed households were particularly characteristic of immigrants and city dwellers. Most saw single mothers as victims, either
of death or other undesirable mishaps, or of male irresponsibility. All
agreed that single motherhood was a temporary and unusual misfortune which, although perhaps it could never be abolished, could be
drastically reduced in incidence in a society providing greater physical and economic security.

Lithuanian Immigrant Mothers Learn "American" Childraising in a
Settlement Class, Chicago, Early Twentieth Century

3
=

State Caretakers

Maternalism, Mothers' Pensions,
and the Family Wage

Raising an alarm about single mothers worked: It created the first modern public welfare in the United States. State and local governments established programs to aid single mothers, mainly in the decade 1910–20. These authorized assistance to "deserving" poor single mothers with children, to defray the costs of raising children in their own homes and to deter child labor and the institutionalization of fatherless children. The enthusiasm for mothers' aid was so great that forty-six of the forty-eight states had passed such laws within twenty years. The design of these programs was so influential that when, twenty years later, the depression provided an opportunity to establish a federal program—ADC—it simply added federal funds to the mothers'-aid model. Mothers' aid became the model not only for ADC but for all the programs today called "welfare."[1]

Not only did mothers' aid shape the welfare state, but the debate about it introduced the themes and questions that still dominate welfare policy discussions today. These include concerns about how to help single mothers without encouraging single motherhood and about the proper role of women, as well as the most fundamental questions about what entitles a person to help. Who is deserving? Who should be required to work for wages? What if wages are too low? Does the state have an obligation to police the behavior of those who receive public funds? What is an entitlement, and what is charity? Today's welfare debates began here.

37

The mothers' aid laws were created by a women's movement, or more precisely by one campaign in a diverse movement that also included woman suffrage, birth control, sexual freedom, child welfare, labor reform, and civil rights. The debate about mothers' aid encapsulated important tensions within the feminist thought of the period. All mothers'-aid advocates wanted the program to signify the public value of the labor of mothering and to recognize public responsibility for needy mothers. The dominant approach continued a maternalist stream of charity activity, using new public funds to rescue poor client families from the stigma of poor relief. Others saw in the campaign for poor single mothers the inauguration of a radical, feminist welfare state and a subversion of women's economic dependence on men.[2] By the mid-1920s the latter visions had been rather definitively defeated, although the maternalist program had also been drastically reduced. By the time of the Social Security Act, it was clear that these programs had been outmoded from the beginning, not only in the inadequate size of their stipends and the proportion of single mothers covered, but also in their fundamental design. Indeed, they had never been appropriate to the problem they were said to address—that of mothers alone with young children. Not only was their scale trivial in terms of the needs of mother-child families, but their basic design would have been unworkable had their scale been adequate. And their whole structure, based on the white racial experience, was oblivious to the considerably different orientation of minority activists.

The inadequacy of mothers' aid should not mask its historical significance as a welfare accomplishment. Breaking with laissez-faire and Social Darwinist assumptions, it not only asserted a public responsibility for the poor but also sought to remove relief from the stigma of pauperism and the poorhouse. It offered, moreover, a feminist version of those principles, honoring the quintessential female labor, mothering. Traditionally in the United States, recipients of poor relief had been disfranchised; with the drive for woman suffrage then in its final stages, feminist reformers were particularly committed to keeping mothers' aid recipients out of the pauper category for this reason too.[3] The program was also a victory in women's struggle for state power. Although established in most places before women could vote, mothers' aid nevertheless succeeded in using the state to support mothers' interests: "By the passage of these laws the

State acknowledged the inviolability of the relation of mother and child, its own stake in the preservation of the home, and the unique social value of the service rendered by mothers in maintaining their homes when fathers 'drop out.'"[4] Mothers' aid was a kind of child custody reform for the poor. When, in the nineteenth century, courts began to award custody to mothers, this meant that prosperous mothers in abusive marriages could contemplate escape without losing their children, a cost most had been unwilling to pay. Mothers' aid extended that possibility to poor mothers. Its inadequacy derived in large part from the fact that the programs were not able to realize their original promise—to support single mothers in a dignified fashion and thereby allow them to care for their children well. This failure resulted in part from the limited vision of their designers, to be sure, but theirs were the limitations of the age. Who in 1910 imagined a world in which half the children live part of their lives with single mothers, most mothers are employed, and mothering is no longer viewed as *the* appropriate life's work for women?

=

In mothers' aid as in ADC there are two figures: mother and child. While the potential appeal and power of the image comes from the relationship as well as the individuals, the meanings of aid to single mothers vary considerably depending on which figure is accented. In the course of the mothers'-aid campaigns the focus migrated from the mother to the child.

This shift in emphasis took place within a charity and social work alliance that always stressed child welfare. A child-saving orientation became particularly prominent in the mid- and late nineteenth century, enacted not only in sheltering orphans but increasingly in intervening against parents who were deemed neglectful or abusive.[5] The women's movement, too, adopted this change, in a shift away from moral suasion, equality, and natural rights as the primary mode of organized female reform discourse to a more pragmatic "political" discourse that emphasized what women could contribute to others and thus made use of a Victorian ideal of women as self-sacrificing. This discursive shift corresponded to an organizational shift from autonomous women's groups to male/female associations—such as the National Conference of Charities and Corrections (NCCC)—social work's national organization—in which women sometimes functioned as auxiliaries but often did most of the work, allowing men to retain leadership roles.[6] In the Progressive Era, reform discussions about child welfare focused on rapidly changing conditions of child labor.[7] Single mothers entered the field of concern because their children were more likely to be in the labor force than other children—about one-third of their children as contrasted to 6 percent of those with fathers.[8] Women reformers argued for aid to single mothers on the grounds that undernourished, neglected children could not learn well.[9] A growing conviction that children's healthy development required mother love particularly anguished reformers because of the numbers of children whose mothers could not both earn and care for them and who therefore had to be institutionalized. Not only did children suffer, but their lack of mothering might prevent them from becoming adequate citizens.[10]

Some mothers'-aid advocates argued on the basis of the women's labor and deservingness. This strategy did not contradict the "putting children first" strategy—it was as mothers that these poor women contributed to society and as mothers that their virtue was measured. The overlap between women's and child-welfare activism was visible not only in mothers' aid but also in campaigns against child labor, for compulsory education, and for protective labor legislation for women and child workers. But the subtle difference between focusing on children or on women in the visual and mental images of single-mother families was extremely consequential. The institutionalization of children could be represented primarily as unhealthy for the children or mainly as pain for the mother. The poverty of single-mother households and the overwork of single mothers could be presented primarily as damaging to children or to mothers; and the women could be presented exclusively as mothers or also as potential citizens, subjects of rights and deserving of sympathy, on their own. Over time a reform campaign that had been oriented to both women and children tilted toward children, although it never lost all of its definition as part of a feminist agenda. For example, mothers'-aid advocates succeeded in getting many states to stipulate that women be represented in the administration of the mothers' aid programs; and the program was popularly called mothers' or widows' "pensions," reflecting the understanding that it was the mothers' labor and deservingness as well as the children's need that was the basis of the claim.[11]

Opponents of mothers' aid knew perfectly well that it was for women as well as children. Anxieties about gender issues vibrated just under the surface of their arguments against mothers' aid. Just as opponents of AFDC claim today, they charged that it would threaten the family by encouraging marital breakup and illegitimacy and the establishment of "female-headed households." (Not even aid earmarked for widows was exempt from these condemnations, because it would encourage men's irresponsibility, diminishing their need to save.[12]) The gender anxiety was not exclusively about women; they were also nervous about "shiftless" men—that is, those who would not sustain their breadwinner roles. It was so vital that relief to women not subvert male responsibility that some argued explicitly that women and children might have to suffer instead, in order to deter unmanliness.[13] Mothers' aid was not "virile"; it was "an insidious attack upon the family," declared its private-charity opponents.[14] Relief to deserted wives could cause an "epidemic" of desertion.[15] In response, defenders of mothers' aid built their argument for state responsibility not only on the basis of children's deprivation, not only on the tradition of poor relief, but also on the state's interest in preserving the family. "Normal family life is the foundation of the State, and its conservation an inherent duty of government," pronounced the influential New York State Commission on Relief for Widowed Mothers.[16]

For both mothers and children, these programs fit within a longer history of singling out deserving groups for public provision. Then, in the late nineteenth century, mothers and children unsupported by men appeared as a social problem of such magnitude that it required public funds. The NCCC discussed public aid for families without male breadwinners as early as 1890, and in 1897 a Destitute Mothers' Bill nearly passed in New York State. Fearing that public aid would threaten their own status, private charities led the opposition. They labeled it the "Shiftless Fathers Bill," manipulating anxieties that it would undermine men's obligations to provide. (The bill passed but was vetoed by the governor and by the mayor of New York.)[17] An alternative proposal, widows' "scholarships," pushed by anti-child-labor activists, intended to replace the earnings of laboring children on whom mothers were often dependent, never caught on.[18]

Poor single mothers themselves seem to have been enthusiastic about public aid, albeit unable to mount a major campaign. During the consideration of the 1897 Destitute Mothers' Bill, New York's mayor received scores of letters regarding the proposal. "I am a scrub-woman in City Hall where you daily come to your office and since the mothers' bill has passed the Senate and Assembly I have watched the papers to see by your inhumanity and injustice how long will the widows and orphans be deprived of the benefits of this bill? I am a widow with seven orphans and their sole support is thirty dollars per month with sixty cents a week deducted for carfare."[19] Caseworkers from private charities and child-saving agencies heard and no doubt passed on mothers' pleas for support that would allow them to maintain households even without husbands.[20] During the mothers'-aid campaign in Baltimore many widows wrote to the mayor urging his support, talking of their heartbreak in having to place their children in institutions.[21] Once the U.S. Children's Bureau was established (in 1912) and gained a reputation, it received many letters from needy mothers, many of which refer to the problems of being without a male breadwinner or of being with one and unable to leave him:

1921, California: My husband lost his job, with about a thousand other men in the Navy Yard . . . we lost our home and furniture and everything we have. . . . Can you give me any information on how to deliver the baby myself? . . . no insurance to cover the hospital at charges [of] six dollars a day. . .

1916, Illinois: Now, Sirs, I am to become a mother again . . . No food for the ones I already have, and nothing to nourish the coming. Only *abuse* and *torture* at the hands of the man who *promised to provide and protect woman* [emphasis in original]. . . . The Soldier receive his pension, What do mothers' receive?

1918, California: I am writing to ask if there is any law in this Bureau that will help me to locate and make my husband support myself and two children . . . I am not able to earn enough to properly support the children. They are being under fed and neglected. . . .

1927, Pennsylvania: I am writing you concerning my children support. My husband died last fall leaveing me with 3 little boys and I am not able to work to support them as I am expecting to take my bed any day now. So I wanted to see if I could get this mothers Pension. . . .

1927, Florida: . . . my self in Family way an[d] i is not able to Bear no Big Exspences. . . . I am a widow. The man that got me this way, he Promes to take Care of me an[d] said he would marry me. But he fail to do so . . . I am the mother of 9, 5 liveing. An[d] Please send m [or] write me what to do about it.[22]

Still, the major pressure for mothers' aid came from middle-class women's organizations.[23] Moreover, the women's movement was unified on this issue, despite its split over the proposed Equal Rights Amendment (ERA). Philosophically this division replicated and intensified one of the most profound and abiding fissures in feminist thought: Colloquially referred to as equality vs. difference, it can be better expressed as a question of the relation between formal and substantive equality for women. Proponents of an ERA believed that no policies should treat one sex differently than the other, and indeed that social policy should insist on identical treatment; anything else would be subverted by male power to women's disadvantage. Opponents of an ERA believed that women's subordinate social position required differential treatment in order to advance substantive equality; that identical treatment would reinforce existing inequalities.[24] But both sides liked the mothers'-aid laws, partly because it appeared that the programs could be made gender-neutral, offering support to single parents of either sex.[25] In fact, the programs were inherently gendered inasmuch as they promoted maternal domesticity; but even ERA feminists at this time believed that mothers belonged at home.

This united support for mothers' aid reflected distance from those who might themselves claim public aid. The activists in this cause were overwhelmingly prosperous, married, and/or childless. Altruism was a potent force in their activism; many had had some direct experience with needy single mothers and their compassion was palpable. But they also had, collectively, subjective interests in mothers' aid, interests deriving from their social position. Like the men of their class, they worried about the threat to the social order created by the new immigrant urban masses. Reforming the socialization of poor urban children was a major social-control strategy.

Their social-control agenda targeted both children and women. They feared that the child-raising practices of the poor might produce adults lacking in discipline, independence, and impulse control. The child-savers' increasing demands for public responsibility for children rested on genuine pity for children's suffering, but also on anxieties about the potential social disorder that could be stimulated by poverty and unrest in the immigrant ghettos. The child-savers' standards about what counted as neglect, abandonment, or inadequate support were of course class, ethnic, and religious constructions that did not always coincide with those of the children or parents being "saved." Child-saving was thus a form of social control as well as charity.[26]

So was their work on behalf of poor women. Beginning with antebellum campaigns against slavery, prostitution, and drink, middle-class women reformers indulged in rescue fantasies, imagining themselves raising downtrodden women up to the norms of respectability they deemed essential to proper family and polity. In letters to the U.S. Children's Bureau, poor women concentrated on asking for financial help while middle-class women writing on behalf of the poor were convinced that education was their most urgent need.[27] There were complexities and double meanings on both sides of the transactions between helpers and helped. Poor, victimized, and deviant women welcomed—even longed for—help and uplift; they often also expressed, more through action than words, alternative definitions of respectability and criticisms of the reformers' norms. Middle-class women reformers misunderstood, disregarded, and condescended to those they wished to "rescue." "These mothers are so ignorant, so pitifully helplessly ignorant, that in the great industrial world there is no place for them."[28] But they often also empathized with the female victims they sought to help, the more enraged by their oppression and exploitation because these insults reverberated with their own experience of subordination. Middle-class women's magazines of the period frequently complained about women's economic dependence on men's capricious gifts, a lament particularly explicit among black women.[29]

Women reformers of the Progressive Era sought not only uplift for others and harmony for the society but also a role for themselves, whether as objects of gratitude or figures of authority. Unlike the men of their class, the female reformers needed legitimation for their public-sphere activism and a forum in which they could get respect and status. Male reformers were usually already professional or otherwise publicly active men aggrandizing their role, while the women were still elbowing their way into visible public activity and defensive about their right to be there. As Hull-House founder Jane Addams so delicately explained in an 1892 speech on the settlement movement, reformers had a "subjective necessity" for their activism. All reformers define problems and pursue solutions that amplify their power and solidify the need for their work. Child neglect among the "dangerous classes" at midcentury was constructed so as to justify a large "placing-out" program, as foster care was then called. The "discovery" of cruelty to children in the 1870s built a role for energetic child protection societies. Progressive Era women were attracted (and confined) to those arenas that put them in most direct relation to "clients," as in public welfare reform and the helping professions. Not only do problems create the need for problem solvers, but those who can define themselves as problem solvers are able to define what counts as a social problem. The mother's-aid campaigns benefited not only some poor single mothers but also some professional and protoprofessional women, just as their child welfare program also involved a strategy for women's welfare.[30]

The women reformers' mothers' aid agenda shifted the focus from deserted women to widows in the second decade of the twentieth century. The widow discourse, emphasizing impeccably deserving and "innocent" supplicants, was simultaneously an instrumental approach to state building and an expression of ambivalent, perhaps transitional, gender attitudes. In emphasizing widows, mothers' aid campaigners implicitly conceded that other categories of single mothers were guilty of something. The widow focus also expressed their gradualist approach to building a welfare state: bringing one group at a time into the house of public care. Meanwhile, a program focused on needy widows might allow other categories of lone mothers to be served with minimal negative publicity.

Yet despite the spotlight on "innocent" widows, mothers' aid was never meant to be open armed or trusting toward those it helped. To the contrary, mothers' aid functioned and was intended to superintend and discipline as well as support its recipients. This is evident in its scrutiny of recipients' morality—not only in its effects on children but as a value in itself—and in the assignment of many mothers'-aid programs to be administered by the juvenile courts—an arrangement that placed single mothers and their children in the same arena as juvenile delinquents, and also allowed for the particularistic, punitive, and/or rehabilitative judgments in which the courts specialized.[31] Most laws had "suitable home" provisions, refusing aid to any mother who failed to provide an environment meeting social workers' standards. Such provisions, strongly supported by the child welfare establishment and the women's organizations that campaigned for these programs, gave relatively unfettered discretion to social work administrators and judges as to what constituted proper family life.[32]

Illegitimate children or male friends, alcoholic beverages, boarders, or alien methods of housekeeping and child care might disqualify a home. In at least one jurisdiction, eligibility was dependent on the children getting satisfactory school reports.[33] Moralistic and condescending attitudes, and the assumption of supervisory and reforming responsibility, characterized mothers' aid designers and administrators (who were sometimes the same). The conviction of superiority inherent in this sense of responsibility was equally a class, ethnic/racial, and religious one. The programs got their start in big cities, which in this period were packed with immigrants, often non-Protestant and non-Anglo-Saxon. Many mothers'-aid advocates hoped to use the promise of pensions as a reward to immigrant and other poor single mothers who allowed themselves to be "Americanized" and otherwise reformed.

The impulse to help single mothers in nonfinancial ways was not in itself invasive. Some were depressed, some were alcoholic, some were abusive to their children; more were at times neglectful because they did not understand the dangers of industrial urban life and the need to take precautions against harm from such sources as streetcars, germs, or the gas in kitchen stoves. But social work assistance and supervision, aimed at making sure that children had "suitable homes," could not help but offer a vision of proper home life particular to those who designed these programs. Recipients were often required to keep a religious presence in their households, and once religion was admitted as an area of concern, social workers' anti-Catholic and anti-Semitic attitudes entered clients' homes. Mothers were urged and sometimes coerced into classes in English, citizenship, infant care, nutrition, cooking, and sewing. There they were taught to keep milk fresh but to avoid garlic, a dangerous aphrodisiac; that diapers should be clean but also that pacifiers would spoil babies.[34] The stipends given had strings attached: Social workers "helped" recipients create budgets and then supervised their adherence to them.[35]

The helping and controlling motives united in these Americanization campaigns had strong currents of racial thought. Today popular usage distinguishes fairly sharply between races—often perceived as people of different "colors"—and ethnic groups; by contrast, in the early twentieth century Americans of Anglo-Saxon backgrounds perceived southern Europeans, for example, much as they perceived

Latinos or African Americans; no doubt there was more prejudice against non-Europeans but there was a continuum, not a break, between European and other minorities. The word "race" was used ambiguously, sometimes referring to humans, sometimes to whites, sometimes to a nationality. Heavy immigration between 1880 and 1920 produced a nativist response, and eventually led to restrictions on immigration designed to retain Anglo-Saxon supremacy in the United States.

Virtually all positions in the political spectrum perceived these second-wave immigrants as a problem, but the proposed solutions varied greatly. Conservatives tended to view non-Wasps as irremediably inferior. Liberals tended to regard them as inferior in culture but potentially responsive to a socialization that could bring them "up" to "American" standards. The social feminists who backed mothers' pensions were mainly of the latter perspective. While their language would strike late-twentieth-century liberals as racist and condescending, their main argument was usually to defend the potential of these unfortunate refugees from less free, less advanced civilizations. Mothers' aid supporters frequently spoke of building citizenship as one of the goals of the program, and they meant raising not only children but also mothers to that level.

The supervision embedded in the mothers' pension plans aimed at raising recipients to "American" standards. Of course many of the needy mothers were Anglo-Saxon or from other northern European backgrounds. But reformers' sensibilities and the solutions they designed were colored by their sense of new urban poverty as primarily an immigrant problem. And in big cities, mothers'-aid recipients were predominantly immigrants: That is, two-thirds of Chicago's in 1917 were foreign born, while less than one-third of the population was foreign born. As late as 1930 in Philadelphia, 36 percent of mothers' aid recipients but only 19 percent of the population as a whole were foreign born. The greater proportion of immigrants receiving help was hardly a sign of preferential treatment. It showed rather the deeper poverty of immigrants, and budgeting practices were themselves discriminatory. A 1922 study showed that eleven of thirty agencies figured that minorities (for example, Mexicans, Italians, Czechs) needed less money to live on.[36] In Washington, D.C., social workers had two standard budgets, a higher one for whites and a lower one for blacks; and the white visitors called "colored" mothers by their first names, discouraged them from educating children, and "suggested sleeping apartments in cellars."[37]

Groups today regarded as minorities received only a tiny proportion of mothers' aid. In Chicago, for example, in 1911, when blacks were 2 percent of the population and 6 percent of those on relief, they got no mothers' pensions. By contrast German immigrants were 7 percent of the population and got 20 percent of the mothers' pensions; Irish Americans were 3 percent and got 22 percent; Italian Americans, 2 percent, got 8 percent; Polish Americans, 6 percent, got 14 percent.[38] In Los Angeles, Mexicans were excluded from the mothers'-aid program on the grounds that their inferior background made it too likely that they would abuse it.[39] Sometimes minorities were excluded from programs; at other times programs were not established in locations with large minority populations.[40]

The nature of this discrimination is visible only in context. The small population of blacks and Hispanics in the North meant that most northern Progressive Era white reformers did not perceive blacks to threaten social disorder to the degree that immigrants did. Those blacks who did live in northern cities were invisible to most elite white reformers. For example, of the many reviews of mothers'-aid programs, few even mentioned blacks or reported on them as a category. Not until 1931 did any national survey of mothers' pensions provide a breakdown by race; then we learn that 3 percent of recipients were black.[41] Even in studies of illegitimacy, which have been intensely racialized in the last few decades, before the New Deal there were few mentions of race.[42] As northern black populations grew, they were able to get somewhat larger shares of aid. For example, by 1917 Chicago blacks accounted for 3.8 percent of the population and got 2.6 percent of the aid; Philadelphia blacks, who were 11.2 percent of the population in 1930, got 18.5 percent of the aid.[43]

Still, however self-righteous and culture bound, the most prominent mothers' aid reformers were distinctly racial liberals. In their emphasis on education and uplift they were promoting a vision of political equality, as political scientist Gwendolyn Mink has argued: They assumed that "with proper instruction and protection, women from different backgrounds could become 100% mothers of fully American children . . . that immigrants and African-Americans could both earn and learn equality—if with the helping hand of social mothers and the state . . . [and] thereby questioned the rigidities of caste and the racial geology of citizenship. . . . The linchpin of this program was political reproduction, through the social mediation of motherhood," of democracy.[44]

=

Yet there remained an unwillingness to make things "too easy" for aid recipients. Even supporters of mothers' aid, such as Julia Lathrop, first head of the U.S. Children's Bureau, worried about its pauperizing tendencies.[45] The mothers'-aid programs were hardly generous, not even to the most "deserving" category of single mothers. The pity expressed for widows did not reduce opponents' fear of making things too easy for them; pity brought no higher stipends. Widows were not treated significantly better than the few other types of single mothers who managed to get relief.[46] Widows were not exempt from moral suspicion and supervision, the responsibility to make sure that mothers' aid recipients were "pure."[47]

Perhaps the fullest measure of the controlling use of mothers' aid was in how few needy single mothers ever received any. Most states had a residency and some a citizenship requirement, thus excluding most recent immigrants and preventing even domestic migrants from turning to this program for help when they needed it most. All the programs operated with very small appropriations. In 1931, 93,620 families received some mothers' aid; in 1930, according to U.S. Children's Bureau figures (certainly underestimates), there were 1.5 million female-headed families with children. The majority of counties in the United States had no public aid programs before federal ADC. In Los Angeles—which had a reputedly generous program—in 1920 only 24 percent of female-headed families received any public *or* private assistance.[48] Mothers'-aid administrators often used suitable home provisions to exclude those who needed aid most; illness, especially tuberculosis, or poor housing might make a home "unsuitable." In Philadelphia in 1918 the waiting list dated back to 1914.[49]

Everywhere the relief actually given out was so meager that only those women with additional resources could live on it. Unlike ADC, mothers' aid was never intended to allow mothers to stay home with their children[50] or to eliminate the class double standard between expectations for prosperous and poor mothers.[51] The latter and their children were always expected to earn. Pension applicants were often rejected if they had children who could work. Most mothers'-aid recipients, including widows, continued to work for wages—for example, 84 percent in Philadelphia, 66 percent in Chicago and San Francisco, 57 percent in Los Angeles. (These figures are usually underestimates, since women's employment was chronically and notoriously underreported.[52]) And mothers' aid did little to suppress child labor. A 1925 Women's Bureau study showed that in Philadelphia and environs the median wage of working widows was just under $16.00 per week while a working-class family needed $31.42 per week to sustain a minimal standard of living.[53]

This employment was not usually cheating (mothers' aid thus differed from ADC), but was part of the terms of the grant. These terms had been common among private charities and they were continued by mothers'-aid programs. When Mrs. C. applied for a Cook County, Illinois, pension, the court (which administered the program) concluded that the family needed $34.00 but granted a pension of $20.00, expecting her to earn the difference cleaning offices.[54] The terms applied even to supposedly deserving widows, and many charity volunteers believed that employment was beneficial.[55] But they permitted or advocated only certain types of employment for their recipients, in line with their overall views that maternal employment should be exceptional, never normative. For example, mothers'-aid administrators often prohibited full-time daytime out-of-home employment such as factory work; they preferred part-time, seasonal, or homework—such as piece-rate garment finishing, night cleaning, or taking in laundry. These choices were almost always the most exploitative, certainly the least remunerative options, and homework had the additional disadvantage that it often drew children out of school and into tedious, physically damaging labor.

Most mothers'-aid programs were stingier than their advocates had hoped. This was, of course, a typical form of political "compromise" in the United States: An opposition not strong enough to defeat the groundswell of popular support for these laws was able to reduce their funding. Opposition had come not only from conventional conservatives but also from the private-charity establishment, which did not deny the existence of the problem but wanted it handled by the private sector. They feared not only loss of their own funding and positions but an undermining of the spirit of voluntarism, which was to them a basic, almost constitutional principle. They were equally fervent in a mirror-image objection, opposing the expansion of the powers of government that such a public relief program implied. Some charged that mothers' aid represented "'an entering wedge towards State socialism.'" They harped on its corruption of the poor, charging that "outdoor relief" (that is, aid to the poor in their own homes) as opposed to almshouse care would allow the poor to cheat, fritter away their aid on inessentials, and lose the incentive to work.[56] The only existing public pension program, Civil War veterans' pensions, had demonstrated the potential for corruption and patronage in the awarding of grants, which created another source of opposition among Progressive reformers in particular, concerned as they were about clean government.[57] These opponents, too, did not give up with the passage of laws but worked to contain the size and scope of programs. In fact, many of their opponents ended up running them.[58]

=

The mothers'-aid supporters cannot be entirely absolved of responsibility for the program's inadequacy. While a few women's organizations continued to work for legislation to expand eligibility and funding, most of the leadership of the alliance that had lobbied for the programs moved on to other issues.[59] But the shortage of funding merely strengthened a preexisting commitment to morals testing and supervision of clients and potential clients, pursued through narrowing eligibility to an ideally respectable few. It was a strategic design, based on the belief that single motherhood was more exceptional than it actually was, and on the implicit assumption that single motherhood would decline as a product of the Progressive Era reform program. Widowhood, after all, generated most single mothers and could be reduced by better industrial and public health and safety. "The thing to do for widows and orphans," reformer Florence Kelley proclaimed, "is to abolish them!"[60] Mothers'-aid advocates never believed they needed a very large program.

Not only was mothers' aid too infrequent and insufficient, but it also placed some recipients in double binds. On the one hand the aid was highly conditional, dependent on the recipient's ability to demonstrate a class- and race-defined standard of maternal success measured on a scale difficult for many mothers to perceive, let alone achieve or accept. Such standards were sometimes defended by analogy to the requirements made of an employee: The mothers were hired by the state to care for children, and their continued employment was dependent on satisfactory performance.[61] (The state then put into place supervisors for these "employees," positions assumed increasingly by female social workers.) "As a care-taker paid by the state, a widowed mother should be expected to manage her home comfortably, and to give care and training to her children."[62] A 1920s social work textbook instructed caseworkers to refer to the aid as wages: "Both mothers and social workers are referred to as employes of the state, engaged in the care and training of the fatherless wards of the state."[63] On the other hand the very terms of aid often increased the difficulty of meeting those standards, even if recipients tried. The stinginess of stipends did not help women avoid the "temptation" to find another man—that is, to behave immorally. The terms of women's employment frequently made them by necessity child neglecters—very little day care was available—and many women were in fact so labeled because of their poverty or inability to remain home to supervise children. Many children suffered from the contradictory expectations placed on their mothers.[64]

The mothers'-aid vision seems regressive today also because of its implicit opposition to collective child care provision, or "day nurseries," as they were called. The positive side of this emphasis on mothers staying with their children was the decreasing population of orphanages, which had mainly been filled not with orphans but with children of single mothers; the negative side was the view that mothers' pensions and, later, ADC, should be an alternative to day care.[65] Even supporters of child care services, such as settlement workers who often provided day care themselves, were boxed into an assumption that child care was distinctly a second-best option after mothers' aid. Some feared that child care would make things harder for women, allowing greater exploitation of their labor. In 1910, Boston's Tyler Street Day Nursery closed "because its promoters became convinced that it was doing more harm than good." An alternate response to this anxiety was the same as in mothers' aid itself: restricting access to day nurseries to "worthy" mothers.[66] Later the very existence of mothers' aid created the illusion that deserving single mothers were taken care of by pensions, so that those who sought child care in order to work were even more stigmatized.[67] This hostility to day care had lasting effects. A quarter of a century later Grace Abbott, head of the Children's Bureau, was arguing that such provision might lead mothers to collapse under the double burden of earning and domestic labor.[68] As recently as the 1970s some argued that child care provisions might serve to force mothers into work[69]—although now this was an argument among conservatives, not among feminist social workers.

This historical shortsightedness rested not only on inadequate information but also on a dominant family norm, the family-wage system, shared by most of the reform and charity population, including feminists and antifeminists. "Family wage" means the sex/gender/family system that prescribes earning as the sole responsibility of husbands and unpaid domestic labor as the only proper long-term occupation for women. Early-twentieth-century reformers evolved the idea still farther to that of the "living wage," which explicitly entitled a man to a dependent, service-providing wife.[70] The architects of mothers' aid believed this sexual division of labor to be best for everyone, and that families that did not reproduce it not only were exceptional but should be treated as unfortunate accidents.

Women activists in the Progressive Era and the 1920s were engaged in a thoughtful and sometimes radical discussion of the family-wage system, about which they were increasingly skeptical. Many social surveys showed that the system didn't work—that most working-class men could not support families on a single wage. The corollary was that women did not work for "pin money" but in order to support themselves and their families; single mothers needed to be able to earn a family wage as much as men.[71] Studies of single mothers revealed, furthermore, how many men would not meet their support responsibilities even if they could. "The theory that 'every man supports his own family' is as idle in a district like this as the fiction that 'every one can get work if he wants it,'" wrote the Hull-House women about Chicago in 1895.[72] Thirty years later Hull-House alumna and social work leader Sophonisba Breckinridge suggested that the whole family-wage ideology was a rationalization for women's subordination: "The demand by women for equal pay . . . has resulted in an attempt to put a social and ethical content [that is,

the family-wage idea] into the discrimination practiced in the past
. . . the argument on which that attempt rests, is at present grounded
in no sufficient body of facts."[73]

The family-wage disputes revealed some class differences. For example, consider a dispute over maternity benefits in a New York
State public health insurance proposal during the years 1916–18.
The bill called not only for coverage of childbirth expenses but also
for benefits replacing wages lost by working women during confine-
ment. Reformers Florence Kelley, Frances Perkins, and Mary Van
Kleeck (then head of the U.S. Women's Bureau) feared that such a
benefit would encourage husbands to send their already overbur-
dened wives into the work force. By contrast union leaders Alice
Henry, Pauline Newman, and others closer to working-class women
defended the maternity wage benefits.[74] The most thoroughgoing rejection of the family wage came from Charlotte Perkins Gilman, who
identified more as a socialist than as a feminist:

> The first steps of working motherhood, usually enforced by extreme
> poverty, bring the woman and the child in contact with some of our
> worst conditions; and we, in our dull social conscience, seeing evil fall
> upon mother and baby, seek only to push them back where they came
> from—instead of striving to make conditions fit for them.
>
> What we must recognize is this:
>
> Women; wives and mothers; are becoming a permanent half of the
> world workers. . . . That children should be forced to work for their liv-
> ings is an unnatural outrage. . . . That adult women should do it, is in no
> way harmful, if the hours and conditions . . . are suitable; and they never
> will be made suitable until overwhelming numbers of working women
> compel them.[75]

But the only group to reject the family wage altogether and call
for women's economic independence from men was the National
Woman's Party ERA supporters.[76] Their view was of course rejected
by the mothers' aid coalition, whose strategy was based on accepting
gender difference and a division of labor in which women were responsible for child care and housekeeping. Labor-oriented reformers
also rejected the pro-ERA position because they believed that inferi-
or wages and jobs made it cruel and even misogynistic to expect
mothers to earn for their children; they considered the ERA a dangerous dream that would at best benefit childless or well-to-do

women who hired domestic servants. Thus some supported the family wage in principle, and others supported it because no alternatives seemed practicable for the poor.[77]

=

Both positions can be usefully called "maternalist" if that concept is carefully and historically defined.[78] Three tenets characterized most maternalists. First, they regarded domestic and family responsibilities and identities as essential to the vast majority of women and to the social order, and strongly associated women's with children's interests. Maternalists did not necessarily approve of the family wage but they accepted it as likely to remain the dominant form in the foreseeable future. Second, maternalists imagined themselves in a motherly role toward the poor. Viewing the poor as in need of moral and spiritual as well as economic help, middle-class women sometimes imagined giving that help as a mother to a child, combining sympathy with authority. Third, maternalists believed that it was their work, experience, and/or socialization as mothers that made women uniquely able to lead certain kinds of reform campaigns and made others deserving of help. This perspective had been adopted on and off for centuries but reached a peak of politicization in the nineteenth and early twentieth centuries—nowhere more militantly than among feminists.

Acceptance of the family wage and adoption of a parental mode toward the poor also characterize what is usually understood by paternalism, making it difficult to distinguish it from maternalism. What makes maternalism more than just a women's paternalism, however, is its rootedness in the subordination of women. Maternalism showed its standpoint—its view from underneath—and from there built a strategy for using the space inside a male-dominated society for an activism that partially subverted male power.

Maternalism was a hegemonic—though not a universal—approach precisely because it could encompass different interpretations. Maternalist figures of speech were so common that even the radical Charlotte Perkins Gilman used them, praising "social motherliness" as the source of social improvement.[79] Progressive social work leaders Edith Abbott and Sophonisba Breckinridge used maternalist arguments for protective legislation and mothers' aid but situated them within a fuller, more utopian vision: a gender-neutral system of universal provision that could respond to gender-differentiated needs, including therefore the specific needs of single mothers. The left wing of the National Woman's Party broached a "wages-for-housework" vision (a 1970s phrase), flowing from the idea that mothers' pensions recognized the social value of domestic labor.[80] But the more characteristic arguments for mothers' aid came from Julia Lathrop, who explicitly dissociated mothers' aid from socialism or from maternity insurance and rather declared her faith in the family wage; cash maternity benefits might be necessary in Europe, but the "American way" was just to raise men's wages.[81]

Under the maternalist umbrella, and within the pro–mothers'-aid coalition, the most important division was between those with labor and those with charity/welfare priorities. While both groups were oriented to the poor, the labor group concentrated on regulation of working conditions while the latter envisioned their clients only in their homes. Differences of emphasis could be significant: Although they agreed that it was best for mothers to stay home, labor reformers like Kelley were quicker to accept a mother's decision to seek work and to demand workplace reform, while welfare reformers, usually social workers, were quicker to conclude that moral reform of the mother herself was also necessary.

The labor/welfare division intersected another division, between two strategies of argumentation for mothers' aid. One, encapsulated in the notion of "pensions," was that children were a social "resource" and that raising them was socially necessary labor, which could logically be supported by tax money. The other continued to argue for charity on the basis of the deservingness of single mothers and the innocence of their children. But the debate was actually farther reaching and more complex, involving the intersection of gender/family norms and state responsibility.

The first argument justified mothers' aid as an entitlement, as a compensation for women's labor and/or as a guarantee of children's well-being. American feminists frequently pointed out that motherhood was work from which the whole society benefited, and socialists added an analysis of how capital profited from women's unpaid labor. Working-class activist Theresa Malkiel wrote ironically of housewives as the "lowest paid workers."[82] (We see here the roots of 1970s "wages-for-housework" and welfare-rights analyses.) Hannah

Einstein, an early New York mothers' aid advocate, argued that becoming a mother and caring for children constituted service to the
state.[83] H. G. Wells called for "paid motherhood"; Charlotte Perkins
Gilman, responding to him, argued to transform child raising into specialized and waged labor for some, thus leaving other women free
from mothering. Though hers was not a mothers'-aid position, she influenced the campaign through her insistence that motherhood should
be recognized as skilled and socially useful labor.[84] Socialist William
Hard, former head of the Northwestern University Settlement, used
his position as editor of *The Delineator*, a popular magazine, to argue
for the pension analogy. Hard liked to describe mothers as "employes"
of the community.[85] He opposed conditioning such relief by supervision of recipients: If the state was concerned with inadequate mothering, he insisted, let it supervise all mothers, including those with husbands, the wealthy as well as the poor.[86] Along with other feminists,
Hard, a staunch women's rights advocate, leaned toward the radical
position that all enforced distinctions between men and women
should be erased and envisioned what we might today call parents'
aid.[87] But above all this group of reformers advocated precisely what
opponents feared: that mothers' aid should become a right.[88]

The argument for an entitlement was more developed in England in
a campaign that coalesced around "the endowment of motherhood."
Among the British feminist activists were some who sought a grant for
all mothers, married and single. In the name of children's welfare their
discourse carried further the critique of marriage itself. A stronger
working-class women's voice created a feminism that challenged the
family wage more sharply than was done in the United States.

The British discourse questioned not only the efficacy of the family
wage but also men's willingness to share it. Some British feminists extended their concern about dependence to married as well as single
mothers, suggesting that the family wage was a problem for all
women. Rejecting romantic assumptions about husbands' protection
of women and children, breaking the silence about intrafamily relations, British class-conscious feminists began to inquire how the "family wage" was actually distributed within families and found frequent
examples of great inequality. Anna Martin, who organized working-
class women in the East London dock neighborhoods, argued that
although "the rearing of the child crop is, confessedly, the most vital
to the nation," the worker doing that job has the worst working

conditions.[89] One feminist submitted a proposal for legislation that would have had the state guarantee a wife's entitlement to a share of a husband's earnings.[90] In fact British feminists were divided about what kind of aid would be appropriate; some supported "endowment of motherhood," but some objected that this would "institutionalize women's 'parasitism.'"[91] But their discourse did not render needy single mothers as alien or "other" to the degree that the American version did. The British campaign protested the effects of the family wage system on *all* women—lowering wages, instituting dependency.

The British debate about family allowances reached American feminists through international women's rights networks.[92] Harriot Stanton Blatch, daughter of Elizabeth Cady Stanton, lived in England with her English husband from 1882 to 1902 and was active in socialist and feminist groups. Back in the United States she supported the ERA, criticized the family-wage assumptions of the leading activists, and insisted that married women's employment was by no means always a misfortune. She wanted the state "to pay the mother of small children the equivalent of the wage she is earning, and allow her to choose whether she will remain at home and take the pension, or refuse it and continue her gainful pursuit."[93] Suffragists Crystal Eastman and Anna Howard Shaw also supported universal maternal entitlements, viewing them as a new right inherent in the extension of full citizenship to women. To quote Eastman, writing in 1920:

> The only way we can keep mothers free, at least in a capitalist society, is by the establishment of a principle that the occupation of raising children is peculiarly and directly a service to society, and that the mother upon whom the necessity and privilege of performing this service naturally falls is entitled to an adequate economic reward from the political government. It is idle to talk of real economic independence for women unless this principle is accepted.[94]

Katharine Anthony, niece of Susan B. Anthony, became an insistent American publicist of European "endowment of motherhood" ideas, challenging the family wage but calling for state subsidies for all mothers. "The mother is still the unchartered servant of the future, who receives from her husband, at *his* discretion, a share of *his* wages. . . . At some time in the future, it will seem amazing to ordinary people that children under six were not considered by the community as having any claim on their taxes."[95]

Critiques of the family wage stimulated discussion of wage discrimination against women. In England and the United States feminist activists pointed out a variety of incongruities in the prevailing wage system. Since all men were supposed to receive a "family" wage, many single or childless men could be said to be overpaid. British reformer Eleanor Rathbone pointed to the existence of "3 million phantom wives, and over 16 million phantom children."[96] On the other hand the system denied a family wage to women who did support dependents. Had the family-wage system actually existed, it would have provided an incentive to men not to marry or reproduce, and if wages were to vary according to workers' needs, then employers would favor unmarried workers.[97] The family-wage system divided women, because female wage-earners with dependents were objectively pitted against childless women workers and against nonemployed women who were dependent on men with whom working women competed. These divisions in turn influenced women's political outlooks, leading housewives to look upon working women as their enemies. Where small bits of aid were given out to supplement the inadequate wages of working mothers, the aid functioned to keep wages low and to encourage employers to substitute low-wage for higher-wage workers.[98]

These contradictions in the family wage system also worried reformers concerned with working-class men's wages. For this reason, and no doubt influenced by the participation of his wife, Dorothy Wolf Douglas, in the mothers' aid discourse, leading U.S. economist Paul Douglas proposed a family allowance system. Only with such an allowance would it be possible to stipulate an equal minimum wage without penalizing those who had families to support.[99] But because such a program was precisely a system of government support for low wages, it was understandably not supported by unions.

This swirling discourse revealed dilemmas that were insoluble within the gender order of the time. The mainstream mothers'-aid agitation stopped well short of arguing for state support for all mothers or all poor mothers. Paul Douglas was virtually ignored. Even Katharine Anthony's proposal for across-the-board endowment of motherhood remained a proposal for subsidizing children, not mothers' labor (a distinction of great consequence for the Social Security Act). The focus remained on widowed mothers—a category more mythical than empirical, which served to obfuscate rather than to educate—and symbolized passivity, self-sacrifice, and victimization.

=

The vision of mothers' aid that predominated in the United States ultimately created a more extensive charitable sector rather than a welfare state. This vision, formed within the charity organization movement, incorporated mothers' aid as an earmarked form of public charity.[100] Supporters and opponents in unison stressed the dangers of pension talk.[101] Although most supporters believed that mothers' pensions should serve to legitimate public aid, their sense of "public" was quite different from that of an entitlement or a public good. They saw the state as standing for and, to a degree, replacing older private charitable groups, a replacement desirable because of greater access to funds and the possibility of creating a more rational, scientific, systematic dispensation of resources. Their conception of the relation between helper and helped did not change fundamentally because of the entrance of government. Moreover they expected mothers' pensions both to relieve distress and to provide a lever with which to effect moral reform. The moral component was essential to their first goal, because legitimizing public aid required the identification of a group of nonstigmatized recipients, and getting rid of the stigma required that these women's behavior be beyond reproach.

Public funding for this charitable enterprise did not decrease the self-interested investment of the reformers; rather, it underscored their emphasis on moral uplift and supervision. Without the element of uplift, public funding would have left these women reformers without a role, without a gift to give. Their activism represented an effort that was particularly appealing to relatively privileged, non-employed women—to claim respect by emphasizing the virtues, skills, and necessities of their maternity and mothering other mothers. By earmarking a program of aid for single mothers they sought to control such deviations from maternal virtue as child neglect, maternal employment, female-headed households, and resultant juvenile delinquency.

In part, the "entitlement" view of mothers' aid was weaker in the United States due to the relative weakness of a working-class women's voice and the racial structure of the entire debate.[102] Ironically, another factor was a stronger middle-class women's movement. The movement gained its strength in part from its breadth, encompassing a wide continuum of political positions that created a place for almost everyone. It was a movement that established ties even between rich, conservative charity contributors and socialists, between those who scrutinized charity applicants for their deservingness and those who themselves moved to the slums. And on this continuum, mothers' aid was at the conservative edge. All supported it, but those who concentrated on it were the conservatives—women in the National Congress of Mothers or the local affiliates of the General Federation of Women's Clubs, for example.

Those in the vanguard of the campaigns for public welfare—working through organizations like the National Consumers' League, the Women's Trade Union League, and the settlements—focused more on what lay beyond. They had in mind a second act to which this was an opener. Many American activists believed that mothers' aid was a first step in acclimating both citizenry and politicians to public welfare. Leading social-work theorist Mary Richmond, an opponent of mothers' aid, was right in charging that many supporters regarded it "as an entering wedge to another and quite different social policy."[103] To the supporters of "socializing democracy," as Jane Addams had put it, mothers' aid represented the "passing of the assumption that economic need is to be regarded as an evidence of some inadequacy in the person."[104] They considered this assumption outmoded because of how the world had changed, and they were convinced that the sufferings wreaked by industrial capitalism were neither exceptions nor could they be counted on to improve on their own. There were causes of poverty against which individuals could not protect themselves, which required collective help. As Julia Lathrop wrote in 1915, "The [Children's] Bureau is doing no work at present on social insurance but, of course, it does recognize that mother's pensions are an awkward first step in that direction."[105] Welfare leaders imagined mothers' aid to be one of a number of pilot projects in a general social and moral reform and child welfare program, in which the state would expand its responsibility for the general welfare. The projects included protective labor legislation for women and children, tenement and housing codes, minimum-wage laws, and maternity and general health insurance (all of it categorized then as welfare and as social work). To a large extent they left the mothers' pensions programs to others, hoping that the programs would "pave the way for a far more dignified and democratic attitude in public relief administration."[106]

Because of this division of labor certain contradictions in the general feminist program of the early twentieth century remained suppressed. Many reformers knew well that the family wage was a myth, yet they supported a program like mothers' aid, which rested on family-wage assumptions. Thus, for example, Sophonisba Breckinridge acknowledged that mothers' aid would be only a poor substitute for insisting on decent wages: "The remedy applied [to the needs of single mothers], however, has been not that of the equal wage but the allowance out of public charitable funds. It is clear, however, that if these subsidized mothers are allowed to remain in the labor market, their presence can be prevented from becoming a catastrophe only by the payment of a family wage."[107]

Ironically, the success of mothers' aid contributed to the receding of these larger goals. The momentum of the mothers' pension wave was so strong that as early as 1912, one year after Illinois passed the first law, its opponents were entirely on the defensive, struggling to affect the design of the programs rather than resisting public programs altogether; within a decade they had been entirely silenced.[108] But the structure of the new programs was momentous. Previous studies have too simply attributed the quick victory of mothers' aid to the strength of the movement or the transparent need it identified. It is equally important that opponents were disarmed precisely because the more progressive model, across-the-board aid given as an entitlement, was definitively defeated. The smallness and cheapness of the programs guaranteed that they would not threaten private charities, and they left discretion in determining who was deserving and in supervising recipients to social workers who often came from the private charities.[109] Edith Abbott expressed some of this skepticism about the nature of the victory as early as 1917:

No other form of social betterment legislation has been so popular. . . . The [reason] is, of course, that mothers' pensions do not interfere with any great vested interests, and they do not even interfere with the taxpayers' interests, since the laws are largely optional and local authorities are not required to appropriate . . . or may make their appropriations as niggardly as they please.[110]

As mothers' aid programs operated, even the rhetoric of entitlement dwindled. The National Congress of Mothers (NCM), the main lobby for mothers' aid, had at first discussed providing support for all mothers of "the race," in that ambiguous phrase that at the time signified both humanity and its Anglo-Saxon subgroup. By the time the actual mothers' pension laws were being passed, the NCM was emphasizing control of juvenile delinquency and ending child labor.[111] By the end of the 1920s the rhetoric about mothers' aid as a right had virtually disappeared—except among poor mothers themselves. Mrs. M. S. from Minnesota wrote the Children's Bureau in 1927 complaining that she could not get a pension unless she sent her two teenage boys out to work: "Why cant a mother alone get it . . . her Mothers pension that every singel mother with minor children is entitled to."[112]

The disappointment of women like Mrs. M. S. was part of the reason for the success of the mothers' aid laws. Their small stipends, narrow eligibility criteria, and personal supervision represented a political compromise. Measured against the goal of providing support for poor children and allowing poor single mothers to stay home with their children, the mothers' aid programs were a gesture rather than an achievement.

Nevertheless, as a gesture they legitimized public assistance. The continued usage of the phrase "mothers' *pensions*" is a sign of this legitimation.[113] The usage may also have reflected the clients' preference to define themselves as entitled: Grace Abbott reported that the word "pension" was "greatly preferred by the mothers."[114] In operation the mothers' aid laws demonstrated that public programs could be run without corruption and thus lessened resistance on those grounds to future public welfare programs. The debate about mothers' aid spread information about the prevalence and predicaments of single mothers and thus inevitably raised questions about the reliability of the family wage as a method of provision. Indeed, the mothers' aid debate was the first of several national waves of concern about single motherhood that, taken together, provide marker flags designating transition points in the process of industrial and postindustrial gender and family transformation.[115]

Mothers' aid politics also produced at least two other major legacies for the New Deal and contemporary welfare policy. Along with a variety of other Progressive Era reform causes, it accelerated the development of interactive national networks of women welfare reformers and professional social workers. It promoted social work as a key route to political influence for women, and set guidelines for welfare state development—state and local discretion, the incorporation of casework, and the identification of particular welfare clients as within women's sphere. The whole experience of mothers' aid, from its conception to the evaluations of its administration, helped congeal a particular view of public welfare which conditioned, more than any other single factor, the future shape of ADC. It was a view that continued, with some adaptations to a different economic situation, the nineteenth-century moral-reform charity tradition.

A 1918 Perspective on Women's Reform Agenda

4
=

"Pity Is a Rebel Passion"

The Social Work Perspective

Mothers'-aid influence did not just seep into ADC; it was not just a debris of precedent deposited in the 1930s. It was actively transported there by a coherent network of welfare agitators rooted in the Progressive Era reform tradition. While the women's movement receded during the 1920s, many of its older leaders actually increased their national influence, cultivating a new generation of leadership. They nurtured their welfare vision primarily from their federal nest, the U.S. Children's Bureau (in the Department of Labor). Thus, when the depression hit, they were the leading federal welfare promoters and—for better and for worse—their perspective determined the shape of ADC.

Their ideas were stubborn because they were not only a legacy of the past but were reinforced in the present, in their own lives and the close community of reformers in which they lived.[1] At first scrutiny the relation between their welfare ideas and their personal lives may appear paradoxical, even contradictory. They lived within a women's community that must be considered unorthodox, possibly even subversive, toward the normative family system, resting as it did on an unusual degree of independence from men and rejection of marriage. Yet they ultimately put into place a welfare program that reinforced a conventional, even outdated gender system and disrespected other women's preference for such independence.

=

The mothers'-aid movement was so localized and protracted that no individuals truly stand out as its national leaders. Two of them, however, Julia Lathrop and Grace Abbott, were primarily responsible for bringing the mothers' aid legacy into the Social Security Act. Vivid and powerful, not only can they can be taken as representative of the female social reformers who contributed so much to the origins of our welfare state, but their stories can be regarded as a microcosm of that female social reform network, whose strength came not so much from the sum of its individuals as from their multiple relationships—a veritable web of intertwining personal and political commitments.

Julia Lathrop came from Rockford, Illinois, and few had more elite credentials—she was a direct descendant of Rev. John Lothropp, who immigrated to the New Plymouth colony (Massachusetts) in 1634. She attended Rockford Seminary and then Vassar, graduating in 1880. Returning home, she found herself, like so many college women of her generation, at loose ends. She worked in her father's law office and with him in some local Republican party activity, encouraged by her suffragist mother. After ten years, she changed her life by joining her Rockford classmate Jane Addams at the newly founded Hull-House in 1890. The alliances and friendships she formed there—notably with Addams, Florence Kelley, and the sisters Grace and Edith Abbott—structured the rest of her life. From that settlement she embarked on a reform career: Appointed to the Illinois Board of Charities in 1893, she visited Europe to study the treatment of dependent groups there, lobbied for the establishment of a juvenile court, and helped found the Illinois Immigrants' Protective League, aimed at Americanizing poor immigrants and defending their interests. In 1912 she became the first head of the U.S. Children's Bureau, the highest female official in the federal government. Beginning with a staff of fifteen and an appropriation of $25,000, she led the bureau until 1921, making it a center of welfare thought and plans. A charismatic speaker, learned and intellectually sharp, she may have received less scholarly attention than some of her Hull-House colleagues because of her tactful, strategic approaches and her long career as a public servant. But her background involved direct action in her work as a factory inspector in 1893 recalled by a Chicago judge years later:

I knew Florence Kelley at the time of the smallpox epidemic when both she and Julia Lathrop were risking their lives in the sweatshop districts of Chicago and were fearlessly entering the rooms and tenements of the west side and not merely alleviating the sufferings of the sick but preventing the sending abroad of the disease-infected garments to further contaminate the community. I saw these two women do that which the health department of the great city of Chicago could not do. The authorities were afraid not only of personal contagion but of damage suits if they destroyed the infected garments. They therefore said that there was no smallpox in Chicago. . . . Julia Lathrop, the diplomat, reasoned and cajoled. Mrs. Kelley, the fighter, asked me to file a mandamus suit to compel action.[2]

At the Children's Bureau, Lathrop undertook a particularly visible campaign to investigate and reduce infant mortality, resulting in the Sheppard-Towner Act of 1921, the first federal welfare program, supporting public-health nursing for mothers and infants. Always a single woman, Lathrop was nurtured by a close circle of women friends and a particularly strong bond with her married sister. When she retired in 1921, she returned to Rockford and lived for the rest of her life with her sister; she had a strong, maternal relationship with her niece. She remained active in Illinois and, through correspondence and travel, in national and international women's reform.

Grace Abbott was not only Lathrop's protégée, but she might have been her daughter, so similar were their backgrounds. Twenty years younger, Abbott was also from a prosperous, midwestern, political, Republican family, also had a lawyer father and a suffragist mother. Born in Grand Island, Nebraska, Abbott graduated from Grand Island College and then taught high school for six years. She followed her older sister Edith to graduate school at the University of Chicago in 1907; they then moved into Hull-House. Like Lathrop and her sister, Grace and Edith were in a lifelong partnership, although Edith remained in Chicago and became primarily an academic. At Hull-House, Grace Abbott was tutored by Addams, Lathrop, Kelley, and Breckinridge, who then promoted her to head the Immigrants' Protective League in 1908. She moved to Washington in 1917 to become Lathrop's assistant as head of the Children's Bureau's child labor division; Lathrop skillfully engineered her appointment as head of the bureau in 1921.[3] Although Abbott retired in 1934, just before the Social Security Act was passed, she helped draft ADC along with her hand-picked successors. Then, from retirement in Chicago, she served President Roosevelt as a key lobbyist for the Social Security Act. While Abbott's personality was vividly different from Lathrop's—more forthright and direct, sometimes even abrupt—they shared what Supreme Court Justice Felix Frankfurter called "a rare degree of disinterestedness and indifference to the share of her own ego in the cosmos."[4] Although Frankfurter's reference point may have been more visible and individualist male egos, he accurately captured the dedication, and the unity between friendships and social commitment, that typified these two and many others of the women's reform community.

Campaigning for Welfare: A White Women's Network

Despite the extraordinary individual talent and skill of Lathrop and Abbott, it was their network that gave them clout and elevated them to power. There is no more apt historical example of a whole greater than the sum of its individuals than this white women's reform community of approximately 1890–1935, sometimes called "social feminists."[5] Its members spanned a variety of causes, united by their own integrated understanding of what they were doing, of what "welfare" meant. As Lathrop wrote, explaining the breadth of her conception of the Children's Bureau's jurisdiction:

> There is no dividing line between so-called economic legislation and welfare work. Everything which affects the life of the nation—be it agricultural relief, taxation, labor, or railroad legislation—affects the lives of children and the welfare of citizens. It is all, in a way, welfare legislation, and conversely there is no such thing as pure welfare legislation which is all fundamentally economic.[6]

Still, this reform community was internally differentiated. Nationally there were three magnetic poles. The most purely feminist—and the only group that called itself feminist—cohered around the National Woman's Party and supported an ERA. At the labor pole, primarily oriented to working women and with some prominent figures leaning toward socialism, were the National Consumers' League (NCL), the National Women's Trade Union League (NWTUL), and

"their" federal agency, the U.S. Women's Bureau. The Children's Bureau group, focused on welfare—although they did not use that
word in its current meaning—concentrated on mothers and took a
dimmer view of working women. On balance the welfare group was
considerably more conservative—less feminist and less left than the
other two. Yet they shared some common purpose, and the boundaries often blurred.

Many working-class, immigrant, and minority women participated in these social reform campaigns, but the national leadership was
dominated by privileged white Protestant women, whose bonds and
affinities were so strong that they formed a close comradeship and
even, however inadvertently, made it difficult for women from different backgrounds to participate.[7] There were some major and
many minor political differences among them, but relative homogeneity allowed them to develop enough of a consensus, and sufficiently cooperative methods of work, to gain substantial power.

The main power base for the welfare advocates was the U.S. Children's Bureau. It was their creation, a presidential concession to the
achievements and demands of the Progressive Era women's network,
a "national settlement house with a specialty in children."[8] What was
extraordinary about the Children's Bureau was a tense balance between two opposite forces: one centripetal, toward professional or
bureaucratic exclusivity; the other centrifugal, toward the civic organizations of the women's and welfare movements. Children's Bureau
staff were responsible to the Department of Labor and the president,
but they were also accountable to a reform movement because they
depended on that movement's support for their policy agenda. If they
had had any doubts that the survival and advance of the bureau's
agenda depended on public support, these were erased during several
waves of conservative attack on the Children's Bureau. Both accountability and support waned over time, and the Children's Bureau lost
power through the 1920s and 1930s. But until the Social Security Act
it remained the heart of white women's welfare thought, a command
center for promulgating a variety of welfare proposals.

The women's unusual ability to construct and maintain activist associations, and thus to maximize influence despite the generally
weak position of women in the political system, derived in part from
their alternative gender system. Let us not exaggerate: It was only
slightly different from the dominant gender system, affected only a

small minority of women, and was relatively short-lived. Yet it left a lasting imprint on the American welfare state. In this system a majority of unmarried women became "married" to their female allies, and thereby to their work, escaping the "family claim" that bound most women. Ironically the very women who continued to base their welfare proposals on family-wage, breadwinner-housewife marital norms removed themselves from these norms.

=

To get a bird's-eye view of the network, I compiled a collective biography of a sample of its national leadership—seventy six women.[9] Their constituency numbered many thousands. For example, in the Northeast alone in 1911–13, there were eight hundred settlement workers and seventeen hundred paid and volunteer women "social workers" in 49 social welfare institutions. These included private charity organizations, family welfare associations, day nurseries, reform schools, hospital social service bureaus, settlements, juvenile courts.[10]

The coherence of this reform network was cemented by the women's homogeneous class, religious, and ethnic origins. They were all white, and most came from prosperous, even prominent, families. An indicator of their privilege was that a third of the unmarried women were nevertheless not regularly employed—that is, they were able to live without earning. (This underestimates those who could have lived on family money, since many of the women chose to take jobs even without economic necessity.[11]) Virtually all were of northern European, Protestant backgrounds, from the Northeast or Midwest. The nine Jewish members were hardly representative of Jewish immigrants: Five had wealthy German-Jewish parents (Elizabeth Brandeis Raushenbush, Hannah Einstein, Josephine and Pauline Goldmark, and Lillian Wald). There were three Catholics (Josephine Brown, Jane Hoey, and Agnes Regan), but they were hardly the typical U.S. Catholics of the period: They were all U.S.-born of prosperous parents. The shared Protestantism among the others was more a sign of similar ethnic background than of active sectarian commitment, for few were churchgoers and churches did not organize their welfare activities. Some among them, of various denominations, were deeply influenced, however, by religious commitments to social justice.

These women were the beneficiaries, and the products, of a major transformation in American education. By 1880, forty thousand, or one out of three, undergraduates were women.[12] But this network was exceptional both in class and in gender terms. While less than 1 percent of all American women held college degrees, 86 percent of these women were college educated, 37 percent at one of the elite New England women's colleges, and 66 percent had attended graduate school.

Had they been born in the second half of this century, many of these women might have become academics or lawyers. But the fact that these professions were closed to most women added to other motivations in turning them toward charity and reform work—a kind of activism generically called "social work" in this period and with which a great majority of this network identified.[13] (Prior to the Progressive Era, "social work" did not refer to a profession but to a range of helping and reform activity; the word "social" originally emphasized the reform rather than the charity component.) Many had mothers active in social reform.[14] The early-twentieth-century professionalization of social work did not create a sharp break with amateur charitable "friendly visiting" or with political activism.[15] On the contrary, well into the 1930s these women considered casework, charity, and reform politics all to be "social work." Frances Perkins called her work as secretary of labor "social work."[16] Amy Maher, chairman of the Ohio Council on Women in Industry, wrote of her pleasure in a brief that women from the NCL had written: "Its a great piece of work . . . and as feminists we're proud of it, and as social workers, and as litterateurs!!"[17]

More than two-thirds lived and worked in the New England and the mid-Atlantic states—hardly surprising since the national headquarters of the organizations they worked for were usually located there. Hull-House long remained a fundamental influence, and national meetings drew midwesterners into contact with easterners. But it is significant that 57 percent of this network were in New York City during the Progressive Era or the 1920s. The city was not only the headquarters for a number of influential organizations but also played a vanguard role in the development of public services and regulation in the public interest, and women in this network were influential in city welfare programs.[18] New York City had established the nation's first Bureau of Child Hygiene in 1908; by 1923 all the states had such bureaus. The city pioneered in promoting welfare through regulation—of prices, milk quality, tenement apartments, midwifery, working conditions, and public and occupational health and safety.[19] New York City settlement houses specialized in demonstration projects, beginning programs on a small, private scale and then getting them publicly funded: The settlements initiated vocational guidance programs, later adopted by the public schools; they initiated the use of public schools for after-hours recreation programs and visiting public health nursing; Lillian Wald, head of the Henry Street Settlement, was a key figure in the city's response to the 1918–1919 influenza epidemic.[20] In 1917 the Women's City Club of New York City opened a maternity center in the Hell's Kitchen neighborhood, where they provided prenatal nursing care and education and housekeeping services for new mothers. Expanded to ten locations in Manhattan, this effort served as a model for the bill that eventually became the Sheppard-Towner Act. The Women's City Club, which provided an important meeting place for many of these women, can serve as an indicator of their prosperity: Members had to pay substantial dues and an initiation fee, and in 1917 the club purchased a mansion on Thirty-fifth Street and Park Avenue for $160,000.[21]

Some of these women had been active in party politics even before they could vote. Some had been in the Socialist party, many identified as Republicans (reflecting their abolitionist heritage), and many were active in the 1912 Progressive party campaign. Most, however, preferred nonpartisan public activism. During the late 1920s and 1930s they transferred their allegiances to the Democratic party. Here, too, New York was important, because the political figure who most attracted these women to the Democrats was Franklin Roosevelt, from his governorship (1928–32) and then his presidency. Several women who had been active in reform in the city, notably Belle Moskowitz, Frances Perkins, Rose Schneiderman, and Eleanor Roosevelt, took on statewide roles. Al Smith's 1928 presidential campaign promoted more division than unity, however, because most women "social workers" were critical of his "wet" positions and his association with machine politics. The reassuring presence of his aide, Moskowitz, and then Franklin Roosevelt's "aide," his wife, Eleanor, was critical in bringing their circle into the Democratic party.[22]

Given these common experiences, it is not surprising that the network was dense with personal acquaintance. Half worked with the NCL and/or the settlements. They met in a variety of other organizations as well, such as the NWTUL, the Progressive party of 1912, and the National League of Women Voters. The settlements in particular encouraged intergenerational connections and intimacy, because the younger or newer volunteers actually lived with their elders, seeing them in action.[23] When Julia Lathrop passed the Children's Bureau on to Grace Abbott, she also passed on her apartment.

Leaders groomed, protected, and promoted their protégées: Jane Addams did this with Alice Hamilton, Lillian Wald, and Florence Kelley; Grace Abbott's entire career was orchestrated by her Hull-House seniors; all of them campaigned for Abbott and then Perkins for secretary of labor, and continually tried to promote women for any accessible government offices.[24] The Children's Bureau staff worked to get jobs for their political friends: Anna Louise Strong, for example, got her position with the Legislative Reference Bureau because of Lathrop's intervention.[25] Those in the national leadership were quite successful in placing their comrades in state-welfare-related positions.[26] And mentoring continued within the government in the treatment of employees. The chiefs of the Children's and Women's Bureaus—the two key federal agencies run by women—manifested extraordinary involvement in the personal lives of their employees. Mary Anderson, for example, head of the Women's Bureau, corresponded frequently with her employees in other parts of the country about their family lives, advising them about such concerns as the care of aging parents.[27] The network developed job sharing, a practice often associated with the women's movement of the 1970s, as a means of bringing in married women who could not manage full-time employment: When offered the position of administrator of the District of Columbia's new minimum-wage law for women, economist Clara Beyer split it with her friend Elizabeth Brandeis.[28] For the first few years after Grace Abbott took over the Children's Bureau, she wrote a stream of letters to Julia Lathrop seeking advice and commenting on how much she appreciated being able to pour out her complaints.

Government and civic leaders consulted regularly about appointments to offices. Grace Abbott consulted Julia Lathrop about who should become chairman of the League of Women Voters' Children's

Committee: "I have been trying to go over people in my mind and have wondered about Dr. Mendenhall or Katherine Dummer Fisher. . . . Dr. M is one of the few people ready for that. Do you think her temperamental difficulties are too many. . . . Amy Field has as many children hasn't she as Katherine Dummer [?][29] I know she has not been able to do the Women in Industry [now the Women's Bureau] things in which she has been vitally interested. Both really are too busy."[30] The female leadership's active promotion of their "sisters" worked in part because their methods were not very democratic. As Grace Abbott wrote in a private letter: "Talking over the question of a representative from the Women's Joint Legislative Committee on the Advisory Committee. . . . it seemed a good plan to have the Committee elect a person at the next meeting. . . . I am wondering if you would serve. . . . We shall appoint you anyhow but I think it would be of great help if you had that relationship to that Committee. I'll be *very* discreet about anything you say about it."[31] Their cooptive method reproduced an "old 'girls' club" and only some women were invited to join. But the homogeneity they replicated through this method added to the network's internal coherence and loyalty, which then further reinforced its exclusivity.

=

If the circle put up a fence against those who did not belong socially, it continued to include volunteers as well as bureaucrats and professionals. Its welfare vision continued to value ordinary, untrained pity and the desire to help along with professional skills, and its evaluation of women's place in a political field led to the conclusion that volunteer support was indispensable. Julia Lathrop's 1912 defense of pity is instructive: "Pity is a rebel passion . . . it does not fear the forces of society but defies them . . . it is the Kingdom of Heaven working within us. The justice of today is born of yesterday's pity. . . . It will need as perhaps no other bureau of the government will need, the continuance of the popular pity which demanded and secured it."[32] Alliance between professionals and volunteers was a defining practice of this early-twentieth-century women's political culture.[33]

Indeed, these women's arenas and mode of operation suggest why the "state" often includes more than government. In the Progressive Era the powerful settlement houses, such as Hull-House and the

Henry Street Settlement, became virtual parts of municipal government and sometimes virtually ran publicly funded programs. When women gained governmental positions there was as much extra as intra-agency consultation and direction. Julia Lathrop's first act as chief of the new Children's Bureau in 1912 was to confer with her constituency.[34] In its first project, collecting data on infant mortality, the Children's Bureau used hundreds of volunteers to help.[35] In 1920 Florence Kelley of the NCL listed investigations the Women's Bureau should undertake, and these were done; Mary Anderson of the Women's Bureau wrote comments on a bill for the protection of female employees that she had arranged for the NCL to draft for the state of Indiana. In 1922 Anderson wrote Mary (Molly) Dewson of the NCL asking her to tone down her critical language about the National Woman's Party, and Dewson complied; in 1923 Dewson asked Anderson to help her draft a response to the National Woman's Party that was to appear in the *Nation* under Dewson's name.[36] In 1923 some women's organizations proposed that they privately raise the money to construct a new building for the Children's Bureau, a suggestion Abbott vetoed.[37]

This kind of cooperation continued through the New Deal. A good example was the Women's Charter, an attempt made in 1936 to negotiate a compact between pro- and anti-ERA factions. Representatives of the usual white women's civic organizations—the YWCA, the League of Women Voters, the Women's Trade Union League, the NCL, the Association of University Women, and the Federation of Business and Professional Women—participated, as did several state and federal government women; the first draft of the charter was written by Mary Anderson, still head of the Women's Bureau; Frieda Miller, then head of the women's section of the New York State Department of Labor; Rose Schneiderman, president of the NWTUL, formerly of the National Recovery Administration (until the Supreme Court declared it unconstitutional), and soon to become head of the New York State Department of Labor; and Mary Van Kleeck.[38] (The drafting of the charter exemplifies, again, the importance of New York and the predominance of single women.)

When the women didn't know each other personally, they presumed that their similar class and educational backgrounds created trust. As Gertrude Gogin of the YWCA National Board wrote Julia Lathrop offering the volunteer services of her organization, "May I just add that I am a Vassar woman, class of 1908, and while you do not know me I do feel acquainted with you thru Katherine Davis and Mary Vida Clark."[39] And they considered their class privileges and affiliations important, working steadily at integrating younger members of the network into their private clubs, for example. Both Julia Lathrop and Grace Abbott not only recommended new women for membership but solicited supporting letters from others. Responding to Abbott's request to recommend Children's Bureau employee Dr. Martha Eliot to the New York City Cosmopolitan Club, Alice Hamilton replied with relief that she could just manage to get the endorsement done by the deadline: "I am sure Dr. Eliot will get in easily. She is much more desirable than the great majority of applicants."[40] The clubs were of practical as well as symbolic importance. When the retired Julia Lathrop came back to Washington for a brief visit, Grace Abbott—who had inherited Lathrop's apartment—offered to vacate it temporarily and move to her club so that Lathrop and her sister could stay in a familiar place.[41] In 1936 Abbott nominated her successor, Katharine Lenroot, for Cosmopolitan membership, explaining: "As Miss Lundberg [Lenroot's partner] is no longer in New York . . . [the club] affords a type of resource for meeting people or having them to lunch or dinner."[42] These class understandings may also have included some suspicion of the "idle rich." As one correspondent wrote in a letter of recommendation, "She is of the Boston aristocrats but a very level headed woman and has done a great deal of fine work in getting better milk standards in Boston."[43]

Further tightening their connectedness was the fact that the great majority of the women in this network were "single"—that is, not married. Only 34 percent had ever been married, and most of those were divorced, separated, or widowed; only 18 percent remained married when they were politically active. Only 28 percent had children.[44] (By contrast, women reformers active at state and local levels included more married and less elite women.[45]) Despite their singleness—indeed, perhaps *because* of it—their efforts were very much directed toward family and child welfare, as a way of connecting with women's traditional role.[46] It is remarkable to contemplate that so many women who became symbols of matronly respectability and asexual "social motherhood" led such unconventional private lives.[47]

Many of them were not really single. More than a quarter (28 percent) were in relationships with other women that might have been called "Boston marriages" a few decades before.[48] This figure is a conservative one, including only those women known to have a specific partner. It does not include women like Edith Rockwood who lived, until her death in 1953, with Marjorie Heseltine of the Children's Bureau and Louise Griffith of the Social Security Agency, and who built and owned a summer house jointly with Marion Crane of the Children's Bureau.[49] Nor does it include Eleanor Roosevelt, who had very close relationships with two different female couples, Esther Lape and Elizabeth Read, and Nancy Cook and Marion Dickerman.[50] At the time these relationships were mainly not named at all, although Molly Dewson referred to her mate as her "partner." Most of their contemporary acquaintances perceived them as celibate.[51] Today some of these women might be called lesbian, but we know little about their sex lives and, in any case, they certainly did not use the term, rare at the time, about themselves. What is relevant here, however, is not their sexual activity but their dependence on other women economically, for jobs, for care in grief, illness, and old age, for vacation companionship, for every conceivable kind of help.

Moreover, they turned this mutual dependency into a political caucus.[52] They experienced their life choices in a manner that could be compared to nuns' sensibility—they were dedicated to a great cause, and family obligations must not interfere. They sometimes addressed letters to close friends, "Dear Sister."[53] A leading social worker of the younger generation reminisced that women grew anxious if they had to tell Edith Abbott or Sophonisba Breckinridge, core faculty at the University of Chicago's social work school, the leading training center among this group, that they planned to marry.[54] And with good reason. Molly Dewson responded to Clara Mortenson's wedding announcement, "Your wedding announcement certainly gave me most mixed feelings. . . . wishing you all good luck. . . . *BUT* at the same time it is no joke for the M.W. [minimum wage] cause to have you leave your post."[55] The women's female bonding did not disadvantage them but brought them political power, and they got it without making the sacrifices of personal intimacy that men so often did. Privileged women that they were, several of them had country homes, and groups would often weekend together; we can be sure that their conversation erased distinctions between the personal and the political, between gossip and tactics.

Almost all Americans at the time considered marriage to be the normal and proper arrangement for all, and family the main nexus of connection between men and women. Unmarried women were often valued and respected, but also often pitied. To the women reform leaders, wife-and-motherhood did not necessarily add to women's status or make them happier, nicer, more attractive, or more moral. To consider marriage the highest state for a woman was ipso facto to consider as given and inevitable some levels of deference, indirection, self-effacement, and/or weakness. Their own avoidance of marriage did not mean that they were like contemporary feminists, challenging gender itself. On the contrary, they were convinced that their notions of the feminine flowed in parallel with those of the majority of married women, and they felt quite comfortably feminine. Those who lived as couples with other women considered themselves to be living in respectable, womanly arrangements. Their backgrounds of privilege, naturally, contributed to their confidence that they were always proper. And lesbianism, despite its occasional "comings out" in selected social groups early in the century, had not yet been much stigmatized—indeed for many it had not yet been named. Like nuns, they created and understood their commitments to one another through their commitment to a cause.

They were aware of the political implications of the rejection of marriage in favor of a community. Some of them might be considered the granddaughters of Susan Anthony, acting out her remarkable 1877 speech, "Homes of Single Women." Unmarried, frequently on the road lecturing and organizing, Anthony was dependent on the local hospitality of women's rights activists wherever she went, and warmed by the single women's homes she visited. She anticipated exactly what came into being—a generation of educated women who did not marry: "The 'logic of events' points, inevitably, to an *epoch of single women*. If women will not accept marriage *with subjection*, nor men proffer it *without*, there is, there can be, *no alternative*. The women who will *not be ruled* must live without marriage." Middle-class women who would not suppress their interest in public-sphere activism—whether professional or volunteer—would live without marriage. Anthony's story was that their homes were as domestic, as charming, warm, and settled as those of married women, never perceived as sad or inferior. "Men go to these homes as they do to their gentlemen's clubs, to talk of art, science, politics, religion and reform. . . . [The women] are not halves, needing complements."[56]

This gender system did not last; by the 1930s it was already breaking down as employment of working-class women expanded, as middle-class women demanded both marriage and career, as same-sex relationships drew more criticism. In the 1920s conservatives began attacking their singleness. Democratic Senator James Reed of Missouri, arguing against the Sheppard-Towner Act, derided the leadership of "female celibates:" "It seems to be the established doctrine of the bureau that the only people capable of caring for babies and mothers of babies are ladies who have never had babies."[57] Julia Lathrop's defensiveness (and contradictoriness) in 1927 was revealing:

> I usually refuse to address myself to this subject partly because it is not worth while to invite the ridicule which attaches to an unmarried woman. But . . . it occurs to me that the fact of decent lives without marriage . . . affords a warrant for urging the value to the individual and to society of the power of self-restraint. . . . Do not misunderstand. Marriage is essential to the happiness of the individual and to the existence of civilized society.[58]

The ideology that made the public a male sphere and the private a female one was never perfectly enacted, and practice was considerably more complex; indeed the public/private separation was often honored only in rhetoric. But the rhetoric was nonetheless influential. In the nineteenth century there was pressure on women active outside families to interpret and explain that activism within women's sphere of interests. Welfare activism was construed as an extension of women's domestic labor, as "social housekeeping."

In the 1930s a different orientation became increasingly evident. While women continued to use their maternal and housework responsibilities to justify their authority in matters of welfare, they also sought "careers" just like men. The transformation was gradual and halting: There had been full-fledged career professionals in the field in the second decade of the twentieth century and full-time activist volunteers long before that. But the norm tipped at a certain point. If the quintessential leader of the white women's reform network in the 1920s was Florence Kelley, head of the female-dominated NCL, her counterparts in the 1930s might be Molly Dewson, by now the leading woman in the Democratic Party, or Grace Abbott and Katharine Lenroot, federal bureaucrats. The new leaders were, first, answerable ultimately to male bosses. Second, they worked within the rules and limits of large bureaucracies: What they wrote, said, and did had to be approved at several levels; and their decisions had implications for mainstream politics. Third, they were increasingly professionals—as trained experts and as politically neutral. Thus they operated with a continuing tension between their allegiance to a women's movement and their professional and bureaucratic responsibilities.

This gradual shift in public position was accompanied by an equally influential private transformation. As time passed, particularly from the 1930s on, women's sense that marriage and public-sphere activity were incompatible choices diminished, and more married activists appeared.[59] Their situations were new, even to other women, and they frequently had to explain their needs and limitations. Clara Beyer, one of the pioneering few to hold a professional job while still taking care of small children, mentioned these issues frequently in her correspondence. In April 1930 she explained to Elizabeth Eastman that she could not come to a late-afternoon meeting because she had to pick her son up from school—an almost heretical refusal among this set of women, who worked day and night:[60] "We poor married women have a hard time measuring up to standards set by our unencumbered sisters."[61] And their single sisters were suspicious of the dedication of their married comrades. Clara Beyer had suggested to Grace Abbott in 1932 that the Children's Bureau hire Jane Flexner (daughter of renowned medical leader Abraham Flexner), but Abbott replied that Flexner would not be able to travel freely because she was married.[62] The ultimate resolution of these tensions in later decades included both changes in marriage and a less total commitment to "the cause."

The women's singleness was a phenomenon not only of a particular period of time but also of a limited class. Marriage was far less dispensable for women without money, education, or connections. Yet this female political culture was not just handed to these women along with their other privileges; rather it was their initiative that turned a limitation—the middle-class taboo on married women's employment or public-sphere activism—into a source of power. And, of course, their community of women was particularly visible because they took their prominence with them to their well-documented jobs. Their friendships transcended boundaries between the public and private sectors, between government and civic organizations.

Being unmarried did not keep these women from useful connections with men, connections simultaneously professional and personal; this system was not what recent feminists have called "separatism." On the contrary, their connections to men, which came with kinship and class as well as reform connections, were important to them. Clara Beyer got her "in" when Felix Frankfurter recommended her for a job administering the 1918 District of Columbia minimum-wage law. She then brought in Elizabeth Brandeis, daughter of Justice Louis, to share the job with her. Louis Brandeis's two sisters-in-law, Josephine and Pauline Goldmark, were also active in these circles. Sophonisba Breckinridge, Florence Kelley, Julia Lathrop, and Katharine Lenroot were daughters of senators and congressmen. Loula Dunn's father and two grandfathers had been in the Alabama legislature.[63] These women often learned politics in their households and knew where to get introductions and referrals to other politically influential people when they needed them. When Clara Beyer said, "It was my contacts that made [me] so valuable, that I could go to these people,"[64] she was speaking about both her female and her male connections. One example is how Julia Lathrop contrived to name her successor. Her letter to Republican Senator Robert La Follette Sr. of Wisconsin is a gem: she had no wish to name her successor, she wrote, but if asked who was best qualified to do the job she would have to name Grace Abbott; she wondered if the senator might provide his opinion? (How convenient that La Follette did as she asked and also recommended Abbott!) Two months later she wrote to her influential friend Ruth Hanna McCormick, daughter of Republican bigwig Mark Hanna and wife of Republican Senator Medill McCormick:

> Senator McCormick suggested the other evening that it would be extremely helpful if Senator Lodge was favorable to the appointment of Grace Abbott, and that it would be well to have someone see him. . . . Of course I could find some New England friend to send to Mr. Lodge, but . . . no one who knows the whole situation as well as I do myself. Since Senator Lodge has always been friendly to the Bureau, I am inclined to venture to ask him to see me, if Senator McCormick and you think well of that, and if the Senator will be good enough to give me a note to Mr. Lodge so that he can be sure of your husband's opinion and of yours.[65]

These women not only benefited from men's help; they also pressed men into service. The famous "Brandeis brief," for example, successful in getting the Supreme Court to uphold protective legislation for women and children, was not only written for Brandeis by women in this network; moreover, it was conceived by women, and Brandeis was persuaded to do it by women. Women were active in convincing men of the importance of social legislation.[66] Frankfurter recalled how he was organized into the cause: "Mrs. Kelley . . . tried one so-called eminent lawyer after another to argue the ten hour law. . . . [It always required a] good deal of contrivance on the part of Mrs. Kelley to get the state to invite us to be of counsel." He remembered working with Josephine Goldmark, "a distinguished product of Bryn Mawr, a charming, handsome, sensitive creature, with a literary and scientific bent of mind, a disciplined mind she had."[67] Paul Douglas, a leading proponent of unemployment insurance and later to become a senator, credited his first concern with welfare legislation to Jane Addams's influence when he was a student in Chicago.[68]

=

The women's welfare network also functioned within a racial system of thought, and its political activities helped to construct and reconstruct that system. In this system racial beliefs intersected with gender norms: Motherhood was a key factor in both, as were questions of women's employment, sexual morality, and patterns of fatherhood and male dominance. The sense of community, common purpose, and identity among them was based not only on class, religious, and political homogeneity but also on race.

The whole outlook of the reformers, their very identity, was formed by the country's transformation in ethnic makeup. In the Progressive Era elite reformers usually considered the new European immigrants to be of a different race. While their terms often sounded biologistic, as in, "Anarchy has become hereditary from generation to generation among the [Italian] immigrants and their children,"[69] they were not necessarily eugenical in the contemporary sense; except for public health experts, few reformers of this generation distinguished between genetic and environmental influences.[70] For the welfare reformers, who were the liberals of racial discourse, the aliens were changeable, salvageable; indeed their presence created an urgent need for reculturation.

The early-twentieth-century social work/welfare vision expressed a consciousness that the United States was in a social crisis created in large part by the new immigration. The survival of the democratic republic seemed to depend on turning the new immigrants into democratic citizens—educated, self-controlled, disciplined. The content of these goals was gendered. Most of the new immigrants came from patriarchal cultures, in which the women and children were subordinated and prohibited from developing as individuals. Campaigns against child labor and domestic violence expressed female reformers' antipatriarchal strategies. In such campaigns social workers walked a winding path between helping and controlling, often responding to immigrants' own expression of their aspirations but also comfortably assuming that their own elite Protestant culture was self-evidently superior.[71] The force of this orientation can be seen in the fact that even in the southern states, where there were few immigrants (less than 2 percent of the population in the 1920s), white women's reform activism was nevertheless primarily directed at recent immigrants, not at African Americans.[72]

The elite liberal attitude toward the new immigrants was complex. Jane Addams, the most universally beloved woman in this network, was extraordinary in her consciousness of the values of the immigrant cultures as well as their lack of fit with urban industrial life; she believed that all would benefit if the new citizens could preserve their heritages with pride. Yet few reformers lived up to this standard of openness. Their very desire to help convinced them that the immigrants needed to be able to fit in. Thus appraisals like this (of a job applicant) were commonplace: "While of south italian [sic] parentage [he] is American in looks (not dark) and manners (excellent) and is one of the ablest young persons I have met in a long time. . . . Would get along well with a rich Commissioner as well as with the immigrants."[73]

The complexity of their attitudes can be seen in their thoughts about Jews. Several wealthy women of German-Jewish background, such as Lillian Wald and the Goldmarks, were integrated into this set, but this did not alter their overall tendency to perceive Jews in general as "other"—alien but not necessarily inferior. Most Jewish women, even middle-class, German-Jewish women, organized independently of Christians, and felt they had to prove themselves.[74] The Protestant leaders offered positive as well as negative generalizations about Jews, revealing complex feelings. Settlement founder Mary Kingsbury Simkhovitch was fascinated but apprehensive: "The

Jewish mind is centripetal; everything it discovers it appropriates."[75] Similarly Florence Kelley, discussing possible immigration restriction in 1913:

> It is obvious that every nation profits by welcoming the victims of *religious* persecution (Huguenots, Waldensians, Pilgrims, Puritans, Quakerts [*sic*], even Mennonites, [illegible] and Jews). But exactly how can we technically draw the line to get to admit the Russian Jews yet exclude the Catholic Slavs? . . . Surely our Yankee ingenuity ought to enable us to draw the difficult exclusion line above suggested. I am convinced that the Pacific Coast people are right about the Mongolians; and I am sure we are utter fools to endure the ruin of the Atlantic Coast by the invasion of Asia Minor and South Eastern Europe. My record of twenty-one years of intimate contact with the immigrants should safeguard me against any charge of race or religious prejudice in this.[76]

These aggressive categorizations softened and blurred over time, but this generation of reformers never lost confidence in their own style and behavior as normative. The remarkable collective unanimity in these attitudes is well illustrated by a batch of letters concerning the possible appointment of Sophie Loeb to a League of Nations child welfare committee in 1927. Three people asked for evaluations contributed remarkably similar comments. Arthur Kellogg, of the social work journal *Survey*, wrote: "Miss Loeb . . . is an annoyingly efficient person. . . . a hard-working, successful, competent Jewess. . . . admiration for her efficiency and acute distress at her personality." Graham Romeyn Taylor, active in the settlements and then director of the Joint Committee on Methods of Preventing Delinquency, wrote:

> . . . unfortunate choice . . . she is a person who primarily enjoys publicity for herself, but has sincerely ridden one hobby—that of mothers' pensions. . . . I know not of my own knowledge but have heard from others. I have no hesitancy, however, in saying that due to the fact that she is very unrepresentative of the most intelligent social effort in America my judgement is that she would be a very unsuitable member of an international body.

And Florence Kelley: "Miss Loeb is a typical New York Jewess of the most "pushful kind." . . . Her appointment to such a position would be an international calamity. . . . Quote me at your own discretion! I am perfectly willing." The criticism of Loeb in these letters included concrete complaints, and it is possible that she *was* a difficult and self-serving person. The point here is how the reformers' dislike was experienced in racial terms.[77]

Their attitudes toward blacks and Hispanics were considerably different, and it is important not to oversimplify or dehistoricize them. For the white northern reformers early in the century, the primary fact was that they did not notice these minorities—did not imagine them as indicated objects of reform.[78] For the southerners, the immigrants appeared reformable and integratable as blacks did not. The exceptions, such women as Sophonisba Breckinridge, Florence Kelley, Frances Kellor, and Mary White Ovington, who did become concerned with African Americans' problems, were in the vanguard of racial liberalism and offered valuable white support for civil rights organizations such as the National Association for the Advancement of Colored People (NAACP). Kelley withdrew her support from a federal aid-to-education bill in 1923 when it became clear that state control would prevent any money from reaching black schools.[79] Several key white reformers initiated major social research projects collecting information about blacks in the north. Several African American reformers visited settlements, but not as residents. The remarkable Lugenia Burns Hope got a small taste of Hull-House by being brought there weekly as the personal secretary to a wealthy reformer who attended meetings there.[80]

Though liberal southern white women activists engaged in some cross-race discussions through the Council for Interracial Cooperation, established in 1920, overall the record of this white women's reform group on race was dismal. White settlements ignored and excluded blacks; those few that included them were segregated. As the Great Migration began, settlement workers worried lest their efforts attract blacks into their cities.[81] They responded to blacks moving into formerly immigrant-dominated neighborhoods by closing down and following the white immigrants elsewhere, conducting segregated activities or simply excluding blacks. The National Federation of Settlements established standards for admission of projects that often excluded poorly funded black ones.[82] The white women's organizations practiced exclusion of blacks, as has been well documented with respect to suffrage groups and the Women's Christian Temperance Union (WCTU).[83] Segregation was growing during the Progressive Era—indeed segregation *was* a Progressive reform among whites, who believed it would strengthen social order. The Children's Bureau had no black employees and its research rarely looked at racial minorities. Even the most antiracist white reformers could be ignorant of the problems blacks faced and thus come to prejudiced conclusions, as for example when Florence Kelley blamed black men for exploiting their wives by sending them out to work.[84]

The first significant involvement of this white welfare network with racial minorities was through the Sheppard-Towner Act, because it was their first national program and therefore the first to reach the South and the West. The Children's Bureau insisted on serving minority women, to their credit, but their insistence on state autonomy in developing local programs allowed great discrimination against African Americans and Mexican Americans. The program's agents were often disdainful and racist (refusing, for example, to recognize any value in traditional healing practices).[85] National Children's Bureau leaders sometimes complained about southern racial policies, but they needed southern political support.[86]

By the 1930s growing black civil rights agitation was making it harder for women in this group to remain oblivious. The Children's Bureau included blacks in the 1930 White House Conference on Children.[87] But Secretary of Labor Frances Perkins was baffled by black demands for representation, telling Eleanor Roosevelt that she saw "no real reason for having a negro" in the Women's Bureau and feared that doing so would create difficulties.[88] Lorena Hickok, a close friend of Eleanor Roosevelt, defended the racial double standard in the administration of New Deal relief.[89] The welfare-oriented network was more recalcitrant toward minorities than the labor network. In response to black women's attempt to organize domestic workers' unions, the New York City WTUL pushed for a state law for the protection of domestic servants (they asked for a sixty-hour workweek, a minimum wage, worker's compensation and old-age insurance provisions.)[90] But the Children's Bureau never focused a study on the child welfare problems entailed by domestic service, although that was the single most common job for women.

The Children's Bureau

The single biggest political influence on the welfare network's ideas was the Children's Bureau. Established in 1912, the bureau is evidence that women exercised political power before they were enfranchised.

The fact that this agency antedated the Women's Bureau, established (also in the Department of Labor) in 1918, reflects the earlier acceptability of federal action to protect children than involvement on women's behalf.[91] Nevertheless, the Children's Bureau was as much a (generic) women's bureau as the Women's Bureau itself; the two agencies achieved a practical and for the most part amicable division of labor, with the latter focusing on employment issues while the former ranged widely into other areas, despite its location in the Department of Labor. Indeed the Children's Bureau founders hoped that it would become a kind of Department of Health, Education and Welfare within the Department of Labor.[92]

The Children's Bureau was the child primarily of Lillian Wald and Florence Kelley, whose work encapsulated the most productive of the vast array of woman-powered reform activity of the Progressive Era. Wald, from a wealthy German-Jewish merchant family, was a nurse who then entered medical school; one day in 1893, or so she told the story, she was called from a classroom to tend a poor woman in the New York immigrant slums. Her emotional response to this direct exposure to extreme poverty and suffering led her to drop out of medical school and begin a settlement. She turned to two other prominent German-Jewish families—the Loebs and the Schiffs—for backing, and no doubt the presence of so many poor Jews in New York particularly stimulated their sense of responsibility. Her Henry Street Settlement became a powerful influence in New York City for many decades, and she lived there until illness forced her into retirement in 1934. Public health nursing was her major emphasis, and within this work—which was of pioneering influence in many areas—she took particular concern for the problems of children. In 1904 she, Florence Kelley, and others founded the National Child Labor Committee.

Kelley was the daughter of a Protestant Irish Republican congressman known as Pig Iron Kelley due to his advocacy of protective tariffs. Her mother brought Quaker influence to the family. Kelley attended Cornell and tried to gain admission to graduate school at the University of Pennsylvania in 1882, but it would not admit women. Traveling in Europe, she fell in with socialist students, became a Marxist, and did the first English translation of Engels's *The Condition of the Working Class in England in 1844*. She married a Russian medical student but, returning to the United States, soon left him and went to Hull-House in Chicago with her three children. Hull-House leaders arranged for her to board out her children, and she was able to live with the group, experiencing the intense bonding of the settlement. (Kelley's personal life thus echoes a pattern characteristic of the group, contributing so much to child welfare and using maternalist argumentation so effectively while not actually raising her own children.[93]) The group of women she met through that nexus was to form the center of her political affinity group for the rest of her life. Moving to New York to the Henry Street Settlement in 1899, she became the paid executive for the NCL, a position she held until her death in 1932. Many members of this women's reform network considered Kelley its leader.

A charming but possibly apocryphal story has become the legend of the origins of the Children's Bureau. In 1903, at breakfast at Henry Street, Kelley read a letter decrying the high summertime death rate of children, and then saw an article in the newspaper announcing that the U.S. secretary of agriculture was investigating the damage inflicted on the year's cotton crop by the boll weevil. She pointed out this juxtaposition to Wald, who suggested that the federal government should have a bureau to look after the child crop.[94] That Kelley and Wald turned this thought into a major ten-year campaign is emblematic of their astuteness; the time was certainly right, given Theodore Roosevelt's sympathy for expanding the federal government and the upswing in Progressive reform. And the issue was right. They called in support through all their connections: Jane Addams and her Chicago group; the various NCL members and branches; Edward Devine, the editor of *Charities*, the leading social work/reform periodical; the National Congress of Mothers and the General Federation of Women's Clubs. They asked the National Child Labor Committee to draft the legislation, a political move because this was one of the few organizations of their network with substantial southern backing and with a much higher proportion of men than the other groups whose backing they won.[95] They achieved a national forum in the White House Conference on Children in 1909, and the pressure mobilized there contributed to the establishment of the Children's Bureau in 1912.

The establishment of the Women's Bureau six years later brought the distinction between welfare and labor priorities into the federal government. The Women's Bureau focused on employed women, and was therefore more positive about them; in attacking unequal pay and unequal opportunity as well as trying to police working conditions, it was more feminist in the contemporary sense, implicitly supporting women's economic independence. By contrast, the Children's Bureau's welfarist strategy retained the norm that wives should not work outside the home.[96] Moreover, the Women's Bureau worked with labor unions while the Children's Bureau people remained suspicious of workers' self-organization, especially when it made demands of capital rather than concentrating on uplift and improvement. In 1934 Molly Dewson complained that the head of the Women's Bureau had to be a "labor woman."[97] This division between agencies devoted to women's interests helped redefine welfare in a way that gradually separated it from the regulation of employment. The very impact of the Children's Bureau, moreover, tended to confirm a definition of women as quintessentially mothers. The constituency mobilized by Wald and Kelley considered child welfare inseparable from women's welfare; they saw parenting as women's responsibility and women's welfare as inextricably connected to that of their children.

The Children's Bureau also believed that welfare programs for children could be an opening wedge for the development of expanded and general government social provision. Their maternalism thus served as a strategy not only for child welfare but for welfare in general. "I think it is unquestionably true that if a person wishes to do any constructive social work in a community that the confidence of the people . . . can best be secured by beginning with work for the children. Work for children is so disinterested and must make an appeal to all classes," wrote a Children's Bureau staff member in 1919.[98]

The Children's Bureau was firmly connected to the social work establishment, which in turn saw the Children's Bureau as its representative in federal government.[99] Social workers frequently asked the Children's Bureau for advice on casework technique and submitted casework plans for comment.[100] This is important to how we understand the gendered meanings of the bureau, because all of social work, male and female, was part of the bureau's "constituency." The strong female friendship network opened out into a social work/welfare network that included men. These men were not

merely allies but also frequently friends, trusted advisers, and ad-
visees. The perspective of the men closest to the Children's Bureau
might be said to be feminized, for such was the meaning of social
work in this period. Many male social workers shared hands-on experiences with women: Some, such as Graham Taylor, Robert
Hunter, or Robert Archey Woods had been influenced by the settlement experience; others, like Edward Devine and Homer Folks,
came out of the charity tradition and became leaders of the campaign against child labor. In entering close working relationships
with these active women reformers, the men were also participating
in a new gender system, one that involved sharing the public sphere
with women, acknowledging and even depending on their leadership. This is not to say that there was sex equality in these reform
groupings. On the contrary, the usual pattern was that men occupied
positions of public leadership disproportionately to their abilities
and their numbers in reform circles, while women were underrecog-
nized. This made the Children's Bureau even more exceptional and
important.

Its social work professionalism, then, contributed to making the
Children's Bureau the main enclave of the welfare reform community. State and local welfare agencies of all sorts looked to the Children's Bureau for advice and support. So did private social work and
charity agencies and civic and women's organizations. The World
War I Woman's Council of Defense for Colorado, for example,
sought advice about how to proceed.[101] A Jewish Social Service Bureau worker from Chicago asked for the Children's Bureau's opinion
on issues of naturalization of aliens.[102] John Andrews of the American Association for Labor Legislation consulted with Grace Abbott
on mine safety legislation.[103] John Hall of the Norfolk Council of Social Agencies consulted Abbott about how to handle his congressman's attack on the anti-child-labor movement.[104]

Professionalism did not stop the Children's Bureau from its highly
consultative style of work, constantly crossing the boundaries between state and society. Having formed a political culture outside
the electoral process, these women did not regard voters per se as
their constituency. Long after woman suffrage they continued to understand that political power was exercised more commonly through
civic organizations than through ballot boxes. Often they turned their
old friends and organizational allies into official members of advisory

committees. Perkins introduced the "conference method" into the New Deal—creating advisory committees that drew in representatives from a variety of interest groups; this method conditioned Roosevelt's remarkable success at heading off or at least overcoming political conflicts. The method also served to heighten executive over legislative power.[105] Within the Children's Bureau network the method arose not from any essential female style, but from the experience of being relatively politically powerless and dependent on broad civic support.

Another measure of the Children's Bureau's influence was the fury of its opposition. During the 1920s the Right, galvanized by the Russian Revolution and intoxicated by its successful repression of radicals during the Red Scare of 1919–20, directed many attacks against domestic progressives. One of the favorite propaganda devices was identifying the "Reds" in positions of power, sometimes in the form of a "spiderweb" chart, first drawn in 1923. The Children's Bureau and its network figured prominently. Julia Lathrop and Grace Abbott were the only federal officials on the list. Women social reformers accounted for eight of the ten listed as key financial backers, one-third of the officers of organizations, and 28 percent of the category "professionals," including Jane Addams, Sophonisba Breckinridge, Alice Hamilton, Helen Keller, and Lillian Wald.[106] The campaign against the Children's Bureau heated up later in the decade, with Florence Kelley often singled out as a Lenin: "Practically all the radicalism started among women . . . centers about Hull-House, Chicago, and the Children's Bureau at Washington, with a dynasty of Hull-House graduates in charge of it since its creation."[107] Some of their own acquaintances joined in the red-scare hysteria. Grace Abbott wrote of her summer resort neighbors, "the gray haired old ladies who rock on the porches . . . are the most bloodthirsty . . . nothing is bad enough for the trade unionists."[108] The attacks could be comical: When Julia Lathrop was compared to Russian Bolshevik and sex radical Alexandra Kollontai (a more unlikely analogy would be hard to imagine), she had to turn to the Librarian of Congress to find out who that was.[109]

Attacks on the Children's Bureau escalated because it won a significant victory—the first federal welfare program—the Sheppard-Towner Act of 1921. Fearing the power of newly enfranchised white women, Congress authorized a program of matching funds to the states for programs in maternal and child hygiene. An excerpt from the congressional hearings hints at the mood:

[Wife of Republican Henry Keyes of New Hampshire, and an antisuffragist:] . . . the time has come, not when it is expedient to pass it, but when it is dangerous not to pass it.

Mr. [Edward] Denison [Republican Representative from Illinois]. How do you mean it is dangerous . . . ?

Mrs. Keyes. Because I think it is dangerous to arouse the feeling of antagonism between men and women.

Mr. Denison. Do you mean that if we do not pass this bill women are going to make war on us?

Mrs. Keyes. I think you are denying a feeling which is very strong, and if you have not discovered it, you are either very fortunate or blind. That feeling is going to be very much increased as time goes on. It is a feeling that there should be a woman's party instead of a general party for men and women; a feeling that men and women should vote against each other, which would seem to me to be the most calamitous thing that could possibly happen. And I think there is not only a possibility of that but a probability.[110]

When organized medicine, led by the American Medical Association (AMA), resisted the stampede, Abbott declared, "My answer to the doctors is that the Act was passed at the request of the women of the country and its immediate success i.e. securing state acceptances depends on them and that in the final analysis they are the ones to be pleased."[111] Sheppard-Towner passed the House 279 to 39 and the Senate 63 to 7, a rousing ovation for the Children's Bureau.

But the AMA did not capitulate entirely, and the Children's Bureau was forced to give up direct provision of medical care under the program. This compromise may not have been terribly difficult, because an emphasis on health education as opposed to services was consistent with the bureau's analysis of ignorance as the source of infant mortality, and with the mothers' aid legacy. Notwithstanding this limitation and its very small size—only about $1.25 million a year in federal funds—Sheppard-Towner had a significant impact on women's and children's health, lowering infant and maternal mortality rates in the areas where it concentrated despite its brief period of work.[112]

The Children's Bureau intended Sheppard-Towner as a first step in federal welfare, not as an isolated experiment. It represented a cautious and partial break with the mothers' aid legacy, in that it provided non-means-tested assistance. Its state agents established public clinics, and those who asked could get help. But it retained the social-control aspects of mothers' aid. Nurses often made home visits, offering inspection, advice, and help according to bureau norms of good child care. These did not always correspond with those of clients: The bureau advised, for example, against feeding or cuddling babies on demand.[113] In continuing the casework approach, Sheppard-Towner did continue the dangers of cultural domination and privacy invasion, but because means-testing was not required, the program did not seem to be stigmatizing its beneficiaries.

The program might well have introduced a new and promising line of development toward more democratic welfare programs had it not been crushed. In the course of the 1920s the opposition to Sheppard-Towner grew, engineered by a coalition of physicians and ideological conservatives, while fear of the women's vote shrank. The law was repealed, effective as of 1929. The Children's Bureau was bereft, deprived of its hope and strategy for the future.[114] With this loss the bureau's functions were limited to research and consultation. Yet the defeat of Sheppard-Towner occurred in part because the Children's Bureau insisted on running it. The bureau rejected several compromises proposing to renew Sheppard-Towner and transfer it to the Public Health Service (more trusted by the AMA).[115] This stubbornness expressed the collective self-interest of the Children's Bureau staff and its loyalists—an atypical all-or-nothing approach. It also communicated women reformers' sense of the vital importance of the Children's Bureau to a welfare state and as a power center for women. Kicking the downed fighter, the PHS attempted in 1930 to swallow up the bureau. This proposed rearrangement, supported by President Hoover and the mainstream of the AMA, was beaten back, however, by a mobilization of private supporters of the Children's Bureau, the strength and size of which took the PHS and the AMA by surprise.[116] As a result the bureau entered the depression hungry for power and opportunity but still confident that under crisis circumstances it could mobilize considerable public support.

Legacy of the 1920s

While the 1920s have usually been described as a thoroughly conservative decade, and the setbacks for welfare advocates were considerable, looking at the history from the standpoint of this women's network makes the balance sheet somewhat more complex.

Although the federal role in welfare did not expand permanently, that of state government did, influenced by Sheppard-Towner and the Children's Bureau. State agencies expanded and developed national coordination of welfare administrators in the public and private sectors—state commissioners of welfare, city relief directors, executive officers of large charities or community chests, often together with key academics in social work, public administration, and industrial relations.[117] (The resultant alliance would support but also limit federal welfare initiatives in the New Deal.)

Of particular import for the history of ADC, administering Sheppard-Towner made the Children's Bureau staff adept at working in cooperation with state officials even where state provision was unusual, such as the deep south or rural areas.[118] Indeed the Children's Bureau significantly nurtured the development of many state welfare departments.[119] Meticulous cultivation of state and local officials and reform organizations then produced loyalty to the Children's Bureau, which called in these debts to support its budget requests, for example, through congressional lobbying.[120]

It was in the 1920s that states rather than municipalities or counties became fixed as the governmental level primarily responsible for welfare. Mothers' pensions had been administered by a variety of government and private formations. Geographer David Ward has suggested that in the Progressive Era there was an opening to a variety of social welfare experiments, often local, which might have created a pattern of decentralized, creative, and varied programs of social provision. This was the meaning of the settlements and of experiments such as the Cincinnati "Social Unit Plan," which proposed and for a time practiced a kind of neighborhood socialism. Welfare programs with municipal and neighborhood foci might have made a difference had they had access to large-scale public funding, which could only have come from the federal government. The 1920s developments confirmed what was to become, in the New Deal, the fixed design for U.S. welfare programs—federal aid to the states.[121]

Professionalization and bureaucratization among social work and welfare advocates proceeded steadily throughout the 1920s. The Children's Bureau worked to impress its standards of professionalism on the many state public health and welfare agencies and private charities with which it worked, advocating social work training and technique and then bringing these standards into government personnel policy and administration.[122] Its staff saw themselves as the very models of expert, nonpartisan civil servants; and being mostly women, their average level of competence and training was higher than that of most male federal employees of comparable rank.[123] In this respect they were typical Progressives, dedicated above all to the eradication of corruption and patronage from welfare activity, and to assuaging anxiety that government provision would necessarily enlarge their scale.[124]

Professionalism simultaneously reflected and aggravated a decline in popular movements for social provision and an increase in the distance between the poor and those with policy influence. At the same time the professionalization of welfare work stabilized some civic organizations, cemented the capacity for government response to poverty, and established social provision as a public rather than a private responsibility. By 1923 Belle Moskowitz could assert that the question of social welfare had been "permanently implanted" in the U.S. political process, and that a consensus for state responsibility had forced the two major parties to join the minor ones in this commitment.[125] Although private charities were defending themselves as innovators and developers of pilot projects for which government would lack flexibility,[126] the growth of the social welfare professional establishment created ever-greater ties to public and academic intellectuals, and these groups together reinforced each other's optimism that the social problems of modern society could be solved "scientifically," through the application of expertise: Constitutional obstacles to regulation could be overcome, institutional care could be improved, and professional standards in social work would spread.[127]

This adoption of social welfare as a quotidian rather than just an emergency responsibility produced a new kind of welfare worker and leader. More often salaried and, for that reason, less elite, women and men who needed to earn helped force the traditional women volunteers out of social work and charity. The leadership was simultaneously more political and more bureaucratic, a characteristic particularly visible in Children's Bureau correspondence with the public. Always the recipient of a large volume of mail, throughout its first decade the Children's Bureau had designed its responses to appear personal, answering appeals with warmth and concern. In the 1930s its replies became shorter and less individualized. As social work leader Gertrude Vaile described the transformation in 1926, instead of trailblazers and visionaries, such as Addams and Lathrop, she saw leaders with "executive powers who may or may not have powers of social insight."[128] But this was not entirely a loss. The pioneers had worked in grassroots organizations trying to lobby from outside political structures; the new leaders were much closer to political power.

The 1920s offered this women's network a unique conjuncture—a waning women's movement and a waxing female bureaucracy. Women had previously become prominent in welfare activity largely because it was not governmental. Their own victories in winning recognition of state responsibility threatened to deprive them of a place in the welfare establishment. Adapting to these new conditions in the 1920s, they were learning a new language, a language of politics rather than morality. They spoke more often tactically and lost interest in celebrations of charitable virtue. They learned to deal with congressmen and state legislators, cabinet undersecretaries and budget officers. "I was proud to be a bureaucrat," said Clara Beyer about her job on the District of Columbia minimum-wage commission.[129] They created the Women's Joint Congressional Committee in 1920, which four years later included twenty-one organizational members and orchestrated joint campaigns. Its program covered the range of the decade's reform agenda: a federal department of education, Sheppard-Towner, defending the Women's and Children's Bureau appropriations, enforcement of Prohibition, a pure-milk law, regulation of the coal industry, Muscle Shoals (the first federal and hydroelectric power plant), federal control of water resources in national parks, property rights and medical and educational services for American Indians, prison reform, civil service reform, and ending lame-duck congressional sessions. Above all, women learned to lobby in the 1920s, and a few learned to use governmental power. Had the velocity of the early 1920s continued, the women's network might have provided the United States with a set of "femocrats," as the many women government officials are called in Australia.

A Progressive Vision of Welfare Persists

Responding to these influences, the women's welfare network had developed a stable vision of welfare by the end of the 1920s. Constant even within their new political world was a commitment to the family wage, enduring despite the steadily increasing proportion of women in the paid labor force. This myopic devotion was not universal but had been contested in the Progressive Era and the 1920s. While the National Woman's Party and its pro-ERA followers had dwindled in size and creativity by the end of the decade, organizations much closer to the Children's Bureau, such as the NWTUL and the NCL, were also increasingly dubious about family-wage assumptions. The limited vision of the Children's Bureau sorority derived in large part from the separation of labor from welfare. In addition, the Children's Bureau's studies of the conditions of the poor continued to confirm its older view that to expect working-class mothers to earn and at the same time to raise children was cruel. Even the Women's Bureau, dedicated to the advancement of employed women, defended women's domesticity as the desirable arrangement, and argued that the ERA would undercut men's obligation to support their wives. By emphasizing that women took jobs only out of dire necessity, historian Nancy Cott pointed out, "the Women's Bureau and other female labor reformers in the protective legislation camp opened no door to the possibility that a wife's or mother's earnings gave her a sense of personal accomplishment or autonomy."[130] No women's organization tried to develop proposals that recognized the whole lives of poor women, at home and in employment, with the family and with the market economy.

The Children's Bureau adapted to increased women's employment by separating the interests of women and children. Its policies were increasingly justified by a conception of child welfare that removed women's own problems from consideration. The labor as well as welfare reform community adopted this strategic shift, and its results were visible in the courts and the legislatures. The anti-child-abuse movement, dating from the 1870s, had begun to question the naturalization of motherhood, identifying some mothers as neglectful. The campaign against child labor accepted the distinction between parental and children's interests, asserting that it was better for mothers than for children to be employed, and that parents could not be trusted to make the best decisions for their children.

The decline of the women's movement contributed to separating women's from children's interests in several ways. Feminist victories—notably the woman suffrage amendment—removed women from the category of minors, thus separating them legally from children. As women gave up their status as victims in need of protection, welfare reformers responded by legitimating welfare in the name of (helpless) children. The social-feminist network shifted its discourse away from motherhood. The 1908 victory in getting the Supreme Court to uphold an Oregon law regulating women's working hours had rested on appeals to women's special social responsibility as mothers, a responsibility situated in women's very bodies. By contrast, in 1923 the network built an argument for a minimum-wage law in the District of Columbia—which would have been an important precedent—on the grounds of women's economic disabilities in the labor market, not on their vulnerability as mothers. (They lost the case.)[131] Meanwhile the sea change in American Progressive thought about birth control, effected by a powerful women's movement in the World War I Era, similarly contributed to an identification of women's interests separate from those of children. And increasing awareness of a "sexual revolution" reconstructed womanhood, even respectable white womanhood, as compatible with sexual desire and activity distinct from reproductive intent.

The influence of this growing analytical separation between women and children in the welfare system may seem paradoxical, given the centrality of ADC, a program directed precisely at women and children together. Because of this shift, ADC only *looked* the same as mothers' aid; in practice it had quite different implications. In an effort to make ADC maximally acceptable, it focused exclusively on the child and did not include support for the mother herself—a fateful decision that became one of the primary causes of its inferiority in comparison to other programs of government aid.[132] The problem was that the mother-child separation occurred not in a feminist discourse that would have validated women's needs and the work of parenting, but in a discourse that treated children, quite unrealistically, alone, as a group with a unique claim on the state.[133]

Another, related split within the Progressive labor/welfare–reform community arose from social work's separation from social reform. Social work had developed a professional identity (although the phrase "social work" was still used very loosely) produced in academic training centers. In 1930, 31,000 workers were categorized as "social and welfare workers," a number which had grown by two-thirds in ten years.[134] The expansion of higher education was creating cohorts of skilled women eager for such jobs. Settlement work, the original neighborhood organizing, had settled into a mode less of reform advocacy and more of service provision, which reduced the ties it established with other groups.[135]

The Children's Bureau played a double role in this regard. It provided a vital connection between social work and reform, keeping alive a language that still labeled welfare agitators as "social workers."[136] But at the same time its professionalism was delegitimating participation by civic organizations and individual activists. For example, in the late nineteenth century "scientific charity" and reform activism began to rely on quantitative, scientific social research to legitimate policy demands. Many civic organizations did empirical studies of contemporary social problems, such as poverty, crime, and immigration, and professional agencies often employed volunteers in research. But in the 1920s this research was increasingly done by professionals. Settlement workers were less likely to initiate the influential social surveys and legislative agitation than they had been two decades previously, although they and other volunteers still participated in some. The surveys were more often organized by paid and experienced or trained workers, who were increasingly specialized and technical and removed from organizing.

The Children's Bureau people knew that the professional welfare research and services they wanted required federal funding, and thus a national system was fundamental to their welfare vision. The collapse of local revenues during the depression was not a surprise to them. Grace Abbott insisted repeatedly that local units of government could not keep up with need even in normal times.[137]

However, the Children's Bureau continued stubbornly to favor joint federal and state funding.[138] Part of their concern was constitutional: Abbott argued that by preserving federalism, state programs would remain even if federal laws were struck down. They also believed, as did their sisters in the NCL, that they had good relations with state administrators of welfare and labor and could influence them to maintain professional, nondiscriminatory standards, while they were unlikely to be able to retain control of a large federal agency. Katharine Lenroot, Abbott's successor, later came to regret this matching-grant structure, because she believed they had had to spend too much time in administration, negotiating with the states; but in the New Deal she and all the Children's Bureau strongly supported state participation.[139]

They did not expect to give up any measure of control in a joint federal-state schema because they envisaged federal standards as the condition of matching funds, a vital plank in their welfare platform. These conditions would require, above all, civil service and professional administration of programs. In this emphasis they continued their Progressive Era legacy of struggle against patronage and all politics in social services. Throughout the New Deal, Children's Bureau spokeswomen used the bogey of the spoils system to argue for their vision of nonpartisan, expert administration.[140] The federal standards they wanted also included minimum levels of support, statewide coverage, the right of appeal in cases of denial or reduction of support, coverage of all needy children (including the illegitimate), and a prohibition on residency requirements. Abbott even proposed a plan in which the federal share would increase as the size of the grants did, as a way of encouraging high stipends.[141] The Children's Bureau staff had confidence that the states would approve of such standards because state agency staff would have become professionally trained social workers. They envisaged a closed circle of professionals reinforcing professionalism.

These professional social workers were to be caseworkers. Although it was an often unstated assumption, by the end of the 1920s casework had become a virtually defining feature of social work. The dominance of casework was not uncontested: Some leading social work reformers promoted social rather than individual knowledge and remedies. Indeed Grace Abbott's sister, Edith, and Sophonisba Breckinridge, dominant in Chicago (through Hull-House and the Chicago School of Civics and Philanthropy), struggled against the casework dominance.[142] Moreover other wings of the Progressive Era white reform coalition definitively rejected the casework approach and concentrated instead on legal protections and public health regulation. It is hard to imagine that Florence Kelley at the head of the Children's Bureau would have continued to champion an exclusively casework approach to helping poor women and children. And within the Children's Bureau, some continued to hope for a Sheppard-Towner, modified casework approach, emphasizing public facilities and open access along with the home visits and education in child raising, housekeeping, and morals characteristic of classic casework.

But even this modified approach was defeated. The Children's Bureau retained its central identification with professional social work, and the depression did not shake its commitment to providing case-work along with relief. Rejecting nineteenth-century diagnoses that poverty emerged from character flaws, the Children's Bureau never-theless believed that poverty damaged the character and the spirit as well as the body, and that social work expertise was needed to help people cope with stress and break with bad (immoral and/or self-de-structive) behavior patterns. Hence its preference for what came to be called the "budget" approach in ADC. Rather than flat grants, it preferred that caseworkers negotiate individualized family budgets because the process could then be integrated into holistic counseling about personal, moral, and social as well as economic matters.[143] As Frank Bane, first head of the Social Security Board, put it, "It was thought that if a person were dependent, he was therefore *per se* un-able to handle money, and therefore he should be very carefully su-pervised."[144] They believed that social workers' discretion and the tutelary relationship worked to beneficiaries' advantage. Katharine Lenroot liked to tell a story about a mothers' aid recipient speaking knowledgeably to a caseworker about child development. The work-er asked, "'Where did you learn all this . . . ?' 'Oh, I'm a state moth-er. I have to know these things.' So they really did feel, under the best conditions, that they were partners with the state."[145]

Casework was the professionalized form of maternalism. In the Pro-gressive Era, maternalism had animated a wide range of progressive re-form, deployed to support demands ranging from higher wages to tene-ment regulation. But it had conservative potential, too, as demonstrated in the career of Elizabeth Lowell Putnam, a maternal and infant health activist from Massachusetts who spent the 1920s allied with the PHS, protesting the growth of public welfare, and Red-baiting the Children's Bureau women.[146] The force behind progressive maternalism—the ma-ternalism of arguments for protective legislation, mothers' pensions, and the Sheppard-Towner Act—was a women's movement, a vibrant, decentralized, mass social movement. Behind that movement and con-tributing to its vigor were a variety of other more radical activisms, no-tably the intense labor struggles and the growth of the Socialist party in the pre–World War I era, which contributed to a general sense of the necessity and urgency of public action to ameliorate economic suffering and inequality. By the 1920s that very imperative had produced a wel-fare bureaucracy (albeit a small one by today's standards) that had the incentive to maintain and legitimate their positions. Welfare states, after their first inauguration, have always had as their functions not only providing public aid but also empowering and supporting professionals and bureaucrats and nourishing a culture that seeks official/professional solutions to social problems. Thus 1920s maternalism was increasingly becoming a state-building impulse.

This impulse marked the women's social work/welfare platform in a number of ways. Entering the New Deal, women welfare supporters took for granted the need for casework. Where they expected to have to struggle was in persuading the private social work establishment that public agencies could do casework and that material assistance and economic security could be integrated into treatment plans.[147] But they saw economic aid as a "tool in treatment," not as the whole treatment. They criticized many of the mothers' aid programs in states and localities for insufficient expenditure on administration, because this indicated failure to deliver casework services along with cash grants.[148] Clearly they knew that a federal program would also have substantial administrative costs, because of the necessity of hiring skilled personnel and keeping their supervisory loads manageable.

The social work vision incorporated casework and professionalism into its emphasis on preventive medical care. This health strategy even predated the Children's Bureau: The NCL campaign for protective legislation for women argued that threats to women workers' health represented a danger to the public health. The first project of the newly formed bureau was to investigate infant mortality and to use the evidence—of appallingly high rates in the United States—to justify federal programs. The Children's Bureau women built a strong alliance with such public health and health insurance–lobbying groups as the Milbank Fund and the American Association for Labor Legislation.[149] They used the drive for "preparedness" during World War I to argue for health insurance. Sophonisba Breckinridge wrote the head of the Children's Bureau in 1915, "I wish very much to work out a program of what I should call 'Conservation versus Preparedness.' . . . In such a program I should demand federal aid to local effort in the prevention of infant mortality, the anti-tuberculosis movement, the various public health activities, the movement to do away with illiteracy on the part of children in the South, and adults in our northern cities. There are other items but these are the most significant."[150]

It was this health emphasis, of course, which created the Children's Bureau's worst enemies—the PHS and the AMA. Social work leaders were well aware of this, but health seemed to them so fundamental that it could not be given up. They assumed that a program of public medical care was inevitable in the United States and viewed their own work as pioneering something that would later be organized on a mass scale. Above all, their health emphasis grew from their woman-centered approach to welfare. They understood that health issues, particularly those surrounding reproduction and child development, were central to women's unique problems of poverty.

If their commitments to casework and to universal provision seemed to be in tension, yet another complication was added by their commitment to provision of aid by categories. Separate treatment of different groups of the needy had been a trend in social work since the mid-nineteenth century, when charity volunteers campaigned to remove certain groups from poorhouses—children, the insane, and unmarried mothers, for example—to provide for them separately. Categorization was at first an attempt to keep the more deserving from pollution by the undeserving; then the casework approach required separation of groups because different problems required different treatment. In the Progressive Era a strategic motive was added: to remove children and single mothers from the stigma of general relief. "Get the children out of the breadlines," Grace Abbott urged.[151] Lacking the power to create universal welfare provisions without stigma, these ever-practical activists sought to remove a particular program from the pejorative meaning of welfare. So in defense of one group of the needy, the Children's Bureau returned to the classic distinction between the deserving and the undeserving: All should be provided for, but not all at the same social level. In arguing to the House Ways and Means Committee that ADC was a modest and reasonable program, Edith Abbott predicted that only 50 percent of needy single-mother families would qualify and promised that these would be "really nice children and the families are nice families."[152]

Commitment to categorical and casework treatment of relief clients moved the women's welfare network to the right, as the general continuum of welfare thought and social work moved to the left during the depression. The preference for dealing with clients in categories was essential to the social workers' power in determining who was worthy. As the depression escalated demands for broad emergency relief, the Children's Bureau women feared the loss of these categorical separations and opposed across-the-board unified relief.[153] By 1937 the inadequacy of relief efforts had convinced even the American Association of Social Workers (AASW) that a general assistance program, incorporating all the different categorical programs, was advisable. By contrast, Edith Abbott, in her presidential address at the 1937 National Conference of Social Work, was in a minority in defending the categorical strategy.[154]

A more ambiguous part of the Children's Bureau's welfare vision was its feminism. Most of this group was old enough to have been active during the final years of the woman suffrage campaign. Some called themselves feminists and some did not, but all believed that women's power was vital to improve the world. Florence Kelley concluded, after the Supreme Court invalidated a minimum-wage law for women in 1923 in what she called "chapter Three of the Dred Scott decision," that "we must have women in all federal courts."[155] Virtually all were conscious of sex discrimination and complained about it in private. In a note Grace Abbott copied a section of a *New York Times* editorial—"'In addition . . . there will be many jobs . . . for women. They will do much of the house to house canvassing and a large share of the clerical work will fall to them.'"—and added, "That, I think, describes the situation in most Government bureaus."[156] When in 1933 the male-only Gridiron Club gave a dinner for the cabinet from which Frances Perkins was excluded, Eleanor Roosevelt responded by giving a White House dinner the same night—for women only. Sometimes the old feminist spirit emerged in a wisecrack—when asked by a reporter if being a woman was a handicap in government, Frances Perkins said, "Only in climbing trees."[157]

In the Progressive Era some had indulged in more capacious, open-ended feminist thought, diagnosing the problems of the world as creations of excessive masculine influence. Jane Addams spoke of the prevailing ruthless and disastrous technical and social conditions to which a narrow, mechanical, and commercial approach to social life had led.[158] But by the 1930s their primary feminist practice consisted of campaigning for welfare for poor women and for appointments to high positions and public office for middle-class women.[159] They no longer spoke about women's rights or sexism in public.

Some part of this retreat from feminism resulted from the fact that they were so busy in their women's enclave they didn't have time to concentrate on what they were excluded from. Indeed, they were sometimes concerned to protect the egos of men who were often outnumbered by women in meetings.[160]

Their view of proper gender and family relations (for other women) was relatively conventional. They hoped that mothers' pensions would really make it possible for mothers to stay home with their children. Even for prosperous women, they doubted the compatibility of motherhood with career or public-sphere activity, and the majority who were unmarried and childless considered that choice the condition for their work. Their "feminism" had put them in the left wing of reformers in the Progressive Era. Yet by the New Deal they were being criticized as too conservative by other welfare advocates, including many women and many social workers, who were much less feminist.[161] Their sexual attitudes were hardly radical. Neither the nineteenth-century "Free Love" tradition, brought into the women's rights movement by Elizabeth Cady Stanton and Victoria Woodhull, nor twentieth-century sexual bohemianism attracted them. Julia Lathrop and Grace and Edith Abbott protested proposals for liberalizing divorce and prostitution laws.[162] The Children's Bureau remained extremely timid to the end of the New Deal regarding birth control. It was constantly pressured to include birth control information among its services, an activity that might have been defended in terms of its promotion of child welfare. Bureau responses suggest that its resistance grew not only from efforts to protect itself against political attack but also from doubt that birth control was central to desirable family life.[163]

Above all the welfare reformers' feminism was characterized by a class double standard. Only this ultimately makes sense out of the paradox of their unconventional private lives and conventional views about what was right for other women. For women of education and high status, they supported careers, public-sphere activism, and economic independence. For poor women, they recommended domesticity and economic dependence on men. They continued to view career and motherhood as by and large alternative choices. Their view also rested on the assumption that a whole society could never run with working mothers as the norm; the children would not be properly raised or homes properly maintained. Even their view of marriage remained that of a labor contract in which the wife performed certain unpaid services for husband and children in return for financial support. (Without that support, they may have wondered, why should women marry?)

By the 1930s, the women's welfare network had developed a full welfare platform. But it was not the only one. They knew and rejected alternative proposals; by examining some of these other streams of welfarist thought, we will better understand their own outlook.

Meeting of the Women's Auxiliary of the Edgecombe Sanitarium,
Harlem, 1925

5

"Don't Wait for Deliverers"

Black Women's Welfare Thought

B lack women, like white, pioneered in welfare advocacy. In the 1890s they organized themselves nationally, just as white "social feminism" gave rise to national organizations. The different groups of women shared many priorities but the blacks, incorporating a distinct African American legacy and facing larger problems of poverty and discrimination, also produced unique priorities and strategies. By taking the standpoint of this network of black women activists we gain a different view of the possible shape of a welfare state.

Among African Americans welfare activism during this period was even more dominated by women than it was among whites. American black women have a long and rich tradition of public-sphere activism and work, a tradition both freely chosen and at the same time an adaptation to poverty and discrimination; the normative femininity they created was never as subordinate or as confined to the domestic as was the white, and these ideas about womanhood affected their welfare thinking.

American black men had somewhat different welfare priorities, which arose from the circumstances of white tyranny in which they constructed masculinity. Not only did they conceive of race leadership as a masculine responsibility and prerogative, but they sought above all to establish themselves as economic heads of families.[1] Even the black elite often lacked economic security (not to mention political and legal rights) and men in particular lacked assured status

111

as breadwinners. Whether following Booker T. Washington's advice and aspiring to become self-supporting freehold farmers, or W. E. B. Du Bois's and seeking industrial wage labor or a profession, they challenged the white economic discrimination that kept them from achieving manly earning power. They concentrated more on establishing economic independence and less on helping the dependent than did black women. Indeed, as the Great Migration brought millions of African Americans to the North, their activism increasingly focused on struggles against discrimination in jobs and housing. While black men were not always comfortable with the visibility of women's activism, it was not until the New Deal that they built organizations, such as the National Urban League, that challenged female leadership on welfare issues.[2]

Black and white female welfare projects were by no means always distinctive. On the contrary, what is known about the welfare activism of other minority groups, such as Hispanics and American Indians, makes the African American and the European American visions seem similar by contrast.[3] Both were feminist in a broad sense, striving to raise women's status and power. Both groups tried to deploy political power despite not having political rights, which they did through formal organizations. Both gave a special priority to, and assumed a special responsibility for, children. Both believed that welfare was a spiritual as well as an economic matter, and that poor women needed education and training as well as material provision. Both networks experienced a similar waning of feminism and a male "takeover" of welfare, a previously female sphere. Both suffered from masculinist cultural movements in the 1920s: Among whites a heterosexual "sexual revolution" made autonomous women's organizations seem outmoded to many, while among blacks the "New Negro Manhood Movement" reinvigorated nationalist definitions that equated race uplift with male authority and impugned female leadership.

Yet there were considerable differences. Black women's activism was born in an era of radically worsening conditions for most African Americans, in contrast to the improving conditions for white women. The National Association of Colored Women (NACW) formed when segregation was intensifying and blacks were being stripped of the modest political gains facilitated by Reconstruction. As white women got the vote most blacks remained disfranchised. In the South the sharecropping system deepened poverty. By 1924 the second Ku Klux Klan claimed 4.5 million members. The Great Migration of African Americans to the North promised at first an opening into a free, meritocratic economy, but it was soon clear that economic apartheid remained and northern racist violence was growing. Black women had no reason to identify with the exclusively white definitions of women's "interests" that dominated in the white women's welfare network.

Despite change over time, each network's politics was characterized by certain continuous themes. The white women reformers practiced norms of femininity, of "true womanhood," that were slightly off-center—not sharply contrasting, just at an angle—in relation to dominant norms. They did not accept marriage and family work as women's inevitable destiny and fulfillment; they did not consider that women's strongest emotional ties and allegiances were inevitably with husbands and children. They saw femininity as a public as well as a private virtue, suspecting that the accumulation of more political power by women was not only desirable but might actually perfect, or at least greatly improve, the world. A strong sense of their own class and ethnic/religious identity allowed them to consider themselves exceptional and to advocate for others a somewhat more conventional gender system than they were willing to practice themselves.

Black women welfare leaders also shared an autonomous gender system, one distinct not only from white mainstream norms but also from those of white feminists. Recently this black perspective has been called "womanism," signifying an assertion of women's rights that does not attempt to isolate gender from race or class issues. "Womanists" valued marriage and women's sexual propriety, women's responsibility for home and children. But they had some distinctively feminist values too: respect for the public achievements of women, in professions or civic activism or both; a definition of marriage that did not send wives into domestic seclusion; and a conviction that women could lead the whole African American "race" as well as men, and perhaps better. They had a strong distaste for positioning themselves only as victims. Although these women, like the whites, were often at a class distance from the women they sought to help, it was a much smaller distance than that of the whites. In the context of the 1920s ebb in feminism, they grew particularly sensitive to a unique erosion of masculine pride that derived from the violence of slavery and postslavery racism. At the same time they defended their right to leadership. These concerns led to some ideas about welfare that were a little different than those of white welfare leaders.

The white women's ideas created a substantial, if minority, influence during FDR's New Deal administration; the black women's, as a result of discrimination, almost none. Today, as we try to envision a welfare system that will create well-being and independence rather than adversity and dependence, the black legacy of welfare thought contains ideas that may be of relevance. Because minorities and minority women in particular are disproportionately represented as clients of our welfare system, because they are disproportionately poor and disadvantaged, this history is particularly vital today.

Campaigning for Welfare: A Black Women's Network

The white experience defined the boundaries of what we understand as welfare.[4] Whites were by 1890 campaigning for and winning government programs of cash relief and regulation, such as the Pure Food and Drug Act and mothers' pensions. By contrast African Americans, still concentrated in the South (90 percent lived there in 1910) and in rural communities, had been largely disfranchised by this time, and even in the North had much less power than whites, certainly less than elite whites, to influence government. Southern states had smaller administrative capacities and were more paltry in their provision of public services, even to whites. African Americans did campaign for governmental programs, but got little. Black welfare activity, especially before the New Deal, consisted to a great extent of building private institutions. Black women welfare reformers created schools, day nurseries, old people's homes, medical clinics, and community centers to care for their own.

Attempting to provide for their people what the white state would not, they even raised private money for "public" institutions. A 1901 Atlanta University study found that in at least three southern states (Virginia, North Carolina, and Georgia) the private contribution to the black public schools was greater than that from tax monies.[5] For example, an appeal for funds from a teacher in Lowndes County, Alabama, in 1912:

> Where I am now working there are 27,000 colored people. . . . In my school district there are nearly 400 children. I carry on this work eight months in the year and receive for it $290, out of which I pay three

teachers and two extra teachers. The State provides for three months' schooling. . . . I have been trying desperately to put up an adequate school building for the hundreds of children clamoring to get an education. To complete it . . . I need about $800.[6]

Thus a large part of black political energy went to raising money, and under the most difficult circumstances—trying to collect from the poor and small middle class to help the poor.[7] White women raised money, of course, but they also lobbied aldermen and congressmen, attended White House conferences, and corresponded with Supreme Court justices; black women had little access to such powerful men and spent proportionally more of their time organizing bake sales, rummage sales, and church dinners. One detailed example may illustrate this: the Gate City Kindergartens, established in Atlanta in 1905:

Another method of raising funds was through working circles throughout the city. . . . From Bazaars held at Thanksgiving time, lasting as long as a week, when every circle was responsible for a day, one day of which a turkey dinner was served. Money was made by sales in items of fancy work, aprons, etc., canned fruit, cakes and whatever could be begged. The association realized as much as $250.00 at a Bazaar. From track meets sponsored by colleges, and participated in by the children of the public school, $100.00 gate receipts were cleared. Food and cake sales brought at times $50.00. April sales brought $50.00, and one time the women realized as much as $100.00 from the sale of aprons. Sales of papers, magazines and tin foil brought as much as $50.00. A baby contest brought $50.00. Intercollegiate contest brought $100. Postseason baseball games realized as much as $25.00. Sale of soap wrappers, soap powder wrappers, saved and collected from housewives, and baking powder coupons brought $25.00. . . . [The list is twice this long.][8]

Some black welfare activists were adept at raising white money, but not without having to accept sometimes humiliating strings, and even the most successful tried to shift their economic dependence to their own people.[9] No doubt some of these money-raising activities were also pleasurable and community-building social occasions, but often they were just drudgery. Jane Edna Hunter, a Cleveland black activist, wrote: "This money getting business destroys so much of ones real self, that we cannot do our best."[10]

In 1890 black women's welfare activity took three primary forms: mutual benefit societies, often referred to as "fraternal" societies even when women were active in them, church groups, and women's clubs.[11] All aimed at "uplift"—a phrase denoting simultaneously charity, self-improvement through education, and campaigns for more respect for the race.[12] But the different forms divided along class lines. Middle-class women organized clubs; the black working class and rural poor relied on mutual benefit programs, offering insurance for sickness, burial, and other misfortunes; and poor women in particular were likely to be in church organizations, with the last two forms by far the more extensive. In turn-of-the century Manhattan, poor black women were more likely than any other group to join mutual benefit associations. The female "fraternal" societies kept up with their male counterparts—remarkable when one considers how much less money women had. One such order alone, the Household of Ruth, the female affiliate of the Black Odd Fellows, had 197,000 members in 5,000 lodges in 1916, two-thirds the male membership.[13] Church groups were also substantial. The Women's Convention of the Black Baptist Church alone numbered 1 million members in 1903, 1.5 million in 1907.[14] The three streams of organization were not mutually exclusive. Most organization women at the turn of the century, black and white, were religiously affiliated. But as an educated and feminist stratum of the middle-class black women developed, secular clubs proliferated. They raised funds to support substantial institution building and formed a national federation. Women were attracted to them precisely because of their double agenda: providing a social space and status with an elite and ambitious group of friends and offering help to the black poor.

Although the formation of a national black women's network of welfare activists was in part a product of white racism, which included a series of painful rejections of black clubs and individuals by the white women's movement, black women were not simply reacting. The rejections were a response to black women's own escalating demands, seeking out affiliation with events and organizations that identified themselves as representing "women," expressing a growing feminist and class confidence among blacks. For example, at the 1893 Chicago World's Fair, white women's organizations prepared an exhibit for the Columbian Exposition; black women asked for a representative on the board of the project but were turned down.[15] Ida B. Wells's campaign against lynching, which she took not only to the Columbian Exposition but also to England in 1894, led her to make a well-deserved attack on Frances Willard for the racist policies and rhetoric of the WCTU.[16] In that same year Josephine St. Pierre Ruffin, representing the (black) Woman's Era Club of Boston, requested and was refused admission to a General Federation of Women's Clubs convention.[17]

The white women engaged in welfare activity were not all racist, and their racisms were not all the same. Women from the most progressive edge of the reform movement, notably those working in settlements, began to understand the difficult conditions of blacks migrating to the North; some helped form the NAACP. Nevertheless most settlements maintained segregation. (A few opened separate branches for blacks, and a very few, such as Henry Street and Hull-House, were open to all.) One settlement committee preferred to keep blacks out of the whole city, announcing in 1910 that Boston was not a "healthy or suitable home for the Negro race."[18] White welfare organizations and projects were segregated, so white and black women rarely interacted. Even the day nurseries were almost always segregated.[19] As white women gained some government offices, they accepted the exclusion of Blacks from state power, however much they might have deplored it privately.[20] Informally the national network of white women reformers usually excluded black women. Even in the 1930s, one of the most important women in the New Deal—Mary McLeod Bethune—was not invited into the network of white New Deal women.[21] There were important counterexamples, interracial efforts of significant impact, particularly local ones: in Chicago, for instance, white settlement and charity workers joined black reformers in campaigning for public services for dependent children, establishing the Chicago Urban League, and responding to the 1919 race riot. In the South interracial efforts arose from evangelical religious activity, and some white women activists worked with the Commission of Interracial Cooperation, forming a Women's Council within it which had 805 county-level groups by 1929. The national YWCA became a forum for communication between black and white women.[22] But these efforts were limited by serious and sometimes crippling white prejudice, and the core networks of women remained segregated. Separation and prejudice meant that white and black women could not easily learn from one another. Even progressive, class-conscious white reformers ignored and trivialized such life-and-death black issues as lynching.[23]

The first organization of this black women's network was the NACW. The first national civil rights organization, it claimed 45,000 members in 1911.[24] The national organization further stimulated the growth of local groups. By 1913 Chicago alone had forty-one NACW-affiliated clubs with 1,200 members, by 1921 sixty clubs and 2,000 members.[25]

The NACW represented a major change in race as well as gender orientation, away from clerical, black male, and white female leadership. The NACW was also a landmark in class terms: It represented the attainment of a critical mass of middle-class black women. Its program was complex, since it simultaneously served to distinguish its membership from the uneducated, impoverished black masses and to work among them. As one historian described this dual meaning: "Their patronage roles toward others less fortunate than themselves not only dramatized their relative superiority within the minority structure, but also gave them the claim to leadership and power positions."[26] Elite black women were proportionately more committed than whites to uplifting the poor, partly because they knew well that whites did not often make class distinctions among blacks, but viewed the whole race like the poorest and least educated among them. Thus their personal ambition required them to help the less privileged: As Mary Church Terrell put it, middle-class black women "cannot escape altogether the consequences of the acts of their most depraved sisters. . . . even if they were wicked enough to turn a deaf ear to the call of duty, both policy and self-preservation demand that they go down among the lowly . . . to whom they are bound by ties of race and sex, and put forth every possible effort to reclaim them."[27]

The uplift strategy did not produce unanimity. Increasing militance against racism produced sharp differences among these black activists just as their movement cohered. At the integrationist end was, for example, Josephine St. Pierre Ruffin, of a small, wealthy, and light-skinned Boston elite; accustomed to relatively respectful treatment and inclined toward assimilationism, Ruffin supported strong efforts against lynching and against the lesser forms of racism so common in the white women's movement. At the conservative end was, as one would expect, Margaret (Mrs. Booker T.) Washington, who advocated a female version of her husband's program that blacks should improve themselves and thus convince whites of their worthiness: "Our poor need to be clothed. Our women must be taught to study for their own achievement. They need inspiration and encouragement to keep a brave heart. Homemaking must be thought about, child rearing needs attention. Our girls need social purity talks. They must be warned of evil company. They must be brought in closer touch with more that is good and pure."[28] Encompassing such differences, the NACW functioned mainly as a federation of local clubs, and usually the local clubs were less political and less ambitious than the national leadership. Nevertheless the NACW was the first national organization of and for African Americans.[29] It might be tempting to describe these two tendencies as leaning alternately toward civil rights and welfare, but this would be a distortion—indeed, this dichotomy arises precisely from applying a white notion of welfare.

The unity of the NACW arose from two shared lines of thought: that altruism was part of the female sphere and the female nature, and that progress and political equality for women were not only intrinsically just but would benefit the whole race. The division that was to characterize many white activists by the 1920s—between those "social feminists" who supported special protective programs for women and the pro-ERA feminists who called for an end to all gender-specific programs—did not develop prominently among blacks.[30] Racism guaranteed that few black women would find it sensible to focus their reform activity on gender oppression only. By the 1890s black women were becoming so active and hopeful that they referred to the birth of a "women's era."[31] "Nothing in the whole realm of questions that effect home, religion, education, industry and all phases of sociology commands more interest than the growing power of woman," Fannie Barrier Williams declared in 1896. "We are preparing ourselves . . . to use and exercise the privileges and responsibilities of that larger and more inclusive citizenship. . . . Is it too much to say that no class of women in the world have such rare opportunities for signalizing their worth as the colored women of America?"[32]

For black women as for white, personal experience influenced the gender and family assumptions in their vision of welfare.[33] While the black group was created in part by white racism, it was also created from the inside, by friendships and networking.[34] Often these relationships were born in schools and colleges, then strengthened by the development of black sororities after 1908.[35] The new national organizations extended ideas and connections across regional boundaries. For

example, the Phillis Wheatley Home for the protection of single
black urban women, established by Jane Edna Hunter in Cleveland
in 1911, spurred the opening of similar homes in Denver, Atlanta,
Seattle, Boston, Detroit, Chicago, Greenville, Winston-Salem, Tole-
do, and Minneapolis by 1934.[36] The YWCA, persuaded to support
and incorporate some early black settlements, drew together many
of these women—roughly one-third of them participated in it at one
time or another (a much higher proportion than that of white
women, who had so many more venues).[37] The women began to
travel widely; northern blacks even traveled south—acts of great
courage, given the difficult and humiliating conditions of travel for
black women.[38]

The experience of mobility, both geographic and social, contributed to the coherence of the black women's network. Although a
majority was born in the South,[39] two-thirds of those migrated north.
They constituted a kind of intellectual brain drain from the South,
an elite of the Great Migration. They literally spread their network
as they fled Jim Crow and sought wider opportunity. Still, because
they did not have as many of their collaborators located in a few
large cities as the white network did, their political groupings were
not so thoroughly solidified by personal intimacy as those of white
women. Yet their mutual support was strong. In the 1930s, for example, the president and trustees of Howard University, led by Abraham Flexner, tried to force Howard's Dean of Women, Lucy Slowe,
to live on campus with her girls (something the Dean of Men was
not, of course, required to do), and she refused to comply. A supportive women's network responded so vehemently that Flexner
must have wondered what hit him: They demanded a large group
meeting with him, intervened with Howard's trustees in New York,
and lobbied Howard faculty, all the while in constant communication with Slowe herself.[40] The network was divided by cliques and
encompassed conflicts and even feuds; women engaged in power
struggles, vindictiveness, and promotion of protégées just as men
did.[41] But loyalty endured, produced in part by adversity and in part
by the thrill of experiencing the individual and collective intelligence, energy, and bravery of black women.

Unlike the whites, their reform careers were not an alternative to
marriage; 85 percent of this network were married.[42] Nor was marriage
a drawback for them. More than half of the married women had

prominent men as spouses, and their marriages sometimes promoted their leadership positions.[43] Lugenia Burns Hope was the wife of John Hope, first black president of Atlanta University; Irene Gaines, of an Illinois state legislator. Ida Wells Barnett's husband published Chicago's leading black newspaper. George Edmund Haynes, husband of Elizabeth, was a Columbia Ph.D., professor at Fisk, assistant to the secretary of labor from 1918–1921, and a founder of the Urban League. George Ruffin, husband of Josephine, was a Harvard Law School graduate, member of the Boston City Council, and Boston's first black judge. This is not to say that they were "coattail" women. Most had been activists before marriage, and many led lives quite independent of their husbands. Some were separated from their husbands; whether due to the location of employment opportunities or deterioration in marital relationships, in either case these separations represented women's independence.[44]

Their fertility pattern was related to their independence—43 percent had no children. What is more striking, 34 percent of the *married* women had no children,[45] about the same proportion as among the whites. It thus seems likely that these activists used birth control, although the marital separations obviously contributed to their low fertility.[46] In their contraceptive practices these women were at least as "modern" as white women of comparable class position at this time.

Most African American women were employed due to economic necessity, but this group was different in that respect. Many of them had prosperous parents.[47] Crystal Fauset's father, born a slave, became principal of a black academy in Maryland. Elizabeth Ross Haynes's father went from slavery to ownership of a 1,500-acre plantation. Addie Hunton's father was a substantial businessman and founder of the Negro Elks. Mary Church Terrell's mother *and* father were successful in business. Most of these women had husbands who could support them; 51 percent of the married women had professional husbands— lawyers, physicians, ministers, educators.[48] Several of the northern-born women learned for the first time in adulthood of the conditions of poverty in which most African Americans lived. Alfreda Duster (daughter of Ida Wells-Barnett) recalled, "It was difficult for me to really empathize with people who had come from nothing, where they had lived in cottages, huts in the South, with no floor and no windows and had suffered the consequences of the discrimination and the hardships of the South."[49] The women of this network were often very class conscious, and many of their clubs were exclusive, such as the sororities or the Chautauqua Circle and "the Twelve" in Atlanta.[50] Yet even among this elite group only a tiny minority—12 percent—were not employed.[51] They were privileged only in comparison to the whole black population, and on average, they were less wealthy than their white counterparts. Even those who were born of middle-class status were usually only a generation away from slavery and without much cushion against economic misfortune.

In fact the drive for and success in professional accomplishment was particularly marked among black women in this period. From 1890 to 1910 the number of professional black women increased by 219 percent, while that of black men rose by 51 percent. In 1890 women were about 25 percent of all black professionals; in 1910 they were 43 percent.[52] This achievement reflects their high level of education: 83 percent had a higher education, comparable to the proportion of white women, and 35 percent had attended graduate school. Patterns of discrimination and opportunity have often made black women's educational and professional achievements—although not their salaries—higher relative to men's than those of white women.[53] The full meaning of these statistics emerges when they are compared to the average educational opportunities for blacks in the United States at this time: In 1940, the earliest year for which we have figures, only 1 percent of African Americans, male and female, had four or more years of college. It must be remarked that many of the black southern colleges were really secondary schools, but only 41 percent of the women in this sample attended black colleges, while those colleges conferred 86 percent of all black undergraduate degrees in the period 1914–36.[54]

Snobbery and class conflict created division and conflict within this network. Not all the women active in welfare causes were from privileged backgrounds. Some of the most influential, such as Victoria Earle Matthews, Maggie Lena Walker, Jane Edna Hunter, Janie Porter Barrett, and Mary McLeod Bethune, had "climbed" upward from slavery and sharecropping, and they could be critical of some of the more status-conscious women. Class markers such as skin color had a powerful resonance.[55] A high proportion of these leaders were very light skinned and several regularly passed for white when it was convenient. Though color was not a perfect proxy for class—some women from very poor backgrounds, such as Jane Edna Hunter, were quite light—but it was close. The fact that Bethune was so dark gave additional meanings to her high position. Color consciousness intensified the race debate about terminology, between "colored," which had implications of mixed blood, and "Negro," which was assertive of race pride. Nannie Helen Burroughs's condemnation of black efforts to look more white (bleaching, hair straightening) could have been published in the 1960s. Whatever their perspective, color was a major issue for these ambitious women.[56]

Education and privilege brought with it an obligation to serve and a justification for leadership. Like Du Bois, many women emphasized building an intellectual and professional elite.[57] Most thought of their obligations in personal terms. "I was going to multiply my ability and my husband's by six," said Alfreda Duster in describing her decision to have six children.[58] However, race prejudice made it difficult even for members of the elite to escape the discrimination and pejorative stereotyping that held back all African Americans, even in the North. Prosperity could not make up for exclusion from citizenship. High levels of skills and education were often frustrated. Sadie Alexander, from one of the most prominent black families in the United States, was the first black woman Ph.D., with degrees from the University of Pennsylvania, but could not get an appropriate job because of her color and was forced to work as an assistant actuary for a black insurance company.[59] Anna Arnold Hedgeman, one of the youngest women in this sample, from a small Minnesota town, where she had attended integrated schools and churches, graduated from Hamline University in St. Paul and then discovered that she could not get a teaching job in any white institution. Instead she went to work in Holly Springs, Mississippi, until she found the Jim Crow laws intolerable.[60] Despite the relatively large black middle class in Washington, D.C., women there could not generally get federal clerical jobs until the 1940s.[61]

A Black Feminist Vision of Welfare

The mixture of privilege, high ambition, frustration, and humiliation experienced by black women welfare leaders structured their reform priorities. In the 1890s and for several decades thereafter the first was education. Although most Americans do not consider education a part of "welfare," that distinction was particular to the white experience, in which public education had been a relatively early development;[62] for blacks, who lacked educational opportunity, schools were an antipoverty program. The majority of the black women in this network taught at one time or another, and 38 percent were educators by profession.[63] Their most important welfare work was in establishing schools, from kindergartens through colleges, like Nannie Burroughs's National Training School for Girls, or Lucy Laney's Haines Institute in Augusta, or the Saints Industrial and Literary Training School in Mississippi, built by Arenia Mallory, who moved there from Jacksonville, Illinois.[64] Women's organizations then supported black students in various ways, from scholarships to school lunches.[65] The emphasis on education was particularly urgent, expressing not only the typically female welfarist concentration on children—a priority visible also in the day nurseries, playgrounds, and settlements they built—but also a race uplift strategy. A 1906 account of a Washington, D.C. settlement concludes with the inspirational story of "a brave little man of eight, penny in hand, come to make his savings deposit. Asked if he is attending school . . . he answers brightly, 'Yes ma'am, I ain't missed a day since you started me,' and I look in my mind's eye past the little children before me to . . . the man with broader, better views of living, the citizen, the Christian!"[66]

Another early black welfare priority was the establishment of old people's homes, considered by Du Bois the "most characteristic Negro charity." These too were predominantly organized by women.[67] But the welfare cause second to education in this period was health. Between 1890 and 1930, African Americans created approximately two hundred hospitals and nurse-training schools, and women often took charge of the community organizing and fund-raising labor. Over time black women's health work changed its emphasis, from providing for the sick in the 1890s to preventive health projects after about 1910. Already in the last century, most locations with a considerable black population had mutual benefit societies that paid sickness as well as burial insurance. In several cities the societies also paid for medicines and actually created their own HMOs. With member dues they hired physicians, annually or on a quarterly basis, to provide health care for the entire group.[68] Many women's clubs concentrated on health programs. The Indianapolis Woman's Improvement Club focused on tuberculosis, attempting to make up for the exclusion of blacks from the services of the Indianapolis Board of Health, the City Hospital, and the county Tuberculosis Society.[69] Atlanta's Neighborhood Union surveyed health conditions in the black schools in 1912–13 and established a clinic in 1916 that offered both health education and free medical treatment.[70] Possibly the most extraordinary individual in this public health work was Modjeska Simkins, who used her position as director of Negro work for the South Carolina Tuberculosis Association to inaugurate a program dealing with the entire range of black health problems, including maternal and infant mortality, VD, and malnutrition as well as TB.[71]

The depression stimulated the most ingenious and dramatic health initiative of all. Black sorority Alpha Kappa Alpha's Mississippi Health Project operated in Holmes County for several weeks every summer from 1935 to 1942. On the eve of their departure for Mississippi, a railroad agent refused to sell them tickets because he decided there were too many of them to fit in the segregated compartments. So they borrowed cars and drove to Mississippi, despite the terrors of being excluded from restrooms, sleeping accommodations, and even gas stations. Arriving, they found clinic attendance low because plantation owners intimidated "their" sharecroppers. So the AKA women turned their cars into mobile health vans and took clinics to the sharecroppers, usually setting up in black churches, the only black-controlled public spaces. Beginning with some prejudice of their own and a lack of sympathy toward the ignorant poor they encountered, they quickly learned that poor, untrained midwives were the only possible health care providers among Mississippi sharecroppers, and that their ability to attract patients depended on their relations with these midwives. The midwives, in turn, overcame their initial fear of a threat to their own positions and to their traditional healing method from these outsiders and demonstrated their commitment to better health care for their people. With the encouragement of the midwives, people came to the clinics, despite the occasional presence of observers sent by plantation owners, "'riders' with guns in their belts and whipping prods in their boots . . . straining their ears to hear what the staff interviewers were asking of the sharecroppers." The women were of course labeled communists, coming into the Delta to incite. Nevertheless, the AKA project immunized more than 15,000 children and provided services such as dentistry and treatment for malaria and VD to 2,500–4,000 people each summer.[72]

Like their white counterparts, black women welfare activists in this period can be described, cautiously, as maternalist.[73] Through maternalism their commitments to helping others and to activism were assimilated to their gendered sensibility. The "others" they sought to help were often constructed as younger, weaker, in need of gentle protection and motherly guidance. Consider Anna Julia Cooper's rhetoric: "When went there by an age when so much time and thought, so much money and labor, were given to God's invalids; the lowly and unlovely, the sinning as well as the suffering. Homes for the inebriates and homes for lunatics, shelter for the aged and shelter for babes, hospitals for the sick, props and braces for the falling, all show that a mothering influence . . . is leavening the nation."[74] Or Frances Batholomew's description of a Philadelphia settlement that "took the neighborhood as a mother takes a naughty, dirty child and washed its face."[75] Although "maternalism" is usually pejorative, referring to unwanted supervision, condescension, infantilization, its meanings vary in different contexts, with particularly different racial implications. Black women reformers believed that slavery had undermined the bases of maternalism—home and family ties, the sanctity of marriage, and the instincts of motherhood.[76] Their view that maternalist reform could benefit the whole race was accompanied by arguments for the strategic racial importance of work with children.[77] Indeed, sometimes the trope was reversed and the speaker presented herself as the child in order to evoke maternalism in others. Jane Edna Hunter titled a chapter of her autobiography "I Feel Like a Motherless Child," describing her arrival in Cleveland, as a penniless, homesick adolescent alone and in need of care.[78] At other times women spoke of their organizations as children they had nurtured. Illinois women writing a history of their Federation of Colored Women's Clubs talked of its "adolescent period"; and according to one comment on the NACW, "So tenderly has this child of the organized womanhood of the race been nurtured" that its "fond mothers have every reason to be proud."[79]

Black maternalism had an even stronger feminist or womanist slant than did the white version. Particularly striking in black rhetoric was the way in which the blessings of the motherly were contrasted to the failures of the fatherly, to which were attributed the problems of the world: "Since the idea of barbarian brawn and brutality in the Fifth century, the civilized world has been like a child brought up by its father. It has needed the great mother-heart to teach it to be pitiful, to love mercy, to succor the weak, and the care for the lowly."[80] The same thinking prompted a Boston group to name itself "The Woman's Era".

They say the Woman's Era dawns at last
When now this century draws near its end
Old nations of man's lordship fading fast
Make way for woman's aid to help to mend
Affairs that sorely need her presence bright.[81]

Thus black maternalism was in part an expression of sharp criticisms of men. Conflict with men pervaded the black women's discourse, far more than among the whites who were more circumspect in their criticisms and claims. Black women legitimated their own leadership with extensive complaints that black men had failed to lead the race; some even accepted white historical myths (albeit for different reasons) that black men had sold their votes away. Women leaders were particularly critical of ministers, who had so much power among African Americans and often used it to suppress race activism. Fannie Barrier Williams condemned ministers "unworthy of their calling . . . responsible for the fact that our church women generally take less interest in the large field of practical religious work outside of their particular churches than any other class of women," and who devoted themselves only to raising money for the church trustees.[82] Women resented the fact that men ran the churches while women kept them alive; one pamphlet referred to the "sleek and comfortably housed pastors [who] would be in a sorry plight, were it not for the loyal women members of their congregations."[83]

In short, women reformers claimed leadership of the race and equality with men.[84] Charlotte Hawkins Brown declared that her own work and thoughts were just as important as Booker T. Washington's.[85] Leading Black feminist Anna Julia Cooper considered women to be at the center of the race experience.[86]

White maternalism was also a way of separating helper from helped, of constructing those who needed welfare or charity as "other." Their poor, immigrant "children" were, at the closest, "adopted." But black women's "children" were very much "family." There was little chronological distance, because the privilege of elite blacks was so recent and so tenuous. There was little geographical distance, because residential segregation did not allow the black middle class much insulation from the black poor.[87]

Closeness to the poor influenced what the black women wanted to give and how they wanted to give it. Concentrating their efforts more on education and health and proportionally less on charity or relief meant that they were responding more often to universal needs than to the particularly unfortunate. They preferred universal programs, such as clinics open to all, or a system in which potential recipients selected themselves, as in homes for working girls. This did not mean that black welfare reformers ignored the classic deserving/undeserving distinction. Although many institutions and programs admitted only the "worthy," their concern was less to weed out disreputable applicants than to prevent beneficiaries from misusing resources or to make sure that they could contribute something. For example, the Sojourna Lodge, a women's affiliate of the Black Odd Fellows, ran a sickness insurance program in many of its five thousand local lodges; in the early twentieth century it required monthly dues of fifty cents and a signed statement from a doctor before a member could collect. Occasionally it refused to pay for those who, it believed, were cheating.[88] Few black welfare programs were means-tested; indeed some had to do the opposite—to exclude the most destitute who could not make any financial contribution themselves.[89] Projects sometimes targeted the needy, but the needy were upwards of 95 percent of the black population. As Fannie Barrier Williams put it, "Among white women clubs mean the forward movement of the best women in the interest of the best womanhood . . . the onward movement of the already uplifted. . . . Among colored women the club is the effort of the few competent in behalf of the many incompetent.[90]

Considering the white women's approach through a black lens shows racial characteristics that have passed unnoticed. The perspective of the white network had been shaped by the turn-of-the-century immigration and residential segregation, which grouped these immigrants in ghettos not often seen by the white middle class.[91] The apparent alienness of these newcomers, constructed of overlaid racial and class difference, not only discouraged the reformers' identification with their subjects but also retarded their development of a more structural understanding of the origins of poverty, as opposed to one that blamed individual character defects. Racial attitudes help explain the whites' commitment to means-testing, "morals-testing," and expert supervision and rehabilitation so as to inculcate into the poor the work habits and morals they so often (or so the reformers believed) lacked.[92]

Blacks, and whites, differing analyses of the causes of poverty were a matter of degree. On one side most white welfare reformers focused on environmental, social change; on the other blacks also engaged in attempts to correct weak character. Many black clubs engaged in "friendly visiting" to guide the poor toward respectability and clung to Victorian notions of womanly gentility. In the 1890s in Washington, D.C., black women volunteered to work with Associated Charities in its "stamp work," a program designed to inculcate thrift and saving among the poor.[93] Black and white clubwomen shared the conviction that the poor needed training, not only in skills but in moral and spiritual capacities. Mary Church Terrell could sound remarkably like a white club woman:

> To our poor, benighted sisters in the Black Belt of Alabama we have gone and we have been both a comfort and a help to these women, through the darkness of whose ignorance of everything that makes life sweet or worth the living, no ray of light would have penetrated but for us. We have taught them the A B C of living by showing them how to make their huts more habitable and decent with the small means at their command and how to care for themselves and their families.[94]

Black clubwomen counseled the poor, as Deborah White listed, "to keep themselves and their homes clean, to bathe their children regularly, and provide them with music, games and books . . . to stop sitting on stoops and talking and laughing loudly in public. Girls had to be kept close to home, boys had to be kept from wandering. Families had to live within their means, domestic workers had to stop buying clothes they could not afford. Women had to choose their husbands more carefully, money had to be saved, and homes had to be purchased."[95] Fannie Barrier Williams declared that the colored people's greatest need was a better and purer home life.[96]

This vision of uplift included particular concern for improving the sexual morals of their people.[97] Such a moral-reform orientation has sometimes been priggish and victim-blaming, and sometimes deflected attention from the fundamental problems of poverty and imposed the values of a dominant group without respect for cultural difference. These perspectives were found among blacks and among whites. For example, Du Bois's 1896 Atlanta University study reported that women's sexual immorality was the "greatest single plague spot" in the reputation of African Americans.[98] But black women reformers knew that sexual abuse of women was not a priggish fantasy, and that such abuse was one of the fundamental problems of poverty.[99] Maternalist anxiety about sexual respectability was prudish, yes, for white as well as black women, but it also recognized that sexual abuse was a major form of women's oppression.

Dismissing the sexual purity emphasis as only prudish also misses its race-specific meanings. Not only were black women more severely sexually victimized, but combating sexual exploitation was for blacks inseparable from race uplift in general, because white sexual assaults against black women had long been a fundamental part of slavery and racial oppression. Protest against sexual abuse of women was at the root of the modern civil rights movement.[100] Indeed, black feminists were quicker than white ones to campaign against rape and to identify it as part of a system of power relations.[101] This was a radical and daring move, for it involved inverting the racist calumny against black women as sexually immoral and identifying white men as the sexual assailants.

Resistance to sexual slander lay at the heart of the black women's welfare vision. In the folklore of the movement, it was a libel of the sexual purity of black women that had first motivated the national organization of clubs.[102] The Negro Health Movement in the 1920s and 1930s, largely constructed by women, used cleanliness as its major theme and constructed it to have double meanings, referring to moral as well as physical purity.[103] Elsie McDougald, writing in 1925 in an anthology on *The New Negro* (referring to urban militants and sophisticates), still had to fight the vicious stereotype, arguing that there was no proof of inherent moral defect in the women of the race.[104] The maternalist metaphor had similar functions—to counteract charges of immorality, since in the gender discourse of the time, women's sexuality was an opposite to women's motherliness.

Standing up for women's sexual honor also required, at times, defying black men, and it is a measure of the feminism of these welfare activists that so many of them did so, and bluntly. They had cause, because black male leaders sometimes repeated slurs on black women's sexual morality that were at once sexist and self-serving, functioning as they did to protect men's sexual behavior from scrutiny. Black women reformers assumed the task of educating men about the racial treason involved in this defamation.[105] And they protested the sexual privilege of the men. Black women leaders frequently attacked the sexual double standard: "Too often the mother who is careful of her daughter's environment and . . character, is negligent as to her son's," Lucy Laney charged.[106] Mary Terrell condemned the atmosphere that "turn[ed] the cold shoulder upon a fallen sister, but greet[ed] her destroyer with open arms."[107] Many criticized black men's hostility to black women and their failure to defend black women's beauty and morality.[108]

Nevertheless, given the difficulties of effecting change in the aggressors, black women reformers focused on protecting potential victims and reclaiming those who had already been victimized. Just like black welfare activists today, they tried to reduce out-of-wedlock childbirth and help unwed mothers. This presented them, again, with the task of institution building, since white institutions would not accept blacks. In Chicago in 1906 there were a hundred homes for single women, only one of which admitted blacks.[109] These institutions had a protective but also patronizing and conservative agenda. The Chicago Phyllis Wheatley Women's Club believed that "many of our girls coming from small towns and the southland are unused to life in a great city and find themselves . . . helpless, ready to fall an easy prey to the human vultures ever ready to destroy young womanhood."[110] In Denver the "girls" living in the Negro Women's Club home were governed by strict rules: For examples, lights out at 10:30; rooms must be kept tidy; dishwashing to be done in a pan instead of a sink and must be done with soap; bath times were assigned.[111] Some homes engaged in supervisory methods that seem excessive by today's sensibilities. Jane Edna Hunter, for example, made a practice of listening in to telephone conversations through the switchboard at her Cleveland Wheatley Home.[112] Black women's considerable contribution to the founding and development of the Urban League was motivated by concern to protect women newcomers to cities, as were clubs for younger girls, given the belief that respectability, self-respect, and purity needed to be learned early.[113]

Protective projects, perhaps inevitably, contained a degree of victim blaming among Blacks as among whites. Sexual exploitation reflected class differences: poor women, black or white, were more vulnerable to assault and to slander; black like white women defined their middle-classness in part by their sexual respectability. But black sexual protection efforts were so connected to uplift for the whole race that victim-blaming was a smaller part of their message than among whites.

Moreover, the drive to enforce sexual respectability was never a monopoly of the middle class; it had more to do with aspirations than with status, with a dynamic than a static position. Jane Edna Hunter came to Cleveland from a poor southern background, and her first attempts to build a home for working girls joined together domestic servants, seamstresses, and other working women. Their preference for a black institution was opposed by the integrationist view of "a small group of [black] club women who, blessed with prosperity, had risen from the servant class and now regarded themselves as the arbiters and guardians of colored society." It was Hunter's own sensibility, not a middle-class imposition, that was shocked by what she saw in the city. "A strong intimation of the evil influence of this rooming house [where Hunter first stayed] came when I observed the pink silk undergarments of the landlady's daughter who went out regularly every afternoon and returned home quite late at night." She worried about the "great temptations that beset a young woman in a large city. At home on the plantation, I knew that some girls had been seduced. . . . In Charleston I was sent by the hospital to give emergency treatments to prostitutes, but they were white women. Until my arrival in Cleveland I was ignorant of the wholesale organized traffic in black flesh."[114]

Despite the necessity of creating segregated institutions, black reformers could not separate welfare from civil rights agitation, any more than they could separate the defense of black womanhood from the defense of the "race."[115] Race issues were poverty issues, and women's issues were race issues. Race uplift work was usually welfare work by definition, conceived as a path to racial equality. And black poverty could not be ameliorated without challenges to white domination. A nice example: In 1894 Gertrude Mossell referred to Ida Wells' antilynching campaign as "philanthropy."[116] Fannie Barrier Williams described her settlement work thus in 1906: "It is not organized to do slum work . . . but to be a center of wholesome influences to the end that well-disposed white people may learn to know and respect the ever-increasing number of colored people who have earned the right to be believed and respected."[117] Civil rights and uplift intersected even in the activities of black elites for themselves because claims to status and respect required resistance to white hegemony.

The women's network was affected, as were all black reformers, by the split between the militant integrationism proposed by W. E. B. Du Bois and the emphasis on self-help and accommodation to segregation preached by Booker T. Washington. Although there are dangers in exaggerating the antithetical nature of these viewpoints, it is hardly possible to exaggerate the importance of these strategic questions within the early-twentieth-century black activism, and they absorbed women as much as men. Several of these women, notably Mary Church Terrell and Anna J. Cooper, were among early rebels against Booker T. Washington's political machine, attracted to both academic educational goals for their people and to challenges to segregation. (The NACW had to struggle to protect itself from Washington's control, because its national organ, *The Notes*, was originally paid for and published by his wife, Margaret.)[118]

But the internal splits did not create two stable sides, and they had unique female meanings. Most of the educators, for example, recognized simultaneously the importance of liberal arts education for women—for example, in training teachers—while also clinging to attempts to raise the status of domestic service through education.[119] Most used separate institution-building and antisegregation tactics at the same time. Nannie Burroughs, noted for her work as an educator promoting Christian and vocational education, urged a boycott of Washington, D.C.'s segregated transportation system in 1915.[120] In the 1930s Burroughs defied the Baptist leadership so strongly that the church almost cut off financial support for the National Training School for Girls in Washington, D.C., which she had worked so hard and long to build. "'Don't wait for deliverers,' she admonished her listeners. . . . 'There are no deliverers. They're all dead. . . . The Negro must serve notice . . . that he is ready to die for justice.'" The Baptists relented, but Burroughs was still provoking white churchmen a decade later. In 1941 she canceled an engagement to speak for the National Christian Mission because the hierarchy insisted on precensoring her speech.[121] "The Negro is oppressed not because he is a Negro—but because he'll take it."[122] Yet in 1938 Burroughs was still rejoicing when a new work relief program earmarked funds for training blacks as domestic servants.[123]

On the other hand, civil rights militance did not eclipse uplift strategies. A sense of responsibility to represent the race at all times in the best possible way was ever present. Women put tremendous pressure for perfection on themselves and others. A reminiscence of Mary McLeod Bethune by one of her students (between 1904 and 1918) communicates the spirit of these demands:

> With Mrs. Bethune, there were just no short cuts, and another part of the character training, shall I call it, would be through these phrases that she would use, like "Whatever you do, do it to the best of your ability." Over and over, . . . "Whatever you do, do it to the best of your ability." And so this feeling about the thoroughness—to this day, any kind of sloppiness disturbs me greatly. . . . Orderliness was another concept that became a part of my life, and even as I grow to be almost eighty years old, I cannot bear to be disorderly. It may be just a tiny thing, but it does become a part of the expression of your living. I can remember many times, as adolescents will, we'd be tired at night and we'd sort of just drop our clothes anywhere. This is when I became a boarding student at the school, and she would come around and look in our rooms at night. . . . Gently we were awakened, we had to get up and put those clothes in a neat way on our chairs.[124]

Another reason for a blurred line between militance and accommodationism was a continuing sense of connection to the white women's movement. Despite insulting treatment, many black feminists did not simply write off white women's organizations but continued to contend with them. The very feminism of the black women forced them to contest segregation and prejudice—yet another example of the unity of antiracist and feminist causes for them. Many were active suffragists, despite the fact that most black women could not vote even after the amendment passed. Those who considered themselves particularly involved in women's rights agitation were vehement in protesting the hypocrisy of the white feminists' language of sisterhood and their practice of black exclusion. A poignant example was Terrell's struggle, as an elderly woman, for admission to the Washington, D.C., chapter of the AAUW. Fannie Barrier Williams, for example, as early as 1896, insisted that white women needed to learn from blacks.[125] Eva Bowles, Lugenia Burns Hope, Addie Hunton, and others fought against discrimination in the YWCA.[126]

Protests against race discrimination were often intensely personal; black notions of femininity did not proscribe militance. Charlotte Hawkins Brown, who was noted and sometimes criticized for her snobbery and insistence on "respectability," nevertheless "made it a practice, whenever insulted in a train or forced to leave a pullman coach and enter the Jim Crow car, to bring suit." At least one lawyer, in 1921, tried to get her to accept a small settlement, but she made it clear that her purpose was not financial compensation but justice.[127] Anna Julia Cooper, whose flowery and sentimental prose style might lead one to mistake her for a "soft," accommodating spirit, rarely let a slur against blacks go unprotested. She wrote to the Oberlin Committee against Al Smith in 1928 that she could not "warm up very enthusiastically with religious fervor for Bible 'fundamentalists' who have nothing to say about lynching Negroes or reducing whole sections of them to a state of peonage."[128]

Black maternalism differed most sharply from white in its approach to women's economic role. The white women, with few exceptions, tended to view married women's economic dependence on men as desirable, and their employment as a misfortune, unless their children were grown; they accepted the family-wage system and, while they frequently complained that it did not work well they rarely questioned it as an ideal. Black women reformers also held up breadwinner husbands and nonemployed wives as ideals; black and white women spoke very similarly about the appropriate "spheres" of the two sexes, equally emphasizing motherhood. Lucy D. Slowe, Dean of Women at Howard, believed that working mothers caused urban juvenile delinquency and called for campaigns to "build up public sentiment for paying heads of families wages sufficient to reduce the number of Negro women who must be employed away from home to the detriment of their children and of the community in general."[129] Personally, many of the married black activists had trouble prevailing upon their husbands to accept their activities, just like white women, and some were persuaded to stay home. Ardie Halyard, recollecting the year 1920, described the process:

INTERVIEWER: How did your husband feel about you working?

HALYARD: At first, he thought it was very necessary. But afterwards, when he became able to support us, it was day in and day out, "When are you going to quit?"[130]

Dorothy Ferebee's husband could not tolerate her higher professional status.[131] Inabel Lindsay promised her husband not to work for a year and slid into a lifelong career by taking a job that she promised was only temporary.[132]

But black acceptance of married women's employment as a long-term and widespread necessity was much greater than among whites,[133] so much so that it requires a redefinition of "maternalism." Black women's views were in large part adaptations to necessity— from as early as 1870 black mothers were employed at three times the rate of white—but theirs was also a principled, feminist position. Fanny Jackson Coppin had argued since the 1860s for women's economic independence from men, and consciousness of the need for such independence was a force behind the great emphasis on education for women. Black welfare activists often organized around employment issues, as, for example, Nannie Burroughs, whose National Association of Wage Earners fought for higher wages and better working conditions for domestics.[134]

The greater black acknowledgment of the existence of working mothers shows in the high priority they gave to organizing "kindergartens" or day nurseries. In major cities throughout the country day care facilities were among the earliest projects of black women's groups.[135] Mary Church Terrell's first publication was a speech she printed and sold for 25 cents a copy to help fund a kindergarten.[136] In poor urban white neighborhoods the need for child care may have been nearly as great, but white activists gave the issue less attention. Few northern white welfare reformers even endorsed day care in principle until much later (the 1930s and 1940s); until then even the most progressive, such as Florence Kelley, usually opposed it even as a temporary solution, fearing that day care would encourage the exploitation of women through low-wage labor.[137] The indifference to child care among white reformers may have reflected the fact that most of the mothers among them had servants to care for their children; while black women, who *were* these servants (domestic service was the most common form of employment for black women), needed affordable care for their children if they had no nearby obliging relatives.

Black women decried the effects of the "double day" on poor women as much as did white reformers. They were outspoken in their criticism of men who failed to support families—Nannie Burroughs wrote, "Black men sing too much 'I Can't Give You Anything

But Love, Baby'"[138]—but their solutions were different. Burroughs's understanding that the great majority of black women would work all their lives underlay her National Training School.[139] Most black women activists projected a favorable view of working women and women's professional aspirations. Elizabeth Ross Haynes wrote glowingly in 1922 of "'the hope of an economic independence that will some day enable them [Negro women] to take their places in the ranks with other working women.'"[140] Sadie Alexander criticized the view that domesticity should be a married woman's ideal. She saw that in an industrial society the work of the housewife would be increasingly seen as "valueless consumption" and that women should "place themselves again among the producers of the world."[141]

This high regard for women's economic independence was reflected in the important and prestigious role played by businesswomen in black welfare activity. One of the best-known and most-revered women of this network was Maggie Lena Walker, the first woman bank president in the United States. Beginning at age fourteen in the Independent Order of St. Luke, a mutual benefit society in Richmond providing illness and burial insurance as well as social activity for Blacks, in 1903 she established the St. Luke Penny Savings Bank. Walker became a very wealthy woman, devoting a great deal of her money and energy to welfare activity, working in the NAACP, the National Association of Wage Earners, and local Richmond groups. In the context of black experience, Walker's business was itself a civil rights and community welfare activity; many reformers, including prominently Bethune and Du Bois, believed that economic power was key to black progress. The St. Luke enterprises stimulated black ownership and employment, opening a black-owned department store in Richmond, thus threatening white economic power, and met intense opposition from white businessmen; indeed a white Retail Dealers' Association was formed to crush the store.[142] Several noteworthy businesswomen-activists got rich from manufacturing cosmetics for blacks: the mother-daughter team C. J. Walker and A'Lelia Walker (not related to Maggie Walker), of Pittsburgh and Indianapolis; Ezella Mathis Carter; and Annie Turnbo Malone.[143] Reformer Jane Hunter was respected not only because of her welfare contributions but also because, once penniless, she left an estate of more than four hundred thousand dollars at her death, as was Sallie Wyatt Stewart, who left more than one hundred thousand dollars from real estate.[144]

The actual marital experience of the black and white activists was clearly pertinent to their attitudes: Most of the black women had the experience of combining public-sphere activism with marriage, if less often with children; most of the whites had not.[145] The fact that most of the white women had ended up, probably largely by choice, dispensing with marriage and family may have made them see the choice between family and work as an acceptable one, oblivious to the different conditions of "choice" among poorer women. (This race difference tended to disappear over time, however; from the 1930s on, white married women more often combined employment and reform activism.)

Still, the African American pride in women's achievements was only one part of the story. Another was the continuing women's longing to be able to stay home with their children. Most black women were neither rich nor professional, but locked in underpaid, oppressive, and sometimes degrading jobs.[146]

Naturally these values and strategies changed over time, particularly for northern blacks, who became more militant, less deferential to elite leadership, and more demanding of government-supported welfare programs. By the 1930s the NACW's elitism appeared archaic to many blacks. Seizing upon the New Deal's promise, grassroots African American groups demanded federal intervention against Jim-Crow local government. Mrs. C. A. VerNooy of the Athens, Georgia, Colored Community Association wrote to President Roosevelt complaining about the exclusion of blacks from local education, recreation, and welfare resources, "Certainly Ambassador Bryce was right when he more than forty years ago declared municipal government the greatest evil in this country."[147] Many of the more left-leaning women shifted their locus of activism to civil rights, through the NAACP, or placed their hopes for advancement in women's integration into industrial labor and unions. But this approach was limited both by black women's limited access to industrial jobs and by the resistance of male unionists to a female-centered agenda.[148] A more mainstream group, led by Bethune, created a new organization, the National Council of Negro Women (NCNW). It broke with NACW traditions in departing from the uplift tradition; showing the influence of Bethune's federal government experience, it focused mainly on lobbying. It did not feature building private institutions but fought for price controls and minimum-wage and maximum-hours legislation for domestic and farm laborers and combated racial discrimination in Social Security coverage, public housing, and New Deal emergency relief programs.[149] As women became not only voters but political party activists, the new generation of black women welfare reformers also adopted the strategy—just as white women did—of campaigning for the appointment of black women to government agencies. In 1925 women from the Republican National Committee wrote President Coolidge outlining the contributions they had made in getting out black voters for him and asking for government appointments for black women. They demanded parallel appointments to those of white women, particularly in the labor and welfare areas, naming the Children's Bureau as one of them (and showing that to black as to white women the Children's Bureau was uniquely important.)[150] In 1930 they got themselves included in the White House Conference on Children; later they campaigned for black appointments to New Deal agencies and protested discrimination in the armed forces.[151] Local women activists were also quick to seize the opportunity Roosevelt seemed to offer and to demand federal support for their projects.[152] Realizing what a good thing they had started, the AKA women tried to interest the federal government in taking over, or just contributing to, their Mississippi health project, but with no success. They also tried the Public Health Service, the Children's Bureau, New Deal relief programs; they appealed to Eleanor Roosevelt personally. All they got was a little surplus food.[153]

Both the NCNW and the black Left deserted the feminist/womanist perspective. Affected no doubt by the masculinist backlash mood of the 1920s, this younger generation neither criticized men nor legitimatized women's leadership on the basis of women's virtues or unique abilities.[154] Moreover, as the use of the term "Negro" rather than "colored" implied, the new mood rejected the emphasis on respectability.[155] That emphasis, calling on individual blacks to serve as exemplars for the reputation of the race, had had both class and gender meanings: It marked the domination of an elite and a strategy of elite leadership, but it also symbolized an argument for women's leadership based on female moral superiority. For both blacks and whites, rejecting it displayed the demise of female moral reform and its replacement by women's participation in previously male politics. For both blacks and whites, in different ways, entering into politics represented a step toward political power—but also the loss of a female sphere of authority to male dominance. Yet there were racially determined continuities, particularly in the unending emphasis on uplift and institution building.[156]

One woman's contributions may illustrate. Lucy Miller, one of the youngest women in this group, was born in 1899 in Daytona Beach, Florida, her father a successful businessman, and was educated from kindergarten through high school in Mary McLeod Bethune's school, the Daytona Normal and Industrial Institute. She graduated from Talladega College in 1922, returned to Daytona, and taught for Bethune one year. She was being groomed for leadership in a manner traditional among the southern women in this network—not informally but explicitly. Bethune offered her the "mantle of leadership." Miller, however, saw more promising opportunity elsewhere. She followed her parents to Boston, exercising the privileges of her class, and there she married a Harvard and Boston Law School graduate, Joseph Mitchell. She did not, however, settle into domestic life. The difficulty of finding a place for her daughter in a nursery school led to Miller's becoming first a teacher and then director of a nursery school at a settlement house. She helped develop a tuberculosis prevention program and made it a model school, where education students were sent for practice teaching. Adapting to a new world in which professional credentials mattered, she earned an M.Ed. in 1935. During World War II she organized training institutes for child care volunteers. Ultimately she was able to exert influence in government: In 1951 she helped create a city agency to oversee preschool services and education and became its educational director; in the 1960s she developed a state licensing law for child care facilities.[157]

Lucy Miller's career illustrates certain patterns common to the black activists of this generation: Many moved north and earned higher educational credentials, some joining the new profession of social work. (Academic positions in colleges other than the traditionally black ones remained very difficult for black women to get.) Although they began to work for publicly funded programs and institutions, they were still required to create their own black institutions as the public sector failed them. They continued to emphasize education and child care centers for working mothers, demonstrating the priority placed on services for children and the understanding that women's employment was both necessary and often beneficial for all.

=

What was the black women's welfare vision? Certainly it required women's leadership. Concern for strengthening the economic position of black men impelled black women to support but not to stand behind their men. In this respect theirs was a feminist vision.

Nonetheless it did not challenge a set of gender norms that defined womanliness in maternalist ways. The black women's leadership claim rested on an understanding of femininity, and of what women could uniquely contribute, that featured motherhood and motherliness—notions of womanhood as especially linked to children and metaphorically to the nurturance of the whole society that were shared across race lines. Black women welfare reformers focused particularly on children's education and health and accepted women's responsibility for children. This maternalism was less contested among blacks than among whites; however, for a variety of reasons among blacks there was no significant equivalent to equal-rights feminism. This did not mean that there was no criticism of men. On the contrary, there was a steady if occasionally private struggle with men in the race movement, sometimes criticizing male resistance to women's influence, sometimes criticizing male failure to perform according to conventional male gender norms, always criticizing male disrespect for women. This criticism appears to have been, during this period, more forthright and public than any by white women. Protecting women against male aggression was a major theme in institution building, signalling that accepting a female gender role that was in some ways conventional was not necessarily inimical to women's rights militance.

Because of this race responsibility, and because for blacks welfare was so indistinguishable from equal rights, black women deemphasized programs for the unusually needy and concentrated on universal provision,[158] creating an important difference between black and white maternalism. Black maternalism operated with less distance and condescension between helper and helped, and combined some romanticization of womanhood and motherliness with respect for women's economic independence. Certainly black, like white, women leaders separated themselves from the disreputable and sometimes treated the needy as children. But only the white women emphasized the use of means- and morals-testing as a way of distributing help, continuing to stigmatize the poor in the process.

The intersection of discrimination and poverty in the black experience meant that welfare claims seemed not so different from the right to vote or to ride the public transportation system.[159] We see here a necessary connection between political and social citizenship: Without some minimum level of security, well-being, and dignity, people cannot function as citizens.[160] And vice versa: To work for welfare was to work against inequality and against discrimination. The fact that this orientation was defeated would have deeply debilitating effects on the society.

Black women had considerably different attitudes toward married women's employment, which constructed an equally different approach to single mothers. Most of the white women welfare reformers retained a head-in-the-sand and even contradictory attitude toward it: It was a misfortune, not good for women, children, or men; aiding working mothers too much would tend to encourage it. Thus they were more concerned to allow—sometimes to force—mothers to stay home than to provide services that would make life easier for working mothers, such as child care or maternity leave. This contradiction became a double bind for single mothers, who most needed to rely on their own employment, given the inadequacy of public provision. Yet the fear of encouraging single-mother households was so strong that the white women's welfare movement succeeded in neither honoring their work as mothers nor creating the conditions in which they could earn adequately. Although black women activists agreed that a male family wage was the most desirable arrangement, they doubted that married women's employment would soon disappear or that it could be discouraged by making women and children suffer for it. They were not paralyzed by fear of single motherhood, although they tried to discourage it. They were less caught up in moralism about illegitimacy than the whites, although they emphasized sexual propriety. Had black women activists had their way, the working mothers of the past few decades would have been much better supplied with child care and other measures to lighten the double day. ADC would have been more balanced and the demand for it possibly reduced.

It is noticeable that neither blacks nor whites made demands for men to share domestic labor or to accept responsibility for children. Many husbands, particularly those in the working class, did contribute considerably to household work, but there were no campaigns to politicize this issue. Yet black women were challenging male behavior in regard to sex, attempting to protect women from sexual exploitation. By contrast whites did not make rape an important issue; when they did concern themselves with protecting women and girls, they treated male sexual activity as uncontrollable and placed the burden of responsibility on women to stay out of danger. It is not clear how the black activists would have translated their antirape consciousness into welfare policy, had they had the power to do so, but it seems likely that they would have tried. In the long run, however, their critique of male privilege was weakened by renewed and even intensified racism and the need for black solidarity in resisting it.

Just as today there is no single feminism, let alone a unanimous women's approach to any social issue, so in the early twentieth century there was no single female vision of welfare. Some of these alternatives clashed and argued with one another—among whites notably the maternalist "social feminism" and equal rights feminism. The dominant African American vision transcended that division to some degree, through its greater support for women's economic independence. There may well have been other distinct perspectives, reflecting other racial/ethnic and class experiences: Little has been written about the welfare activism of farm women, working-class women, Hispanic, Asian, or American Indian women. Unfortunately there was very little cross-race discussion, even between movements as well developed and as similar as white and African American maternalist feminism. That lack of communication contributed to the historical limitations of our welfare system in ways that cannot be undone. Still, reopening that conversation may help us know not only the full historical picture but also the range of alternatives we face today.

Signing Wisconsin's Pioneer Unemployment Compensation Act, January 1932. Left to right: Henry Ohl, Jr., Wisconsin State Federation of Labor; Elizabeth Brandeis Raushenbush; Paul Raushenbush; John Commons; Governor Philip La Follette; Lt. Gov. Henry Huber; and Assemblymen Harold Groves and Robert Nixon.

6

Prevention Before Charity

Social Insurance and the
Sexual Division of Labor

B lack men and women were almost entirely excluded from welfare planning in the New Deal, and white women, despite their
hard-won governmental positions, were marginalized. The center
was occupied by an all-white and virtually all-male group that advocated social insurance. The social insurance vision of welfare was enacted in Social Security's old-age pensions and unemployment compensation, while the social work vision was expressed in Social
Security's public assistance programs, such as ADC. An amalgam of
these two models continues to shape American domestic policy, creating a two-track welfare system. What was previously called social
insurance is now referred to as "entitlements" or just "Social Security"; the social work–inspired programs, such as ADC, are now called
public assistance, or just "welfare."

Social insurance is a little used term today but in the first half of
this century it denoted a distinct welfare vision: government provision to replace wages temporarily or permanently lost through illness, injury, unemployment, or retirement. Directed mainly at full-
time wage earners, social insurance ideas had little direct influence
on ADC; but they had great indirect influence, because the social insurance programs grew stronger in part by distinguishing themselves
from public assistance. Indeed it is the relationship between the two
types of programs that created the contemporary meaning of "welfare." That relationship was constructed in part as a sexual division

of labor, because the two welfare models were to a large extent marked by gender. Social insurance was overwhelmingly a male vision, social work a deeply feminized one. Just as comparing white to black women's perspectives made it possible to identify the racial aspects of both visions, so now comparing social insurance and social work perspectives makes visible the gendered aspects of our welfare system: not only what was female in it but also what was male. This gendered reading will show some of the "deep structure" of our welfare system.

Campaigning for Welfare: A White Man's Network

Social insurance was the collective product of a high-powered group of reform intellectuals, many of whom were as influential in the development of modern social science as in welfare design. Like the social work vision, social insurance ideas expressed the interests and worldview of their authors at least as much as the needs of their beneficiaries.

The social insurance community changed over the years between 1890 and 1935. No one epitomized its first generation better than the Reverend John Graham Brooks, a classic gentleman reformer, American style. Born in 1846, he came, like Julia Lathrop, from one of the oldest European families in the United States. Reform was deep in his upbringing. For example, his abolitionist passion led to an attempt to enlist in the Union Army, which failed because he was underage. Educated at Oberlin (a center of abolitionist and other reform sentiment) and the Harvard Divinity School, he became a Unitarian minister and married the daughter of a prominent Boston family, who accompanied him when he went to study social theory in Germany in the years 1881–85. There he witnessed the establishment of Bismarck's social insurance program. Returning to the United States, he took up another congregation. But the ministry could not satisfy his energy for reform and he began spending more and more time in a group of reform-minded young clergymen. In 1891 he gave up the ministry to devote himself full-time, for the rest of his long life, to social science and reform. He defended trade unions and women's rights and advocated labor regulation and social insurance, vociferously enough to be frequently branded a radical. Yet he always remained an amateur, freelance writer and reformer, never in a permanent job—an option conditioned by his independent income.

Brooks' social insurance ideas, like those of several of his contemporaries, were at first similar to those of his female social work associates and included morals-testing and supervision.[1]

John Commons's mother wanted him to become a minister, but he resisted. One of a second generation in social insurance, born in 1862, Commons was also descended from early American stock and abolitionist parents; he also went to Oberlin, as had his mother. But he came from a more modest background than Brooks, the son of an unambitious small-town newspaper editor. His mother moved to Oberlin and kept a boardinghouse in order to support her children in college; while there, she and John started an "antisaloon" publication. When Commons moved to Baltimore to study with economist Richard Ely at Johns Hopkins, she came with with him and kept his house. He understood his debt and expressed gratitude in his autobiography, even recognizing that she had sacrificed a career of her own for him and his father. In the 1890s his prolabor ideas and rejection of classical economics gave him a radical reputation, and he lost several academic positions in that decade. He acknowledged his intellectual debt to several leftists during that decade. But by the peak of his career, at the University of Wisconsin in the Department of Political Economy after 1904, his reform ideas appeared almost mainstream, partly because they had become more accepted and partly because he consciously modified them to win acceptance.[2] His pro–social insurance views were in the center of Progressive reform; he was sympathetic to labor leader Samuel Gompers although more supportive of government labor regulation. Some labeled his "Wisconsin school" approach to labor history as conservative. From the perspective of social insurance history, however, Commons's most significant innovation was his increasing involvement with the Wisconsin state government, which ultimately laid the basis for the recruitment of his student Edwin Witte to direct the design of the Social Security Act.[3] Commons began by assisting Governor Robert La Follette Sr. in drafting reform legislation, on civil service and establishing public utilities and industrial commissions. He promoted the use of empirical studies by experts as a basis of legislating.[4] In 1906, with his teacher Ely and his student John Andrews, he established the American Association for Labor Legislation (AALL), which was to become one of the most influential social insurance organizations.

As social insurance gained adherents, the network of reformers grew more varied, and no one could be identified as typical. But

Abraham Epstein exemplifies a third generation and the changing constituency and leadership of social insurance. Born to a poor Jewish innkeeper's family in 1892 near Pinsk, Russia, he immigrated to the United States in 1910. Although he was not the first non-Protestant to achieve prominence in reform circles, he was among the first from a nonelite background; men like Brandeis and Frankfurter were wealthy German Jews, not poor immigrants. Displaying prodigious ambition, within eight years of his arrival in the United States Epstein had earned a college degree in business, completed a year of graduate work, and won a position as research director for the Pennsylvania Commission on Old Age Pensions. From then on Epstein remained a full-time, professional reformer. He developed a considerable following for his proposals. Supported by the Pennsylvania Federation of Labor and the Fraternal Order of Eagles, Epstein led campaigns for state pensions in Pennsylvania and Ohio. In 1927 he formed the American Association for Old Age Security (later called the American Association for Social Security [AASS], making it the source of that term as a slogan), which gained support from virtually the entire welfare community; Jane Addams, John Commons, Paul Douglas, Florence Kelley, Fiorello LaGuardia, Norman Thomas, Oswald Garrison Villard, and Edwin Witte were among the members of its Advisory Council in 1927.[5] Soon, however, Epstein's group began to feud for leadership with the Commons/Andrews AALL group, and several attempts at mediation by others failed. Epstein himself always remained somewhat marginal because of his socialist politics, his ties to organized labor, his prickly, combative personality, and very likely his Jewishness. He was conspicuously excluded from the work on drafting Roosevelt's Social Security Bill. But, ironically, it was his rather than the Wisconsin design for unemployment compensation that ultimately prevailed, and his criticisms of Social Security were ultimately validated by the 1939 amendments that broadened its coverage.[6]

=

Despite sharp, even bitter differences, a core of agreement about social insurance had developed by the 1920s.[7] Its proponents were convinced that interruptions of income from circumstances beyond the control of individual workers were inevitable in a capitalist economy, and that public responsibility for the victims of such misfortunes was not only an matter of ethics but also necessary for a healthy economy. This new kind of welfare plan had a few agreed-upon principles: coverage of clearly defined causes of need, such as unemployment or illness, by government provision, with compulsory participation; automatic (that is, not means- or morals-tested) benefits among those covered without discretion on the part of administrators.

Today the distinction between social insurance and public assistance is understood mainly in terms of the "contributory" funding of the former, through special earmarked taxes, but this was not the primary meaning of that distinction before the New Deal. Many social insurance proposals called for funding from general tax revenues, just like public assistance, and proponents never counted on a strict actuarial relation between payments into a fund and payments out to an insured person. The social insurance advocates emphasized not how funds were raised but rather rationalizing and universalizing programs and spreading risk. "It fundamentally aims," wrote Paul Douglas, "to distribute the burden . . . which falls with such a crushing weight upon the minority . . . over a wider group who as a whole are able to bear it. This is indeed the real purpose of all insurance."[8] They took models from private—capitalist or fraternal—insurance schemes and adapted them to state control. Perhaps the most important adaptation was making them compulsory, a decision taken very early and agreed to fairly unanimously.[9]

Social insurance got its name by analogy to private insurance. Defining it a quarter-century earlier, John Commons pointed out that all insurance was really social insurance, since all insurance aimed at "the social distribution of individual loss." At first the notion of social insurance included nongovernmental insurance programs run by such nonprofit groups as unions or benevolent societies. By the 1930s "social" as a modifier of insurance had come to mean "public," as in insurance "made universal by governmental compulsion."[10] Because social insurance would be dignified, advocates envisioned it as a vastly preferable alternative to older poor-relief traditions. And the Social Security Act soon gave social insurance programs, in addition, the status of entitlements as distinct from the discretionary, charitable standing of programs like ADC.

Unlike public assistance, social insurance was not exclusively direct-ed at the poor but rather at wage-earners more generally. One of social insurance's selling points was its benefits to all classes.[11] Its advo-cates proposed not to relieve but to prevent poverty. In an influen-tial debaters' handbook on social insurance published in 1912, only one of thirty two articles mentioned poverty. (It was also the only one by a woman.)[12] Indeed social insurance agitation gained critical support from big business when it became clear that private "welfare capitalism" was inadequate and too expensive; in this re-spect support for social insurance represented an attempt to shift some of the costs of maintaining a labor force to the public purse.[13]

Social insurance proponents aimed at nothing less than creating a perfectly regulated economy. They had no faith that a hidden hand within the market would suffice. They were social engineers, con-vinced that government must regulate the distribution of wealth not only to protect individuals but equally to preserve national economic vitality.[14] Social insurance could achieve this end, they believed, by aiding workers as soon as there was a loss of earnings rather than waiting until they were impoverished, or by providing incentives for employers to maintain steady employment and safe working condi-tions. They shared with most Progressive reformers great confidence in social betterment; they thought big and structurally. In this sense they were more radical, "perfectionist" in the tradition of American Protestant radicals, than the social work network, whose religious orientation was more evangelical: Richard Neustadt, who moved from settlement work to social insurance advocacy, considered the view that [poverty] "is ultimately preventable [to be] a fundamental doctrine of democracy, an axiom of civilization."[15] But their perfec-tionism did not extend to personality or "character," that major fo-cus of nineteenth-century charity; they devoted little attention to in-dividual character flaws.

Social insurance designers saw themselves as pioneers but they lacked clarity or unanimity about the desired results. Some believed that social insurance was a stage in the development of an increasing-ly responsible and beneficent state. Others believed that a few strate-gically placed social insurance programs would obviate the necessity for expanded state provision. None foresaw—or intended—that so-cial insurance, rather then ending poverty, would intensify inequality and thus create greater need for additional welfare programs.

=

Social insurance and social work networks were sex-segregated, but not symmetrically: the former were virtually all male, the latter male and female.[16] Yet in class, ethnic, religious, and political backgrounds the two groups were similar. The majority of both came from rather privileged backgrounds. Many had Republican and temperance allegiances. Most took their Christianity very seriously and considered their reform work part of a Christian moral vision. Nine of the seventy-six in my sample were ministers. Like the women, they were extremely highly educated. Many, like Brooks and Commons, were women's rights advocates.

Yet, as a whole, the men's group was less elite than the women's. For example, although the men had more education, the women were more exceptional in their educational achievements because fewer women had higher education.[17] The women were also, on average, from more elite backgrounds than the men—two-thirds of the women had elite parents, one-third of the men[18]—no doubt in part because lack of access to most vocations sent a high proportion of all educated women into this kind of activity. Ethnically and religiously the men were more diverse than the women. The women's network was more overwhelmingly Protestant and northern European, mostly native born; the men by contrast included more immigrants.[19] One-fifth of the men were Jewish, and in the later part of the period, considering men born after 1880, the proportion went up to one-third; half of the Jewish men were immigrants. The Jews were often from poor backgrounds, several with radical political inclinations. By contrast the Jewish women were primarily from wealthy German backgrounds and were born in the United States. Several of the less elite social insurance advocates were influenced by European social democracy and maintained active ties with the labor movement. This legacy strengthened their sense that workingmen—in both class and gender senses of that term—were their main constituents, the designated beneficiaries of social insurance.

Except for a few of the older men, who were full-time amateur reformers, the social insurance advocates were overwhelmingly professionals who managed to make their advocacy serve their careers—and vice versa. By the early twentieth century, middle- and upper-class men's identities were increasingly defined by a profession, and men with a passion for social justice and mercy fulfilled that mission through a profession, experiencing from their youth the pressure for discipline, specialization, and achievement.[20] More than half were academics for some time during their lives, and while the older men were also likely to be ministers or charity workers, almost three-fourths of the younger men (those born after 1880) were academics.[21] These were often economists or statisticians.[22] By the 1920s nearly three-quarters of even the Jews in this network had found academic positions, despite anti-Semitism. Indeed, for the less-privileged men, social insurance careers became a route to upward mobility. By contrast only 13 percent of the white women ever held regular academic positions.[23] While two-thirds of the men had participated in social work, most had done so as volunteers, temporarily, before or outside their career vocations. The white women with salaried jobs were almost all social workers.[24] For women the activism *was* the career.[25]

The different educational and occupational influences on these men and women affected their welfare visions. The women were much more likely to have had long-term direct contact with the poor, and especially the female poor, through settlement houses or relief agencies. All except the oldest women had personally experienced the transformation of social work from a volunteer to a professional activity, beginning their careers as volunteers for charity or reform groups, ending as salaried workers for the same or similar groups. Women's careers had arisen directly from their charitable and reform activism, and their identities were strongly influenced by their goals and their self-definition as altruists. As academics the social insurance advocates were more insulated from the conditions and aspirations of the poor themselves. Moreover, whether as ministers, academics, or executives of various organizations and corporations, the men were likely to have participated in welfare reform only as leaders, experts, and/or prominent public spokesmen, never having been part of the ranks. The major conduit for discussion and information between the poor and the social insurance reformers was union leadership. Thus the ignorance, manifest in their welfare plans, of the massive poverty problems of non–wage earners such as single mothers, is not surprising.

Proper family life was important to welfare assumptions and values, and activists were surely influenced by their own family experiences. Virtually all (91 percent) of the men were married and 68 percent had children; they were heads of families and few had employed or publicly active wives. Let us recall that only 34 percent of the white women had ever been married, only 28 percent had children, and only 18 percent remained married during their peak political activity. The years in which these women were young (approximately 1870–1915) represented an important transitional period for privileged women, who were entering the public sphere through professions and activism in larger numbers than ever before; but it remained socially very difficult for them to combine this public-sphere activity with marriage. The difficulty arose not so much from the stresses of the "double day" that working-class women faced, because these women in the main could afford household and child care help. Rather the barrier to combining marriage and "career" was created by the cultural expectations that wives should be domestic and should function as support staff for their husbands. Privileged white women faced a choice between two mutually exclusive options.

Thus in the organizations and committees on which they sometimes worked together, married men with nonemployed wives typically faced single women who were extremely publicly active. The men often regarded these women, who were usually middle-aged by the time they reached positions of importance in their reform area, as spinsters. The men were likely to connect the women's singleness with their concern for widows and orphans and to perceive both as quaint, marginal, and decidedly unscientific. The increasing technical elaboration of social insurance designs intensified this perception.

The men's sense of themselves as a vanguard was reinforced by the fact that so many had been influenced by European social insurance thought. In fact, the whole social insurance stream of thought was brought to the United States from Europe, by academics educated abroad. In the 1890s a handful of Western European countries passed social insurance legislation; by 1915 most European countries had such programs.[26] British influence was stronger in the settlement and social work tradition, while the German connection was more prominent among social insurance advocates (and, indeed, its opponents were quick to brand it un-American, a German plot).[27] German economics was highly influential, its ethical content particularly attractive to Americans from evangelical Protestant traditions.[28]

The first to begin popularizing German social insurance ideas in the United States was Brooks. Sponsored by U.S. Commissioner of

Labor Carroll Wright, he published the first scholarly study of German social insurance. Other studies were produced soon after by physician-statistician Isaac Rubinow and the Russell Sage Foundation.[29] In 1902 Charles Henderson of the University of Chicago sociology department induced the NCCC—the main national social work professional organization—to appoint a commission to study social insurance. Soon several states organized studies of European schemes, and in 1906 the AALL became the first national organization to make social insurance a priority.[30]

The most immediately influential of these German programs was workmen's compensation, and the influence was strengthened further by the adoption of the Workmen's Compensation Act of 1897. The AALL's biggest victory was on this issue, and, after fourteen years of agitation, by 1920, forty five states had passed workers' compensation laws. These laws levied payroll taxes on employers and, from the resultant state funds, compensated injured workers according to predefined scales. Since the legal principle of workmen's compensation disregarded the question of who was at fault in an accident, the next logical step was a campaign to extend coverage to occupational diseases, again stimulated by European legislation—in this case a British act of 1906—and in many states the original laws were extended to cover disease. From the insurance coverage of industrial disease grew the first campaign for universal health insurance, spearheaded again by the AALL, beginning in 1912. But the insurance movement got stalled here, and no public health insurance bills were passed.[31]

European ideas fell on different soil when they landed in the United States. Constitutional structures, class and gender relations, and political culture steered ideas differently and constrained outcomes. In Germany and England, for example, pressure for public social provision came from unions and socialist and labor parties; when initiatives came from the Right or from the state itself, they were defensive against union and left-wing strength. In the United States, by contrast, the unions were relatively, or at least formally, disinterested in state welfare provision, and Left political parties were weak. Rather the leading pressure groups for social provision were at first white women's groups or other middle-class reform organizations in which white women were prominent.[32] Social insurance men entered a field in which other groups had already staked out a welfare jurisdiction—notably in mothers' aid, and the restriction of their proposals to wage earners was conditioned by their knowledge that others were campaigning to help the nonemployable poor.

As social insurance gained momentum, two emphases distinguished themselves. John Commons, John Andrews, and their AALL were interested in the potential of social insurance to provide incentives to capital to improve the workings of capitalism. They advocated a workmen's compensation plan that would give employers a financial motive to improve safety conditions in their plants; later they designed unemployment insurance to make it profitable for employers to stabilize employment. At root they were Progressives in their hopes of perfecting the capitalist economic and social order through state intervention.[33] Other social insurance advocates, such as Isaac Rubinow and Abraham Epstein, had socialist leanings. Even a safe factory would always produce accidents and illness; employment in a capitalist order was inherently unstable. For them social insurance was part of permanent government intervention in the economy.[34]

In the 1920s the two social insurance groups developed considerable mutual animosity. The AALL came to be identified with an "American plan," which, in comparison with European plans, deemphasized central state responsibility. Abraham Epstein's American Association for Old Age Security spoke for those who supported a strong national system. The prominence of Epstein and Rubinow on this side brought out latent anti-Semitism as well as anti-Europeanism and antiradicalism in opposition.

By the time the two schools were drawn into New Deal debates, their differences had congealed around alternative models of unemployment compensation. In 1931 Wisconsin adopted a model championed by Commons, which the AALL characterized as supporting the values of individualism and competition while helping the unemployed. It provided employer taxes held in separate accounts for each firm, to be used for benefits for employees laid off by those very firms; the more layoffs, the higher the employer taxes, so that the system encouraged firms to prevent unemployment. This approach was criticized by Epstein, Rubinow, William Leiserson, and Paul Douglas on the grounds that it could never provide adequate relief and that unemployment was beyond the control of individual firms. The AASS offered instead the "Ohio plan" (Rubinow was chairman of the Committee on Research of the Ohio Commission on Unemployment), which provided for a single statewide pool of funds for unemployment insurance. Rubinow and Leiserson insisted on a program funded by earmarked contributions, distinct from taxes, with the compensation in direct actuarial proportion to what was paid in, while Epstein and Douglas preferred funding through a progressive tax.

From the perspective of those concerned with women and children, the difference between the two social insurance streams was small. Neither group displayed any interest in providing directly for non–wage earners. The Epstein/Rubinow faction's view—that the primary goal of social insurance ought to be relief of need—might seem more congenial to the charity and social work tradition. But in fact it was even more distant from the woman-dominated welfare reform network than was the AALL group. One reason for this has to do with class and ethnicity: the leaders of the Children's Bureau network, on average, were more like the "American" group, mainly from elite WASP backgrounds. The women's network, with a few exceptions, did not identify with the Left. On the contrary, their connections—of family, education, and class—with the AALL group proved useful. Epstein's militant, egocentric style particularly repelled these elite women, while John Andrews was married to one of their network, and his commitment to protective labor legislation was more important to them than his unemployment plan.

But a fully "coeducational" welfare campaign never materialized. In the World War I era, many factors pushed women into male-dominated arenas—the woman suffrage amendment, the decline of feminist activism afterward, the sexual "revolution," and the division among women's rights activists about the ERA. But there were countervailing pressures, too. The Red Scare and attack on the Left weakened the Socialist party, thus shrinking one important common ground for men and women reformers. The two centers of welfare agitation—the Children's Bureau and the AALL—did not work together. Social insurance ignored the primary concerns of the women while the women's social work lobby ignored the need for programs more massive and universal than mothers' aid. Although suffrage pushed women toward the political mainstream, women's victories in establishing several federal agencies representing women's power—the Children's and Women's Bureaus—had the opposite effect, keeping alive a centripetal whirl of women's activism. For the social insurance advocates the achievement of workmen's compensation was followed by a long dry period. Momentum declined, and the hoped-for next step, medical insurance, did not materialize. By contrast, the woman-dominated social work–oriented forces seemed on a roll in the early 1920s with the Sheppard-Towner Act, which seemed at first to herald an expansive new welfare state.[35]

Gendered Welfare Strategies

The continued separation of male- and female-dominated welfare campaigns arose from and then confirmed highly gendered modes of welfare work. A comparison of the white men and women is revealing, although it does not yield opposites. More often it shows differences only in the nuances and uncovers many shared goals and assumptions. This is as expected. Comparing male and female ideas implies neither a universal gender system nor that gender was necessarily the determining or even dominant factor in constructing these visions. The values men and women shared were often themselves part of the gender order, such as their joint belief in the family-wage system.

Consider the different rhetorics of welfare advocates. If the welfare writings of the early twentieth century were read with authors' names hidden, we might be able to pick the sex of the writer with a high degree of precision. Women's writing sounded the social work approach to poverty—a concern with personal maladjustment. Among caseworkers and reformers, among those focused on labor legislation, health care, and mothers' aid, women more often used narrative and cited actual cases.[36] They employed sentimentality manipulatively, not naively. In 1923 Julia Lathrop referred to her group's accustomed use of "'sob stuff [and] high ideals afloat.'"[37] Twelve years later, when the Children's Bureau women were drafting ADC and Abbott's colleagues suggested she was asking for too small an appropriation, Abbott responded that to increase their request they should focus not just on children but on crippled children.[38]

But this manipulative rhetoric, this appeal to pity, did not mean rank opportunism. Recall Julia Lathrop's 1912 defense of pity: "pity is a rebel passion . . . The justice of today is born of yesterday's pity . . ." Moreover, because their stories were taken from actual cases they gained the complexity that combats sentimentality. That is, they avoided the dichotomies of good and evil, victim and brute, innocent and guilty, pure and polluted, that characterized some Victorian women's reform rhetoric. Indeed, at its best their distinction between poverty and pauperism was precisely about that complexity, because the concept of pauperism could be used to integrate the "hidden injuries of class" into the understanding of poverty. There were some stereotyped stories of saintly, pale, overworked widows, but there were also stories of child abuse, maternal negligence, alcoholism, demoralization, and dishonesty. Their narratives included condescension and moralism, to be sure, but they were not wrong to recognize personal and intrafamily problems among the poor.

By contrast social insurance rhetoric was more often abstract. When a "case" was used as an example (an infrequent device), it was invented, simplified, or hypothetical, while the women's stories came straight from case records. Social insurance writing addressed incidence of need, costs of various systems, administrative arrangements of various systems, and impact of insurance on economic incentives. It debated why insurance had to be compulsory, why compensation should be based on flat rates, and what classifications of workers and employers were appropriate. Its language was that of actuarial computation and administration, reflecting the economic and academic orientation of the authors.[39] Epstein's *Insecurity: A Challenge to America* (1933), spends more than one hundred pages on low wages, the impossibility of savings for workers, and the inadequacy of relief and private insurance without a single individual vignette or anecdote; instead the text is full of figures: "The number of families in whose behalf Red Cross flour was requested increased from 3,939,757 to 4,488,477."[40] An exception delimits the pattern. William Hard, close to the women's reform community, did use concrete examples but relied on imaginary rather than real cases, for example, longshoreman "Smith," who was burned in an explosion of benzine, naphtha, and gasoline on a ship, and how he would have been taken care of had there been a social insurance system.[41]

These rhetorical differences did not arise from innate gender differences but from social and political context. The women's writing style was influenced by casework training, which emphasized focusing on specific individuals in all their complexity. It simultaneously reflected and reinforced the women's reluctance to recognize that such a system might be inadequate to the scale of the need for welfare.

The contrasting rhetorical styles were also instrumental, deployed to win over potential supporters and to neutralize opponents. Social insurance advocates were likely to write academic texts or reports, while social workers addressed more general publics. Social insurance advocates sought to persuade politicians and scholars to try a new method of provision, while the social workers were defending a traditional form of aid. Among the major opponents of social insurance were private companies that sold insurance for a profit. (The social insurance advocates did not consider routing provision through private corporations.) Since all agreed that social insurance had to be compulsory, reformers had no choice but to challenge the private companies directly. The eleven main companies writing industrial insurance in 1900 reported ten million policies with a value of more than $1 billion.[42] An AALL 1934 study reported that $750 million was spent annually on burial insurance alone, even though five million policies had lapsed through nonpayment of premiums in 1932 alone. Six percent of total income was spent thus in 1932.[43] Brandeis condemned such expenditures as a scandalous waste of workingmen's savings.[44] So reformers emphasized the high cost of private insurance and appealed to the middle and working classes by pointing out how much cheaper a public system would be. By contrast, the mothers'-aid agitation provoked no particularly powerful enemies—the only interest group that fought the laws was private charities.[45] Their small-scale proposals combined with their sob stories were intended to minimize opposition to new taxes and to overcome fears of public corruption.

Rhetorical modes correlated with organizational modes. Women spoke more emotionally because they were trying to build grassroots support; social insurance men, by and large, spoke more coolly because they were not. Lacking full citizenship, women had devised a political practice that took place primarily outside electoral politics and the civil service system. A tradition of civic organizations dating from the Revolutionary Era continued directly into Progressive welfare agitation. The female social reform network rested on membership organizations and the members were active. The NCL, a key organization of the Progressive Era white women's network, at the peak of its power around 1910, had more than sixty locals, its influence felt in every major city, every northern state, and some southern states.[46] It could rely on alliances with the WTUL, the General

Federation of Women's Clubs, the League of Women Voters, the YWCA, and many other membership organizations. The network could call a national pressure group into action, and quite quickly, when faced with an opportunity or a challenge. Unlike the tactics of civil rights or labor movements, theirs were not militant nor disobedient; they were, after all, a group with access to power, influence, and money. Their tactics might be described as halfway between those of the elite and those of subordinated groups.

The social insurance advocates worked through staff organizations, groups run almost exclusively by paid workers. These leaders spoke in the name of the organization, rarely developed local chapters, and, if they reached out more broadly, did so mainly to ask for money. The influential AALL was essentially a small group of experts. When a few AALL locals developed early in the century, the leaders—unable to manage the resultant diversity, dissension, and need for coordination—disbanded them.[47] Epstein's and Rubinow's socialist approach attracted support from working-class organizations such as unions and the Fraternal Order of Eagles, but building large organizations was never their priority, and they did not create strong connections with the Socialist party even when it did have a mass following.

=

When welfare advocates sought to derive their arguments from fundamental principles, gender showed again, although not in a binary, male-female contrast. They used three types of complementary, not alternative, ethical claims—rights, needs, and compensation for services[48]—and many writers used all three.

Men more often made *rights* claims, associating their welfarist ideas with principles of liberal thought about citizenship. Statistician Frederick Wines spoke of a "natural right" to relief came up as early as 1883.[49] In 1920 social work educator Arthur James Todd found the origins of modern social work not in the church, the peasant moral economy, the paternal bond between lord and peasant, or anything of the English tradition, but rather in *The Declaration of the Rights of Man* and Tom Paine: "Modern social-reform movements and social work represent a series of concrete attempts to define and redefine the Rights of Man."[50] Prefiguring Franklin Roosevelt's "Four Freedoms," Todd listed some new "rights": to a decent income, to organize for economic protection (unions), to leisure, to education, to recreation, to health (including sanitation, preventive hygiene, protection from impure and adulterated food), to decent habitation, to a childhood "untainted by unnecessary and preventable diseases or degeneracies" (a eugenics goal), and to women's rights.[51]

In the nineteenth-century woman movement, rights talk was characteristic of the most radical—those we today call feminists—while women charity workers preferred the language of self-sacrifice. Women revived and expanded rights talk in the Progressive Era by announcing social rather than individual rights. Florence Kelley spoke of constitutional rights to childhood and leisure that "follows from the existence of the Republic."[52] But they also relied on appeals to pity and compassion and did not surrender their confidence in altruism. Social insurance rhetoric, on the other hand, hinged on rational-choice assumptions that governing motivations were always self-interested and appealed to mutual advantage, implicitly denying altruism as a social motive.[53]

As women extended their program from charity to welfare, asking that the state provide pity and compassion, they argued that *needs* themselves were a claim on the polity: that fulfilling human needs was necessary to the social order and therefore a public responsibility; in short, they were politicizing needs.[54] Their arguments were explicitly ethical because they were simultaneously campaigning for specific policies and for changing fundamental premises about the boundaries of public responsibility. Child welfare work particularly emphasized needs. Homer Folks talked of children's need for family life, as opposed to institutional care, in the 1890s.[55] Later child welfare workers spoke of children's needs for play and security and used these new diagnoses as the basis for new concepts of child abuse and neglect. The protracted struggle against child labor spread an authoritative discourse about "meeting" children's needs.[56] Sometimes needs seemed to trump rights. In child protective services, for example, a widening variety of children's needs could outweigh parental rights.[57]

The consciousness of needs and the whole casework structure—emphasis on personal, flexible approaches—flowed from a maternalist vision. Indeed, turn-of-the-century social workers often used the words "maternal" and "paternal" interchangeably, referring to an authority that directs, guides, and controls.[58] But the social insurance orientation was not paternalist. It broke away from the personal, caretaking dimension of social work and moved toward a structural relation of social control between themselves and the poor—one that was distant, not individually supervisory.

Needs-based claims flourished as social work became professionalized. Casework, the dominant social work technique by the 1920s, required ascertaining the individual and social needs of clients. Social work begins, said Porter Lee in his 1929 presidential address to the NCSW, "by someone seeing an unmet need." Social workers became reformers, he argued, by rousing others to see the need.[59] This is one of the ways in which casework skills could be said to be feminine, involving attentiveness, empathy, and asking the right questions. Social work leader Bertha Reynolds came to believe that casework was defined by "perceptiveness regarding needs."[60] The variability of needs did not seem to these social workers to make determinations less exact; casework discourse sought to make needs scientific through empirical studies of the costs of living and the making of family budgets.[61] Social insurance plans, by contrast, required no discretionary ascertainment of need.

Reacting against the individualistic approach of casework, a new field of social work differentiated itself in the 1920s, social group work. Descended from the settlements and other community organizing, it too focused on needs—social needs, whose frustration deformed both individuals and community. Women were disproportionately influential here, too. One worker declared in 1931 that "the central objective for settlement programs, which satisfies a no less universal hunger of the human heart, than the love of beauty . . . is the objective of personality through group relations."[62] Although psychiatric influence in social work redefined these needs yet again in ensuing decades, they remained urgent.

The left wing of social work sought to turn needs into rights. Unions frequently based demands for a family wage on needs; John Ryan, a Catholic welfare leader, asserted that "The laborer's claim to a Living Wage is of the nature of a *right*," a theme he repeated from 1906 through the New Deal.[63] The Progressive party platform of 1912 also framed these claims in terms of rights.[64] In the New Deal and World War II, leftist social workers integrated needs and rights principles.[65] The 1940 White House Conference on Children declared that "aid in case of need has come to be regarded more generally as a right, both by those who supply it, however much they may begrudge it and deplore the necessity for it, and by those who accept or demand it, however much they may hate it."[66] Perhaps the ultimate defense of the women's social-work tradition, Charlotte Towle's 1945 *Common Human Needs* tried to unify rights talk with needs talk, arguing that there was a right to have one's needs met: "Public assistance services [the general name for casework-accompanied relief] achieve their broad social purpose only when those who administer them understand the significant principles which make for sound individualization in a program based on right . . . understanding of common human needs and . . . basic principles of human behavior." Due to the depression,

> Want and fear became the base for a progressive curtailment of man's freedom. Today, as repeatedly throughout history, this basic want and fear have engendered hostile feelings which, in turn, have pitted man against man and prompted him to use his scientific enlightenment in that wholesale destruction of life and property which now threatens not only the realization of his social goals but also his very survival.[67]

But the technique nevertheless required an expert to identify a client's needs.

In defining those needs, social work may silence a client's own expression of need and deprive her of access to defending her claims through the adversary proceedings that adjudicate rights. Social work study of family budgets is an example. Attempts to examine how the poor actually divided their money, and thus to estimate actual costs of living, go back to Carroll Wright's initiatives as early as 1875. Such studies often became prescriptive and arbitrary, offering, for example, guidelines for how much should be spent on food.[68] With psychiatric influence, social workers became authorities on what their clients needed spiritually as well.[69] Using needs talk as a means of control fit the skills of social work women. Casework defined a client as multiply needy, not only poor, and this definition gave caseworkers a position of power and authority.

The development of needs talk coincided with the rise of the concept of the "social"—as Hannah Arendt identified it, a concept distinct from the private, from the state, from the economic. Social life generated a range of wants that could be classified as needs, from telephones to styles of parenting. Arendt saw the social realm as oppressive, a space defined by forces outside the individual.[70] Or there is Michael Ignatieff's contemplation about the welfare state:

> There are few presumptions in human relations more dangerous than the idea that one knows what another human being needs better than they do themselves. In politics, this presumption is a warrant to ignore democratic preferences and to trample on freedom. In other realms too, the arrogation of the right by . . . social workers to administer the needs of their clients . . . is in each case a warrant for abuse.[71]

Needs talk, then, was in tension with democratic impulses in reform. Some reformers, of course, resisted the domination potential in needs talk. In the settlements leaders spoke of learning from the poor about their needs.[72] Settlement worker Mary McDowell found it "hard to ask people to 'clean up' in as righteous a manner" as she was used to. "The tragedies in their lives are so very great. . . . When people live in two small rooms, perhaps with a good many children, with soot, and oil, and coal. . . . I look upon dirt now as a very small evil."[73] Or as Jane Addams dryly remarked of one of her less successful gambits, "The experience . . . taught us not to hold to preconceived ideas of what the neighborhood ought to have."[74] The depression social work Left revived that democratic critique, condemning needs talk for its inegalitarian implications, and reclaiming rights rhetoric. Grace Coyle was typical of this tendency in her call to social workers to defend clients' rights as well as their needs—their right to organize, to social security, to free speech.[75] But despite such awareness, egalitarian empathy remained difficult to achieve in casework relations. For social workers distance was created not only by casework theory, not only by their sense of class, religious, and racial/ethnic superiority, but also by their own family situations, which rarely called upon them to combine earning and child raising. Their experience of singleness fit the class distance they felt from their clients, and their acceptance of the premise that children and women needed breadwinner husbands, that children needed full-time mothers, that women should choose between family and career.[76] Overall the continuing premise of the social work mainstream was that welfare clients could not define their own needs properly without professional expertise.

Yet a critique of the language of needs without a gender analysis misses much. Since needs talk often involves bringing into public a previously private discourse, it has often been a feminine discourse, constructed by those who take responsibility for the quality of the private. Needs language was often brought into political debate by women. When women argued for access to political and civil citizenship, such as the voting rolls or juries, they often argued from needs—of the poor, of the children, of the city dwellers. Arendt saw the social only as "one-dimensional space wholly under the sway of administration and instrumental reason."[77] In fact needs discourse has been intensely contentious and mobilized in progressive as well as conservative directions. We see it in campaigns against child abuse and neglect and changing prescriptions about what children "need"; in pressures to raise the minimum provision for the poor in conformity with new social needs, such as telephones; in the as yet failed arguments for public medical provision to meet health care needs. Needs talk was sometimes turned introspective and made subversive, notably by settlement women. One stunning example was Jane Addams's insistence that settlement work fulfilled needs for the privileged women who did it, needs that she considered at once spiritual and "primordial."[78] Needs talk is not inherently dominating. Rather needs and rights talk represented two different kinds of complex discourse, each containing authoritative and democratic potential.

In addition to needs and rights, welfare reformers also promoted *compensation for service* as a principle of entitlement. Mothers'-aid advocates clung to the word "pension" precisely because its association with veterans imbued it with honor. For the women's reform network, however, its masculine overtones were both attractive and disadvantageous. The service for which veterans received pensions was not merely a man's work assigned by a conventional division of labor. Military service was a symbolic basis of citizenship and one particularly responsible for citizenship's traditional masculinity.[79] Feminists consciously constructed a maternal citizenship in opposition, imagining a citizen mother who could stand as an equal beside the citizen soldier. In one prominent line of feminist theory and in the mothers'-aid campaign in particular, women reformers argued that women's work as reproducers (of culture as well as particular children) constituted a service of value to society equivalent to that of the soldier.

The compensation-for-service claim for welfare was a kind of comparable-worth argument about what counted as a "contribution" to society. The welfare advocates who used it saw that the valuation of various social contributions is not fixed or self-evident. For example, in 1935, the group most widely considered deserving of compensation for service was unemployed male heads of families with children, and all welfare proponents considered unemployment insurance the highest priority. The notion that the elderly deserved pensions in recognition of their years of service was not yet widely accepted; the ethical principle that previously enforced care for the elderly was not reward for contribution but filial obligation. The popular notion that the elderly had contributed, "paid their dues" in years of service, and thus deserved pensions from the state was constructed by an active social movement. (One problem with the emphasis on needy children inherent in the mothers'-aid campaigns was that children could not be said to have rendered service.)

Legally the service claim may have been the most important of all legitimations for state assistance. In defending state welfare legislation against legal attack, the most consistently effective arguments were based on remuneration for service. Before the New Deal, key appellate courts accepted no distinction between entitlement programs, pensions, and public assistance, between workmen's compensation, civil service pensions, and poor relief. A wide variety of programs were upheld on the grounds that government could confer benefits on groups of citizens who had served the state. This legal logic rejected rights as well as needs claims, because the public monies were not construed as rights inhering in individuals, even those who putatively earned them.[80]

The emphasis on mothers' service to the state might have proved fruitful had it been systematically maintained. But state mothers'-aid advocates ultimately featured children, not mothers, and appealed to the public sympathy rather than to the sensibility that service deserved compensation. As a result mothers' aid laws were upheld on traditional poor-relief grounds—that states could assist indigents because doing so served a public purpose. This categorization weakened the possibility of claiming mothers' aid as an entitlement, because support of the indigent was an allowable state function but never an obligatory one. Mothers'-aid advocates also neglected opportunities to claim universal children's allowances, and this too was consequential: The means-testing of the programs was a red flag that placed it automatically in the category of poor relief. But women's reliance on need claims was not a "mistake"—the inferior position of programs for women was determined by many factors, most fundamentally poor women's lack of political power. Despite romantic rhetoric about motherhood, women were not able to establish mothering, and especially not single mothering, as honorable state service. In the growing social insurance discourse of the 1920s, men continued to dominate positions from which they could make rights and compensation-for-service claims.

Thus in three modes of claiming, two were predominantly male. Rights and claims on the basis of service to the state were male, if for no other reason than that men controlled the state. Both approaches gained strength from the law of contract in its irrevocability and universality. By contrast the needs tradition called up a female realm of nurturance, and of authority through the power to give. Similarly, the oppositional use of needs talk represented the bringing into public of a private logic, in the way in which family members ask for help because they need it, not because they deserve it or it is their share.[81]

=

The organization of professional/occupational disciplines that shaped welfare thought shows another gendered dimension. Social insurance men were academics, and their disciplinary skills and communities deeply influenced their welfare visions. Just as they participated in the creation of modern social science within the universities, so they saw their welfare proposals as exemplifying the application of that science to perfecting society.

Nothing about this scholarly and scientific approach inherently excluded women. The female welfare leadership was hardly intimidated by the scholarly discourse of social insurance.[82] In the late nineteenth century, women had been prominent among those who envisioned the application of expertise—of science—to society. "The work of social science is literally woman's work," wrote Franklin Sanborn of the American Social Science Association (ASSA) in 1874; it was the feminine side of political economy.[83] Jane Addams even wanted to rationalize children's recreation: "This stupid experiment of organizing work and failing to organize play . . ."[84] Helen Sumner Woodbury called for the application of "scientific methods of invention and experiment . . . to political and economic affairs" and for taking up the science of the "production . . . of happiness."[85] Three decades later Charlotte Towle called for extending the "critical, empirical attitude of the natural sciences . . . to the study of personality."[86]

Despite men's higher professional status, women had at least an equal commitment to authoritative expertise. They favored coercive measures, such as housing codes, wages and hours regulation, health and safety regulation, and food and drug testing and labeling. They sought professionalization of social work and scientific methods of public administration. The U.S. Children's and Women's Bureaus considered themselves pioneers in the incorporation of expertise and meritocratic principles into government. As local and state governments inaugurated welfare programs, after about 1910, women in these agencies were among the foremost proponents of nonpatronage hiring and professional standards.[87] Today we might see an inconsistency between their commitment to civil service and their use of an "old girls' network" to bring women into jobs. However, they believed they needed such a network to help highly qualified women get past discriminatory practices.[88]

Moreover, those who identified as social workers were continually anxious about their status as professionals. The membership of their professional organization, the NCCC, had grown from 300 in 1888 to 4,500 by 1908.[89] Yet in 1915, at its annual meeting, Abraham Flexner declared that social work lacked the characteristics that would allow it *ever* to become a profession, a critique repeated by Maurice Karpf in 1931.[90] This network of women had a triple burden: proving that women, social workers, and government employees could be professionals.[91]

The sexual division among welfare proponents affected the structure and content of the modern social science disciplines, especially sociology, in ways that influenced welfare design substantially. At the turn of the century there was little distinction between sociology and the social research wing of social work, or between social reform and applied sociology. In fact, some who worked for the charities called themselves sociologists, while at the turn of the century Lester Ward acknowledged, albeit critically, that most people identified sociology with philanthropy. "It is the housing of the poor, charity work generally, slumming, reform work in the neglected quarters of cities, settlement work, etc. . . . It is social work, often of a high order."[92] The same motives that led women into social work were drawing them in large numbers into graduate sociology and, to a slightly lesser extent, economics departments, which were rapidly expanding at this time. The understanding of their professors was that they would do "applied" work, research rather than teaching, and research about contemporary social problems, for institutes, government investigations, and the private sector—but not for universities. Thus Ida Merriam, considered a brilliant young economist upon earning her Ph.D. in 1928 from the Brookings Institution,[93] had three job offers: from *The Encyclopedia of the Social Sciences*, from the Committee on the Costs of Medical Care under director Isidore Falk (a leading social insurance proponent), and from Eastman Kodak. In her later memoir she remembered being resigned to not being considered for an academic job.[94] Edwin Witte much admired Elizabeth Wilson's thesis on "Distribution of Disability Costs," and recommended that she seek out a job with the Social Security Board.[95] It is arguable that the development of the entire modern field of social work and the social survey was shaped by the refusal of the University of Chicago sociology department to hire Edith Abbott or Sophonisba Breckinridge; this refusal then impelled them to build the School of Social Service Administration, which dominated social work/social research for many decades.[96]

The definitional boundaries academic/nonacademic and basic/applied must not be taken as given or predetermined, any more than the notion that women did not fit as university professors is accepted as eternal. The definition of "applied" research that excluded it from universities has not been stable; today work that fits that definition is commonplace and respected in social science departments. Moreover, women were active in the infancy of quantitative social scholarship.[97] Up to World War I, social science quantitative work was, in fact, mainly developed outside universities, by reformers, and women were prominent among them.[98] The earliest organization in the field, the ASSA, showed a strong feminist bias from its beginnings.[99] Women's groups tried to influence the design of the censuses in order to advance social research.[100] Massachusetts statistical officer Carroll Wright supported the survey work being done by female investigators.[101] When Wright persuaded Congress to fund investigations into urban slum conditions in the 1890s, he turned to the settlement women of Hull-House to conduct the Chicago survey.[102]

The result, *Hull-House Maps and Papers* (1895), with Florence Kelley as the main author, became extremely influential. Addressed to "the constantly increasing body of sociological students," Kelley's book documented every aspect of an area about one-third of a square mile around Hull-House. It detailed methods of investigation, defined its categories, and reprinted the schedules used. It challenged the 1890 census; to cite but one example, the census had reported 5,426 employed children in Illinois, while Kelley and her crew identified 6,576 in 1894 in only five months of investigation.[103] It featured graphically complex, color-coded maps (inspired by Charles Booth's maps of London) that offered visual representation of sociological conditions, including demography, migration patterns, ethnicity, wages, occupations, and housing conditions.[104]

Hull-House Maps and Papers became the *ur*-work of a new genre, further developed by Du Bois's *The Philadelphia Negro* (1899) and Atlanta University studies (1898–1913), and the Pittsburgh survey (1914), which was also originated and executed mainly by women.[105] Florence Kelley, through her work on this Chicago study, as an Illinois factory inspector, and later in developing projects funded by the Russell Sage Foundation, was one of the definers of modern standards for social research along with Wright and Du Bois. The women's network led in persuading the embryonic social work profession of the importance of social data, and in establishing its first committee on statistics in 1905. The single greatest impetus to the development of the survey was the establishing of the Russell Sage Foundation by Margaret Slocum Sage in 1906; its staff and funding did far more than American universities to nurture and sophisticate social investigation. By 1920 it had already invested $223,000 in social surveys.[106]

The women's reform network pioneered the practice of making social surveys the bases for policy proposals.[107] Their belief in the power of data to persuade was of a piece with their rhetorical preference for the concrete, the specific. Doing social surveys became so common that it could be called a social movement; at least 2,775 were completed by 1927.[108] An indicator of the growing importance of surveys was the renaming of *Charities and the Commons*, the key journal of the social work establishment, as *Survey* in 1909, newly supported by a grant from the Russell Sage Foundation.[109] The women's network became a center of authority in the discipline of "social statistics,"[110] and by the 1920s the Children's Bureau became the federal government's leader in statistical research.[111] The test for applicants to the Children's Bureau required outlining a statistical table from raw data and a plan for investigation of a social problem.[112]

Within the developing field of sociology, women's overrepresentation in quantitative research was such that it was sex-typed: Empirical study of contemporary social problems, such as poverty, crime, and immigration, was increasingly considered a branch of (female) social work, while (male) sociological scholarship remained more theoretical and/or qualitative.

The story of the relationship between Hull-House, arguably the most important enclave of the women's welfare network from 1890 to 1910, and the University of Chicago Sociology Department may serve to illustrate.[113] Between these two centers of social research and scholarship there arose close cooperation and division of labor. The first sociology faculty were from the social-work, Christian reform tradition, such as Charles Henderson, Graham Taylor, and Dean of Women Marion Talbot, who also taught in the department in its first years. They greatly admired Jane Addams, who lectured in university sociology classes frequently enough for one historian to describe her as "adjunct professor."[114] In 1895 the university tried to acquire Hull-House but was rejected by Addams and Julia Lathrop. Despite the value of durable economic support, they had several reasons for preferring autonomy, one of which was the inevitable subordination that would be the settlement's fate inside such a male institution as a university in the 1890s. Accepting Hull-House's autonomy, University of Chicago sociologists still viewed it as their "laboratory;"[115] considering quantitative work "applied," they preferred to subcontract it, so to speak, to lower-status workers—in this case often the Hull-House women. After about 1915 quantitative work at the University of Chicago Sociology Department was deemphasized altogether, as W. I. Thomas, Robert Park, and George Herbert Mead developed their influential qualitative methods. Instead the School of Social Service Administration, established by Breckinridge and Edith Abbott in part because the Sociology Department would not have them, became the "standard bearer of the social survey."[116] (Ironically, W. F. Ogburn, hired by the University of Chicago in 1927, is sometimes described as the initiator of quantitative sociology.[117])

Nothing illustrates the malleability of gender meanings so well as the transition over the last century from a feminine association with statistical work to today's language about "hard data" and the masculine domination of the "hard" social sciences.[118] One scholar concluded that the social survey "provided the vehicle for the transformation of sociology from a 'soft' to a 'hard' discipline."[119] This gender reversal was completed by the 1930s. Academic sociology returned with enthusiasm to quantitative research, and that work became detached from social action. The social survey tradition, which had become part of social work, was gradually separated from sociological survey research, which defined itself as disinterested.[120] Eventually the survey became categorized as a "quaint piece of muckraking reportage that predates . . . 'legitimate' social science research."[121]

=

Social insurance thought was marked not only by the changing definitions of social science but also by another academic event: the rejection of partisan scholarship in favor of scholarly objectivity. In the 1870s and 1880s reformist motivations had once characterized all social research, of the social insurance as well as the social work persuasion. The ASSA saw itself as promoting not basic research but reform; it was quite unlike a twentieth-century discipline-specialized academic organization. Making no claim that they produced value-free work, its members believed that scholarship could be truthful, moral, *and* partisan. Carroll Wright, for example, never thought that statistics were neutral or inert in respect to social/political controversies. His early focus on "special" groups and "dependent classes" served his desire to demonstrate the need for state intervention; he knew that his improved data on women's employment, controlled for "conjugal condition," would challenge the myth of the family wage.[122] Like his women allies, he took public stands on social and moral issues. A Civil War Union officer devastated by the failure of Reconstruction, he supported studies of Negro conditions, including one by Du Bois.[123] Responding to the allegations that "shop girls" were immoral, he asserted that his study showed that they were rather "honest, industrious and virtuous, and are making an heroic struggle against many obstacles, and in the face of peculiar temptations, to maintain reputable lives."[124]

Wright's "daughters" similarly justified their scholarly work in terms of its contribution to social change, not to knowledge. The premise that welfare policy should be based on empirical data produced the

corollary that the purpose of social surveys was policy recommendations. A bibliography of surveys, for example, refers to them as "Reports of Fact-finding Studies Made as a Basis for Social Action."[125]
The purpose of the survey was to collect reliable, accurate data, but
this did not mean objectivity in the contemporary social-science
sense of disinterest or political neutrality. As the introduction to
Hull-House Maps and Papers put it, "The painful nature of minute
investigation, and the personal impertinence of many of the questions asked, would be unendurable and unpardonable were it not for
the conviction that the public conscience when roused must demand
better surroundings for the most inert and long-suffering citizens of
the commonwealth. Merely to state symptoms and go no farther
would be idle; but to state symptoms in order to ascertain the nature
of disease, and apply, it may be, its cure, is not only scientific, but in
the highest sense humanitarian."[126] Sophonisba Breckinridge and
Edith Abbott, two of the most exclusively academic of the women's
welfare network, insisted on purposeful research—data should be
collected because of their contribution to reform—and required
their students to participate in reform activity.[127] Edith Abbott said of
her mentor, Julia Lathrop that she rejected "the academic theory
that social work could be "scientific" only if it had no regard to the
finding of socially useful results and no interest in the human beings
whose lives were being studied."[128]

But the social surveys were not editorials or policy proposals.
Rather, researchers believed, education itself would bring about better policy. Julia Lathrop argued in 1910 that the United States was
backward in social provision primarily because its public was not being given "ascertained facts."[129] In this respect these social researchers were like muckrakers: They had great faith in the power of
the facts themselves.[130] (Ironically, this belief in the power of facts
was not itself empirically grounded but was a matter of faith.[131])

At the turn of the century no gender difference was visible here, but
academic social science soon created one.[132] The transformation of academic standards of conduct in the late 1880s and early 1890s deeply affected how social science research would be done. The development toward "objective," professional, disciplinary, technical social science
has often been narrated in a determinist fashion, even in teleological
terms.[133] In fact the victory of value-neutral social science occurred
through political battles in which those committed to "objectivity"

used their institutional power to silence radicals and mavericks. "Objectivity" soon became a synonym for research supporting status-quo premises.[134] Successful attacks on several academic reformers, including notably the social insurance advocate Richard Ely at the University of Wisconsin, had a chilling impact, pushing ambitious academic men to define themselves as disinterested, nonpartisan experts. By the 1920s male academic social scientists increasingly denied that their work was value laden; they identified themselves not as reformers but as consulting experts to reform.[135] Women welfare planners escaped this repression—because they were not in the universities![136]

The academic campaign for professional "objectivity" was part of a drive to eliminate "undesirables" from sociology, which served also to exclude women. In his 1929 presidential address to the American Sociological Society, Ogburn insisted: "Sociology as a science is not interested in making the world a better place. . . . It will be necessary to crush out emotion and to discipline the mind so strongly that the fanciful pleasures of intellectuality will have to be eschewed in the verification process; it will be desirable to taboo ethics and values (except in choosing problems) [sic]."[137] The "undesirables" included the largely female "amateur" social scholars, by now openly spurned by some of the very academics who used their work. Robert Park told a seminar that the greatest damage done to Chicago was "not the product of corrupt politicians or criminals but of women reformers."[138] Continuing their reform-oriented research, women were assigned second-class status, their work defined as "applied."[139] As "social workers" they continued to maintain that their studies were intended not only to reveal sufferings and injustices but also to advocate government intervention—"welfare"—and to plead for social cooperation as opposed to social conflict as the basis for progress and order.

Several factors mitigated these gender differences and encouraged convergence among welfare designers. Academic economics became increasingly laissez-faire while the social insurance spokesmen by definition supported government intervention. As social insurance ideas gained support and proponents became involved in campaigning for concrete proposals, they had to reject value neutrality. "One would not be true to one's self or to one's conscience were one, after all the facts have been revealed, to speak calmly and 'impartially' of the injustice now meted out," Abraham Epstein wrote in 1928.[140] As representatives of the women's social work group gained some governmental positions, they too became outspoken supporters of social insurance.

But no convergence developed, and these disciplinary differences contributed to the separation. The increasing domination of social research by professional social scientists deterred women from expanding into large-scale social planning, as the increasing distance of male social insurance planners from individualized casework limited their cognizance of the cultural and psychological damages of poverty. Social insurance designers continued to treat the problems of the female and nonemployed poor as marginal and uninteresting, while the Children's Bureau, despite its location in the Department of Labor, focused only on women's and children's issues. The public health and labor sections of the women's political network pioneered the use of the state for more democratic, universal protection of the citizenry, but the social work group remained oriented to individualized treatment.

=

Perhaps the ultimate difference was that social insurance aimed to prevent poverty, social work to prevent pauperism. Poverty is an economic condition—lack of money; pauperism is also an internal, moral, and/or psychological condition. Thus "prevention" in the social work tradition required environmental and character reform, not just economic tinkering. Both social insurance and social work reformers aimed to help the unfortunate achieve independence, but they defined it differently. For the former independence was a wage; for the latter it remained a matter of character and individual circumstances, and those required casework. Often called "differential casework," this technique required in-depth investigation of a client's background, circumstances, and attitudes. Individualization was in fact the essence of casework: Its guiding principle was "to treat unequal things unequally."[141] The very premise of casework was antibureaucratic, in the pure sense of bureaucracy, since it insisted on the worker's discretion.[142] The caseworker was emphatic that money alone was not enough. The deindividualization of social insurance alone was anathema to social workers.

Casework was nevertheless scientific in an important sense. It derived from the "scientific charity" movement, which equated casework with the scientific method itself.[143] In the nineteenth century charity workers identified causes of poverty which they then counted. As casework expert Lilian Brandt wrote in 1906:

The method consisted in tabulating the opinions of a large number of charity workers as to what was the cause of poverty in a large number of individual cases. . . . [This] meant reliance on opinions, not on facts; and . . . the burden of deciding whether it was intemperance, lack of work, unwise philanthropy, inefficiency or illness, in a given case, that brought the family to dependence, and the conviction arising that the decision could not be of much value, did much to make statistics in general hateful to charity workers.[144]

These single-cause data were then used to separate out the deserving. Thus a table of twenty-eight thousand cases investigated by the Charity Organization Societies in 1887 produced the following results:[145]

Worthy of continuous relief	10.3 percent
Worthy of temporary relief	26.6
Need work rather than relief	40.4
Unworthy of relief	22.7

Progressive Era scientific casework rejected such enumeration of simple, alternative, isolable causes and insisted on the whole context, which might include family, neighborhood, or the whole society. This new understanding did not equate science with single-factor, unambiguous answers.[146] Grace Abbott continued to refer to casework as the basis of scientific method in the mid-1930s, at the bottom of the depression.[147]

The impact of this commitment to casework changed historically. What in the Progressive Era was progressive, even pioneering, was by the 1930s relatively conservative. The thinking of one long-time social work activist Gertrude Vaile is illustrative. In 1915, from her position as Denver's director of social services, she argued thus for mothers' pensions:

Not only should a government, in the mere exercise of its police power, be prepared to see that no one shall be driven to desperation for lack of the necessities of life; . . . The poor and suffering are so, not only by their own fault or peculiar misfortune, but also by the fault of us all. Government permits working and living conditions which create poverty and sickness—yea, even licenses some of them; and it is only just that organized society as a whole should struggle with the responsibility and pay the cost.

She argued, furthermore, that the relief should be "of a pension nature—that is, long-continued."[148] Yet in 1934, even in the depths of the depression, she feared that relief without casework would encourage clients to "lean."[149] This fear of pauperization lost legitimacy over time, and the social work Left in the 1930s became particularly critical of it. By 1940 Vaile was arguing that if public relief pauperized families, it was not because of relief per se but because of inadequate relief and inadequate casework. But she never lost the conviction that individual attention to individual clients was necessary for their rehabilitation.[150]

This did not mean that the social work crowd was opposed to universal provision. Both Children's Bureau heads—Lathrop in the Progressive Era, Abbott in the depression—favored universal guaranteed benefits. They grew more critical of social insurance as it developed, because it helped the least needy and created a regressive tax.[151] In this respect Abbott and those in her camp were to the left of social insurance advocates. The Children's Bureau group particularly disliked plans to insure workers through their employers, since this would render most women uninsurable; contributory insurance would even exclude many wage-earning women who could not afford contributions. They always factored in the impact of low wages on women's choices. Abbott's defense of the mothers'-aid principle rested on "recognition . . . that the contribution of the unskilled or semiskilled mothers in their own homes exceeded their earnings outside of the home and that it was in the public interest to conserve their child-caring functions."[152] Since the majority view among women reformers at this time was that mothers *ought* to stay home, they naturally opposed a welfare system that made staying home economically disadvantageous. Still, they always preferred universal benefits.

The irreduceable conflict, the difference that ultimately necessitated ADC's separation from the Social Security Act's social insurance program, came not from social work rejection of insurance or universal plans of provision, but from social insurance rejection of casework. Isaac Rubinow defined mothers' aid as incompatible with his social insurance principles because it was means-tested, entailed submitting to supervision, offered low stipends, and did not create an entitlement the recipient could enforce through the courts if necessary.[153] Those who wrote ADC also opposed stinginess, but supervision lay at the heart of their welfare program. The contrast was sharp. The social insurance principle had become standard, across-the-board entitlements, while social work's chief diagnostic as well as rehabilitative tool remained differential casework, with individualized, nonstandard treatment at its heart. [154] Even when women sought inspiration from European social insurance programs, they tended to "feminize" the plans, incorporating casework and moralism. Thus Katharine Coman, a Wellesley College economist, concluded, after a survey of European old-age pension programs, that the purpose of pensions for the elderly should be "not merely the comfort . . . of the individual . . . but the influence on the moral fibre of the community. . . . Thrift is an old-fashioned virtue, but it is still an essential element in race efficiency." Rubinow responded that she had confused two projects and that her view demonstrated that the "old ideas of asceticism" were still alive.[155]

Social insurance advocates simply did not think rehabilitation necessary or, more important, respectful to beneficiaries. This was partly because they were not mainly "front-line" social workers, actually meeting the poor; because they did not direct their primary concern toward the most wretched and demoralized, they ignored evidence of need for extra financial help (counseling, education). Imagining men as the primary beneficiaries—they envisioned women and children primarily as dependents of beneficiaries—they no doubt considered the supervision inherent in casework unneeded, demeaning, as an attack on a (largely unconscious) masculinity.[156]

Casework played a paradoxical role in the development of the gendered meanings of social work. Trying to define an objective, professional method and status involved rejecting the practices and values of their legacy of friendly visiting—sentimentality, intuition, personal kindness.[157] Some leaders longed to defeminize their field. When Stuart Alfred Queen wrote in 1922 of making social work "a profession, a 'man's job'," he was speaking for many.[158] In describing 1890s social work, Queen and his coauthor used the pronoun "they," but for 1920s social work always used "he."[159] Yet in attempting to attain professionalism and defeminization through casework, social workers were choosing an approach and a technique that was perceived by many as quintessentially feminine—specific rather than universal, grounded rather than abstract, tailored rather than generalized. Moreover, as a technique that required close contact with welfare recipients, casework served to strengthen commonalities between trained and amateur social workers.

If their commitment to casework was in some ways elitist, women reformers also had a democratic reason for disinterest in social insurance—the fact that it was premised on insuring wage earners, collecting taxes, and administering benefits through employers.[160] The workplace location of social insurance was premised on the assumption that women were economic dependents of male breadwinners, and that women would therefore be taken care of by men's insurance. It is ironic that reformers so dedicated to empirical research would have been so loyal to this fiction in the face of so much contrary evidence.[161]

The family-wage myth was still widespread in the 1930s, but it encompassed different interpretations. The social insurance advocates' family-wage view was a rather conservative version, based on the unexamined assumption that women's full-time domesticity was desirable for all concerned. It was patriarchal to the degree that it continued to view a family, for policy purposes at any rate, as an attribute of a male wage earner. It supported the trade unionist demand for a family wage high enough to allow a husband alone to support his family—a demand that working-class women had usually supported, not least as an escape from the drudgery of the double day. Social insurance proponents also shared the male workers' rhetoric that made the family wage a token of masculinity; aged or unemployed workers were said to need protection from the "impotence" of dependency, for example.[162] It ignored all those whose economic distress was created by long-term lack of access to the steady wages on which they wanted to base social insurance. "What the widow needs is . . . sensible life insurance," Rubinow announced in 1934.[163]

The social insurance advocates cemented the family wage into the fundamental structure of welfare benefits. In doing so they also walled out numerous men as well as women. They neglected what we would call today the "working poor," for they assumed that only the interruption of wages was problematic, while in fact low wages themselves were the problem for many men. Moreover, many workers were not wage earners at all but farmers, sharecroppers, or even small businessmen who also needed help. The social insurance advocates had an extremely urban, industrial view of need, one serving the new professional middle class and the aristocracy of the working class—those with steady jobs for major employers.

For the women the family-wage commitment not only informed their design of ADC but also justified leaving the task of designing an overarching welfare state to the men. While they exempted themselves in some ways from the conventional sexual division of labor, by remaining single and/or pursuing public careers, they accepted it in their deference to the social insurance men. They never challenged the men's ultimate responsibility and authority to take care of the whole, as they cared for the women and children. Women's welfare job, like that of women in families, was to care for the husbandless and their charges, dependents of dependents, conceived as a small residuum. Although they wanted to treat these single mothers and their families well, their continuing fear of pauperization made them oppose long-term public provision to establish female-headed families on a stable or permanent basis.

Their family-wage commitment was illogical in several respects. They knew the error of assuming that resources sent into a family through its male head would necessarily be shared fairly among family members. Many among them had worked for agencies dealing with family violence, desertion, and drunkenness, and they knew the fallacy of considering men the universal protectors of women and women the beneficiaries of male support. It is not surprising that the male social insurance advocates were uninterested in directing grants to women. Abraham Epstein argued, "Nor is it the mission of family allowances to usher in a new relationship between man and wife . . . no apparent reason why the alleviation of this particular form of insecurity should have to carry with it a general reformation of the world."[164] But the women welfare advocates did want to reform the world, and the family in particular, and thought the state could do it. Nevertheless they refrained from challenging the family-wage principle.

If this shared gender system was inadequate to help the poor, it worked rather well for the welfare advocates themselves, and this helped keep it unchallenged for so long. Male-female relations among these activists were usually smooth and effective precisely because of their sexual division of labor. While economically many women reformers were condemning poor women to a life of dependence that they themselves had escaped, politically they were in the same position as their poor "clients." They designed programs that would benefit women directly when male wage earners failed them, but did not encourage women's independence from men.

Thus it arose that both tracks of the two-track welfare system were designed to maintain the family-wage system. (That they did not succeed is another matter.) The very process of a gender analysis reveals the inaccuracy of dichotomizing men and women: The gender differences were actually part of a *shared* vision of the ideal gender structure of the society and family. Where the men and women differed was in analyses of the nature of poverty and how to help the poor. The social insurance advocates tended to assume that the damages of poverty would be cured by money and jobs. The social work advocates had a more complex view, in part a feminist one. They attempted the difficult and perhaps counterhistorical task of defending the value of women's traditional domestic labor in a capitalist industrial context. They also tried to integrate a social, psychological dimension into an economic theory of poverty. Influenced by the experience of social workers combating drinking and domestic violence, and particularly by their clients, they believed that the injuries of class were experienced through problems like alcoholism, defeatism, and violence as well as through inadequate food and shelter. They considered the social insurance definition of poverty partial, reductive, and naive. Despite the social distance between them and the objects of their concern, they identified with the women and children who were hurt by intrafamily abuse perhaps even more than with those hurt by societal abuse. But they did not, in this period, suppose that economic independence might be a precondition for the self-esteem and self-development they sought to give poor women. Nor did they develop a system of casework suitable to conditions in which public assistance took in millions of clients. Nevertheless their vision at its best—articulated most vividly not in their words but in, for example, their settlement-house work—foreshadowed more recent projects for the empowerment of the poor, such as community organizing, far more than did social insurance schemes.

But it was the social insurance advocates who moved toward what British welfare state theorist T. H. Marshall called "social citizenship," the notion of public provision as an entitlement.[165] And it was these men who argued that only in this way could the stigma of the dole and the humiliation of dependence be removed.

Unemployed Women Demonstrate at New York City Hall, 1932

7

The Depression Crisis
and Relief Politics

As important as the various approaches to welfare was the fact that they came together in a crisis—the most severe and protracted crisis the economy and society had yet experienced. The Great Depression jolted politicians and bureaucrats into quick action and produced therefore some jerrybuilt structures of provision. Both social work and social insurance programs now intersected with demands for immediate relief and schemes not only to end this depression but to prevent others. Because the short-term needs were so pressing, government policy designers were less concerned than usual with the long-term merits and effects of these proposals and programs or their consistency with ideological positions. They concentrated their attention on the immediate compromises that could get the bills past powerful antagonists in legislatures. In order to put the results into the right perspective, and to evaluate their hold on us yet today, we must experience just some of the stresses of the depression.

Social workers were already worried in the spring of 1929. The usual warm-weather seasonal decline in relief requests did not happen. In October, before the stock market crash, a sharp upturn in relief expenses appeared.[1] By the spring of 1930 everyone was calling it a depression. By 1933 in New York "there were so many evictions on the East side you couldn't walk down the streets without seeing furniture on the sidewalk."[2] But even pessimistic economists predicted it would hit bottom in early 1931 and recovery to occur in 1932.[3]

That it would endure twelve years was still unthinkable. "The Depression was a way of life for me, from the time I was twenty to the time I was thirty. I thought it was going to be forever and ever and ever. . . . You know, *fear*," an elementary school teacher reminisced. A farmer thought that "The majority of people . . . were mentally disturbed you're bound to know, 'cause they didn't know when the end of all this was comin'. There was a lot of suicides that I know of. From nothin' else but just they couldn't see any hope. . . . Part of 'em were farmers and part of 'em were businessmen, even. They went flat broke and they committed suicide on the strength of it, nothing else."[4]

The data most commonly used to describe the depression's effect are unemployment figures, and the most common image is men in breadlines. Unemployment was alarming in the first year of the depression and staggering by the end of President Hoover's term in 1933: An estimated thirteen to sixteen million—one of four—workers were out of work by then. One or two million were homeless and wandering. These figures, furthermore, underestimate workers' problems. Many who had been marginal or seasonal workers, or who worked in the informal economy, went uncounted. Those lucky enough to be employed often suffered radical earning declines—ruinous for the many who were already low-wage workers. In Ohio workers' average incomes dropped by 69 percent from 1929 to 1932.[5] There was great concern for the mental health of unemployed men, for joblessness was devastating.

But representing depression suffering so exclusively in terms of unemployment images and statistics creates a misleadingly partial understanding of the crisis. This interpretation puts men at the center and marginalizes women. It is particularly distorting because the depression is so often conceived as a democratic, collective crisis, one that in some ways bound Americans together. Calculating its human costs only in terms of unemployment makes the majority of Americans less visible, because most of the poor were not employed even in good times—for example, nonemployed women, sharecroppers, domestic servants, children, and so on. In both contemporary and historical descriptions of the depression, it is remarkable how little attention was paid to the problems of women, let alone single mothers. For example, stories commonly captured sympathy for unemployed heads of household, especially if their wives were supportive; but no one asked whether husbands were supportive of housewives or laid-off women.

The relative invisibility of women reflects the low ebb of the women's movement in the 1930s. The depression is a rare example of a period of militant social movements that did not produce a feminist upsurge. On the contrary, in gender terms the 1930s was a conservative decade. The crisis strengthened the 1920s reassertion of "traditional" family norms. Prominent women's organizations lost power during this decade. In popular culture and professional discourse alike, the emphasis was on family togetherness and domestic roles for women. To family caseworkers, preventing marital dissolution was a major, overriding goal; even in cases of abusive families, agencies responded with pressure toward reconciliation rather than prosecution or separation.[6] The popular iconography of the period, whether of suffering or of heroism, featured monumental male (white) workers and placed women in positions of domesticity and support. Even in images of rural life, where women's farm labor was economically as productive as men's, families were signified as composed of farmers and farmers' dependents.[7]

These values were not new, but their reaffirmation in this period impressed them on welfare provision. The focus on unemployment represented not merely a deemphasizing of other suffering but a structural principle for government action: that honorable poverty derived from disrupted wage earning, a premise that remains fundamental today in our welfare system.

Depression Relief and Women's Poverty

Despite the greater prominence of unemployed men, single mothers and children were impoverished in large numbers and they were exhausting existing poor relief and mothers'-aid appropriations. Most of these programs were funded not by the states but from county and municipal sources, which were least able to maintain the revenues they needed when unemployment rates grew. In 1931, although forty-six states had mothers'-aid programs in operation, only seventeen programs received any state funds. Only eight states assumed administrative responsibility for the programs, while the rest had county or municipal administration.[8] Since most of the statutes were permissive rather than mandatory, most local areas had no programs at all. Any hope that they would inaugurate them was thwarted by the depression.

The total spent on mothers' aid was puny even in good times. During the last predepression year, 1929, approximately $17 million were spent throughout the United States on mothers' aid in urban areas; rural programs are less well documented. By 1932, the peak year of spending, approximately $34 million went to mothers' aid nationwide, after which the amount dropped slightly until ADC went into effect.[9] In the context of the depression, $34 million increasingly began to seem negligible. While stipends shrank, demand exploded. In Los Angeles between 1929 and 1933, the number of families served expanded 110 percent.[10]

Under the depression's impact, some mothers'-aid programs contracted not only relatively—in relation to need—but also absolutely, because state and local revenues, usually based on property taxes, declined precipitously. Moreover, many states had borrowed heavily in the 1920s and loan repayments now ate up much of the revenue they did get. Even the five richest states—New York, Massachusetts, Illinois, Pennsylvania, and California—could not cope, partly because relief demand was greatest in the big cities located in the rich states. Total relief stoppages occurred several times in big cities. In New York after bankers refused to advance any further credit to the state, the Department of Public Welfare decided arbitrarily to cut the monthly food order for every tenth family, and to allocate funds for rent only *after* the family was evicted.[11] In three states (Arkansas, Mississippi, and New Mexico) and sixty-nine counties inadequate revenue led to eliminating mothers' aid altogether.[12] By early 1933 nearly one thousand localities had "defaulted" on these programs.[13]

Just as male unemployment was multiplying the numbers of children and women without access to male wages, single mothers were losing ground relative to other categories of relief claimants. Before the depression, mothers' aid accounted for by far the greatest proportion of all state and local aid, greater even than other programs (general relief and aid to the elderly and the disabled) combined.[14] Now other forms of aid expanded both absolutely and relative to mothers' aid. In urban areas, for example, state-funded work relief—primarily directed to men—had expanded tenfold by 1932 while mothers' aid was only 1.4 times greater (1,000 as compared to 44 percent).[15]

The downward spiral of privation caused public demand for more poor relief to grow and become militant. Particularly visible nationally was the Bonus March. In 1931 veterans' groups demanded and won a loan of 50 percent of the bonuses due them from a 1924 law; when Hoover vetoed it, Congress overrode him. But as conditions grew worse, the veterans asked for cash payment of the bonus in full, which Congress refused to authorize. Thousands of veterans with their families then encamped on the outskirts of the capital, demanding payment of their bonus, until they were forcibly evicted by the police and army, leaving several dead and many wounded.

Social workers, who among middle-class people were most aware of the desperate need for help, began to pressure the Hoover administration for federal relief. The NCSW lobbied, and in October 1931 a group of state welfare administrators formed the Social Work Conference on Federal Action on Unemployment. (Here we meet the common gender assumption that defined the problem as [male] unemployment, ignoring the impact of the depression on the nonemployed.) These initiatives led to an agreement that Senator La Follette of Wisconsin, supported by Senators Costigan of Colorado and Wagner of New York, would get the Senate Committee on Manufacture to appoint a subcommittee on federal aid with himself as chair and to hold hearings, for which the social workers would gather the witnesses. This subcommittee then sponsored a bill drafted by the Social Work Conference on Federal Action, which provided for $375,000,000 in federal aid for relief, in the form of grants to states, to be administered by the Children's Bureau. Forty percent of this amount was to be distributed to states in proportion to the population, the rest according to need. The proposal incorporated the characteristic social work network approach: federal-state cooperation, and the assumption that the Children's Bureau would be in control of all federal welfare. Opposed by the president, the bill was defeated, along with a more generous substitute that would have distributed federal relief money to the states with no federal control. This Congress did pass the Federal Emergency Relief and Reconstruction Act, which provided loans, but only to those states that could come up with a repayment scheme and only after state relief had been cut to the bone.[16]

Social workers had been let down by their President, Hoover. Given his social work background as a relief administrator in World War I, they had expected much of him. Many social workers had expected that he might treat this depression as an emergency equal to that of the war and give up his hostility to government "handouts."[17] Instead he appeared hostile to public aid, indifferent to suffering, and paralyzed by indecision. As late as May 1932, Ray Lyman

Wilbur, Hoover's Secretary of the interior, in addressing the National Conference of Social Work, spoke of the benefits of the economic hard times—"Our children are apt to profit, rather than suffer from what is going on"—to cries of "Shame" from the audience. One journalist headlined "Secretary Wilbur and Marie Antoinette."[18]

During the 1932 presidential campaign and the long four-month wait between the November election and March inauguration, social workers saw a rapid increase in suffering. The numbers of children removed from their homes because of lack of support was growing.[19] In 1933 the Pennsylvania Department of Public Welfare surveyed eight hundred thousand children and found 20–40 percent undernourished. Company towns were particularly badly off: in one Pennsylvania town 65 percent of the population was living on Red Cross free flour.[20] State programs continued to collapse. In New York, Governor Franklin Roosevelt's Temporary Emergency Relief Administration (TERA) had $20 million, which was completely inadequate. City governments were the hardest hit. Even New York, by far the best prepared for the task of provision, was overwhelmed. In Chicago some public employees had not been paid for eight months, and the city owed its employees more than $44 million.[21]

The crisis was so severe that when Roosevelt took over in March 1933 he took action in his first day in office. Relief was not his highest priority; first he ordered a bank holiday, began federal budget cutbacks, started the process of repealing Prohibition, and abandoned the gold standard. His was, originally, an orthodox fiscal policy: he favored retrenchment, not spending. The first federal aid program, the Federal Emergency Relief Act (FERA), took two months to emerge but it made a difference immediately, thanks in large part to Roosevelt's choice for FERA administrator, Harry Hopkins. A former social worker who had run the relief program in New York during Roosevelt's governorship, Hopkins thought big and fast. The choice of Hopkins showed Roosevelt's desire for control and the value he placed on the experience of New York. Long before Roosevelt's governorship, New York City had been a vanguard in the development of municipal welfare programs and regulations; like his gubernatorial predecessor Al Smith, Roosevelt took that legacy to the state, relying on many City experts, including Frances Perkins; Roosevelt then appointed her head of the New York State Industrial Commission.[22] New York's Temporary Emergency Relief Administration was in some ways a model for the FERA, not only in large-scale provision but also in its assertion of a larger over a smaller jurisdiction. The Act provided that, because of the existence of an emergency situation, no local ordinances would be allowed to nullify TERA or otherwise interfere with it; FDR wanted that boldness in Washington. By bringing Hopkins in outside the control of any existing department or cabinet secretary, Roosevelt licensed him to spend the half billion dollars authorized for the FERA quickly. The Hopkins folklore has it that one half hour after his appointment, still lacking an office, he set up a desk in a hallway and spent $5,000,000 in two hours.[23] Half of the FERA's funds were supposed to be matched by state and local funds, but half were direct federal grants.

The federal money was like rain in a drought. Local welfare administrators and politicians, even those who had been strong states'-rights defenders, were at first delighted with the FERA.[24] As soon as federal relief funds became available, many local authorities literally transferred their mothers' aid and other public-assistance caseload to the federal government; in many areas the intensity of need and the suddenness of federal money overflowed budgetary separations between mothers' aid and general relief.[25] Even this first small wave of federal relief demonstrated how inadequate mothers' aid had been. A conservative estimate for 1934 suggests that three times as many children and almost three and a half times as many single-mother families were receiving federal emergency relief as had received any mothers' aid.[26] Thus the federal government was supporting state dependents in general and single mothers in particular *before* the Social Security Act, and relief administrators were well aware of this fact. This meant that if Social Security had not included an ADC program, federal funding would have been *removed* from existing beneficiaries. As it was, ADC merely meant transferring relief funds from one federal program to another, and making the contribution of state matching funds a condition of federal aid to these families.

A states' rights response to federal relief did come, and rather quickly. Not only did many local politicians and charity executives fear federal takeover, but so did many federal officials because Roosevelt's emergency response bypassed existing executive agencies. Harry Hopkins became the "czar" of federal relief as an entirely new layer of federal agencies was created, the so-called alphabet soup of FERA, CWA, PWA, CCC, NYA, NRA, NIRA, WPA and so on.* One historian described this as the construction of a new parallel government alongside the old.[27] Especially offensive to the private-charity and social work establishment was Hopkins's decision that the FERA would distribute funds only through public agencies, cutting any of the existing private-charity and social work organizations out from the thrill, the power, and the overhead of administering so much money. There were few existing public relief agencies so new ones had to be constructed quickly, staffed by people who were not professional social workers, setting up a rivalry with the private agencies. Loula Dunn, FERA director of employment under Hopkins, later recalled how "we found people who were nonentities but suddenly were able to do a magnificent job on a crash program . . . great pioneers. . . . There were many of the voluntary agency workers that were excellent. There were others that couldn't deal with the mass, quick-moving program that had to get underway right away."[28] In some places the private agencies fought back successfully and got themselves designated as public for the purposes of dispensing federal relief,[29] but their opposition and their political involvement had been quickened nonetheless.

Hopkins's personal style further stimulated opposition to federal relief. Decisive, in a hurry, he was not always consultative, but he evoked great loyalty as well as hostility:

> For a social worker, he was an odd sort. He belonged to no church, had been divorced and [psycho]analyzed, liked race horses . . . and had little patience with moralists. . . . As he talked to reporters—often out of the side of his mouth—through thick curls of cigarette smoke, his tall, lean body sprawled over his chair, his face wry and twisted, his eyes darting and suspicious, his manner brusque, iconoclastic, almost deliberately rude and outspoke, the cocksure Hopkins seemed, as Robert Sherwood later observed, "a profoundly shrewd and faintly ominous man. . . . By Roosevelt's second term, he would be the most powerful man in the administration.[30]

---

*FERA = Federal Emergency Relief Administration
CWA = Civil Works Administration
PWA = Public Works Administration
CCC = Civilian Conservation Corps
NYA = National Youth Administration
NRA = National Recovery Administration
NIRA = National Industrial Recovery Act
WPA = Works Progress Administration

But Roosevelt was too political to seek totally centralized federal control. He needed the loyalty of his state and local legions. In the fall of 1933, much to the dismay of the national leaders in welfare agitation, FDR was already insisting that local responsibility for relief was the only basis for a permanent system. Edith Abbott called this "probably the most reactionary pronouncement that has come from the White House," labeling it the motif of the "old poor masters."[31]

Despite its limitations, the new federal relief was particularly important to single mothers and their children, whose numbers and need continued to grow not only absolutely but also proportionally to others. Twenty percent of all urban relief families had female heads in May 1934.[32] Even in rural areas some 13–14 percent of relief families were female-headed and about half of those had children under 16.[33] Many "male-headed" families were female supported. One letter of complaint about relief discrimination referred matter-of-factly to "women with families and dependent husbands."[33] Single mothers with young children were conventionally classified as "unemployables" (along with the disabled and the aged) at the time, because it was then assumed that they could not both earn and care for their children. Frances Perkins testified in 1935, for example, that "you take the mother of a large family, she may be able-bodied and all that, but we classify her as unemployable because if she works the children have got to go to an orphan asylum."[35] Of the "unemployables" on relief in cities in 1934, 45 percent were mothers alone with children.[36] Most of the female unemployed were hidden because no one, often including themselves, considered them as customarily employed or entitled to employment. Substantial numbers of women heads of household did manage to get themselves classified as unemployed—25 percent of a national sample of those on relief in 1934—and these certainly included some single mothers.[37] But even those women householders who got relief averaged consistently poorer than the male. This was the case both in urban and in rural areas, both among tenant and among owner farmers.[38]

A measure of the poverty of single mothers was that relief held together families that might otherwise have been separated—reducing, for example, the number of children taken from parents and placed into fosterage.[39] Yet the assistance remained much too little. In 1934 federal relief was providing for 358,000 female-headed households with children under sixteen, mostly urban.[40] This was only 1.2 percent of the approximately 29.9 million households in the United

States, while a minimum of 8–9 percent of them were probably female headed.

Conservative gender and family norms structured the relief women did get. Despite the theoretical break with old poor-law traditions Hopkins seemed to stand for, in many localities relief to women was still being "morals-tested," far more than that given to men. Journalist Lorena Hickok found that state relief officials retained the deserving/undeserving distinction. From Maine she wrote, "To be a 'deserving case,' a family has got to measure up to the most rigid Nineteenth Century standards of cleanliness, physical and moral. . . . As a result, a woman who isn't a good housekeeper is apt to have a pretty rough time of it. And heaven help the family in which there is any 'moral problem.'"[41] Even at the depths of the economic crisis, means and morals-testing humiliated female relief recipients: "The investigators, they were like detectives, like I had committed a crime. . . . I had to tell them about my life, more than if I was on trial . . . the investigator searched my icebox . . . I was ashamed of my life . . . that's how you're made to feel when you're down and out like you're nothing better than a criminal."[42]

Relief checks intended for families usually went to men as heads of households, but their families did not in fact always share in this welfare. As one letter of complaint put it bluntly, "Every since you all started sending their check . . . he move and left me. . . . When he was out of work I washed and iorn [sic] to help him."[43] The norm of domesticity for women also meant that those who left their homes were suspect. There were homeless women, like men, albeit in smaller numbers; by one estimate there were 45,000 transient women and girls in 1933. These women were treated less well than men. There were fewer shelters, proportionately, for women. Homeless women were often afraid to seek public assistance because relief workers were likely to send them "home," although many women had purposely left their homes in order to search for work or to escape abuse.[44]

The most overt discrimination may have been that in the public works programs. The FERA, the CWA, the PWA, and WPA all inaugurated federally funded projects that hired millions of the unemployed. These jobs were the best source of public aid, both because the wages were higher than public assistance stipends and because so many people preferred the greater dignity of working for a wage.

In North Carolina, for example, WPA wages were three and a half times higher than old-age assistance and six times higher than a mothers'-aid grant for one child.[45] Of 1.6 million collecting work relief in 1934, only 142,000, or 11 percent, were women.[46] The CWA gave women only 7 percent (300,000 of 4 million) of the jobs. The FERA did little better, giving women 12 percent of the jobs, while women were 25 percent of the unemployed even in official figures. Discrimination in public jobs was directly relevant to single mothers and mothers'-aid programs, because jobs might have been an alternative to aid as a way for single mothers to support their families.

One factor in excluding women was a masculinist vision of useful labor, and therefore of what public works should be. The largest, best known, and least-criticized projects were quintessentially male: building dams and bridges, for example. Construction jobs were for men, of course, and the monumental public works design style perpetuated a masculinist vision of what work was essential, of what the society needed. Feminists of this period were not yet arguing that women could do heavy construction work, so there were few complaints about women's exclusion from these projects. But the society also needed more teachers, nurses, and child care workers, and public health workers, and there was no reason why public jobs in these areas could not have been funded.

Equally influential was the view that women were not entitled to jobs as men were, so women's unemployment did not really count as a problem. Quite to the contrary, the depression produced an agitation to eliminate married women from the labor force. Sixteen hundred female federal employees were fired for this reason; 77 percent of local school systems would not hire married women and fired female teachers who married.[47] The WPA allowed only one job per family and always assumed men were the breadwinners. The discrimination was not confined to married women. Men were universally favored, even those with shorter work histories than women. The sex discrimination was so notorious that even the AFL, hardly a champion of women's rights, criticized the policy at its 1936 national convention.[48]

Yet another factor was Hopkins's personal disinterest in providing work to women, and former domestics in particular; he accepted the argument that they were not accustomed to real jobs and/or were accustomed to low wages and poor working conditions. In dealing with the "women business," as Hopkins disdainfully called it, he actually defied the WPA's own regulations, dumping women in the category of unemployables along with "derelicts." Hopkins set an arbitrary ceiling on women's employment in the WPA at 16 percent. In Baltimore, for example, while women had accounted for 25 percent of family heads on relief, they got only 10 percent of the jobs.[49] Throughout the country women applicants consistently had difficulty getting themselves defined as employable or as having sufficient work experience to be hired. A Russell Sage Foundation study listed the reasons for women's lack of access to WPA jobs:

> (a) a desire to compel WPA and relief officials to exert greater care in determining whether the women seeking work are indeed the economic heads of their families . . . (b) a desire to avoid substituting the wife for the husband who is thereby enabled to seek odd jobs which might enable him more easily to supplement the wife's earnings than she could supplement his if he were the only employed [sic] . . . (c) a desire to put some brake upon the women's eagerness to be the family breadwinner, wage recipient, and controller of the family pocketbook; (d) an effort to reduce expenditures for materials; and finally (e) a desire to protect the WPA program against possible public criticism.[50]

WPA officials frequently claimed difficulty in establishing "female" works projects because of the nature of the work, claiming less "need" for such projects and that the cost of materials—for example, fabrics and machines for sewing rooms—was too high. There are no published data comparing materials costs for male or female projects, but one can legitimately wonder about the price of material for heavy construction projects. Attitudes toward the cost of materials were surely affected by the view among some WPA officials that the sewing rooms were a charity rather than employment in the public service.[51] Racial motives were also involved, as in a Fayetteville, North Carolina, decision to close a sewing project and send all the black women to janitorial work at white schools.[52]

At the root of this alleged materials problem was the government's consistent commitment to sex and race segregation of jobs. Women and minorities who did get work relief were segregated into stereotyped, tedious, low-wage jobs. In 1936, 56 percent of all women on WPA worked in sewing rooms. This proportion was greater in states with a high proportion of minorities, like New Mexico, where it was 84 percent.[53] Women and minorities could not get access to better jobs. The Civilian Conservation Corps (CCC), for example, was initially only for men. A meager counterpart for 8,500 women (as compared to 2.5 million men) was set up just before the program was abruptly ended in 1937.

The Children's Bureau and its allies, especially the Women's Bureau, vigorously protested sex discrimination in the New Deal.[54] They objected to the sex-based wage differentials in the NRA. They got Ellen Woodward appointed as assistant WPA administrator in charge of women's and professional projects, and she worked to alter the conception of women as choosing, rather than needing, to work. WPA women workers *were* heads of families. "The real sufferers, perhaps the greatest sufferers in this depression have been women . . . trying to keep a home together on little or nothing."[55] Mary Anderson, head of the Women's Bureau, criticized the gender wage differentials in the NRA codes and WPA projects, and got an equal minimum wage written into the Fair Labor Standards Act. Eleanor Roosevelt was prominent in opposing prohibitions on married women's employment.[56] The informal New Deal women's caucus got the FERA to sponsor a White House Conference on the Emergency Needs of Women in November 1933, and it prodded Hopkins to do a little better. In 1934 the women's network considered forming a Coordinating Consultant Commission on Economic Welfare of Women, which would include representatives from the FERA, Departments of Labor and Agriculture, NRA, and others, but this did not take off.[57]

But on the issue of job discrimination, the difference between the Women's Bureau's stronger orientation toward sex equality and the Children's Bureau's maternalism showed vividly. The Children's Bureau continued to soft pedal criticism of job discrimination, paying relatively little attention to the problems of working mothers and their children. In its symbolic language, "working woman" meant single childless woman, while "mother" meant unpaid domestic worker. As Gwendolyn Mink puts it, "In maternalists' view, the strength of woman's labor rights faded as she approached marriage and motherhood."[58] To some degree the Children's Bureau group seemed to support the WPA's discrimination against women, although for different reasons. Grace Abbott, for example, condemned the fact that so many women were on WPA jobs who should have been home with their children supported by mothers' aid.[59] The principle of equal wages did not require identical treatment of women and men in access to jobs or type of jobs, and the Children's Bureau may have accepted that men had a right to a job that women held only contingently. In this way the maternalist legacy of discouraging working motherhood fit with New Deal strategies to promote wage-earning manhood.[60]

There was no equal treatment for minority men either. The black press was filled with articles denouncing race prejudice, exclusion, and insulting treatment in New Deal programs.[61] There was similar, if less widely protested, discrimination against other minorities. In California impoverished Mexican Americans were heavily represented on the relief rolls at the beginning of the depression—hardly surprising, since the average wage for farm workers went from thirty-five cents an hour in the 1920s to fifteen cents in the 1930s, and the average time worked was also drastically reduced. The response was a massive campaign to "repatriate" Mexican Americans, even though many were citizens. (The same impulse was expressed toward New York Puerto Ricans, even though they, too, were citizens.)[62] Some 130,000 to 160,000 were coerced to "return" to Mexico by 1936. American Indians were also discriminated against, sometimes on the excuse that they already received special federal resources, sometimes because they often lived in remote areas where no one went to set up WPA projects.[63] A number of western states actually argued that American Indians were not entitled to any of the benefits of the Social Security Act.[64]

A large part of the problem was the federal structure that shaped most welfare programs, the shared funding and control among national, state, and local governments. The very few programs that were directly run by the federal government gave blacks a better deal. The most shining example was the PWA, whose director Harold Ickes was, after Eleanor Roosevelt, the most publicly civil-rights-committed white in Washington. He stipulated that all PWA contractors hire at least as many blacks as their proportion in the 1930 census, one of the first uses of affirmative action quotas.[65] However, many federal administrators were prejudiced, and many others declined to control the racism of local project staff. When blacks and whites were equally badly off, the former were sometimes denied jobs on the grounds that they were used to poverty and had less need. Minority workers were required to accept less skilled and lower-wage jobs than were white workers; in New Mexico, for example, Hispanic women could never get the supervisory or desk jobs sometimes given to Anglo women.[66] The public works programs actually depressed the black occupational structure by refusing to give blacks jobs at the level they had held previously in the private sector.[67] At times there were dual wage scales for the same jobs. State and county administrators determined that blacks could get by on less than whites in the same area, and by as much as 50 percent.[68] Local control also meant large differentials in the level of stipends; in North Carolina, for example, typical of the South, public assistance benefits were about half the national average.[69] In the southern states, racism combined with inadequate resources deprived many blacks of relief entitlements altogether, forcing them to depend on private charities. In Birmingham, Alabama, for example, destitute blacks were shunted to the Red Cross, whose relief payments were the lowest in the country, often paid only in kind; on its work projects, supervisors treated workers like a chain gang, literally standing over them with pistols.[70]

Above all, local control allowed major employers to dictate relief policy that would not interfere with hiring at very low wages. Big western growers forced relief agencies to refuse relief when pickers were needed.[71] In some places WPA administrators regularly laid off women when there was a demand for domestic servants, whose wages were typically down to $1.50/$2.00 per week—many receiving no money at all but leftovers and cast-off clothing.[72] Where layoffs or discriminatory wage rates could not be used, the WPA local officials made sure workers had short hours so they would have to accept private low-wage employment in addition.[73]

But federal agencies were by no means free of discrimination, and the Children's Bureau was no better than most and worse than some in its treatment of minorities. As of October 1935 it had no black professional employees, despite complaints from the Urban League.[74] The Children's Bureau responded with chilly politeness to requests and suggestions for work centering on African Americans.[75] Lenroot similarly parried grievances from a Puerto Rican group: "It does not seem practicable to set up a separate relief program for Puerto Ricans."[76]

A sense of how this discrimination felt comes from letters of complaint to federal officials. One official, the "Negro Advisor" to the WPA, Alfred E. Smith, got an average of seven thousand letters a year.[77] The grievances implicate both overall policy and petty harassment. Relief programs refused to hire qualified colored caseworkers. "If a person refuses any type of job, even if it doesn't pay more than $3 per week, he cannot receive employment on a WPA project. On the other hand if he accepts a job for $3, which no one can live on, then he cannot receive aid." Workers were harassed, baited, even whipped by public works foremen. Blacks were fired to make room to hire whites. In a project for the blind with thirty-two black and five white pupils, three trained black Braille instructors were laid off and replaced with untrained whites. Black WPA workers were sent to the homes of local officials to do domestic service. An elderly couple, the man about sixty-five, was denied aid because they could not produce a marriage certificate. Complaints usually went unanswered, even after federal officials directed that responses be made.[78]

Race and sex discrimination could not always be distinguished. New Mexico relief workers rationalized discrimination against Hispanic women by arguing that they, unlike Anglo women, needed to stay in their homes to care for families because of their cultural traditions.[79] African American letters of complaint included many about unfair treatment of women—proportionately more than did white letters. Not only did minority women suffer from a double discrimination, but the fact that proportionally more black women needed work than white women made it worse. Their need was greater because of race-based poverty and discrimination and because there were proportionately more single-mother families among African Americans.[80] Moreover, the fact that black women's previous work experiences were so often in domestic service (82 percent of black women wage earners in 1930) was used to lock them into the unskilled category.

Still, provision for minorities and for white women would have been far worse without federal assistance. Although never enough and never stable, federal relief was nevertheless a major achievement. It worked—at keeping people alive, at giving people hope, at preventing disorder, at demonstrating that the government could manage a huge distribution system. Federal relief also raised expectations. The very existence of these federal programs awakened civil rights consciousness and prompted demands for equal treatment.

African Americans in particular protested prejudice militantly and patiently and did in fact gain a great deal of help (though not in adequate proportion to their need).[81] New York Puerto Ricans organized to condemn the city's neglect and demand a survey of economic and social conditions among their people.[82]

Thus both the successes and failures of federal relief strengthened support for permanent welfare programs; both good and bad experiences made many people want more. Federal relief also produced criticism, less of corruption than of partisan politics in distribution—inevitable, given its decentralized control. The patronage opportunities afforded by relief also had their positive aspects, because patronage beneficiaries then became political supporters of welfare programs. For Roosevelt, insulating welfare provision totally from politics and from patronage was not a goal. Instead the relief experience showed that welfare could further brace his political coalition.

Toward a Permanent Welfare Program

The 1932 Democratic platform had pledged Roosevelt to produce unemployment and old-age insurance. His "brain trust" was also advocating public medical insurance and a permanent public works program. But the immediate needs could not await the design of a complex permanent system and, on the other hand, Roosevelt's emergency provisions took some of the urgency out of social insurance. So Roosevelt waited more than a year, until summer 1934, before even appointing a group to prepare a proposal for a permanent welfare structure. That hiatus allowed several groups to jockey for influence and lay claim to the expertise and authority to design an economic security system. One group was the women in and around the Children's Bureau; another was the social insurance lobby.

The Children's Bureau group had made gains and suffered losses in the 1920s. The biggest loss was the repeal of Sheppard-Towner. Without any compensatory expansion of federal welfare program, the Children's Bureau had no momentum or current track record. On the other hand, its approach was based on cooperation with states, and these relationships grew steadily stronger through the 1920s. The federal women's network thereby built connections with women in local government and private agencies, and they all gained skills and confidence as bureaucrats and politicians. These strengths were illustrated by the campaign to get Hoover to appoint Grace Abbott as secretary of labor in 1931. It failed, but not before Clara Beyer had mobilized a national political effort drawing in thousands not only from women's organizations but also from academia, the Urban League, and influential men in various areas of reform. Beyer later reflected that this campaign was a rehearsal for the successful struggle two years later to get Frances Perkins appointed.[83]

More ominous for the Children's Bureau, however, was the attempt of the PHS to swallow some or all of its work. Sheppard-Towner—a step toward publicly funded medical care—had antagonized not only the conservative medical leadership represented by the AMA, but even the more progressive PHS. Weakening the Children's Bureau would weaken the whole Department of Labor, the major source of initiatives toward expanded governmental intervention and regulation. But the PHS offensive against the Children's Bureau had layered motives: It represented both a fundamental conflict of political values, and a jurisdictional power struggle imbued with hostility to the women's reform community. The PHS wanted to control all health-related activities and to cut down the Children's Bureau. The AMA and the PHS labeled the Children's Bureau women as a bunch of radicals, even Reds; as unnatural, nosy women; and as simultaneously dangerous and incompetent.

These attacks crested at the 1930 White House Conference on Child Health and Protection. Since 1909 such conferences had become decennial. The Children's Bureau grew out of the first one and planned the second, but it was entirely excluded from the planning of the third. The PHS had gone directly to Hoover to get authorization to run this conference. Several key committees were packed with physicians, with little or no representation from the social work/child welfare network. The major recommendation of the conference was, unsurprisingly, to transfer all child health work to the PHS.[84] The denouement was dramatic. Dr. Martha Eliot, later to become head of the Children's Bureau, told the story in an interview: Having filed a minority report as a lone dissenter, Grace Abbott rose to present it; she was ruled out of order. But the plenary session had been packed by Children's Bureau supporters, and they began to object. Dr. Haven Emerson, PHS leader, climbed onto a chair and attempted to disperse the group, announcing that nothing significant was to happen at this meeting anyway:

[This] didn't quiet the crowd in the least, and after Dr. Emerson was through, the same chair, which stood in the middle of the crowd, was mounted by oth-er[s]. . . . Among them was Josephine Goldmark . . . of the Consumers' League. She just said to the crowd, 'We must stand by. We have to see that this does not take place and that this recommendation does not pass.'. . . There must have been 500 members of the Conference in the room, and peo-ple were standing all around the edge. It was quite an event. . . . Surgeon-General Cummings was the chairman. The majority report was given and then the protest came from the floor vigorously, people standing and speak-ing from all over the floor, including doctors. Many people rose to protest . . . and finally there was a call for the minority report and the chairman had to permit Grace Abbott to read her minority report. It was then moved that the minority report be substituted for the majority report. In the meantime, the chairman ruled that there would be no votes taken. This did not please the au-dience, but the end result was that the whole thing was tabled. . . . it was per-fectly clear that the people who had come to the . . . Conference . . . were not for splitting up the CB.[85]

This episode was a reminder of the continued strength of the woman-dominated welfare lobby. Even President Hoover was spooked by the display of women's power at the conference; in 1932, frightened of what the women's vote might do to him, he dictated a memo for Grace Abbott's signature to the effect that he had played no part in the attempt to transfer Children's Bureau programs to the PHS. Ab-bott refused to sign it.[86]

But despite this victory over the PHS, the main trend put the Chil-dren's Bureau on the defensive. The PHS continued to lobby to take over Children's Bureau functions,[87] and the bureau had to struggle for paltry appropriations year after year. Without a major program to administer, without major funds to distribute, it was losing its base of support.

What salvaged the Children's Bureau's role, at least temporarily, was that so few other welfare experts had federal positions in the Hoover administration. Social insurance proponents had no represen-tatives in the federal government at all—or, that is, none for whom so-cial insurance was their primary reform. Social insurance advocates were relatively uninterested in relief or public assistance and, unlike the Children's Bureau group, made no bid to run an entire system of government provision. In this respect their concerns were still narrow-er than those of the women and their child-welfare network.

Social insurance men did have significant support in several states and among businessmen, which they might have transformed into influence in Washington had they not been so divided. Not only did they have differing proposals, expressing alternative political positions, but they bickered, insulted, and undermined each other. By 1932 there were two camps offering proposals with different names—"reserves plans" versus "insurance plans."[88]

One woman from the white women's social feminist network, Elizabeth Brandeis Raushenbush, was central to social insurance schemes, and her double role is revealing of the highly gendered assumptions that underlay both networks' operation. She was the wife of the chief designer and then administrator of the Wisconsin system, Paul Raushenbush, and the daughter of Supreme Court Justice Louis Brandeis, and she used both connections effectively. But she was also in her own right a full member of the social work network—a close personal friend of Clara Beyer (they had shared a job in the early 1920s) and editor of Josephine Goldmark's biography of Florence Kelley. She was herself a social insurance expert, coauthor of the Wisconsin act. In 1934 she was a central go-between in an attempt to unite both sides (the Wisconsin or "reserves" and Epstein or "insurance" groups) in the unemployment insurance dispute in support of a compromise, the Wagner-Lewis Bill, conceived by herself and her husband and written by her husband. It called for a federal tax on employers as an incentive to get states to adopt unemployment compensation; any employer paying into such a state fund would be exempt from the federal tax. It was neutral in that states would be free to adopt any sort of plan they chose. With help from her father and from department-store magnate A. L. Filene, Brandeis Raushenbush arranged a private meeting to sell the scheme to the other social insurance group, to businessmen, and to the administration. The meeting succeeded in winning support for Wagner-Lewis but did not promote a long-term rapprochement; the social insurance men continued to malign and abuse each other.[89]

Elizabeth Brandeis Raushenbush's importance in unemployment politics points out that there was nothing inevitable in the male/female, social insurance/public assistance division of labor. Neither she nor her female network expressed doubt or aggravation about her double loyalties. In fact, she tried to draw her women's network into the design of unemployment provision. She called on her Children's Bureau colleagues to lobby for the Wagner-Lewis Bill; one of them,

Lavinia Engle, was responsible for getting Lewis as a cosponsor of the bill.[90] Her attempts to integrate her worlds failed, not because of conflict but because of the pervasive and shared assumption of a division of labor among welfare advocates. The Children's Bureau network supported social insurance and thought it appropriate for men to design it, just as the men thought the women would take care of public assistance. That division of labor, which had developed over several decades, was now going to lead to a bill with separate insurance and assistance programs. Had either group been less energetic, there might have been a unified rather than a stratified economic security bill.

Although the Children's Bureau left social insurance design to others, it still wanted to direct the whole federal program. Women leaders worked hard for FDR in the 1932 campaign and came to believe they could collect on his debt to them. His appointment of Frances Perkins as secretary of labor confirmed these hopes; she was "their" candidate, and her appointment arose from a massive lobbying campaign conducted by the women's network.[91] Its explicit message to FDR was that Perkins was the wages owed to the women's network for their mobilization of support in the 1932 election—a campaign that brought first-time "conversions" to the Democratic party among many previously loyal Republicans. Moreover, Molly Dewson, chief of Democratic party women's activities had proven herself an extraordinary politician and Roosevelt promoter in 1928, 1932, and in the 1934 congressional elections, and FDR understood her value for the future (in the 1936 election she was to repay him handsomely). The Children's Bureau women's network worked steadily to draw all their contacts away from the Republicans and toward FDR.[92] Eager to appear a team player at this juncture, Abbott, who was retiring, gave Perkins authority over the choice of a successor.[93]

The New Deal continued the Hoover administration's reliance on the Children's Bureau for welfare leadership and social and economic statistics. Roosevelt and his cabinet consulted the bureau about a wide variety of problems and proposals relating to domestic policy.[94] Despite its tiny appropriation of $375,000,[95] the Children's Bureau published the *Monthly Relief Bulletin* and throughout 1933 supplied the only national statistics on state and local public assistance. (Defending its turf, the bureau would criticize statistical reports done by others.[96]) In 1934 Clara Beyer set up a Bureau of Labor Standards for the Labor Department and in effect ran it until 1958, although a man was always titular director.[97] The Children's Bureau took the lead in reviving the anti-child-labor movement as a means to help counter unemployment. Calling an emergency conference on child labor together with the AFL, the Children's Bureau contributed to the revival of state laws and ratification of the federal amendment.[98] It was the conduit used by civic organizations pressuring for social legislation and the addressee of thousands of letters from the public asking for relief. Letters to Perkins or FDR concerning any aspect of welfare needs, including old-age pensions, were referred to the Children's Bureau.[99] Moreover, the bureau was the main federal agency pressuring FDR for a more aggressive federal response to the economic crisis. Grace Abbott was agitating for low-cost public housing in 1934.[100] The welfare promoters organized in and through the Children's Bureau thus arrived at the New Deal eager for the expansion of welfare services and assuming that their growth would also expand the bureau.

But in his year and a half in power, Harry Hopkins had become a contender for controlling a new welfare program. Although Hopkins was himself from the same social work tradition as Abbott and her friends—and their first response was to praise his appointment—he quickly broke with that orientation. His preference for massive, immediate relief suggested a view that lack of money was the only source of problems, making casework unnecessary or, at least, outside the appropriate sphere of government relief-giving activity. Hopkins preferred direct federal control, offering a minimal role to the states, a strategy opposed by the Children's Bureau and many social insurance advocates. The FERA laid out extensive requirements, including uniform minimum benefits, public accountability, the setting up of separate emergency relief agencies in the states rather than working through existing welfare departments, for example. He got little resistance at first, because local desperation was so great, but the Children's Bureau group suspected, on the basis of experience, that this easy compliance would not last long. Moreover the very emergency, temporary nature of the structures Hopkins (and other New Dealers) created seemed to engender more vested interests that would be hard to integrate into the permanent welfare system both social work and social insurance proponents wanted. The two groups were often united in their criticisms of Hopkins.

Both Hopkins and the Children's Bureau had good arguments. Hopkins's care rested on humanitarianism and a simplified Keynesianism, his object being to get as much money distributed as fairly and quickly as possible. He was critical of both the "old-line" Children's

Bureau group and the social insurance people. A social worker, he nevertheless rejected the Progressive Era social control orientation more radically than the bureau women did. Hopkins saw the Children's Bureau group as snobs and elitists in their emphasis on their own expertise and condescension toward the poor. At the same time he condemned their willingness to cooperate with corrupt, patronage-appointed state and local officials. By his insistence that only public agencies should dispense public funds, he set up his operations as rivals to the private-charity establishment, which had been assiduously courted by the Children's Bureau group. At the same time he believed the social insurance advocates were far too slow-moving and undemocratic in their coverage designs.[101]

On the other hand, Children's Bureau predictions that Hopkins's methods would produce state and local opposition were soon realized. Grace Abbott believed that he antagonized state administrators and failed to understand the widespread hostility to apparently wasteful spending.[102] Reflecting their emphasis on professional administration, the Children's Bureau group accused him of amateur, slipshod, and inefficient management. Established welfare advocates of all camps questioned whether his relief programs contributed to the ultimate creation of a welfare state that they envisioned. Frances Perkins complained that Hopkins saw "almost everything in terms of relieving starvation" and that he was not aware of the "larger permanent implications of problems of employment . . . some of the people who work for him have sold him a counsel of despair."[103] These welfare advocates disliked his propensity for makeshift, emergency programs.

The women's complaints about Hopkins were sometimes jealous and small minded (and Hopkins's attacks on the Children's Bureau group were disdainful and insulting), and their jurisdictional rivalry with Hopkins meant that they never gave him a fair chance. But they were right to notice his limitations: He passed by an opportunity to iron out the "archaic patchwork" of public welfare in the United States and to develop a plan for a permanent system of economic security.[104] Edith Abbott's view, as paraphrased by her biographer Lela Costin, says a great deal about the inadequacy of the welfare system we are stuck with today:

Each state was required to set up its own emergency relief administration, which mean that "one state after another carefully avoided laying the groundwork for a new public assistance administration [to] perma-

nently supplant the inadequate and inefficient local poor relief system."
. . . Allowing Hopkins to use half of the federal funds as unmatched
grants to states . . . [meant that] each governor felt impelled to drive the
best possible bargain with Hopkins. . . . Thus "the game of 'pull and
haul' between the federal and local relief authorities [came into] full
swing again," Abbott said. When Hopkins . . . said that "the unemployables" were to "go back to the states," Edith Abbott entreated him to
take a position of leadership and demand that the states abolish their old
pauper laws. . . . "It is hard to believe that the President can wish to per-
petuate the old theory of local government which makes the small prop-
erty-tax payer responsible for the relief that his poor neighbors need."[105]

Perhaps Roosevelt shared some of this view, for when he finally
moved to produce the promised permanent welfare programs, he
passed over both the Children's Bureau network and Hopkins's FERA
group and chose the social-insurance group. Characteristically, he set
up the Committee on Economic Security (CES) outside any existing
government agency, and to staff it he turned to academic social insurance advocates—relative outsiders to capital infighting—"experts,"
not politicians. Wisconsin controlled the CES. Edwin Witte, executive
director of the CES, had been chief of Wisconsin's Legislative Reference Library, where he had become skilled at legislative drafting,
wrote the Norris-LaGuardia Act (limiting federal injunctions in labor
disputes) and helped design the state unemployment compensation
program. Arthur Altmeyer, who was chief statistician and then executive secretary of the Wisconsin Industrial Commission, was appointed
chair of the technical (drafting) board of the CES. Witte also brought
from Madison his student Wilbur Cohen, later to become President
Lyndon B. Johnson's Secretary of Health, Education, and Welfare, as
his personal research assistant. As Eveline Burns, an independent consulting economist, put it: Witte did what "the Wisconsin boys wanted,
and . . . Miss Perkins wasn't going to buck the Wisconsin boys and . . .
Altmeyer . . . wasn't going to buck Wisconsin. He was Wisconsin."[106]
Ironically the new head of the Children's Bureau, Katharine Lenroot,
could qualify as a Wisconsin person, if not a Wisconsin "boy"—a native of that state, her father a U.S. senator from Wisconsin (1918–27),
she had also been a student of John Commons. Under his tutelage she
had made her political debut, speaking to the state legislature in favor
of a minimum-wage law in 1910. But her loyalties lay elsewhere now,
and she was not invited into the CES group.

Thus, despite the major victory of the social work and women's network in the Perkins appointment, the enormity of the economic crisis of the 1930s eventually weakened its position and reduced its influence over welfare policy. The "women" were asked to contribute *only* to the small programs they were expected to run. Behind this shift lay a deeper pattern: In periods of relative prosperity welfare had seemed a marginal governmental concern, in part because its recipients were less politically powerful, and it thus seemed appropriate to leave welfare programs to women and the quintessentially women's profession, social work. The depression brought welfare policy into the center of governmental activity, and encouraged its integration with macroeconomic policy.

Moreover the social work network was timid in what it asked for and in spelling out large-scale proposals embodying its vision of public social provision. Developing in the 1920s, the network had to fight to hold its own in the absence of expanding government or expansive reform thought about welfare. Led by women who had been socialized to think small rather than big, the group defended itself by defining an increasingly "small" area in which it could claim expertise—women and children—not really small at all, being the great majority of the population, but small in political importance and influence. Some in this network had truly visionary ideas about a welfare state, developing over the generations, from Jane Addams to Florence Kelley to Edith Abbott. But they did not generate concrete plans for an overall welfare system. Their biggest political campaigns, in which they mobilized popular support, focused on the defense of Sheppard-Towner and the Children's Bureau and the appointments of Abbott and Perkins. They did not make use of the depression to mount a substantive campaign. At a time of crisis and new possibility, their most prominent welfare advocates had become bureaucrats and organization women, neither making common cause with the rising social movements of the 1930s nor attempting to nourish a social movement more to their liking.

Townsend Movement Caravan Leaving Los Angeles
for Washington, 1936

8
=

New Deal Social Movements and Popular Pressure for Welfare

The program we call "welfare" today was created not only in the context of suffering but also in the turbulence of vociferous protest. While the labor movement may be the most well known of the depression-era social movements, rebellion among social workers was equally militant; one of its explosive moments—at the 1934 annual meeting of the National Conference of Social Work—may serve as emblematic of the anguished yet hopeful mood.

The conference opened to general excitement, with Assistant Secretary of Agriculture Rexford Tugwell and "relief czar" Harry Hopkins in attendance; as one participant put it, many social workers felt that "we had arrived and could give a leadership in welfare matters which had hitherto been denied to us."[1] With "rumors sweeping the hall," fifteen hundred people jammed into a room meant for five hundred to hear Mary Van Kleeck speak. A prominent social work leader, feminist, and now an elder stateswoman, Van Kleeck was an impressive figure, at her zenith in the 1930s: regal, with the confidence of a daughter of the upper class, supremely well educated, her ambitions disciplined to her high sense of moral responsibility. The first head of the Women's Bureau and then director of research for the Russell Sage Foundation, she was rapidly moving to the Left now, as were so many other middle-class intellectuals.[2]

209

Her topic was "Our Illusions Concerning Government." One illusion, she argued in this charismatic address, was that government is a neutral force, an illusion derived from the thinking of Fabians and the Progressive party; she referred to the tragedy of the German Social Democrats' faith in government, which "paved the way" for fascism. Others had rejoiced in the increased public responsibility for welfare, but Van Kleeck raised critical questions about the new government jobs social workers, including her friends, had got from the New Deal. Did the shift to public social work commit social workers to the preservation of the status quo, separate them from their clients? Was social work now an instrument of class domination? With whom should social workers ally themselves, government officials and agency directors or clients and the working class? What was needed, she concluded, was not the NRA, not relief, but a comprehensive income maintenance program financed by progressive taxation and—administered by workers.[3]

The atmosphere was already explosive, and Van Kleeck's speech struck a match. Gertrude Springer, a close friend of the Abbotts and by no means at the radical end of the NCSW political continuum, said she had never witnessed such a prolonged ovation. "The effect on her hearers was electric. The younger and more volatile rose as to a trumpet call. The soberest were shaken." Bertha Reynolds thought the effect like a strong wind.[4] The majority at the conference probably preferred a more moderate vision, an evolving welfare state rather than a revolution. But it was Van Kleeck who set the terms of the debate. As Springer put it, "This year the radicals had the big tent and the conservatives were in the sideshows."[5]

The social work support for Van Kleeck's alternative welfare proposals sprang from several years of militant social protest in the early 1930s. Roosevelt's election accelerated rather than subdued that spirit. His administration's commitment to change only intensified the insurgencies coming from a wide variety of social groups.

Much of this social activism concerned welfare. While the visions of welfare we have examined came mainly from elites, depression social movements afford a glimpse of some of the welfarist impulses of the less privileged citizenry, and their influence on government and experts. As welfare reformers constructed their visions of the problem of poverty, its causes, and remedial proposals, the objects of their gaze also contributed to what they saw. Poor people offered their interpretations of the problem through social and political activism that helped to redefine the causes of poverty and the criteria for who deserved help. Traditionally the primary form of mass protest against impoverishment and inequality was "bread riots," collective civil disobedience in which protesters defied laws of property to take what they considered theirs according to a higher moral-economic understanding. The "bread riots" of the depression—sit-ins at relief agencies and resistance to evictions or mortgage auctions—also asserted moral entitlements as superior to property law. Sensitive to these manifestations of popular sentiment, political leaders of various sorts offered welfarist proposals designed to win support.

Our welfare state, and particularly the Social Security Act, cannot be understood without a careful look at this popular activism.[6] Civic associations as well as many spontaneous and even individual protests influenced public policy in a variety of ways. They constituted a form of lobbying, impressing demands, definite or vague, upon those in power, with implicit or explicit threats of withholding votes or other resources of popular power. Demonstrators disrupted economic and governmental processes, thus stimulating welfare proposals in attempts to restore order.[7] Social activism also contributed to a rapid shift in "public opinion" regarding government responsibility, drastically expanding the range of the the realistic, making possible the previously unimaginable.[8]

The focus here is not the specific design of alternative proposals, but their visions of possibility and justice. For example, depression social movements specifically valorized the elderly and those defined as "unemployed," designating them as quintessentially deserving groups of welfare recipients, in contrast to other social groups that might also have been candidates for that position (such as children or single mothers). Social movements helped Roosevelt create the electoral coalition that not only brought about his repeated reelection, but also allowed the relative stability of the New Deal programs for several decades. Protests deeply affected the Social Security Act and ADC within it.

Examining the influence of social protest requires interpreting silences as well as cries. Doing so risks imposing ahistorical expectations onto the past, projecting one's own "noise" into the silent field. Still, silences cannot be ignored: They remind us of hidden assumptions and of the existence of the powerless, the unmobilized, the alienated. And the quietness of some groups makes the demands of others relatively louder.

=

The "silence" of the women's movement was particularly consequential. Although the program that was to become the epitome of "welfare" focused on single mothers, that social group created no activism to represent its needs. By contrast, thirty years later, in the 1960s, single mothers organized and effectively pressured the welfare system for better treatment, through the National Welfare Rights Organization (NWRO). The NWRO arose in large part *because* of the welfare system, which brought women together and gave them shared problems and even a location in which to meet each other, broader bases for collective action than those created simply by a common economic and social experience. The mothers' aid recipients in the 1930s were too few, too scattered, and too lacking in a sense of entitlement to create collective activism. The home visits that caseworkers still made before the depression precluded recipients meeting each other in the waiting rooms of "welfare" offices, thus creating a community or group identification. When single mothers did articulate grievances, they did so primarily to individual caseworkers.[9] Twenty years earlier, in the decade 1910–20, there had been an agitation for mothers' pensions. Not even a ripple of such a campaign was evident in the 1930s. No crusades for any women's interests reached anywhere near the size that creates a social movement.[10] Women were active in many movements—disproportionately in relation to their general social influence and power—but they did not lay claim, as women, to designation as deserving sufferers entitled to relief.

There *were* functioning women's organizations in the 1930s. Many of those who had created mothers' pensions were still active—a few of them in government jobs, and others in such associations as the League of Women Voters, the Women's Trade Union League, the National Consumers' League, the settlements. But these organizations were at a low ebb of vibrance and popular support. Though they did some effective lobbying, and though their leaders had some success in promoting women into jobs and public appointments, they had become mainly staff rather than membership organizations. Most of their members contributed only money, with the work done by paid staff or top leaders. This network formed a Women's Joint Congressional Committee, consisting of representatives of various organizations, which mobilized letter-writing campaigns, personal lobbying, or behind-the-scenes visits to key politicians. Black women's organizations were only slightly healthier, because the most politically energetic women tended to work in civil rights, notably in the drive for a federal law against lynching, or in labor groups. Some women worked in the main political parties, particularly for Roosevelt, and Molly Dewson was able to organize broad participation for the Democrats. The Women's Division, which she headed, recruited fifteen thousand women to educate themselves about New Deal policy and then to canvass voters and propagandize for Roosevelt; in the 1936 election campaign sixty thousand women were mobilized. The National Woman's Party continued its steady campaign for an Equal Rights Amendment, and by the late 1930s was making more progress in getting its bill at least onto the floor of the Congress, but this group was small and not growing.[11] None of these women's activities could be said to constitute a mass movement. None conducted a lobbying or even an educational effort on behalf of single mothers. And the white women's organizations did not consider poor women central in their constituency.

Labor, on the other hand, did create a mass movement during the 1930s, which had a substantial impact on welfare expectations. But it forfeited some influence on welfare programs because its national leadership was only gradually emerging from its tradition of hostility to public welfare provision. The AFL's official condemnation of government intervention was inconsistent, since it accepted state regulation of women's and children's wages and hours and was enthusiastic about the use of the state to exclude competition for jobs from immigrant workers.[12] Gompers's own opposition to public welfare grew from programs such as workmen's compensation, which, by interposing government between capital and labor, defined certain issues as outside the realm of collective struggle; he was less alarmed by provision for workers already out of the labor force. For example, the AFL usually backed state and federal old-age pension proposals between 1907 and 1932, when the Dill-Connery Bill, solidly supported by labor, became the first federal pension proposal to be reported out of committee.[13] The AFL had accepted workmen's compensation, in a masculinized form that defined most women's jobs as nondangerous and therefore excluded from coverage. But labor's national leadership resisted health and unemployment insurance and never identified any welfare programs as a central labor demand.

Concerned that government insurance would weaken workers' loyalty to unions and interfere with union recruitment, the AFL feared increasing workers' "social wage"—that portion of the working-class standard of living that did not derive from wages.[14] "Compulsory unemployment insurance," AFL President William Green wrote, "was a union wrecking agency."[15] Gompers did not want "decommodification—the removal of various goods and services from the market.[16] The decommodification of education was an old tradition (for whites at least), removed from what was typically considered a welfare state. But whether other services—such as health care, pensions for the aged, child care, or wages during disability—should remain items to be purchased privately or should be removed from the market and provided as part of a social wage by the government was precisely the issue. From the AFL perspective on class relations, the more that remained commoditized, the more was at stake in its collective bargaining with capital and thus the stronger the union. When, as in the United States, unions were not themselves political, expressing part of their strength through political parties, an expanding welfare state undercut workers' dependence on the unions.

Thus the depression at first deepened organized labor's suspicion of unemployment insurance, because such programs seemed to sell out its goal of full employment by making large-scale unemployment more tolerable. In September 1930 AFL President Green went so far as to propose voluntary agreements between employers and workers in seasonal industries for setting up private insurance funds, shorter workdays and workweeks so as to divide available work, and stabilization of production. But in 1932 the AFL Executive Council could still declare, "Failure of industrial management to provide and maintain work opportunities through the distribution of the amount of work available . . . is resulting in the crystallization of public opinion in favor of Unemployment Insurance. . . . The American Federation of Labor wishes very sincerely that the enactment of such legislation could be avoided."[17]

This position, however, may not have characterized the majority of union members. Many state federations championed state assistance and social insurance, including health insurance.[18] Locals rarely polled their members and local leaders' positions often depended on approval from above. Even those locals that went on record against social insurance may have done so without the informed consent of their members. There was a revealing moment, for example, in the 1918 convention of the International Typographical Union (ITU). First a resolution was passed against health insurance, saying that it was "advocated mainly by socialists and theorists [*sic*], who, for the most part are not affiliated with the labor movement." Later in the same meeting another resolution was passed: "Resolved that the . . . [ITU] herewith endorse health insurance for wage-earners and their dependents, with equal contributions from employers and employees, the funds democratically administered."[19] The speculation that the first resolution emanated from the leadership is unavoidable, particularly given the Red-baiting language at this moment of intense labor radicalism.

It would be useful to have a gender analysis on this question. There is a large gender gap on issues of welfare today, with women considerably more pro-welfare, and some of its contemporary causes were present sixty years ago, notably women's greater responsibility, and internalization of responsibility, for families. But women were underrepresented in unions, and often effectively disfranchised even when they were members. The AFL's notion of full employment had a silent modifier—"male."

In the depression majorities in many locals supported welfare programs, particularly health and unemployment insurance. A United Mine Workers delegate to the 1931 AFL convention estimated that 90 percent of the miners wanted unemployment insurance. Other large unions, such as the United Textile Workers; the Iron, Steel and Tin Workers; the Aeronautical Workers; the ILGWU and the Amalgamated Clothing Workers; and numerous municipal Central Labor Councils called for unemployment insurance. Where left-wing influence was robust, locals openly broke with the international; for example the New York Carpenters Local called a citywide conference in January 1932 to establish an AFL Trade Union Committee for Unemployment Insurance and Relief. Soon this committee became national. AFL President Green at first cried communist, but he admitted to his Executive Council that there was a growing demand he would have to face, and by July the council had indeed changed its position to advocate an unemployment insurance program.[20]

It was probably the combined pressure of some unionists who had never fully accepted AFL hostility to public provision, and others who shifted because of the hardships of the depression, that forced this change. From the point of view of leadership, the decisive factor was that mass unemployment created a nearly irresistible pressure on laid-off workers to take nonunion, low-wage jobs. The only evident way for unions to maintain their strength was to make it possible for some of the unemployed to remain jobless, and this required some kind of provision for the unemployed. AFL backing was never enthusiastic. Altmeyer complained that in testifying for Social Security, William Green made so many suggestions for improving the bill that he seemed to be against it.[21]

No matter how tepid, AFL support for welfare proposals seems to have been a necessary condition for the Social Security Act.[22] And vice versa: Rexford Tugwell considered Social Security the main factor in winning labor votes in the 1936 election.[23] The leadership of organized labor threw its weight not only against conservative objections to the bill but also against the more inclusive left-wing alternative. Organized labor was becoming part of Roosevelt's indispensable electoral base. The Great Depression in this sense marked a sharp break with the Progressive tradition, moving the center of gravity in the reform coalition away from the professional and other middle classes and toward the working class.[24] By 1936 Altmeyer, speaking to labor from the Social Security Board, was already rewriting AFL history, finding quotations from Gompers that made him out to have been in favor of some welfare programs.[25]

But the AFL's blessing was less influential in passing Social Security than were new forms of workers' militance developing outside the AFL. Although the culmination of this movement—the creation of the CIO—took place later, after Social Security was passed, it had been visible since the beginning of the decade: a militant, uncontrolled, erratic, powerful labor movement. Steel workers, auto workers, movie actors, newspaper reporters, migrant farm workers, miners, clothing workers, store clerks, tenant farmers, teamsters, and longshoremen were highly mobilized by 1934. Union-organizing struggles took place in industrial and commercial cities, in rural California, in the mountain valley mining towns. AFL leaders themselves referred to it as the "uprising." In 1935, as the Social Security Bill moved slowly along the congressional belt, this mass movement became even more widespread, and the CIO secession was underway.

These organizing drives did not directly make "political" demands—that is, demands on the state—but they were quickly learning to rely on the state, dependent as they were on the National Industrial Recovery Act of 1933 and then the Wagner Act of 1935, which guaranteed to workers a right to organize. Moreover, if the struggles were not explicitly aimed at welfare, they were very much directed at the redistribution of wealth.[26]

=

Other members of the working class, ignored by the unions and the union drives because they had no jobs, were participating in another militant social movement—that of the unemployed. Often organized by Communists and Socialists,[27] unemployed councils in many locations were creating new forms of protest. The councils were more effective at resolving individual grievances than at developing enduring organization, but they made a lot of noise through demonstrations and prevention of evictions. When evictions were scheduled, they would block the sheriff's entrance, return the furniture to the house, reconnect gas and electricity, and then pack the courts to pressure judges on behalf of the ousted tenants. In Chicago one council would put a sticker on the door of an apartment where they had moved a family back in after an eviction: "This furniture was moved back by Local 23 of the Unemployed Council."[28] To protest relief cutbacks they held sit-ins in relief bureaus.

Membership in the unemployed councils was rarely stable but estimates range from 100,000 in 1933 to 450,000 in 1935.[29] Particularly remarkable was the widespread racial integration in these actions, based of course on the disproportionate unemployment among blacks. (In Harlem, for example, unemployment reached 60 percent by 1933.) Just as striking, if less novel, was the participation of women, including those not technically "unemployed" because their previous work had not been consistent enough, well paid enough, or full-time enough to make them considered employed.[30] Sometimes the groups were ad hoc, but sometimes they were citywide, stable organization, involved middle-class people, and developed full platforms. The Baltimore People's Unemployment League, for example, forced the reluctant AFL group, known for its antiradicalism, to join it in a Citizens' Alliance for Social Security.[31] In 1931 critic Edmund Wilson reported that the councils had virtually stopped all evictions in Detroit.[32]

These groups, by contrast with unions, focused primarily on welfare issues. In attempting to bring collective force to bear on individual grievances, they frequently confronted caseworkers directly. Many caseworkers sympathized, and many others got the message. The councils also agitated for more relief and for more equitable, less humiliating relief procedures.

They were the first groups to organize on a mass scale for unemployment insurance, by which what they meant some system that would help those who were *already* unemployed, a need the Social Security unemployment program never did fill.[33]

The demands of the unemployed groups circled back to affect the labor movement. Many of the unemployed activists came from unions and/or went into the CIO[34]—hardly surprising when, in 1935, 26 percent of AFL members were unemployed. *The Rank and File Federationist*, newsletter of AFL dissidents from 1933 to 1935, had welfare first on its list of demands and consistently attacked AFL leaders for their failure to push for better welfare programs.[35] The militant spirit of the unemployed councils sometimes took over unions themselves. In Baltimore, for example, in 1934 the Marine Workers Industrial Union, furious at the "grafters" and "hypocritical tyrants" who were not providing adequate relief, seized control of relief administration from the FERA agency; an elected committee of union members ran the program, offering relief to strikers in the process.[36]

But unemployed-council welfarism, reflecting its union orientation rather than the interests of its many female participants, was male in its assumptions: Its priority was insurance for the unemployed, not for women doing unpaid domestic labor. Indeed, despite the greater militance of the unemployed councils as a whole and of their considerable female membership in particular, they ultimately reinforced a view of workers as male family heads, and of the needs of the poor as restoration of male employment.

=

The closest thing to a pressure group for poor single mothers was organized social work. Professional organizations like the American Association of Social Workers played an important role in a chain of communication, allowing clients' wants, first transmitted to caseworkers and then to their supervisors, to reach a larger public.[37] The AASW and the annual National Conference of Social Work became the country's major organizational spokespeople for federal welfare. In 1929 only a minority of social workers favored federal relief; by 1932 a majority, including even the more conservative Family Welfare Association, called for it; and by 1935, when FDR announced that the federal government would "quit this business of relief," there was a mass social work outcry.[38] Groups and individuals from all parts of social work cried out. "DON'T DO IT MR. HOPKINS!" was the headline over Edith Abbott's article of protest in *The Nation*.[39] The AASW demanded non-means-tested work relief for all the unemployed at prevailing wage rates; federal standards for public assistance including provision for medical care; universal rather than categorical assistance under a single federal agency. In the fall of 1935 many AASW chapters held protest meetings about the ending of FERA and the resultant suffering. Critics included even such establishment figures as Joanna Colcord of the Russell Sage Foundation and Solomon Lowenstein, executive director of the New York Federation of Jewish Philanthropies.[40] The American Public Welfare Association, representing mainly state and local welfare officials, joined the clamor, accusing the administration of imposing "a starvation scale" of relief. While social workers of various political tendencies had criticized relief as a weak substitute for long-range services, the profession was unified, and loud, in its condemnation of the FERA cutoff. The timing of the protest was advantageous because it occurred just as Roosevelt was trying to mobilize public pressure to get his Social Security Act through Congress.

The background to this outcry, and one of the factors that amplified it, was the development of an organized Left within social work. The Left social work caucus created such an expansive and militant political network that it was in itself a social movement. Known as the rank-and-file movement, it was in large part a union-organizing drive. Its members struggled to maintain wages and working conditions for social workers as caseloads soared and agency resources shrank. The movement criticized the professional orientation of social work, particularly its casework emphasis, arguing for a social work that was simultaneously an advocate for social change. As one spokesperson put it, social workers must be involved in struggles for "better housing, protection of the rights of free speech, the right to organize and the right to social security on an adequate level. . . . Social workers cannot escape . . . reality by . . . drugging themselves with techniques."[41]

The context of this movement was a rapidly expanding profession. One observer estimated that there were 150,000 full-time employed social workers in 1939, and public-sector social workers alone grew in number from 31,000 in 1930 to 70,000 in 1940.[42] Meanwhile social work had become more stratified and disunified than it had been in 1920. One stratum included specialized, college-educated workers, such as those specializing in psychiatric casework. The powerful Russell Sage Foundation subsidized this tendency, distributing $5.8 million between 1907 and 1931 to private agencies working on scientific charity and casework models.[43] Yet this was not the status of most social workers; as late as 1925, sixty percent had no more than a high school education, and only one-third had any social work training at all.[44] Moreover, the professionally trained cadre shrank during the depression as private agencies were forced to constrict because of reduced budgets.[45]

The different strata of social workers were inclined toward different politics: The more elite, usually found in private agencies, were likely to be Republican Protestants from relatively privileged backgrounds; the public-sector social workers generally had less formal education and included more Catholic and Jewish Democrats from modest, often working-class or immigrant backgrounds. Meanwhile the role of volunteer social workers diminished. The settlements declined, in the less altruistic mood of the 1920s, because of their frequent association with radical causes and bottom-up movements, and because the newer volunteers came from less-privileged backgrounds and brought in fewer resources.[46] The old-guard professionals were alarmed and threatened by the rapid influx of untrained workers in the depression: "We have seen social work diluted by . . . inexperienced and untrained persons; . . . disastrous as it is that so many millions . . . have been forced to accept relief . . . it would be even more disastrous if . . . the relief . . . were to be left in the hands of those who have acquired little or no social work knowledge or skill;" "These hundreds of emergency workers should be helped to realize that . . . they have no place in the [future] social work picture."[47] Such attitudes were on a collision course with the new breed of social workers who not only intended to make a future for themselves in social work but did not consider themselves apprentices. The combination of their own upward mobility, the economic hardships they saw all around them, and their disinclination to identify with elites made them a militant and radical group.

Mary Van Kleeck's 1934 speech was a kickoff event for the rank-and-file movement. Social work by this time had three political camps: the profession had been pushed so far to the Left that the *conservatives* were those who gave full support to the New Deal; the center offered critical support; and the Left demanded radical measures of redistribution. Even the centrists wanted something far more ambitious than Social Security. Social work "has had enough of patching up," charged the executive secretary of the Hartford Council of Social Agencies. "Henceforth, the central purpose of social work is going to be the development of a social order in which every honest and industrious citizen will be forever freed from the menacing shadow of economic insecurity."[48] In 1933 the NCSW presidential address, delivered by Frank Bruno, redefined pauperization in the service of social reform: No longer were paupers created primarily by too-easy handouts, the older social work anxiety. Rather, "It was the experience of defeat, the emotional frustration, the unrewarded effort . . . to gain a foothold upon the slippery industrial banks, which finally broke their spirit. . . . And as if that were not enough, we have erected . . . a condition of eligibility for relief which still further convinces them that struggle is useless."[49]

The movement Van Kleeck helped detonate defined much of the social work discourse for the next decade. These left-wing social workers never created a stable national organization but remained a movement. (Their journal, *Social Work Today*, had a peak circulation of six thousand, compared to *Survey*'s twenty-five thousand.) Still, their militancy frequently won support from many more cautious social workers. Initiated by the Social Workers' Discussion Club of New York in 1931, the movement held its first national convention in February 1935 and set up a National Coordinating Committee. Like the rest of social work, it was female-dominated—but the rank-and-file movement had more women in leadership than did the mainstream organizations. By 1935 there were social work unions in seventeen major cities with a combined membership of 8,200 as compared to the AASW's 8,600; by 1938, 14,500 belonged to the social work union, as compared to the 10,500 in the AASW.[50]

Rank-and-file social workers' low wages and poor working conditions tended to make them identify with their clients. The radical social workers' antiprofessionalism was not a denial of the need for high standards of treatment of clients but rather a critique of casework technique as condescending, controlling, and disrespectful towards clients. Caseworkers resisted enforcing means-testing investigations and forcing relief clients to divest themselves of all resources. Even Gertrude Springer in her personal and professional advice column for caseworkers in *Survey* began to denounce these practices. "Are Relief Workers Policemen?" she asked, answering in the negative; in "When a Client Has a Car," she didn't see why she or he should give it up.[51]

The radicals saw "professionalism" as an excuse for not working with clients to achieve social change. Some social workers, especially relief caseworkers, did begin to make common cause with their clients. The much-publicized case of Sidonia Dawson, a New York City relief casework supervisor, offers a particularly militant example. In September 1934 a delegation from an unemployed council visited her relief bureau to register complaints. They pushed into the waiting room and were forcibly ejected by the police. The next day Dawson joined a demonstration of approximately one hundred relief workers at the central relief office denouncing police brutality. She gave a public speech charging discrimination, indifference, and callousness toward relief clients. She was fired. This stimulated more protests, and ultimately a social work committee of inquiry investigated for the Executive Council of the New York AASW. This body issued a fence-sitting report, neither condemning Dawson nor calling for her reinstatement either—which produced yet more resistance. As the inquiry noted, the case was "repeatedly matched in various large cities."[52] Dawson's behavior could be placed on a continuum with settlement work, which had two decades earlier been central to the women's social work network. Carrying on that tradition, Helen Hall challenged social workers at the NCSW to organize clients to work for social change.[53] But unlike Hall, most of the new social work militants were too young to have been inheritors of the settlement tradition (which had paled by the 1930s); they were reinventing forms of direct action with beliefs quite different from those of the settlement tradition—seeking not social peace, but fundamental redistribution of resources through mass mobilization and social conflict.

The social work rank-and-file movement's militance peaked by 1936 and then declined rather quickly, as its members became exhausted, defensive of the little they were able to give as social workers, and grateful, too, for the jobs they had. But at its peak it was able to influence the Social Security Act and the 1936 elections. The social work shift leftward pushed the social work leadership to a more progressive stance and contributed to the overall pressure for welfare and redistribution, and for an end to the invasive, humiliating practices of old poor relief.

But the social work Left did not break with the family norms that dominated the union movement. Social work had been changed by the decline of feminism. The younger generation—those not part of Progressive Era social feminism—tended to be suspicious of feminism as a middle-class tendency that was out of touch with the needs of the poor. Moreover, social work was a predominantly urban and white operation. Few at the conventions worked with sharecroppers or migrant workers; few were people of color. There was probably more antiracist, prowoman sentiment in social work than in any other profession at the time, and relief caseworkers denounced the exclusion and unfair treatment of women and minority men. But social work leaders were not influenced by any thinking that challenged the norm of women's dependence on husbands. Nor were they thinking about how to make sure that a new welfare state would include everyone in its reach.

—

The labor and social work agitation of the depression was explicitly left of center. The movements that focused most directly on welfare, and that more immediately threatened Roosevelt and the Congress, defy any easy Right-Left categorization. These "welfare populisms" cohered around welfare proposals but were more influential as inchoate social movements than as articulations of specific alternative proposals. The populist label fits these movements only partially; they were not exclusively agrarian, and their leaders did not all have direct roots in populism.[54] They all used the typically populist rhetoric of attacks on big business but without a Marxian class analysis; their key social categories were big against small, parasites against producers.[55] And they shared with populism the belief that not having enough money in circulation was the basis of the country's economic problems, to which they offered inflationary solutions: some called it "money radicalism."[56]

The first groups to take organized, direct action for federal government relief from the depression were farmers. By the 1930s the agricultural depression was already a decade old. In the 1920s the average value of a farm had dropped 25 percent—more in the Midwest, due to falling produce prices and rising transportation costs—while farmers' indebtedness and tax burdens had grown sharply.[57] Half the midwestern farms were threatened with foreclosure by late 1932.

Farmers in the three most common United States agricultural positions—sharecroppers in the South, wage workers in western agribusiness, and farm owners in the Midwest—were all becoming demonstrative. In California ten major strikes took place between 1930 and 1932; in 1933 there were thirty-seven strikes, including the largest agricultural strike in U.S. history, involving eighteen thousand workers. In the South the sharecroppers' and tenant farmers' unions were so threatening that planters responded with "slave law, mob violence, and Fascist methods," according to the *New York Post*; a U.S. Department of Labor study called it a "miniature civil war."[58]

Less repression could be mounted against the midwestern activism of farm owners who directly confronted banks and agribusiness. The legacy of the populist call for federal government intervention against banks was alive here, nurtured by the successful Farmer-Labor parties. Bankruptcies, increasing as a result of steep price declines in 1930, stimulated local, spontaneous direct action as farmers stopped auctions, held "penny sales" in which farmers repurchased their property for very low amounts, and blockaded roads. Milk was dumped on highways, poured into ditches, or distributed free. Farmers made a mighty local impact and learned that direct action paid off.[59] The demand for federal relief, particularly against mortgage foreclosures, grew rapidly.

By summer 1932, with wheat selling at thirty cents a bushel (down from three dollars in 1920), the Farm Holiday Association was born in the Midwest, its slogan patterned after the closing of the banks known as the bank holiday. Its leaders derived directly from populism.[60] The "Holidayers" demanded federal agricultural relief or else, threatening to keep produce from the market until prices rose.[61] Their direct action created a virtual moratorium on foreclosures from the Rockies to the Appalachians by the winter of 1932–33. Midwestern capitols were besieged by thousands of farmer demonstrators. The Farm Holiday group claimed to represent over one million farmers and had put together a program designed to build coalitions with other groups, a program including federal operation of banks, a sharply progressive income tax, veterans' bonuses, and relief for the urban unemployed. In May 1933 a "Continental Congress" of workers and farmers, sparked by the midwestern "Holiday" group, demanded immediate agricultural relief and called a farm strike to begin October 21. An Agriculture Department historian believed that midwestern farmers were at this time "nearer armed revolt than that any group had been since the Whiskey Rebellion of 1794."[62]

Roosevelt headed off the strike by his capacity for quick, decisive, experimental action. On October 22 in a radio "fireside chat" he announced that the Reconstruction Finance Corporation would inflate the currency through buying gold, and that the Agriculture Department would furnish loans on stored grain. In fact he had been working to avert this strike earlier by rushing through the Agricultural Adjustment Act in May, the Farm Credit Act in June, and the Commodity Credit Corporation in October, which collectively helped farmers refinance mortgages, subsidized crop limitation, provided loans secured by crops, and promised inflation through devaluation of gold and free coinage of silver. In other words Roosevelt offered much of what the midwestern farmers' movements were demanding (although the inflationary promise was never fulfilled). "USDA checks were descending on the land in a gentle, pervasive rain, damping the prairie fire."[63] The success of the Holidayers in getting federal help by means of disruptions was widely publicized, influencing the tactics and goals of other welfare activisms.

Simultaneously the first of a series of movements for old-age pensions arose in California. The most famous of these programs was that named for its founder, Townsend, but in fact they were numerous: the General Welfare Federation Plan, the San Diego Income Idea, the National Annuity League, the American Pension Union, the Ham and Egges [sic] movement, the McLain movement, to name but a few.[64] These movements not only fostered the general demand for federal government help but also created an extraordinary and long-lasting shift in definitions of entitlement, making of the elderly a group quintessentially deserving of that help. The movements have generally been labeled crazy, absurd, and even unethical and dangerous by contemporary opponents and by historians[65]—harsh judgments focused partly on their inflationary aspects, something they shared with the midwestern farmers' movements. The emphasis on condemnation has prevented historians from registering fully their influence on Social Security in particular and attitudes toward government provision in general.

Demand for government old-age pensions had been gathering strength before the depression. Even the AFL endorsed state pensions in 1929. Eight states had enacted programs in the 1920s, and then, with the depression, more than a hundred state bills were introduced in the 1930–31 congressional year.[66] Starting early in the Roosevelt administration, however, this developing pattern became a mass movement.[67]

In 1933 Christian socialist Upton Sinclair drafted a program for a group of Los Angeles liberal Democrats that was to propel the state, and the national Democratic party, into a political crisis. Sinclair's plan, to be known as EPIC (End Poverty in California), had multiple parts—it was no single-tax panacea. It called for making the million-plus people on relief self-sufficient by establishing them on unused land to farm, or in idle factories to be operated at public expense. These people would then engage in a statewide barter system using scrip instead of money. The plan included a $300 million bond issue and a progressive tax reform as well as a land tax. And it offered an old-age pension of fifty dollars a month to all the needy over sixty.[68]

EPIC seized control of the California Democratic party, in part because it was already split, and Sinclair's plan was inserted into the party platform. Sinclair himself became an effective campaigner. But the main reason for EPIC's popularity, possibly not understood by Sinclair himself, was the backing of the elderly. He was defeated because of an expensive Republican smear campaign, the first modern election won by professional men.[69] His supporters might even have withstood that onslaught of misinformation—for example, that Sinclair was an epileptic, a communist, an atheist, and a "free lover"—had it not been for Sinclair's own decision to downplay his call for pensions because Roosevelt had promised to recommend a federal old-age pension law.[70] By contrast his opponent, Frank Merriam, endorsed virtually every pension program, no matter how practical or impractical, while Sinclair tried to explain what was wrong with them. Sinclair lost with 37 percent (880,000 votes) to Merriam's 48 percent (1,140,000), although several other EPIC candidates did better, notably Sheridan Downey, who had endorsed the Townsend plan.[71]

EPIC's performance shook up California politics; its successor movement, that of Francis Townsend, had an equivalent effect nationally. An elderly physician who had worked as teamster, schoolteacher, miner and ranch hand, once in California he practiced both medicine and real estate sales. In other words, he combined the social idealism and entrepreneurialism that has often characterized American reform. Unlike EPIC, which had socialist or at least left-wing identification, Townsend was quite conservative. And unlike EPIC, his plan was directed only to the elderly: Every nonemployed person over sixty without a criminal record was to receive a pension of two hundred dollars every month—twice the average wage at the time—provided the entire previous payment had been spent within thirty days. It intended to provide relief to the elderly, to stimulate consumption, and to reduce unemployment by encouraging those over sixty to retire.[72] Townsend's plan was classically populist in its proposal to increase the amount of money in circulation. It also had a typically populist combination of radicalism and conservatism: democratic in its universal inclusion of all over sixty, regardless of need or occupation, its financing provisions were extremely regressive, based on a transaction or sales tax, and it proposed to abolish all other federal relief.[73]

Townsend was equally ambiguous in its gender implications. The plan included all women, employed or not, compared to the one in six who qualified for Social Security pensions. In doing so it recognized non–wage-earning labor, such as housework and parenting, as a contribution to society meriting a pension. And it offered women equal pensions, as opposed to the Social Security plan, which tied pensions and contributions to earnings and therefore perpetuated the effects of women's low wages. Townsend literature emphasized the discriminatory aspects of Social Security. Townsend's plan undercut the family-wage system by providing older women with their own pensions, thereby subverting their dependence on husbands, although it is not clear that Townsend followers had considered the potential of women's economic independence to erode masculine authority. These woman-friendly provisions may have been responsible for attracting a striking participation by women, but they played typically subordinate roles, usually in auxiliaries. And the explicit gender ideology of the movement remained essentially conservative. In its leaflets and brochures, elderly women were pictured always on the arms of men, always white, while young women alone with children represented what was wrong with the New Deal's palliative relief system.[74] And Townsend's reckless insistence that old-age pensions would eliminate the need for all other relief would have been detrimental to women and particularly to single mothers.

Townsend's size and growth rate were spectacular. There are uncertain and conflicting claims about its size, from one million members and five million adherents, to 3.5 million members and 30 million petition signers. At one point Townsend claimed seven thousand clubs.[75] In 1934 Townsend threatened the "Biggest Mass Meeting Ever Held in All the World"—a call to its supporters to organize simultaneous meetings throughout the United States on a Sunday afternoon shortly before Election Day.[76] The electoral clout of this cause had already been demonstrated in California by EPIC. The Townsend plan was introduced into the House for the first time in January 1935 by California Democrat John McGroarty. In the hearings, conducted by a hostile Ways and Means Committee, the administration denounced it. Perkins called it "a fantastic dole," Hopkins called it "cock-eyed" and dependent on "miracles," and Witte euphemistically Red-baited it ("not within the structure of our present economic or governmental system").[77] The private papers of the administration's welfare specialists leave no doubt as to their fear. Edwin Witte wrote in 1935: "Regarding the Townsend plan, I run into Townsendites wherever I speak. Frankly, I fear that the Townsendites will decide the next presidential election, putting into office again the most extreme conservative interests. . . . It is truly remarkable that a movement of this kind, which would surely mean the end of our present economic system, has reached such proportions."[78] Witte and his staff kept up a large correspondence attacking Townsend, including letters to newspapers. He tried to convince the Post Office Department to indict the leaders of Townsend and other pension movements for mail fraud because they solicited donations and/or charged a fee for their literature.[79] All told, many hours went into studying and damning this proposal.[80]

Townsend, ironically, helped get Social Security passed.[81] A 1936 poll showed that 56 percent of Americans favored the Townsend plan.[82] Congress was deluged with letters, telegrams, and petitions for Townsend in 1935, communications that "terrified representatives and drove senators to distraction," reported Richard Neuberger, later a Democratic senator from Oregon.

The messages demanding passage of the Soldiers' Bonus . . . were mere rivulets compared with the [Townsend] torrent. . . . These letters at the start took the form of pleas and requests, but later they became outright threats. And after a member of the state legislature of Oregon had been re-called by an overwhelming majority for voting against a memorial favoring the Townsend Plan, shivers began to travel along Congressional spines.

Rexford Tugwell later observed that Roosevelt "knew that the 'movements'—like EPIC in California—however irresponsible and unrealistic, came out of a deep source." Witte believed that the Townsend movement weakened the cause of Social Security by building the vote for more radical programs, but he was mistaken. Contemporary observers as well as later historians were sure about the ultimately positive impact of Townsend on Roosevelt's bill—par-ticularly, as Paul Douglas put it, in "obtain[ing] support for the idea in quarters which would have been unaffected by more soberly drafted proposals."[83] Frank Bane of the Social Security Board, remi-niscing thirty years later, felt that "we had two great allies that were helping us put Social Security legislation through. They were far more important, I think, on the Hill, than any of us were. Those two were a gentleman by the name of Dr. Townsend, and the second one by the name of Huey Long."[84]

From a different geographical base, in the southern states, the Share Our Wealth (SOW) program of flamboyant populist Louisiana senator Huey Long extended to the creation of a comprehensive welfare state. Long broadcast his plan for the first time on the radio in February 1934, although he had been enunciating much of it in the Senate since 1932. It called for:

1. a homestead allowance of three to five thousand dollars (multiply by 10 to get the value in 1990 dollars), including a home, an auto-mobile, and a radio;
2. a minimum guaranteed annual family income of two to three thousand dollars or one-third the average U.S. family income, with no income to be larger than one hundred to three hundred times this—that is, none above six hundred thousand dollars to $1.8 million;
3. regulation of working hours to balance production with consump-tion, sometimes specified at thirty hours a week and eleven months a year;

4. pensions to all over sixty, sometimes specified at thirty dollars a month;
5. government purchase and storage of agricultural surpluses, to be held until needed to maintain prices;
6. veterans' bonuses paid in cash;
7. universal free education to all those qualified, including free schoolbooks, and college education for some boys (Long promised to create one thousand new colleges);
8. drastic taxation of income and inheritance; and
9. public works whenever necessary.

Later he promised a job to every American man, the election of the secretary of agriculture by farmers, a pardon for anyone caught stealing food, and a federal program against disease, insanity, and drug addiction. And no one earning less than one million dollars would pay taxes.[85]

Long openly defended redistribution as the only means to improve the welfare of those on the bottom, since he believed the nation's resources to be finite and its economy a zero-sum game. His statistics were extremely outmoded or fabricated. Huey's son, Senator Russell Long, described the plan's redistributive impact as "for one-third of the nation's money to be divided among all the people, [although] the other two-thirds [had been] captured by the upper one percent."[86] Nevertheless, the plan was denounced as socialistic. Eager to defend himself, Long agreed to debate American Socialist party leader Norman Thomas; at an event in New York City that drew an audience of 2,500, Long sought to distinguish himself from the "Reds" (read: intellectuals) by his bellicose, rustic, and uncouth style. Yet one astute observer noticed that when analyzing his SOW proposal he talked like a college professor.[87]

The Share Our Wealth scheme was more sharply attacked from the Left than from the Right. Thomas understood himself to be debating a serious rival. The Communists were particularly nervous because their strategy involved riding on and leading what they believed would be a mass movement to the left of Roosevelt; Long threatened to lead it himself, in what they feared was a fascist direction.[88]

The Share Our Wealth movement expanded in much the same way as Townsend—by the formation of local clubs, and it only took two people to start one. Clubs met in homes, churches, lodge halls.

They arose in response to Long's radio broadcasts; after each one he received on average sixty thousand letters through the club networks and another sixty thousand at his Senate office. The Long machine claimed 200,000 members within one month and 20,000 more joining daily. It claimed 3 million by the ends of 1934 and even more spectacular growth in 1935—27,431 clubs with 4,684,000 members and 7,682,768 on the mailing list. (One wonders, of course, how these were counted.) In January 1935 the SOW movement claimed 12 million followers, while a critical historian credits it with 7.5 million. Long's volume of mail rivaled that of Roosevelt himself; by mid-1934 he was receiving more mail than all other senators combined. It was said that two trucks delivered mail to the U.S. Senate, one for Long and one for everyone else. His following was not confined to the South but was considerable in the Midwest and the mid-Atlantic states as well.[89]

Long's welfare program, combined with his decision not to mount a specifically racist appeal, attracted even blacks to the SOW cause.[90] Black Louisiana politicians claimed that 90 percent of blacks would back Long if they were enfranchised. However, although Long refrained from the virulent race-baiting that so many southern politicians engaged in, he did nothing to encourage black voting. When he was elected in 1928, 2,054 of Louisiana Blacks, or 0.5 percent, were registered to vote; by 1936 black registration had declined to 0.3 percent.[91] Moreover, Gerald L. K. Smith, later to become a leading anti-Semite and Nazi sympathizer, became Long's chief lieutenant. A minister who attracted fundamentalists and combined the Share Our Wealth promises with Jesus, racism, and patriotism, Smith increased Long's appeal. As a social movement Share Our Wealth was not democratic, intensely participatory, or persevering, but it was indeed a mass movement.

Roosevelt considered Long a direct electoral threat. Anticipating the 1936 election, the Democratic Party had a secret poll taken of Long's strength in early 1935, which predicted that he could take 3–4 million votes on a third-party ticket; Roosevelt feared that "Huey" could do what Theodore Roosevelt had done to Republican president William Howard Taft in 1912—split the party.[92] By April 1935 FDR's advisers expected Long to defeat two of the most powerful men in the Senate, upon whom Roosevelt relied heavily, Pat Harrison of Mississippi and Joseph Robinson of Arkansas. Long threatened to be "political master" of the whole Lower Mississippi Valley. Then, in May 1935, Long moved to challenge the president from his position in Congress. Long denounced the president's opposition to the Pat-man veterans' bonus bill, demanding a congressional override when it was vetoed. When FDR requested permission to read a message to a joint congressional session to explain his veto, Long filibustered to try to keep the president from using this political platform. FDR won by a bare majority, with forty eight senators abstaining.[93]

The presidential initiative most associated with the New Deal's "turn to the Left" of 1935 was a direct response to Long and the similar "welfare populist" movements: the June tax bill calling for heavy inheritance taxes, a sharp increase in income tax on those earning more than fifty thousand dollars, and graduated taxes on corporate income and surplus. Senator Paul Douglas credited Huey Long's movement with converting the president to the use of federal power to build a welfare state.[94] In Will Rogers's words, "I would sure liked to have seen Huey's face when he was woke up in the middle of the night by the President, who said, 'Lay over, Huey, I want to get in bed with you.'"[95]

Paired with Long as a powerful antidemocratic force during the depression was Detroit Catholic priest Charles Coughlin, the first major radio preacher to whom an estimated 30 million people listened each Sunday. Coughlin, too, had a welfare program at the core of the platform of his organization, the National Union for Social Justice. It was less comprehensive and consistent than Long's, but he took it seriously: He reportedly hired students at the Brookings Institution for as much as four hundred dollars each to write papers on economic matters.[96] Like the populists, he was primarily concerned with monetary issues. He called for abolition of the Federal Reserve system and establishment of a government-owned Central Bank, printing greenbacks and remonetizing silver. His commitment to decentralization was little more than rhetorical. Although Coughlin condemned big government he sought support from an urban, working-class constituency and called for a large and potentially permanent public works program that would provide a minimum wage of fifteen hundred dollars a year to anyone not working in private industry. But Coughlin's overall political leanings were more clearly to the Right than Long's. For example, although he frequently claimed to be pro-union—a virtual necessity in Detroit in the 1930s—he consistently preferred company unions and threw his weight behind a rival to the UAW; and he drew working-class support only from the elite of more skilled and conservative workingmen.[97]

As with Townsend and Long, the numbers and intensity of Coughlin's admirers were awesome. He produced and mailed millions of copies of his weekly sermons from his own press. Searching for possible indictments, Postmaster General Farley reported to the president in early 1935 that Coughlin had cashed more than $4 million in money orders in twenty months. Receiving more mail than any contemporary, he had a stenographic staff of 145. The basement of his office "looked like a modern post office for a middle-sized city."[98] Coughlin claimed to have National Union for Social Justice groups in 302 of the 435 congressional districts.[99]

The three populist groupings making prominent welfare demands—Coughlin's, Long's, and Townsend's—came close to joining a third-party effort to rout Roosevelt in 1936. A circle mainly composed of eastern intellectuals, continuing the Progressive tradition, organized a League for Independent Political Action (LIPA) to offer an alternative to the capitalist parties. Welfare demands were a central part of its program, including workers' insurance, old-age pensions, public works, and direct relief to be funded by taxes on the wealthy. In 1932 the League and the Socialist party began to work out an alliance. Farmer-Labor parties held majorities in Minnesota and Wisconsin legislatures, and LIPA for a time negotiated with these for a merger. Their presidential candidate of choice, Republican Congressman William Lemke of North Dakota, seemed for a time able to attract Long, Townsend, and Coughlin as well. Had these groups consistently thrown their votes to a national third party, Roosevelt would have faced a serious challenge. But in May 1932 the Minnesota Farmer-Labor party defected to Roosevelt, and the Socialist party decided to run Norman Thomas, thus foreclosing the league's hopes for that election. Long's assassination in September 1935 ended that particular threat.[100]

Even without this direct electoral challenge, populist pressure on Roosevelt remained strong. In January 1935 press coverage of the administration's Social Security proposal presented it as a response to the demands of the Townsend and Long movements, and the issue of *Newsweek* that covered the story had Townsend on the cover.[101] The Townsend movement in particular not only pressured Congress to pass Social Security but also saw that old-age pensions were a major part of its content and formed the basis for a powerful, ongoing lobby of the elderly that kept old-age pensions politically inviolable. Raymond Moley, member of FDR's "brain trust," considered Long's strength one of six key factors that led to the "Second New Deal," recollecting how Roosevelt spoke of his plans to "steal Long's thunder.[102]

The popularity of these "welfare populists" is evidence that demands for government provision do not inevitably fall on the liberal or democratic end of the political continuum.[103] None of these "populist" welfare programs improved on the administration's with respect to including racial minorities, none covered the particular needs of women, none addressed the critical need for some kind of health insurance. Only the Left took on these challenges.

=

Among the third parties that challenged Democratic control were the Socialist and Communist parties. The Communist party had developed great strength and influence by the time Social Security deliberations were under way in 1934–35. This period also coincided with the Communist switch to a popular-front strategy, impelled by the rise of fascism and the German threat to the Soviet Union, involving alliances with liberals and appeals to American nationalism and pragmatism. Thus the Left augmented its challenge to the New Deal precisely when welfare was central to the domestic political agenda. Both Socialists and Communists had their own welfare platforms.

In the 1920s, the Socialist party was a mere skeleton of its former self. The appearance of prosperity had seemed to refute Marxist claims of the decline of capitalism, and the death in 1926 of Eugene V. Debs, leader of American socialism for thirty years, deprived the party of a popular political and moral leader. Yet at the outbreak of the depression it still had its own press as well as access to the liberal press. More importantly, it had produced a leader to replace Debs. Norman Thomas had moved from Progressivism to the Democratic party to socialism; the sources of his socialism were Christian and pacifist, not Marxist. An eloquent speaker, with charisma both in person and on paper, he appealed very effectively to intellectuals but much less strongly to the working class, becoming still less effective as workers grew more active and more militant. In 1932 he drew 885,000 votes, in 1936 only 187,000.[104] Throughout the depression Socialist party membership never exceeded 21,000.

The Communist party had also been small in the 1920s, its membership estimated as low as 7,500 and as high as 13,000.[105] During the 1930s Communist party membership and popularity increased immensely, influenced by the severity of the depression and the inadequacy of government response, and by its call for resistance to Nazi Germany and other fascist forces. By 1934 membership was around 23,000–26,000; it reached 80,000 by 1944. More significant than membership—never a good indicator of political party strength in the United States—was its ability to command support for its initiatives and ideas and the high level of activism among its members.[106] One historian calculated that in Chicago Communists openly led, organized, or participated in 2,088 mass demonstrations in the first five years of the depression.[107]

Above all the Communist party and the entire Left gained legitimacy in the depression and World War II. More Americans than ever before, even those who disagreed sharply, saw the Left as articulating an honorable political perspective that was entitled to expression. Other radical groups, such as Trotskyists and radical pacifists, also grew, and often made working alliances with the Communist party. Among Catholics there arose a strong movement to the left of the New Deal. It included not only the radical Catholic Worker movement but also broader-based campaigns for social welfare, motivated by the church's efforts to retain the loyalty of the Catholic working class.[108]

The Communist party gained strength as a result of its relief and welfare agitation. For example, in Alabama in 1931 an openly Communist group started calling for free coal and carfare, work relief, free school lunches, and free utilities for the unemployed. Party members, mainly women, also sustained neighborhood relief committees, protesting the racist and otherwise disrespectful behavior of relief agents towards clients. Nationally both the Communist and Socialist parties articulated a shared critique of the New Deal. They criticized the puny amounts of relief, its humiliating conditions, and its use as political patronage; and they decried it as a device to shore up capitalism rather than alter the fundamental distribution of power and wealth.[110] Both groups put foward welfare proposals of their own.

The Socialist party's relief proposals, prominently featured in Norman Thomas's speeches, were not only more generous and more ambitious than Roosevelt's but also more innovative. When in 1932 Thomas called for $5 billion in immediate federal relief and $5 billion more in public works, he anticipated exactly what FDR would do. A journalist imagined FDR saying to Thomas, "Well, Norman, you see we've taken some of your planks from you."[111] Thomas loved to discuss the many areas in which government could put labor to use in improving public life. He anticipated several later achievements: public works, improving highways in order to reduce traffic fatalities, better planning in lumbering in order to protect forests.[112] Best developed was the Socialist party's unemployment insurance plan, which called for government and employers to make equal contributions, unlike the AALL plan, which relied on employers' contributions only and called for supplements to the unemployed worker of 10 percent for a dependent wife and 5–10 percent for dependent children.[113] (The Socialist party plan, like most others, endorsed the family wage and concentrated on male welfare needs.)

Unlike most others, however, the Socialist party's welfare proposals did not separate welfare from the rest of a social and economic program. Its 1932 platform called for public works, public ownership of basic resources (such as minerals and forests) and utilities, socialization of the credit and currency system, steeply progressive taxation, and minimum-wage and maximum-hours laws. In such a context its social insurance program was relatively less important. Welfare was not so central in drawing people to the Socialist party as it was for Long, Townsend, or Coughlin.

Much more influential than the Socialist proposals was the Lundeen Bill, after Ernest Lundeen, the Minnesota Farmer-Labor Congressman who introduced it. This left-wing omnibus welfare proposal gathered considerable popularity just as Social Security was being drafted. Largely influenced by the Communist party in its popular-front modality, the bill's popularity in part reflected the new legitimacy the Communists had gained among the working class and middle-class intellectuals, African Americans notable among them. Support for Lundeen expressed in part a popular yearning for more government responsibility for the whole economy and for individuals' welfare.

Called the "Workers' Bill" by the Left, Lundeen first emerged in 1931 from the Communist-influenced unemployed councils. It provided for a federal system of "insurance" for involuntary unemployment due to sickness, accident, maternity, or old age, to be available to all categories of wage labor, with no one required to take scab jobs or to work for less than union wages. Despite the term "insurance," this program made no attempt to emulate insurance in its literal, actuarial meaning. The payments to citizens would be funded by a progressive tax on all incomes over five thousand dollars. The program would be administered by elected committees of workers. It seems likely that this early version of the bill was written by Communists.[114] It was promptly endorsed by Socialist and Trotskyist unemployed organizations as well and quickly began gathering support from unions. AFL leadership feared it could not stop the flow tide: "Now, what are we to do?" President Green wrote. "I do not know what we can do when the people are hungry. . . . We may have to face the situation some way and make a definite declaration because of the growing demand to do something."[115] A dissident AFL Committee for Unemployment Insurance and Social Security was organized early in 1932. Its energetic head, Louis Weinstock, toured the country in that year and spoke before three hundred unions. At the AFL 1932 convention he gave a five-minute speech hanging from a chandelier because the leadership had refused the recognize him. Union backing for the Workers' Bill grew steadily throughout 1933 and 1934 as Roosevelt did nothing. According to one supporter, the bill was eventually backed by several internationals, six state federations, numerous central labor councils, and several thousand locals.[116]

Meanwhile the bill began to gain favor outside the AFL. The Socialist party endorsed the Workers' Bill. Lundeen adherents claimed that seventy cities and counties, including Minneapolis, endorsed it. Many civic organizations promoted it, especially ethnic and other small mutual benefit societies (for example, the Russian Workers Club of Hamtramck, Michigan; the Polish Republic Society of Milwaukee; and eighteen Lithuanian organizations). In endorsing it, the Fraternal Federation for Social Insurance claimed 25,000 members.[117] And Lundeen had many middle-class champions, notably professionals and intellectuals; the liberal journal *The Nation* advocated it and called for the defeat of the Social Security Act, and the *New Republic* gave it equal billing with three other proposals, including Social Security.[118]

The Workers' Bill was intended to include blacks, the only welfare proposal of which this could be said, and black organizations responded accordingly. Some blacks prominent in speaking for it, such as Dr. Reuben Young of the League of Struggle for Negro Rights, or Ben Davis, editor of the *Negro Liberator*, were in or close to the Communist party, but by no means all. The bill gained the blessing of the Urban League. Its leader T. Arnold Hill pointed out, "there are no workers in America in such desperate need of social protection in the form of adequate unemployment insurance as the five million Negroes."[119]

The Workers' Bill took women's needs more seriously than did any other welfare proposal. The version introduced to Congress was in fact written by social feminist Mary Van Kleeck.[120] It offered fourteen weeks of unemployment compensation for maternity and support for any woman head of household with dependents. But there is no evidence of any autonomous women's interest in the bill, or any "gender gap" in its defense. At the 1934 congressional hearings Communist Ella Reeve Bloor, claiming to represent farm women, rather bravely argued not only for maternity help but also for birth control and aid for single mothers.[121] In 1935 the hearings devoted an entire session to the security needs of women. But all the national white women's organizations who had been active in welfare advocacy backed the administration, and the black women's organizations did not enter this debate.

A gauge of the prominence of the Lundeen Bill was the excitement and effort of its opposition. Ironically, while Lundeen supporters denounced the Long, Townsend, and Coughlin plans in much the same terms as the administration did, administration backers lumped Lundeen in with the others as a quack proposal. Opponents made fun of the bill's generality, not comprehending that its sweeping inclusion of all workers, employed or not, was precisely its point.[122] Generally two kinds of denunciations were made: It was too expensive and would bankrupt the country; and it was a Communist plot. An economist speaking for the bill figured that it would cost $5.8 billion. Alex Nordholm, an assistant to Witte, wrote a detailed report on the bill in which he reckoned the cost at $20 billion. Several opponents charged that financing it would require appropriating all available "surplus" or "cash" or necessitate an annual tax of 25 percent on corporate surpluses (this was understood to be unthinkable).[123] Nordholm calculated that even if the federal government used everything in its treasury and confiscated all individual and corporate net incomes over five thousand dollars and all inheritances and gifts, it would still fail to raise the cost of the program.[124] But these calculations came from political opponents. Lundeen supporters were ill equipped to respond, lacking a corps of economists and budget analysts.[125]

The charge that the Workers' Bill was a Communist plot was correct in that the Communist party was the main organizational force behind the bill and sponsored several of the key forums in which it was touted, such as the 1934 and 1935 Congresses on Unemployment. This is not to say that the Red-baiting used by opponents of Lundeen was accurate: Their logic was that anything Communist was ipso facto wrong, and that anyone that agreed with the Communists was dangerous, a dupe if not an agent.[126] While the Communist party, like all political groups, certainly used welfare agitation to gain support, those in need of relief also used the party's leadership and militance to gain help.[127] All the welfare proposals of the depression, not least the administration's, were similarly used. Indeed, many became Communists precisely because they were disturbed about poverty during the depression, and Communists certainly believed that socialism would include a generous welfare program. Witte's biographer, noting the extraordinary effort Witte poured into attacking Lundeen, characterized his defensive, dismissive response thus:

> Witte's argument was valid on technical grounds, but it concealed the fact that had he and his colleagues and Roosevelt chosen to support the bill's radical principle, they could have worked out the technical details. His emphasis on the measure's subversive support similarly obscured the main issue: whether the country did not need a radical redistribution of wealth, more consumption, and less capitalization. His attack was completely in character with his own technical and nontheoretical approach to legislative programs . . . it revealed how limited was his and his colleagues' conception of social insurance as a measure for basic economic reform."[128]

Lundeen, like the Long, Townsend, and Coughlin proposals, expressed a strain of Keynesianism. Aware that "actuarial insurance . . . applied to unemployment . . . breaks down when unemployment attains mass proportions," Van Kleeck also expected, as did most socialists, repeated and worsening economic crises. "Can the government and owners of wealth pay the bill? In effect . . . given so great a productive capacity that goods must be destroyed, it is a reasonable demand that the unemployed be given the purchasing power . . . in sufficient quantity to buy the goods produced." In 1935 the United States was a "closed economy," having retreated from world flows of finance and goods. Lundeen proposed an intense pump-priming through a higher social wage which, through purchases, would increase investment and jobs. Lundeen's defenders believed that that purchasing power could be provided so as to entail also a "redistribution of national income in proportion to the extent of unemployment . . . diverting funds from higher incomes to workers' purchases."[129]

But however thoughtful the plan, Lundeen's supporters did not believe their bill could be passed and thus had little incentive to figure out a practicable budgetary and administrative plan. As Van Kleeck put it, "The bill . . . in its present form may truly be said to be more of a declaration of principle and policy. . . . Its significance rests upon this different concept of social insurance, . . . to define the obligation of government and industry to compensate for losses through unemployment that is beyond the control of the workers, individually or collectively."[130]

A House Labor Committee subcommittee held hearings on the Lundeen Bill when it was introduced in 1934 and again in 1935. William Connery of Massachusetts, chair of the Labor Committee, and Emanuel Celler of New York, joined as cosponsors of the bill, and it was reported out of committee by a close vote, 7–6, in March 1935. It was killed by the Rules Committee, where the Democratic leaders were committed to support the administration bill.[131] In April, Lundeen tried to attach it to the Social Security Act as an amendment; no discussion was allowed and it got fifty-two votes in favor. Lundeen was optimistic, arguing that if he could get that many votes with no floor discussion his idea was gaining impetus, and he reintroduced the bill in 1936 and 1937. But by then the Social Security Board was successfully using its governmental powers to build support for its program.

There can be no doubt that Lundeen added to the pressure for an unemployment relief program. Although Witte worried that it might undercut backing for Social Security, the opposite opinion was more widespread—that it served to counter the force of Right-wing opposition to welfare provision.[132] But the ultimate influence of the Lundeen Bill was only quantitative, not qualitative. To most support ers it represented a Social Security Act that provided more money. The more significant aspects of its distinctiveness—its universality, its attentiveness to some of women's special needs—were rarely discussed, and its provision for administration by workers' and farmers' councils virtually ignored.

=

Despite the profusion of associations active in the New Deal, only a minority of people belonged. Most people never join organizations, let alone political ones. But informal political voices can also be forceful, and the nonjoiners are not necessarily politically passive. Their opinions, formed by the mutterings and exclamations of family members and friends as they hear the news or the president on the radio, by the nods of workmates over lunchtime talk and the remarks of women in grocery stores, by the shared complaints of those waiting in relief offices, are at times transformed into public collective action and speech.

This kind of public opinion cohered to form a pro-welfare political culture. Of course there can be no objective measurement of "public opinion," because it is so malleable, so sensitive to hegemonic political culture—even to the questions asked by the pollsters. Nevertheless the shift during the depression and New Deal was unmistakable.[133] This support responded both to a perceived need and to a sense of new possibility; a response both desperate and, paradoxically, hopeful and creative. Even the widespread hostility to relief and to taking relief was contingent: much of it was evoked by the terms of help rather than by the help itself, objecting to help that was demeaning and dishonorable. When provision was reduced, widespread and angry protest ensued. Moreover, sometimes the claiming of welfare itself constituted political action. An important part of this politicized welfare claiming took the form of protest against discrimination, particularly by blacks resisting both racial and gender injustices in the administration of welfare. And civic interest in public welfare was not only quantitative but qualitative, so to speak; some citizens wanted not only to receive help but also to participate in designing welfare systems.

Although it is hardly surprising that the public supported welfare programs, it is remarkable how strongly they did so. By 1935 89 percent of the population favored old age pensions for the needy, a very new idea, and 56 percent supported Townsend, the most generous proposal. Forty percent continued to support Townsend, in 1939, four years after Social Security had passed. In 1935, 77 percent thought the government should be responsible for finding jobs for everyone who wanted to work, and 68 percent thought the government should collect enough taxes for public works jobs. Publicly funded medical care was extremely popular: 74 percent wanted entirely free medical care for the poor. Pollsters even got positive responses to questions about increased taxes when the taxes were to be earmarked for welfare purposes. 59 percent said they would personally pay higher taxes for free medical and dental care for those who couldn't afford to buy it.

The polls showed, unsurprisingly, that support for welfare was higher among the poor.[134] More significantly, backing was stronger among those who themselves received some kind of public aid *and knew that they did*. Public opinion polls were new in the New Deal, so we cannot tell how new this pro-welfare opinion was. It is nonetheless likely that prowelfare sentiment was as much a product of the welfare state as a cause of it, constructed by awareness of the possibility of a welfare state. In general the popularity of welfare, and paying for welfare, grew throughout the New Deal and up to the end of the war.

Americans also expressed approval of welfare in voluminous letter writing. Presidents had often received a great deal of mail, but Roosevelt's volume was of an altogether different magnitude. Lincoln had received at most 100 letters a day, McKinley 1,000; Hoover averaged 600 a day. Roosevelt got 450,000 in the first seven days of his presidency and then averaged 8,000 a day. The first rush expressed the hopes that his election germinated, but the high volume was maintained largely because FDR and his assistant Louis Howe constructed an apparatus to answer them all. Roosevelt even invited mail in some of his fireside chats. These were not simply letters asking for help; they were more public spirited and more ambitious. The letter-writing citizens wanted a welfare system, not just a piece of the pie or emergency relief. The most common themes were proposals for relief programs; the second most common, demands for inflation; the third, hostility to "money interests," monopolies, and "big boys."[135]

Many went beyond writing to join activist coalitions that pressured local governments into doing what was necessary to get federal funds. The Baltimore Citizens' Alliance for Social Security ("social security" was at this time still used as a generic synonym for welfare), which included an unemployed league, unions, fraternal and religious organizations, joined in promoting municipal acquisition of federally funded programs. The alliance staged protests against local government inaction and cutbacks, and promoted increased inheritance and corporate taxes, with considerable success. Such coalitions included the Left and continued throughout the decade, by the late 1930s no longer regarding relief "as either emergency or temporary."[136]

Relief cutbacks provoked militance even among Roosevelt loyalists. One Chicago woman, secretary-treasurer of the Workers' Alliance Local 45, recalled, "And we were going into relief stations, sometimes gettin' arrested two, three times a day." She described to Studs Terkel her skirmishes with the police, how the "Polish women" threw cayenne pepper in the cops' eyes in tussles over evictions, how a particularly fat woman used her bulk to intimidate and block the police—yet this is an activist who proudly described how, as assistant precinct captain, she got every vote in her apartment building for Roosevelt in 1936.[137] When Roosevelt announced the end of federal relief he was, of course, drenched with protests; when the CWA was abolished, the downpour amounted to over 50,000 letters and 7000 telegrams of protest.[138] When the WPA announced plans to lay off workers there were widespread protests in various cities, including sit-down strikes by WPA workers. In Detroit the administration responded by shutting down some projects, thus creating what the workers considered a lockout. The protesters won: Washington reversed itself and ordered reinstatement of all discharged workers and no further discharges until other replacement assistance was guaranteed.[139] In Harlem protesters shut down one thousand stores in a sympathy action.[140] Settlement houses often sustained relief protests with space, food, and political pressure.[141] In Minnesota, Farmer-Labor party ward clubs, and particularly women's groups in the party, took on the job of overseeing welfare practices.[142]

Throughout the country, relief claimants were expressing a new sense of entitlement to what they were getting. Even with respect to welfare proposals that never succeeded, such as national health insurance, citizens seemed to expect aid. They criticized the contradictions:

"Mrs. Roosevelt there is so much talk about no American child shall be denied this or denied that, but it is all talk."[143] A journalist visiting New York and New Jersey cities in 1934 reported: "Relief is regarded as permanent by both clients and relief workers. Clients are assuming that the government has a responsibility to provide. The stigma of relief has almost disappeared except among white-collar groups."[144] One woman described her response to being made to wait many hours to see a caseworker who was not busy—a common tactic used against blacks in southern relief offices[145]—"Yes, sir, I let her know that I wouldn't stand up in there another minute. And after that, they certainly did fly right."[146] In 1933 a woman on relief attempted to have her social worker arrested for the "attempted starvation" of her family.[147]

Open thievery by the poor and unemployed was common—often organized, public expropriation of goods. "Grown men, usually in two's or three's, enter chain stores, order all the food they can possibly carry, and then walk out without paying."[148] Stealing coal from the railroads was standard, and firemen sometimes "spilled" coal when they neared towns. Unemployed and antieviction protesters "stole" electricity by putting up their own "jumpers" and reconnecting turned-off water and gas.[149]

Relief claimants forced changes in the terms of their stipends. The Platzke family held their caseworker hostage when she visited them because their food requests had been denied. Mrs. Platzke told the caseworker, "if we are going to starve, you are going to starve with us." Officials decided not to press charges but provided emergency aid.[150] In Birmingham Curtis Maggard, an unemployed steel worker, whose family had not eaten in four days, went to the relief office with a "croker sack"; when told that a relief check was in the mail, he responded, "You been telling me that for four weeks. . . . You got a grocery store up there. . . . When I get home, I'm going to have that croker sack full of food. Ya'll got a grocery store down there, and I'm going to send somebody to hell to get me something to eat." He didn't get a full sack but got an immediate check.[151] Claimants refused to sell personal belongings or to quit growing vegetables for themselves or for sale. They made and sold liquor. They squatted in vacant homes. Some violent protests revealed individuals cracking up under stress, but the definitions of what was normal were fuzzy in such difficult times. A Chicago welfare administrator recalled a mother of nine children, used to receiving two quarts of milk and cut down to one quart when relief funds got tighter: She "raise[d] hell at the relief station. She became vituperative. The case worker wrote her up as a psychotic," but a psychiatrist who evaluated her said that she seemed to him entirely normal.[152] Political scientists Gabriel Almond and Harold Lasswell found that clients who behaved "aggressively" at a relief bureau were by no means more "disturbed" than those who did not; the "aggressives" were those whose previous experience led them to feel both more entitled and more acutedly reduced in circumstances.[153]

African Americans appear to have been particularly quick to organize and work collectively to win or defend relief entitlements. The Athens (Georgia) Colored Community Association wrote to Roosevelt with complaints and proposals two days before his inauguration.[154] In Baton Rouge an Emergency Advisory Council for Negroes formed to fight for fair relief; in Indianapolis it was the Negro Economic Welfare Council of Indiana; in St. Louis the Pacific Movement of the Eastern World, a black fraternal organization, took on the task. A Baptist minister, complaining on behalf of two elderly widows, justified his intervention thus: "I am a colored Baptist Minister, free born as an American citizen. Therefore, I feel that I have a Constitutional right to represent affairs. . . . we as a group should have some voice."[155] Many protested the investigations of applicants. "Your Administrators here in Baltimore take it upon themselves to inquire into the morals of the applicant. . . . The writer does not believe that the letter of the Relief law, or even its spirit gives the Administrators that authority. May I mention that in France, to hold a moral inquest upon the applicant for aid is forbidden by law."[156]

It would be difficult and distorting to try to distinguish civil rights from welfare activism among blacks.[157] The Harlem riot of 1935 was an expression of frustration in part about inadequate relief.[158] In the South the motives for protest at relief offices were simultaneously racial and economic. Black southern Communist Hosea Hudson explained his decision to become "aggressive" in a relief office:

> I said, "Everytime I come out here, "Get back side the wall," and when I get in the office, they tell me "your coal's on the way." When I get home, I ain't got no coal to make a fire." I said, "I'm getting tired of getting back side the wall!" I was talking loud. That was just loud-

mouthing. Let the people know somebody had some courage to speak. And several guys in the line there knew me, had worked in Stockham foundry with me, they said, "Tell them about it, Big Red!" . . . There was about 75–100 people, it was a lot of people there.[159]

To many social workers these attitudes of entitlement proved that recipients were beginning to "lean," lose their work ethic and commitment to economic "independence." FERA reports from local administrators often echoed this fear of pauperization. A Pennsylvania observer reported that relief was "regarded by a great proportion of our clients as a regular and accepted way of life," and another found the same in Detroit. Such reports usually concluded that counting on relief was demoralizing. But these relief administrators did no interviews, assumed rather than tested their ideas that relief claimants were demoralized, and, equally without basis, attributed this putative state to relief. By contrast journalist Lorena Hickok found that demoralization was not caused by relief but by unemployment and low wages and employers who sought to use relief standards as the basis for wages. "I am wondering if the only way to get employers to pay people enough to live on won't have to be for the government to treat the unemployed as labor surplus, take them all out of the market, pay them living wages, and let industry howl."[160]

But regardless of how they interpreted it, observers agreed on the development of attitudes of entitlement among relief and public jobs claimants. It affected casework practice strongly: "One strange phenomenon shook to its foundation the official . . . practice" wrote Bertha Reynolds, a social work leader. "Professional workers in private agencies [used] home visits so that the privacy of the families might be protected. To their surprises . . . many preferred to come to the office . . . getting out of the isolation of their dreary homes to meet others, even their neighbors, who were having similar experiences. They did not seem to feel the 'stigma' . . . The aura of prestige around the private social agencies began to quiver."[161] E. Wight Bakke, author of the best-known study of unemployed male workers in the depression, found that relief did not suppress a recipient's energy, foresight, and initiative but redirected them: "He and his family in their own estimation are not passive recipients of public charity. They are still active citizens . . . 'self-reliance' is not dead . . . relief clients do study and learn the techniques by which to increase the level of their subsistence in the way indicated by their accusers." Bakke devoted a chapter to recipients' techniques of "working" the relief system.[162]

In other words, what appeared as dependence and cheating to some appeared as healthy initiative and even citizenship from another point of view. This is not to say that clients were happy or eager to be on public assistance, but rather that claiming public assistance did not in itself make people feel unworthy, dependent, or helpless.

Not only were claimants rejecting the taint of relief, but their claiming may itself be considered a form of political activism. Through experience with welfare, clients learned that aggressive attitudes worked better, and the longer the experience, the more assertive the client. The more aggressive clients were not only those who had suffered the most deprivation but also the more socially secure—for example, the native born, the well educated—those who felt more entitled.[163] For many, making claims on the state was a fundamental type of citizenship participation. Among the poor it is far more common than voting and may well be equally influential. Clients of services express their wishes through the act of seeking help and then through interactions with caseworkers.[164] For the "new poor" in the depression, seeking relief or a WPA job might reflect a drop in status or sense of self-worth, while for the "old poor," the same actions might signal increased self-esteem. Claiming welfare could make someone feel more rather than less deserving, more rather than less a citizen. How we conceive the meanings of welfare claims depends on how we conceive the values of a welfare state: whether as an unfortunate, emergency necessity, as a charity to the disabled or the lazy, or as an aspect of citizenship.

How does all this sit with the perception of other observers that people were reluctant to take the "dole" and turned to relief offices only when they had exhausted other sources of help?[165] The contradiction disappears when we recall the concrete conditions of relief in the stratified welfare state. There were, of course, some, particularly men, who took any help other than wages as humiliating. The first approach to the relief office was particularly hard. "Though Mr. Putnam had felt that he 'would sooner be shot than apply for relief,' once the first application was made he didn't find it so bad"—this is a typical report.[166] Some even thought of others: "I never applied for PWA or WPA, 'cause as long as I could hustle, there was no point in beating the other fellow out of a job, cuttin' some other guy out."[167]

Many, particularly but not exclusively men, wanted to work; hence the popularity of WPA. An administrator recollected, "The men wanted to work . . . the dominant theme through all the years of the Depression. . . . I'll never forget the morning we opened the office . . . a cold November day. . . . Thousands . . . lined up for blocks. Many . . . carried their tools with them." Most complaints about relief were about its humiliating conditions of delivery and only secondarily about its inadequacy.[168] Clients would often sit all day at relief stations waiting for their turn. "I finally went on relief. . . . It comes as close to crucifixion as . . . You sit in an auditorium and are given a number. The interview was utterly ridiculous and mortifying." Many caseworkers themselves hated the procedures. One recalled how she was told by her superviser that she "had to *see* the poverty. . . . So I looked into this man's closet—he was so insulted. . . . He said, 'Why are you doing this?'"[169]

Women were more likely than men to claim relief, and they gave it different meanings. Many husbands covertly or explicitly relied on their wives to apply. For a variety of reasons women were less threatened by claiming relief than men were. Although many women wanted employment, unemployment was not a disgrace for them. The combination of male unemployment and relief weakened men's authority in the family and frequently encouraged wives and children to assert more independence.[170] For women, dependence on the state was perhaps not such a sharp break with norms that labeled them dependent on husbands. Relief claiming represented an active step, and sometimes a move away from passivity, especially for those responsible for children as well as husbands. Indeed for many women relief claiming was a first step toward citizenship, a first relationship with the state.

The New Deal not only heightened citizens' sense of entitlements, but also their desire to participate. The depth and breadth of the crisis increased commonalities among Americans. This, combined with Roosevelt's informal style and willingness to try programs that appeared risky and ad hoc, produced a new sense of possibility and communication with government. Improvement seemed possible, because people saw money and jobs return to the economy, and new ideas also seemed possible as new programs burgeoned. Many Americans supposed that their own suggestions might be listened to and valued. Citizens not only wanted relief but wanted to shape its struc-

ture; as the federal government expanded, so did the popular imagination of how government might function to improve the society.
Their ideas poured into Washington. Many proposed projects were
quite concrete: "Dear Sir I am begging you please grant me the power as to set up the trust in the United F.T.Y. bank [for orphans]. Sir I
am not asking you for to put up the money."[171] J.S. Hayes from Adel,
Georgia, proposed:

> 1. Is to stop all children under 14 yr old from working [because]
> where I want a $2.00 for a job these children . . . will do it for 75
> cents.
> 2. To set a standard wage for a man to work for and if he be caught
> working for less put in . . . jail for 60 days.[172]

Many proposed public service projects that the WPA could fund.
Rachael Crook, a graduate student in economics at the University of
North Carolina/Chapel Hill, wanted to set up a cooperative truck
farm and canning factory for tenant farmers.[173] P. E. Kelly Shelton of
San Antonio spent eighteen years teaching in the public schools, then
organized a nursery and kindergarten in 1927, and wrote Eleanor
Roosevelt in 1935 asking for WPA money to start a "Free Nursery &
Kindergarten for the colored children"; she enclosed a petition from
"The Child Welfare Group."[174] From Indianapolis: "I want to open
up a place for children, whose parents are unable to provide. . . . I
see a large house just a few houses down from me, a place that I
think would be suitable. . . . It has the toilet and water outside, and
no one seems to stay there. . . . If I could get the real-estate-man to
let me have it for awhile without pay, And then see how I would
progress, I would be willing to pay after that."[175] R. C. Morris of
Starkville, Mississippi, proposed a health survey regarding malaria
and housing that would keep mosquitoes out.[176] Black clubwomen
from Athens, Georgia, proposed a farm colony, school auditoriums,
gymnasiums, parks and playgrounds, necessary "if we want to catch
up with Russia"![177]

The spirit of social invention overtook intellectuals, too. "The
pages of old Progressive–Era journals such as the *New Republic* and
Survey once again bristled with bold ideas for economic planning
and the cooperative commonwealth."[178] "CURES: Three Groups Offer Plans for a National Utopia," headlined *Newsweek* in November
1934, hardly a time when utopia seemed close.[179] In the 1920s social

insurance and welfare ideas had seemed confined to relatively small groups of experts; now such ideas appeared among a much larger population. It was not only the "quacks" who developed schemes; respectable businessmen and intellectuals developed social insurance and welfare plans: the National Retail Dry Goods Association, the Pennsylvania School of Social and Health Work, the Milbank Fund, the National Economic and Social Planning Association, and many individuals. The dean of the University of California Bureau of Public Administration circulated a proposal for self-help cooperatives, building on a left-leaning network that had existed in California since the 1920s.[180] Lewis Mumford and other urban planners and housing experts developed ideas for healthful living spaces. Frank Graham, professor of Economics at Princeton, called for cooperative production units among the unemployed to manufacture goods to be sold for deposit credits, which in turn would be paid to the producers as wages. Various resettlement plans continued the utopian communitarian tradition. Intellectuals resumed intensive study of European social welfare programs.[181] Some of this ferment soaked into New Deal thought, through the edges of Roosevelt's "Brains Trust." On the whole the New Deal was crafted more by politics than by intellectuals, but New Deal politics was sensitive to social and intellectual dissent and the electoral revolts it threatened. From one perspective, depression insurgency was remarkably restrained and limited, relative to the severity of the situation. Third-party efforts and extraparliamentary protests were mainly local and, despite their militance, easily blocked and contained. Despite the widespread class-conflict rhetoric, even in Congress, no mass socialist orientation spread. But the dominant mood of mass activism was not so much against capitalism as it was for a kind of "moral capitalism,"[182] recalling the "moral economy" premises of traditional bread riots. Measured against this goal, depression social movements made substantial gains. They solidified a new understanding that workers were often the helpless and deserving victims of inexorable and overpowering "business cycles"; that economic victims were entitled to collective help; and that the federal government would have to take responsibility for giving that help. Moreover, New Deal policy makers, witnessing these dramatic insurgencies, were not always sure the threats they faced could be contained within the existing political and economic system. They could not see the future.

The limitations of these social movements had to do with their social base and the fact that popular understanding of economic needs was, in some ways, as shortsighted as that of the experts. The weakness of a nonmaternalist welfare approach meant that, even as the frailty of men's ability to support families was being so vividly demonstrated, the public was not hearing any critique of family-wage strategies. Some nonmainstream welfare proposals, such as Townsend, Lundeen, and a myriad local projects, addressed this lack, providing for women and sometimes children outside dependence on a male wage earner. But a critique of women's economic dependence was never articulated publicly and did not enter New Deal thinking. And no one discussed single mothers. There was a vital black movement, arguing for the extension of full citizenship to African Americans, and it included militant protests of their exclusion from such social citizenship rights as welfare. But it could not command mass white attention or win much white support precisely because of the exclusion of blacks from citizenship: their lack of political power, lack of access to education, and the burden of racism they carried. Moreover, exclusion from citizenship was so extensive that blacks had priorities more urgent even than welfare—such as protecting themselves from lynching. For similar reasons other minority movements were marginalized. This silence—or rather deafness—produced portentous omissions. And they were not omissions alone; they interacted with the presence of strong movements, such as those of (white male) labor and the elderly, which were making effective claims of entitlement for others.

Roosevelt Signs the Social Security Act, Surrounded by (left to right) Rep. Robert L. Doughton, Chairman of the House Ways and Means Committee; Rep. Frank Buck (D., CA); Sen. Robert Wagner (D., NY); Sen. Alben Barkley (D., KY); Harry Hopkins (with his bow tie and little else showing); Wis. Governor Robert La Follette, Jr.; Sen. Augustine Lonergan (D., CT); Sec. of Labor Frances Perkins; Sen. William H. King (D., UT); Rep. David J. Lewis (D., MD); and Sen. Joseph Guffey (D., PA).

9
=

The Legislative Process

Reformers Face Politics

When Roosevelt signed the Social Security Act on August 14, 1935, he knew it was one of his major accomplishments—if for no other reason than because of the opposition and crippling amendments his forces had had to beat back. The victory contributed considerably to Roosevelt's repeated reelection and to the Democratic hold on Congress for twenty years. But since he thought of Social Security as a beginning, not a definitive piece of welfare legislation, even he might have understated its importance. Social Security continues today to structure the entire U.S. welfare system. It provided old-age pensions, unemployment compensation, aid to dependent children, and several programs of aid to the disabled, as well as a small program of federal money for maternal and infant health. It has since been expanded but not fundamentally changed, and no new major initiatives were undertaken until President Clinton's medical insurance proposal in 1994.

Social Security provided economic security to many, but it also installed considerable inequities in the welfare system. These arose from a hierarchical stratification of provision based, in part, on an application of constitutional federalism that federalized some programs while allowing substantial local control of others. The law set up two social insurance programs, Old-Age Insurance and Unemployment Compensation, relatively generous and honorable in their terms and restricted in their inclusion. For others, the law provided several public assistance programs, including ADC, with stingy and humiliating conditions. The stratification of programs reproduced and deepened already existing social inequalities. Just as labor-market forces and cultural changes were allowing women and blacks to move onto the main track of citizenship, Social Security created a new hierarchy of social citizenship in which they were on the bottom again.

Some of this stratification derived from the amalgamation of a variety of welfare visions, but the inequities were intensified by, and others emerged from, the legislative process itself. Social Security was not passed by acclamation. It would undoubtedly have passed easily in a referendum, but the structures of Congress allowed the resistance of powerful minorities to exercise great leverage. Roosevelt was at moments quite dispirited about its chances.[1] To get it through Congress he called in many political debts and expended much of his impressive political clout.[2] The bill took more than six months to write and then seven months to get through Congress, and it was amended many times.

Yet ADC, along with the Children's Bureau's program for maternal and children's health services, were the least controversial parts of the Social Security Act.[3] To support ADC was, literally, to support motherhood. Congressman Fuller of Arkansas voiced the sentimental pieties that seemed to him politically necessary:

It is easy to foresee the great good and happiness this welfare measure will bring to the aged, the helpless mother, the dependent, neglected, and crippled children. In visualizing I can see the expectant mother, weak from worry, overwork, and undernourishment, back in the rural district in a little cabin on the mountain side, where the unexpected stranger is met by the friendly bark of the farm dog and where hospitality reigns supreme, joyously explaining to her ragged and tired husband at supper time how the welfare workers have promised relief before and during childbirth. I can see the dependent and neglected boy who never knew the love and guidance of father and mother as he grows to manhood extolling the grandeur of his country and the loyalty due the Stars and Stripes. . . . I can see the careworn and dejected widow shout with joy upon returning from the neighbor's washtub after having received assurance of financial aid for her children. I see her with the youngest child upon her knee and the others clustered by her, kissing the tears of joy from her pale cheek as she explains they can now obtain clothes and books, go to Sunday school, and attend the public school; and as they prepare to retire I can hear her offering thanks to him from whom all blessings flow.[4]

Almost no one opposed ADC. Its symbolic resonance evoked the most generous emotions among voters. Given that consensus, why, then, did ADC emerge so small and niggardly? And why is it so resented by so many today? The explanation can be found in the convergence of reformers' visions, Children's Bureau experience, depression poverty, and social movements with the legislative process. It is a story reminiscent of the struggle for public medical insurance today, and it reveals much about the obstacles to a better welfare system today.

Writing ADC

Roosevelt took his time in developing a welfare program, as distinct from emergency relief. Several welfare bills had been introduced prior to 1935, notably the first Wagner-Lewis Bill, but FDR had avoided throwing his full strength behind them because he did not have a clear vision of what he wanted. When Roosevelt first used the term "social security," in the generic, it connoted primarily health insurance.[5] Yet in recruiting someone to head his Committee on Economic Security (CES), to draft legislation, he turned to Edwin Witte and his Wisconsin colleagues, whose primary concern was unemployment. The unemployment program initially claimed most of the attention of those developing the administration's bill. Old-age insurance became prominent only belatedly. No one could have predicted it would become the best-funded and most popular program, or that the very term "social security" would ultimately come to refer to old-age insurance after the law was passed in 1935.

In his earlier compromises with antiwelfare forces, including prominently organized physicians and big business, the president eliminated two programs that had been an integral part of most welfare planners' vision: public works and medical insurance.[6] Social insurance advocates had accepted time limits on unemployment compensation only because they expected a provision for automatic startup of public jobs when unemployment reached certain levels. By eliminating a permanent public works program and keeping the emergency jobs programs separate from Social Security, the administration implicitly denied that job shortages were an ongoing, recurring problem. This created a contradiction that has plagued welfare ever since, between the realities of the economy and the assumption that unemployment compensation (and "welfare") should be temporary. It hinders the consensus about whether the private sector can generate enough jobs with living wages, or in other words, whether "welfare" recipients are lazy and could be working if they chose to. Had public works been permanent, moreover, gender-conscious reformers might have had a better platform on which to protest the discrimination against women in the design and distribution of jobs. The lack of public medical insurance had particularly negative economic consequences for single mothers because of children's health needs. The deletion of public works and medical insurance from Social Security contributed greatly to the stigma on "welfare" by depriving the poorest of essential supports that might have provided them with the dignity of work and health care.

While Old-Age Insurance and Unemployment Compensation—Titles II and III of Social Security—were extremely controversial, ADC (Title IV) and the other public assistance programs (Old-Age Assistance and Aid to the Blind, Titles I and X) were uncontested. Everyone agreed that ADC would be drafted by the Children's Bureau. No one from the various technical and advisory committees that Witte established had anything to suggest about ADC.[7] Nothing illustrates so profoundly the maleness of the social insurance perspective as does the total silence about single mothers and children in their deliberations about this bill. Witte accepted as given, from the moment he first heard the Children's Bureau plan, that there should be federal contributions to the state and local mothers' aid programs and left the design to the bureau.[8]

So ADC was quickly drafted by Grace Abbott, Katharine Lenroot, and Martha Eliot.[9] Their speed reflects the fact that they anticipated no controversy and that ADC was not even the Children's Bureau's highest priority. On the contrary, the program dearest to their hearts at this time, and the proposal they knew to be controversial, was a renewed Sheppard-Towner program, a national program for child and maternal health services, which would become Title V of the act.[10] This program encapsulated the most ambitious of their welfarist hopes, offering what they viewed as an entering wedge to a large federal public health program. They had been agitating for this from very early on in Roosevelt's administration and ranked this program first in the three-part recommendation they made to Witte. The program faced strong opposition from physicians, as did anything that hinted at public medical insurance.[11] Soon, however, Titles IV and V seemed so minor and innocuous compared to other parts of the Social Security Bill that they were crowded out of the spotlight and received little opposition or attention of any kind.

The proposal submitted to Witte asked for $7 million for child and maternal health services (Sheppard-Towner had appropriated $1.48 million for the first year and $1.24 for succeeding years); $1.5 million to encourage state and local services for homeless, dependent, and neglected children; and $25 million for "mothers' pensions," as they still called mothers' aid. All the funds were to be allotted on a state/federal matching basis with the exception that an additional smaller sum was allotted "for special assistance to states which are unable because of severe economic distress to match."[12]

The small size of its requests reflected both timidity and fear, a faintheartedness that had been growing for a decade. Title V was actually less far-reaching than Sheppard Towner had been, because it restricted services to the needy by requiring means-testing, which was certain to be stigmatizing and to drive many away. But the vitriol and vehemence of the Red-baiting attacks on Children's Bureau people because of Sheppard-Towner had left them perpetually anxious.[13] Indeed, the Children's Bureau had been on the defensive for a decade by this time. It had had to fight hard against cutbacks in its appropriations for fiscal years 1934 and 1935.[14] And the PHS attempts to take over and/or destroy Children's Bureau programs had not let up.[15]

The Children's Bureau's low request for ADC also reflected its inaccurate estimate of the number of fatherless families it expected to serve. The staff estimated adding 179,000 families to the 109,000 then receiving mothers' aid.[16] The total, approximately 288,000 families, was less than the 358,000 female-headed families with children actually receiving relief in 1934. The low figure further expressed their desire to make this an elite assistance program, to serve only the deserving, perhaps even the exemplary.

The Children's Bureau request for joint federal/state rather than wholly federal financing and administration continued unaltered a decades-old preference. They did, however, expect their programs to be one-half federally funded, not one-third as the act ultimately provided. Their resistance to federally administered proposals may have reflected their own sense of political weakness within the federal government; certainly it expressed their optimism that professional social workers, including many women, would continue gaining influence in state welfare departments.

The Children's Bureau people continued to give highest priority to health programs, despite the fact that this choice kept them perpetually embattled with the PHS. It was their long-term conviction, widely shared among welfare advocates before the depression, that a universal public health insurance program was essential to any reasonable welfare system.[17] Maternalists still, they believed that children would provide a foot in the door to winning political acceptance of it.[18] "Which groups in the entire population would be accepted as a group which should have their medical care aided through federal funds?" Abbott asked. The answer was crippled children.[19] Witte believed that they chose this focus because they thought FDR would be particularly sympathetic to it.[20] They reduced by $3 million the amount they asked for general child and maternal health services and earmarked the same amount for crippled children.

The separation of maternal and child health from the ADC program suggested how differently the Children's Bureau people regarded the two: They saw the health plan as innovative, permanent, and opening toward an expanded welfare system; they saw ADC as helping an established program, probably temporarily, a program they did not regard as leading in a progressive direction.[21] Like many of their male colleagues in social work and welfare circles, they believed that social–insurance programs for unemployed and retired breadwinners would ultimately take care of dependent women and children. Assuming that women did not normally face the economy as individuals, as workers, they saw no problem in grounding women's social rights in their dependent position.

The Children's Bureau place at the drafting table derived from its parent, the Department of Labor, which had been the federal authority on welfare before FDR created new agencies. Secretary of Labor Frances Perkins had chosen Arthur Altmeyer as her personal representative and Thomas Eliot, assistant solicitor to the Department of Labor and husband of Martha Eliot of the Children's Bureau, as the counsel to the cabinet committee.[22] It was Thomas Eliot who reviewed and corrected his wife's and Lenroot's drafts of Titles IV and V before sending them to Witte.[23] Wilbur Cohen, Witte's assistant, believed that a decision was "ninety-eight per cent won" if Perkins, Altmeyer, and Witte agreed.[24]

But then the CES excluded the Children's Bureau network from its deliberations.[25] The seven-person Advisory Committee on Child Welfare had only one woman, Jane Hoey, then associate director of the Welfare Council of New York City, and she was a Hopkins employee and loyalist, not tied to the Children's Bureau. Her appointment was experienced as an insult by the women who had for so long been the backbone of all child welfare activity. The general twenty-three-member Advisory Council contained only four women from this network: Abbott, Mary Dewson of the National Consumers' League (and, more importantly for this appointment, the Women's Committee of the National Democratic Party), Helen Hall, president of the National Federation of Settlements, and Belle Sherwin, president of the National League of Women Voters.[26] Lenroot was especially resentful at being excluded because she had written sections of the bill. But the CES preferred Congress to think it had all emerged from Congress's Legislative Drafting Service, and Lenroot dutifully sidestepped the question of her authorship when testifying in congressional hearings.[27] In a pattern common to the way women were often used at the time, despite excluding the Children's Bureau from discussions, the CES and the Social Security staff continued to rely on it for research and responses to citizens' complaints and inquiries about Social Security.[28]

Exclusion of the Children's Bureau may have been affected by straightforward sexism, but it was also motivated by a mutiny against the Children's Bureau's claim to define welfare policy, a revolt beginning to include women as well as men. The New Deal gave rise to a group of Washington women professionals who distanced themselves from the Children's Bureau network, women like Josephine Brown, Barbara Nachtrieb Armstrong, Jane Hoey, Eveline Burns, and Ida Merriam. Either because of their youth or for more ideological reasons, they were not primarily influenced by the first-wave women's rights campaign.[29] They were, arguably, a first generation of "postfeminist" women: accepting and supporting many of the gains women had made over the previous decades, but without emotional ties to a women's movement or conviction that a women's movement should be a priority. Brown and Hoey went on to work for Social Security; Armstrong and Burns, both academic economists, worked for the CES. They did not consider themselves part of the "generation of older people who had bled and died together," as Eveline Burns put it in an interview, with some disaffection:

BURNS: . . . a sort of little group . . .

Q: Almost a conspiracy.

BURNS: That's right.[30]

They were also too young to have been primarily molded by Progressive Era welfare and social work ideas. Specifically they were not maternalist. They were critical of the Children's Bureau's emphasis on casework, more interested in social insurance and employment-based or universal entitlements. The group serves as a foil, showing how out-of-date was the bureau's maternalism.

The exclusion of the Children's Bureau was also determined by the several-decades-long tradition of disassociation of social work from social insurance, of welfare from economics. Abbott, Lenroot, and Eliot were experts on casework, on poverty, and on health and welfare research and provision. They did not do economic planning.

Some members of the social work network tried to challenge this old division of labor, to influence the overall design of New Deal welfare programs. Some were part of the Lundeen "clan," as Burns called it.[31] Even the Children's Bureau loyalists tried to stretch the emerging conception of the economic security bill to include universal and guaranteed benefits for the poor. When the CES rejected this idea, Grace Abbott made a compromise proposal—free, tax-supported pensions for those earning less than one thousand dollars, contributory pensions for those with higher earnings. In her emphasis on tax support she had widespread backing, and not only from women or from the Left.[32] As social work leader Homer Folks put it, a tax-supported scheme would be contributory *and* equitable.[33] Indeed Witte's biographer claims that he at first found the arguments against an insurance approach convincing but was then influenced in the other direction.[34]

Edith Abbott in particular, arguably the most influential social work academic in the country from her base as head of the University of

Chicago School of Social Service Administration, continued to press for a larger program and a more thorough break with the poor-relief tradition. Edith Abbott had frequently served as her sister's spokeswoman, saying what Grace could not because of her public office. With Grace's retirement in 1934, Edith Abbott was freed still further. She seized the occasion to argue that it was possible actually to abolish poverty through public aid—not social insurance—available to all without stigmatizing qualifications. She argued for a policy that would abolish the "pauper laws," condemned private and public charity programs as "disgracefully opprobrious and un-American" and perpetuating inequality, and called for bringing all forms of public assistance together in one welfare statute, staffed by "competent social workers," that would provide general home assistance, mothers' aid, old-age assistance, and pensions for the blind, to which federal, state, and local government would all contribute.[35] But she said nothing about unemployment and health insurance, which were among the most popular and publicized issues, and she never wrote actual designs for programs.

Grace Abbott was also more outspoken from retirement. She was one of several vociferous opponents of the cutbacks in federal relief, skeptical of the view that the Social Security program would meet this need quickly.[36] She criticized the principle of employee contributions to unemployment compensation.[37] She argued for public health insurance steadily, even after Roosevelt had effectively vetoed it. In 1937 she drafted proposals for federally supported sick pay and medical insurance, on a noncontributory and national basis.[38] In 1935 John Andrews of the AALL asked her to help organize a conference on "Forgotten Farmers and Social Insurance," protesting the exclusion of agricultural workers from old-age insurance.[39] And she reversed her earlier insistence on state matching funds.[40]

But Grace Abbott remained a quintessential team player and administration dependable. She attempted to accrue and maintain influence through impeccable party faithfulness, leading, with John Andrews, the lobbying for the Social Security Act despite her disappointments in it.[41] She refused to sign a minority statement organized by social work spokesman Paul Kellogg protesting the inadequate payroll tax for unemployment compensation.[42] She even had to explain away her beloved sister's criticisms of Social Security.[43] She did Witte's bidding in testifying and lobbying for the bill. Witte later asserted that, at a crucial moment when the bill was stalled in the Ways and Means Committee for six weeks under attack from Townsendites, "self-styled 'experts' and 'liberals,'" Abbott's work had been crucial in the bill's passage. Later she provided the same service for the Fair Labor Standards Act.[44] The assistant secretary of labor asked for her advice about tactics in persuading Congress to accept the unemployment program of Social Security.[45] In 1936 Mary Dewson of the Democratic party asked her to take charge of organizing a social-workers-for-Roosevelt campaign and Abbott tried to use this work as a bargaining chip for her demands for the continuation of federal direct relief.[46]

The Children's Bureau did try to widen its influence, but without much success. It ran a conference on child labor with the AFL in 1932. Immediately after Roosevelt's inauguration, it proposed a conference on stopping home mortgage foreclosures, but FDR ignored the suggestion.[47] It tried to persuade the FERA to include child health nursing provisions in the CWA, but this came to little.[48] Its staff wrote parts of the Fair Labor Standards Act of 1938 (which finally outlawed child labor).[49] But despite its recognized expertise on all welfare matters, and its connections with virtually everyone in the field, its influence was on the whole limited to child welfare issues and a few other instances when it was invited to play a coordinating role. A friend of Perkins called her "a half-loaf girl: take what you can get now and try for more later,"[50] and this might have been a slogan for the whole Children's Bureau crowd. It might also have been a slogan for all bureaucrats and government officials, of course, but there were others in the administration who pushed farther-reaching ideas. Mainly men—with all that that meant in terms of greater confidence and greater legitimacy, and mainly higher-ranking than the Children's Bureau women—they included Rexford Tugwell, Harold Ickes, and Will Alexander. Whether the Children's Bureau's efforts were timid in conception or blocked by stronger influences, the fact remains that the women's network did not offer a welfare program equal to the proportions of the crisis.

When the crisis created a need for leadership, the social work network was quickly outstripped in what it could offer by an academic reform elite socialized to think big. On the whole the child welfare network accepted the limitation of its influence to women's and children's programs and the other public assistance programs that were drawn up on the same plan. Its initiatives in other areas were strikingly minor. When its members wrote or spoke in support of welfare initiatives, they revealed a vision more expansive than the ADC and maternal and child health programs they drafted. But they almost never developed concrete proposals. Grace Abbott recognized this as early as October 1934; she complained that Witte was "able" and "nice," but "the insurance crowd has swooped down on them with a program all ready . . . and the rest of us talk on rather general principles."[51] The planners, longing for a controlled economy, also lost some of their dreams.[52] They expected Social Security to include, as a minimum, guarantees for full employment through permanent provision for public works when necessary.[53] But their most ambitious ideas made their smaller ones appear less radical.

=

It was not only the "insurance crowd" that pushed more ambitious programs. During the New Deal a "third force" entered the welfare business, attracted by the whirlpool of energy around Harry Hopkins. As head of the FERA, he represented the most generous, flexible, and above all national (as opposed to state and local) impulses of New Deal Democratic loyalists. He was also personally close to Franklin Roosevelt. He used the FERA to trailblaze a campaign for a unified federal welfare state with cabinet status for its head. A heterodox group, no more attached to social insurance than to public assistance principles, the FERA also began to exert its persuasive enthusiasm on the CES. In fact the CES's own Advisory Committee contained some who welcomed this pressure; its own report argued that the CES basic program—federal work relief and federal aid to state programs for the elderly and dependent children—was inadequate to the needs created in a modern industrial economy.

The FERA produced a draft of a social security plan well ahead of the CES, in June 1934. Contrary to the Children's Bureau's complaints that Hopkins acted only in an emergency framework, his bill rested on the premise that some unemployment and some population of "unemployables" were permanent features of the economy.[54] Moreover it contained an ingenious version of ADC that, through a new definition of dependent children—all children for whom there was no adult person other than one needed to care for the children, able to work and provide a reasonable subsistence compatible with decency and health—would have extended aid to virtually all poor children. This eligibility criterion would have provided federal funding for permanent assistance to all poor families with children under sixteen.[55] Certainly the CES definition could have included, for example, the children of unemployed or underemployed men in two-parent families, children in foster homes, and children staying with relatives; and it was designed specifically to exempt a child's caretaker from employment obligation. So forceful was the FERA group at this time that this definition remained in the draft of the bill sent to Congress.

The crux of events in 1935, from a gendered perspective, was that as the welfare system grew in size and importance, men took it over. This loss to women arose from the limitations of Children's Bureau welfare ideas combined with the influence of societal sexism on both men and women. Male "takeover" has been a standard pattern in professionalization—indeed it has been suggested that the proportion of women in a field is an inverse indication of the degree to which it has been professionalized.[56] This process does not require a conspiracy: Male domination of high-status jobs does not depend on individual misogynous motives or a takeover mentality but merely the normal ways in which men are socialized to greater ambition, assertiveness, self-confidence and women to timidity; and the ways in which even unusually assertive women can be disregarded or disdained. The New Deal was the key turning point in this development: Previously women had dominated the welfare field; afterward they steadily lost their authoritative place.

Bitterly, women's own successes contributed to their demotion as a sex. Women were leaders of the drive for the professionalization of social work and of welfare administration, which then raised the status and the pay of those jobs to the degree that they became desirable to men.[57] Women led campaigns for governmental welfare responsibility, which then made welfare a matter of state and of interest to men. Women's early success in getting some New Deal positions soon became a limit: Previously the white women's network had operated a kind of hiring hall in which they controlled who got jobs because they were asked to recommend people; in the New Deal those they recommended for appointments had to be approved by the Democratic party.[58] Women had been the vanguard of the scientific study of social problems, which helped create academic disciplines and largescale research funding from which they were then excluded. In a variety of professions, women's share of academic degrees and jobs peaked between 1920 and 1940 and then declined.[59] Another aspect of women's dwindling influence was the decline of religious and moral discourse in politics. One source of women's power had been its passionate and adept use of moral suasion. Julia Lathrop was already aware in 1929 of the faltering influence, the old-fashionedness, of what she called, with tongue in cheek, the "'woman's program' . . . Peace Home Children."[60] The early-twentieth-century transfer of responsibility for the poor to the state and experts was one face of a decline of religion, a secularization, in American domestic policy, and this trajectory directly correlated to the ebb of organized women's influence.

Yet another source of the weakening of the social feminist lobby was women's voting. In the early 1920s there were widespread hopes and fears—depending on one's political perspective—that woman suffrage would make a large qualitative difference in voters' choices. Politicians of the 1920s expected a large "gender gap," but it did not materialize. By 1930 the constraining fear of the female vote had dissipated.[61] Women remained vital in the 1936 election, and they knew it. The Women's Division produced and distributed 90 percent of the Democratic National Committee's campaign material, for example. But the direct result of women's loss of political autonomy was that Roosevelt was able to harness their power, discipline, and stamina without repaying his debt.

The New Deal's welfare programs would not have looked substantially different had the Children's Bureau been abolished in 1930. Organized women had little success in preventing or correcting discrimination against women in New Deal programs. But New Deal welfare legislation would have been quite different if the Children's Bureau had *never* existed. Its influence was long-term, not short-term, in its years of lobbying for the principle of federal social responsibility and in its specific endorsement of mothers' aid as the paradigm for federal public assistance.

Social Security and Congress

After drafting ADC the Children's Bureau experienced nothing but defeat. One after another, crucial parts of its plan were shattered. The losses were not caused by CES betrayal. Witte was a social insurance man, to be sure, but he was above all a political compromiser, a wise choice for FDR precisely because he was primarily committed to getting *something* through the Congress. Witte and his staff worked hard to defend the Children's Bureau version of ADC against congressional amendment. As the CES responded to various restrictive amendments, some of the Children's Bureau's priorities always remained on these short lists, especially its request for federal power to supervise state administration of ADC procedures.[62] Witte and Perkins sacrificed provisions the Children's Bureau thought important because, along with Roosevelt, they believed these compromises absolutely necessary to passage of the whole omnibus bill.

Two sources of opposition were particularly responsible for changes in the ADC title: southern Congressmen and the economic interests they represented, who demanded protection of their low-wage labor force; and politicians who benefited from patronage power at the state level. (Had the bill included medical insurance or public works provisions, as originally promised by the administration, still other powerful interests would have been engaged in the opposition.) The first victory of these groups was referring the bill to the House Ways and Means Committee rather than the significantly more liberal Labor Committee. The chair of Ways and Means was Robert L. Doughton of North Carolina, who served in Congress from 1911 to 1953 and represented his own substantial economic interests in agriculture and banking as well as those of his constituents. Reported out, it was passed in the House on April 15 and sent, without further changes to Title IV, to the Senate Finance Committee. Its chair was the powerful Pat Harrison of Mississippi, who had been in Congress for twenty-four years, serving in the House from 1911 to 1919 and then in the Senate until his death in 1941. Doughton's and Harrison's support was essential.[63] Reported to the Senate on May 13, the bill passed on June 20. Then a House-Senate conference reconciled differences, and the president signed the final version on August 14.[64]

Congressional amendments involved two major aspects of ADC: which agency and what kind of experts were to administer the program, and with how much centralized control. The outcomes of these disputes, defeats for the Children's Bureau, marked ADC permanently, creating many of its deficiencies today.

In the intra-administration politicking about control, the Children's Bureau met three challenges to its jurisdiction: from the Public Health

Service, the FERA, and the social insurance group that eventually formed the Social Security Administration. The first two challenges it defeated, but not the third.

The PHS tried alternately to defeat and to seize control of Title V, which included three maternal and child welfare programs. Its constituency was, as before, physicians who had viewed the Children's Bureau, with good reason, as supporters of "socialized medicine" as a result of the bureau's promotion of the Sheppard-Towner Act. The PHS called for a "functional" model of organization—all federal *health* programs should be united in one agency. Grace Abbott responded with a "population" model—services for *children* should be united in one agency. In fact the organizational arguments veiled fundamental political disagreements. The Children's Bureau mobilized the social work network, which was entirely unified in its support, and succeeded in separating some prominent physicians from the PHS lobby, producing a modest victory: Title V survived, and another PHS attempt to restrict or abolish the Children's Bureau was defeated.[65] Martha Eliot later concluded, however, that the Children's Bureau was victorious only because the president had already decided against a substantive health insurance proposal, and the AMA knew it.[66]

Expecting the battle over Title V, the Children's Bureau was not actively campaigning about ADC; it had never occurred to them that anyone else would want to bother with ADC. The CES assumed that the Children's Bureau would supervise ADC; as a continuation of mothers' pensions, ADC was quite simply "theirs."[67] When the CES shifted, assigning the program to the FERA in the version sent to the House, the bureau was surprised and shocked.[68]

The struggle for control of ADC displayed jurisdictional rivalry and a certain amount of personal hostility, but also competing conceptions of social provision. Three welfare visions were in play. The Children's Bureau aimed to strengthen casework in a particular program as a means of moving toward a permanent federal-state program of social work that would combine relief and counseling.[69] The FERA's perspective, critical of the elitism of the Children's Bureau/ child welfare network, was oriented to massive relief programs and direct federal works projects. The social insurance perspective, represented by CES leadership, advocated limits on the assistance programs in order to keep them less desirable and less popular than the new and untried insurance programs. The social insurance perspective thus mandated that the assistance programs should not be independent, and it was the influence of this perspective, not of the FERA, that ultimately cost the Children's Bureau control over ADC.

The FERA's bid for ADC was part of a larger strategy to become the core of a permanent federal welfare agency—a venture that intersected with a major split in the social work profession.[70] While the social work Left was supporting Lundeen, the radical alternative to Social Security, and conservatives were behind whatever the administration offered, moderates looked to the FERA. At first Hopkins was every social worker's hero. In the New Deal's honeymoon period Hopkins made large promises. The honeymoon ended with his abrupt termination of the CWA jobs program in March 1934, a move that put 4 million people back into the relief offices.[71] Discontent among social workers reached a peak in January 1935 in the midst of negotiations over the Social Security Act, when FDR announced federal withdrawal from relief. By the fall of 1935 many AASW chapters were holding protest meetings about the ending of the FERA.[72] These cutbacks did not so much cost Hopkins support among social work moderates as they made him appear to be their best hope within the administration.

While the FERA wanted to unify all public assistance in one program, Children's Bureau women wanted their programs removed from relief so as to protect their clients from stigma and humiliation. They sought the "psychology" of a social insurance program without its contributory or universal nature, Lenroot recalled years later. The Children's Bureau believed that it was best suited to uphold high meritocratic standards in state administration of ADC, because of its long experience with state officials in the mothers' aid laws. It argued that FERA administration, which would take place entirely outside the existing mothers' aid apparatuses, would "necessarily pull down the carefully built standards of the Mothers' Aid program and virtually result in giving children aid which was little better than local poor relief."[73]

The FERA, on the other hand, thought the public assistance programs were "an opportunity to capitalize the recent gains in standards of relief and administration and to use the emergency structure to bridge over the transition period until the states could establish permanent public welfare programs."[74] FERA supporters argued that the rationalization of all federal relief programs under one agency would simplify bureaucracy, preventing families from having to negotiate with a series of agencies. ADC was not, they said, really child centered but should be part of a general program of income maintenance. Their view gathered support from those who resented the Children's Bureau's emphasis on expertise and professional standards. This hostility emanated both from federal and state bureaucrats and from politicians' desire to preserve political control over relief and welfare jobs. The FERA group did not believe that relief ought to be mixed with casework; they did not deny the usefulness of the latter but suspected the social control potential in tying relief to "treatment." Josephine Brown, an important spokesperson for the FERA on this issue, criticized the "individualistic philosophy of the case work field" and called the mothers' pension support network the "spiritual successors of Dorothea Dix."[75] She also challenged the older social work professionalism in another way, calling for the training of social workers at state universities and agricultural colleges. Like others of a slightly younger generation, influenced as much by depression radicalism as by Progressive Era reform, she was developing a different and broader vision of social work, one that questioned the premises of casework and the women's Progressive Era program.[76] She was trying to adapt the social work profession to a welfare state.

From this depression social work dream of a welfare state came the idea of a federal department of welfare, or of health, education, and welfare. The FERA was not the only source of this strategy. Many social work leaders promoted the proposal. Homer Folks, for example, argued for such a department on grounds nearly opposite to those of the FERA, maintaining that welfare work required a "different technique . . . from that of those departments which are direct operating concerns. . . . This technique is primarily that of cooperation with the corresponding State Departments, and, through those Departments, with local governmental activities."[77] But the Children's Bureau opposed the creation of such a department. Lenroot's argument that it would separate welfare from labor concerns may have been a bit disingenuous, but she honestly feared that the FERA legacy, which she considered one of federal arbitrariness and even tyranny in relation to state and local officials, would spoil the cooperative relations the Children's Bureau had built.[78] Central control also meant, to the child welfare establishment, undermining the principles of categorical relief and of casework; it meant the victory of the irresponsible (in their view), no-strings-attached kind of relief with which Hopkins was associated. No less important was their conviction that the Children's Bureau had more power under Perkins in the Department of Labor than it would have in a welfare department. Even after ADC went to the Social Security Board, the Children's Bureau group continued to campaign against a department of welfare because, they figured, Hopkins would be its secretary and the Children's Bureau subordinated.[79] Grace Abbott saw him as an imperialist, attempting to control more and more. "I wish you had some way of keeping Harry Hopkins in bounds," she wrote to Lillian Wald in 1937, long after the Children's Bureau's loss of ADC.[80] The animosity was mutual. Hopkins referred to the social workers in the federal government as "pantry snoopers,"[81] and Aubrey Williams of the WPA vowed to end the "mothers' aid group."[82]

But the Children's Bureau's enmity to Hopkins was also deeply, if covertly, feminist. Abbott and Lenroot knew that Hopkins's power demoted one of the two federal agencies that most represented organized women.[83] When welfare spending was marginal and aimed at an unfortunate minority, it was women's work; when it became large-scale national policy it was men's. However muted the bureau's identification with a women's rights program, the younger generation of women that came into federal welfare work through the CES or the Social Security Board, such as Burns, Hoey, or Armstrong, seemed far less likely to defend the specific interests of women. In the depression context the Children's Bureau's quiet, elite, middle-aged feminism looked conservative from other perspectives. For example, the bureau no longer commanded the support of the professional organizations. The AASW, the American Public Welfare Association, and the NCSW, where the greatly increased numbers of public-sector social workers could be found, supported Hopkins, while the Child Welfare League of America, representing mainly older private charities, and key women's organizations sprang to the support of the Children's Bureau.

Children's Bureau feminism was defeated, but not by the FERA. Rather in the course of 1935 the interests of the third and more conservative group, social insurance advocates, embodied in the new Social

Security Board, emerged paramount. What made the social insurance men "conservative" in this context was not only their lack of interest in women's needs. And they were not as a group opposed to public assistance.[84] Their conservatism was in fact quite similar to that of the Children's Bureau: They were willing to establish a nonuniversal program, to create a plan exclusively for the upper working class and middle class. They did not merely accept exclusion forced upon them by politics. They had never seriously considered a universal program of insurance, one that would include housewives, sharecroppers, domestic servants, for example. Moreover, they tried to make a virtue of these exclusions, building political support among social insurance recipients by denigrating and actually worsening the programs aimed at the poor. Their fundamental programmatic elitism was similar to that of the mothers' aid tradition: Detesting the dishonor of the dole, they created programs that removed some from the stigma while deepening the stigma for others. Like the Children's Bureau in its vision of ADC, but with a different rationing mechanism, the Social Security Board built an elite, restrictive program.

As the bill made its way through Congress there were several about-faces on the question of who would run ADC. The administration bill had assigned ADC and Old-Age Assistance to the FERA; the House Ways and Means Committee, viewing Hopkins and the FERA as a dangerous expansion of central executive power, claimed to be reluctant to assign a permanent program to an emergency agency and gave the program to the Social Security Board.[85] The Senate Finance Committee, subjected to intense lobbying from the Children's Bureau and its supporters, returned ADC to the Children's Bureau and placed the whole Social Security Board within the Department of Labor.[86] But the deal worked out in the conference committee sent all the assistance programs to the Social Security Board and created within *it* a new Bureau of Public Assistance. Witte lobbied without success for a compromise solution, which would have placed the Social Security Board in the Department of Labor.[87] Congressional opposition to this proposal took force from conservative views that the department was entirely too prolabor as well as from specific hostility to Perkins; Altmeyer thought she was disliked both because she was a woman and because, like her Children's Bureau subordinates, she did not cooperate enough with demands for patronage.[88] Loyal bureaucrats to the end, the Children's Bureau network testified and campaigned for the Social Security Act despite their loss of ADC. And the bureau retained control of the maternity and child health services, which it hoped would grow.

What, then, would have been different had the Children's Bureau administered ADC? Children's Bureau ADC agents might have been expected to press for a stronger casework approach. Since the Children's Bureau hoped for the expansion of public provision, its version of casework might have been less often reduced to scrutiny against cheating and more oriented to treatment and provision of a variety of services. Lenroot, upon later reflection, argued that ADC caseworkers would have concentrated less on questions of eligibility and more on "teaching" the women. She also believed that the program would therefore have been less stigmatized.[89] The fact that a maternal and child health program would have been administered simultaneously by the same agency would have promoted casework as well as strengthening its medical component, and would have helped to combat stigma.

There is no reason to think that Children's Bureau administration would have reduced discrimination in eligibility for ADC, given the agency's commitment to building a privileged program for "deserving" single mothers. This is not to say that the FERA would have been better; neither mothers' aid nor FERA local programs had good records for nondiscriminatory administration. Both were biased against "moral" deviance as well as racial minorities; the Children's Bureau had a poor record in regard to the needs of the black population—at best, one of neglect.[90] The casework approach, with its emphasis on the discretion of the social worker and the "family budget" method of determining stipends, might have held back the development of an administrative or legal notion of an entitlement to ADC.[91]

Removing ADC from the Children's Bureau placed it with the other two "assistance" programs as poor stepsisters of social insurance, its fate controlled by a wicked stepmother, the Social Security Board. Children's Bureau administration of ADC would have created resistance, at least, to the invidious distinction that honored social insurance programs and dishonored ADC—in other words, to the stratified system of welfare that was developed. The bureau's emphasis on social work expertise as well as nonpartisan administration might have had an antistigmatizing effect. This emphasis might also have made casework *work*, so long as the ADC rolls remained relatively small. The casework approach might have proved more effective than an administration emphasizing strictly means- and morals-testing in actually helping single mothers to achieve economic independence from government provision, through personal counseling and the provision of education and child care services.

But the "welfare" rolls did not remain small, and their growth made casework impossible. Not only did clients resist the hierarchical and supervisory assumptions inherent in casework, but casework is very expensive. (Means- and morals-testing are also expensive, of course.) Probably ADC would have continued to be starved for appropriations, as it would still have been identified as a noncontributory program supporting "deviant" families, competing with contributory programs supporting conventional ones.

One claim can be made with certainty about the impact of the loss of ADC by the Children's Bureau: It blocked the maternalist strategy that had guided the women's welfare network since the 1890s—that of making children the key to social progress, the first step toward legitimating federal welfare provision for all. The removal of ADC from the Children's Bureau and its placement among the other public assistance programs under the Social Security Board killed the dream of an elite mothers'-aid program. Now ADC recipients were affected by the stigma of the other noncontributory programs and of the poor people not covered by the "nonwelfare" programs like Old Age Insurance. Not only were ADC recipients not elite, they were the opposite, and the children-first strategy was reversed. We got a system in which children are arguably the social group least well served by welfare policy, particularly in comparison with the elderly.[92]

Children's Bureau control over ADC would have strengthened a federal agency representing women's political power. The existence of such a power center might have had far-reaching, if indirect, influence, possibly reducing the extent to which women lost ground politically and professionally during the 1940s and 1950s. But the opposite causality was more consequential: The Children's Bureau lost control of ADC because of the declining dynamism of the women's movement.[93] The women's organizations with welfare concerns were losing energy and clout.

The second major conflict in the legislative history of ADC, concerned what federal criteria local ADC programs would be required to meet. Its outcome not only shaped the welfare system but also influenced the federal structure of the American state.

Federalism has often been misconstrued as a set of federal-state relations, but in fact local governments—municipal or town and county or parish—have been significant in the United States. Poor relief had originally been a local affair. At the turn of the twentieth century the rise of "scientific charity" began to coordinate both private and public relief along broader lines. State boards of welfare systematized indoor and outdoor public relief; charity organization societies rationalized private benevolence. After about 1910 states began to provide public assistance in "categorical" programs for particular types of needy people: most commonly the blind, the old, the children without fathers. But while these were state laws, most of them still left control with local authorities. In fact most of the laws were permissive rather than mandatory: They did not require but only authorized counties and other localities to establish programs with state financial contributions. And most localities did not provide mothers' aid.

The Social Security Act ratcheted these programs up a notch, replacing what had once been state-local relations with federal-state relations. The act stipulated that states had to provide a single state agency to administer public assistance programs. This was a major step toward systematization and homogenization of provision. But it was a step backward from the emergency New Deal programs toward decentralized control. Only one of the five Social Security programs that gave money to individuals—OAI—was entirely federal. The others were all based on federal grants to the states, with varying degrees of control left to the states. One might make the generalization that the closer to federal control, the more respectable and generous the welfare program. Thus the struggle about the strength of the federal guidelines for ADC was momentous, both on its own and as part of the New Deal's construction of a new federalism.[94]

The ADC design did not simply add federal aid to the mothers' aid programs but reflected the 1920s growth of state government capacity and responsibility. State responsibility, in turn, made it easier for federal supervision to be effective. The CES draft of ADC established strong federal standards—strong precisely because they were general—allowing the federal supervisory agency wide discretion to approve or disapprove local programs. These guidelines included a broad definition of eligible children, a general minimum level for stipends, and minimum qualifications for administrators and investigators.[95] Thus, requiring a single state agency to handle the programs also made it more likely that professionals would be in control, an added boost for the Children's Bureau.

But these rules were virtually all removed before the Social Security Act was passed, contributing further to making the assistance programs less desirable than the entirely federal Old-Age Insurance and Unemployment Insurance, which retained more federal requirements.

The attack on federal standards came not only from Congress but also from state politicians. Given the emergency spirit in which the legislation was being considered and the widespread belief that the assistance programs would shrink and possibly disappear over time, saving federal and state revenues was not a dominant motive. The primary motive, emanating particularly from southern politicians, who monopolized crucial committee chairmanships, was to protect employers' access to the primarily black but also Latino agricultural and domestic labor force of the South and Southwest. The threat to this economic system from Social Security was not only that recipients would lose their incentive to perform low-wage labor (it is crucial here that among the southern black poor, single mothers, and the elderly were regular members of the labor force) but also that other wage earners freed from the burden of supporting dependents might similarly become more resistant to accepting low wages. This intention incorporated employers' wish to hold black women in field labor and domestic service.[96] The number of workers at issue was massive: Of approximately 5.5 million African American workers, for example, 2 million were in agriculture and 1.5 million in domestic service. A secondary motive was politicians' desire to retain control over patronage jobs in local assistance programs, a control directly threatened by the federal standards proposed by the Children's Bureau.

Even before it was amended, ADC had been designed to accommodate the southern employing class and other conservatives.[97] A one-year state residence requirement eliminated many migrant workers. States had to take the initiative in developing ADC programs; the federal statute guaranteed nothing. It left to the states the specific determination of eligibility, which encouraged continuing reliance on the "suitable home" requirements encoded in most mothers' pension statutes, the requirement most often relied upon to exclude needy but "undesirable" families. The last was a policy opposed by more progressive social workers but still supported by the Children's Bureau establishment.[98] Indeed federal ADC administrators encouraged it: The model state law distributed by the Social Security Board read, "any dependent child who is living in a suitable family home."[99] In general, localism in the administration of poor relief has long been a method of protecting local employers from the potential of welfare stipends to increase workers' bargaining power, and the Social Security Act was no exception to this tradition.[100]

After the first draft of the bill, but before it was sent to Congress, FDR's men negotiated more changes, private bargains with powerful Democratic leaders.[101] The best known was the exclusion of agricultural and domestic laborers from social insurance. Even ten years after the legislation was passed, after numerous expanding amendments, one-third of black male and two-thirds of black female workers were excluded.[102] Equally important was the sacrifice of federal standards in the assistance programs, deemed necessary to the bill's passage by the administration leadership. Without federal control, state and local agents were free to exclude whoever they wished. Southern administrators typically "could see no reason why the employable Negro mother should not continue her usually sketchy seasonal labor. . . . They had always gotten along." Numerous southern states required ADC mothers to take jobs whenever available, kicking them off the rolls—often called the "farm policy." Blacks were systematically deprived of access to ADC benefits: In 1937–40 only 14–17 percent of recipients were black, far below the proportion of their need.[103] Add to this policy the rationalization that blacks needed less to live on than whites, and the unsurprising result was great inequality in the size of stipends: In 1940 the Alabama monthly average was $13.63, compared to $32.39 nationally; in 1954 Mississippi was the lowest, at $26.20, when the national average was $80.24.[104] This racial double standard was a risk inherent in the Children's Bureau strategy of federal-state cooperation.[105]

Lack of concern about racism contributed to Children's Bureau optimism about working with the states. The bureau staff treated complaints about the mistreatment of minorities as marginal, just as minority mothers and children were marginal in their mental portrait of the desired "clients" for ADC.[106] Lack of class consciousness made them similarly naive: Accustomed to their own rather noblesse-oblige approach to helping the poor, they did not recognize that others had interests in keeping the poor poor. Thus they had no reason to doubt that continued progress in improving the size, extent, and fairness of welfare programs would come about as a natural result of increasing professional standards both in casework and in administration. They had a Whiggish view of historical process as almost inevitable, however unsteady, progress.

But their commitment to federal standards was a principled stand, not just a means to Children's Bureau authority. Even after it was clear that the Social Security Board would control ADC, the Children's Bureau women continued to fight for stronger federal supervision. And they did not enter the battle about standards naive or unprepared; they knew they would meet strong opposition. In designing Sheppard-Towner, which was modeled on the Department of Agriculture's extension activity, its staff had studied the varied precedents for federal-state programs since 1917; this study was repeated in 1935.[107] In reflecting on the final law, Witte concluded that no other federal aid legislation had ever gone to such lengths to deny the federal government supervisory power.[108]

We can get a sense of how the losses were accumulated by looking at some of the amendments. The bill sent to the House defined dependent children in the FERA-proposed language, including all for whom there was "no adult person, other than one needed to care for the children, able to work and provide a reasonable subsistence compatible with decency and health."[109] The Ways and Means Committee specified a more limited set of relatives in whose home the child had to be living, removed the requirement that stipends be high enough to create a "reasonable subsistence," and removed the exemption of the adult needed to care for the children. The Senate Finance Committee then further narrowed the eligibility definition by specifying that the children had to have "been deprived of parental support or care by reason of the death, continued absence from the home, or physical or mental incapacity of a parent."

The administration bill required that state plans "furnish assistance at least great enough to provide, when added to the income of the family, a reasonable subsistence compatible with decency and health." The Ways and Means Committee added maximums—eighteen dollars for the first child and twelve dollars for each additional—which remained in the final act. The CES leadership agreed that this was a disaster; Joseph Harris of Witte's staff wrote Aubrey Williams that the "worst provisions in the [Social Security] bill are those which limit the federal aid to dependent children to the arbitrary amounts."[110] Witte called it "utterly inadequate and completely out of line with pensions of $30 per month to individual old people"; he also called attention to the fact that "the allowance for the first child must include the mother and really covers two persons."[111] The Senate Finance Committee confirmed the maximums adopted by the House and removed the provision that the assistance ought to create "decency and health."

The CES bill provided for federal rules and regulations "necessary to effectuate the purposes of this title." The Ways and Means Committee specified that federal rules could not include the selection, tenure, and compensation of personnel. This was of course a defense of patronage jobs, and deprived the federal agency of any possibility of maintaining professional standards of administration; it was one of the changes most objectionable to the Children's Bureau and the CES. They offered compromise suggestions—to require state departments to set their own minimum personnel qualifications, and to supervise local administrative agencies through rules and regulations approved by the federal agency—but without success.[112]

As federal regulatory power was removed from the assistance programs, the only federal recourse was to disapprove of entire state plans. This meant, of course, that federal officials could face a choice between accepting inadequate, corrupt, and/or discriminatory plans, or denying aid to all the single mothers and children in a state. As the process of removing federal controls continued, the CES tried to get, as a compromise, a kind of line-item-veto power: the ability to disallow parts of state programs. This attempt also failed.[113]

The CES held on to the requirement that qualifying ADC programs be statewide, but the purpose of the rule was soon vitiated. This demand was a floor upon which any further expansion of a welfare state would have to build. (Today there are complaints about "welfare" claimants crossing state lines to get better benefits; imagine if benefits changed across county lines!) The requirement was intended to stop discrimination and patronage from determining who got aid and who didn't; to guarantee that locations where there was little political power—notoriously, minority and rural areas—or locations whose dominant party was out of power, would not be deprived of programs.[114] A variety of procedures soon developed, however, to get around this attempted guarantee of equal provision. Winifred Bell's 1965 study of ADC provides several examples: Despite the existence of a statewide standard of assistance, grants could vary on the basis of cost-of-living variations, which in turn could be (and often were) determined on the basis of extremely subjective values. Even with a single state agency supervising, in fact the programs could be run in a decentralized fashion with the state agency merely claiming responsibility. It was within a state's right to call for counties to initiate programs with their own revenues, which would then be matched by the state, and those in turn matched by the federal government; thus both the proportion of those aided and the level of grants could vary according to local politics.[115]

The final Social Security Act kept the proviso that public assistance stipends, once granted, could not be denied without a fair hearing. In the first decades of ADC this was an almost useless provision, since so few recipients were able to use this right. Later, particularly in the 1960s, it was to become the basis for many welfare rights victories.

Again, what if? How might ADC have been different had federal standards remained and been enforced? Ultimately this greater central control would have altered the entire shape of our welfare state. Given the right political circumstances, federal standards might well have created the leverage to federalize entirely the funding of assistance programs. Higher stipends and wider inclusion of needy single-mother families would have made the program more expensive, by increasing the cost of each client family, and by encouraging many more families to apply. The kind of rapid expansion of the rolls that occurred in the 1960s might have happened much earlier. But such a huge expansion in the late 1930s and 1940s might have had different political meanings and induced a different response. During the depression there was broad support for public social provision and a weakening of the view that the needy were themselves responsible for their predicament. Moreover, it was the very weakness of the public assistance programs—the development of the stratified welfare system—that stigmatized the poorer programs; ironically, if ADC had cost taxpayers more, it might also have been regarded as a more nearly universal program, potentially benefiting the middle and working classes as well as the marginal. At the same time the inclusion of more minority recipients might have resulted in the hiring of more minority people as caseworkers and administrators, thus influencing welfare thought.

Would higher stipends have decreased fathers' support payments or alimony? This has not been studied empirically, but the effect would have been small, since fathers' payments were minimal. Would higher stipends have increased the divorce and marital separation rate? It seems quite likely, on the basis of current findings, that higher public assistance payments would have had a small effect in that direction, particularly among the white poor, where poverty is a factor in coercing women to stay in unwanted marriages. It is not clear how to evaluate such a trend, since there are disadvantages in both directions: Marital separations are hard on the individuals involved and on the children; but the prevention of marital separation often increases levels of family violence and problems, which also damage adults and children.

A different ADC would have affected attitudes about mothers' employment, which deeply influence the program to this day. Lone mothers were caught in a double bind created by the lingering maternalism of its creators. Mothers were supposed to be at home with their children, and depression-stimulated campaigns to drive married women out of the labor force supported that orientation. But low stipends and restriction of availability forced mothers to earn, on or off the books.[116] In 1930, 28.8 percent of employed women were married; in 1940, 35.0 percent.[117] A more generous ADC program would have kept more mothers at home but more likely it would have improved the overall labor-market position of women: fewer would have been forced to take the worst kinds of work, casual labor and home work, while others would have been hired as welfare caseworkers and clerical workers.[118] A nonmaternalist welfare policy might have encouraged some of the supports that make it easier for mothers to earn, notably child care.

Silences

Even more portentous than the amendments weakening the Children's Bureau draft of ADC were the alternatives that were never even considered. Some options were not imagined necessary by the designers of the legislation; some they believed to be politically impossible. The object of discussing these suppressed alternatives is not to blame or criticize the welfare advocates of that time, but to see the structural limitations of ADC.

The law was silent about unmarried mothers. Many social workers knew they existed, and plentifully, but believed that public assistance for them would be vulnerable to political attack and therefore futile to pursue. Nor was divorce in the discourse. There was already enough support-the-traditional-family rhetoric around, and these welfare advocates remembered the charge that mothers' pensions undermined the family. The Children's Bureau group would probably not be surprised by today's conservative charges that ADC creates incentives to out-of-wedlock childbearing and marital disruption. They believed the best strategy was reticence and allowing states to handle these controversies. But they did not conceive how rapid and drastically rates of divorce and then out-of-wedlock birth would grow and become major social issues.

This ticklish problem and its avoidance occurred within another silence about the possibility of universal child allowances, or even allowances to all poor children. ADC was reserved for the children of poor single mothers. It set up a doubly stigmatized group. There is an irony here: The designers of ADC wanted to create a special group because they thought they could thus keep it an elite group. What happened was the opposite: The rapid decline in youthful widowhood and the rise in the "wrong" kind of single motherhood made poor single mothers a suspect group. A European strategy of universal allowances, proposals with which the Children's Bureau group was acquainted, would have obviated this problem of respectability. A program of grants for all children, which could then have been taxed away from prosperous people, might by today have become a commonplace entitlement, like old-age pensions or home-mortgage tax deductions. Alternatively, an allowance for all poor children would have avoided some of the anomalies of ADC. Two-parent as well as single-parent families would have gained, giving the program broader support; the fear that federal aid was subverting the male-headed family would have been muted. In fact the original ADC law did not require means-testing; states could in theory have written their programs as universal. Only in 1939 did amendments require this, and by 1941 every state program had a means test. But it is unreasonable to think that states could have inaugurated universal programs. The limited federal funds available would have made this impossible; such a program required national leadership.

The morals-testing employed in ADC, on the basis of the "suitable home" provision in the law, also had its negative charge strengthened because of the program's association with the poor. It was the particular intersection of means- and morals-testing that so tainted ADC. Adding suspicion of poverty to suspicion of single mothers created not just a sum but a new entity—a new definition of dependency that drew in connotations of laziness, greed, and female sexual immorality.

Ironically, early welfare reformers had hoped to avoid morals-testing by focusing on children, who were ipso facto innocent. But they could not fend off the question, How could immoral women care properly for innocent children? The paradoxical result was that a strategic decision to use sympathy for children ended by disadvantaging children, offering them a welfare program inferior to those offered other social groups, notably the elderly. Morals-testing could have been omitted in a gender-neutral plan to aid all who could not earn a living for themselves and their families—whether through unemployment or domestic labor—as a matter of right. Such a logic required a more fundamental break with family-wage assumptions than the dominant maternalist thinking of the welfare reformers would then allow. Only the Left and the Townsendites were making such claims in the 1930s, and the lack of influential feminist voices limited their appeal. Equally disregarded was a more radical maternalist alternative—that mothers should be paid by the state for their nurturing work, justifying their entitlement on the basis of their contribution as mothers rather than on the basis of their helplessness or virtue. An active principle in the discourse at the time of the mothers' pensions campaign two decades earlier, and a subtext in the contemporary agitation for radical welfare proposals such as Lundeen, this idea was never mentioned by Social Security supporters.

The greatest weakness in ADC, however, was beyond its designers' control because it arose from the relation between the public assistance and the social insurance programs. This relationship did not spring into being full-grown but was constructed by the Social Security Board in the late 1930s and the 1940s. When Old-Age Insurance (OAI) was first introduced to the public, it had many disadvantages:

Workers were to pay six–seven years of taxes before the first pensions would be paid out in 1942, while public assistance old-age assistance (OAA) could begin in 1936; those already elderly had no way of being included; many occupations were excluded; and OAI stipends were not necessarily higher than those from OAA. OAA was funded by general tax revenues and offered a much better bargain for most Americans; OAI required that workers pay a new, additional tax.[119] Indeed virtually every grassroots group campaigning for old-age pensions, as well as Harry Hopkins, had insisted on a "noncontributory" plan.[120] Equally important, on this new welfare field, social insurance had no higher respectability or status than public assistance. Social Security Board staff feared that OAA and OAI would compete with each other among the electorate, and that OAA might win.

The board therefore began a campaign to boost its controversial OAI and to denigrate OAA. Propaganda to legitimate such a program was appropriate and constructive; the problems were created by a competition in which OAI was promoted by creating invidious distinctions with other welfare programs. The start date for OAI pensions was advanced to 1940, and benefits were extended to cover survivors and dependents (thus institutionalizing the family-wage system, covering women as dependent wives rather than as mother-citizens). ADC was caught in this drive, which required worsening all the public assistance programs. Rejecting the principle of New Deal emergency programs, which provided nonrestricted grants, in 1937 the Social Security Board began to institute individual budgeting as a part of its officially recommended casework.[121] This procedure gave caseworkers great discretion in determining the size of a claimant's stipend and required claimants to submit to invasive and humiliating investigations and supplication to get help. From then on, the determination of need considered not only recipients' resources as they applied for ADC but also how the grants were spent. In 1939 for the first time amendments to Social Security required means-testing in public assistance programs. The Social Security Board even campaigned to lower OAA stipends.

Although the material worsening of public assistance alone would have deepened its stigma, the Social Security Board used ideological as well as financial warfare. It operated a large public relations campaign to sell OAI as an honored citizenship entitlement. The separate tax for OAI, which workers first perceived primarily as a disadvantage, was redefined as a token of the superiority of the program. As Theda Skocpol put it succinctly: "Through a clever and widely disseminated public metaphor, Americans were told that their "contributions" insured that each wage earner would be entitled in old age to collect benefits that he or she had 'individually earned.' Actually, benefits are paid out of a common fund."[122] Social Security Board propaganda portrayed the regressive payroll tax it collected as if it were a form of saving in which one got back what one put aside—as if being included in OAI automatically rendered the insured worker prudent. It openly denigrated public assistance programs as the resort of the feckless and the lower class.[123] Above all, it portrayed public assistance as charity and OAI as getting back something of one's own. In truth Social Security OAI (FICA) taxes were no more specific, earmarked contributions than was federal income tax; they were used as part of general revenue, and one's pension was not related to how much one contributed (most people got more than they contributed).[124]

=

What can we conclude from this legislative story? The inadequacy and disrepute of ADC today should not lead us to minimize the achievement of 1935. The Children's Bureau and its supporters installed aid to single mothers within the founding federal welfare law. By producing a separate program they got explicit recognition of single mothers as a deserving group. This attainment required no great contest in 1935 precisely because the network responsible for it had built a federal base for women's and children's welfare over several decades. The Children's Bureau group was limited by a gender vision that was rapidly becoming obsolete, but that relative conservatism contributed to the ease with which the ADC program was accepted. Had ADC not become so stigmatized, and had the Children's Bureau controlled it, amendments might have helped it to change and become capable of helping its recipients out of poverty.

The inferiority of ADC in comparison to other Social Security programs was not created directly by sexism or hostility to single mothers. On the contrary, to most legislators in 1935 single mothers were respectable, pitiable widows. The gender system imported by ADC designers came into play at a more basic level, through assumptions that made the program small and marginal and the programs for men large and honorable. But American politics and Congress in particular brought race into ADC and the whole Social Security package. Indeed one could say that the fate of ADC was defined by the Civil War and Reconstruction—by the economic race relations and party alignments then constructed. These included the South's loyalty to the Democratic party and the party's dependence on its southern support, the retention of strong states' rights in constitutional adjudication and in legislation, and the enforced low-wage labor of black agricultural and domestic service workers.

The factors that made the welfare law so excluding and so inequitable also contributed to creating the need for welfare, because they shored up the systems of race and sex discrimination and class exploitation that engendered poverty. These same systems produced more single mothers and kept them poor and in need of "welfare."

The Family Wage Umbrella as Drawn in 1919

10

Welfare and Citizenship

The Social Security Act was written by two kinds of people—and sometimes by the same people in two different roles—social planners and politicians. It united two great strains of the American reform tradition: a progressive welfare vision that emerged historically out of charity, transforming pity into justice, as Julia Lathrop called for; and American logrolling politics, which evoked the flexibility, patience, cleverness, and willingness to compromise of political leaders from Franklin Roosevelt to Grace Abbott. Lacking either of these, Social Security would not have happened. Readers may not agree about whether that alternative would have been better or worse, but all should agree that Social Security has given us a mixed legacy.

Despite its limits Social Security initiated a welfare state and laid down the premise that the federal government had a responsibility to protect its citizens from the cruelties of poverty. Despite its promise Social Security failed to provide that protection. ADC offered some federal protection to mothers left without male support, providing women a measure of economic insulation against total dependence on men. The legislation was a product of several generations of brave, creative, smart, and feminist women reformers committed to helping the poor, especially women and children. Yet their ultimate creation, ADC, has become one of the most-hated governmental programs, and no group has criticized it more than feminists.

The economic hardships of the 1980s and 1990s have spawned a resentment of entitlements. Millions of people working hard to survive and provide for their children resent the bite of taxes, especially tax money they believe to be benefiting others who, they imagine, may not work as hard. "Entitlements" has become a code word for undeserved benefits. Those who understand a welfare state to be an absolute necessity to a viable nation need to resist this pejorative redefinition.

We cannot do without the concept of entitlement because it is fundamental to citizenship. Citizens have rights to which they are entitled by law, and losing this understanding endangers the republic. As I was devising a title for this book, I looked for synonyms—I imagined "enrighted" and "encitizened"—but found none. We are entitled to due process, fair trials, and legal representation; to vote and to run for office; to security from attack and to protection of our property; to freedom to travel and to publish. As the welfare state expanded, our entitlements grew—extending for example to education, support in old age, protection from environmental hazards and infectious disease, and support for single mothers.

Moreover, the *feeling* of entitlement is also vital to the republic. It is the attitude of citizenship, the essence of independence; without it we would have subjects, not citizens. Of course, entitlements are limited by law, but we may be proud of the concept.

Citizenship also implies that entitlements are distributed fairly. Making fairness a reality depends on openness in government and on a knowledgeable citizenry—not so easily accomplished in a complex, massive state. Today's discussion of entitlements is muddied by the fact that so many of them are hidden. Anyone who examines federal or state budgets sees that most domestic governmental expenditures go proportionally less to the poor and more to the nonpoor. The question is, What counts as an entitlement? The victories of "special interests," as powerful lobbying groups are often called, have not been not only in winning government largesse but in getting it delivered in ways that are not construed as a benefit.

This is why we cannot look at "welfare," or ADC in particular, without considering the larger context of a welfare state and all its recipients. The case considered most closely in this book—ADC and how it was distinguished from social insurance—serves as an emblem of the way that in welfare, as in so much else, the moral question about who is adjudged deserving is often answered through politics. In 1935 the elderly did not appear more deserving than did lone mothers. A combination of militant social movements, voting power, social insurance ideas, and the interests of major employers managed, in part unintentionally, to get them defined as maximally deserving, to win substantial benefits for them, and to get those benefits defined as an entitlement and not as "welfare."

The distinction between entitlement and charity intersects and affects that between deserving and undeserving. In theory the deserving inspire both charity and entitlements. But in history entitlements redefined their beneficiaries as deserving, by the simple act of removing surveillance from recipients; while charity created more of the undeserving by intensifying the surveillance.

Today's "welfare" crisis, then, is as much about values as about costs. Costs and needs are real problems, of course, and tightly connected. The loss of industrial jobs and decline in real wages that have made "welfare" more needed also increased the burdens of paying for it. But the ethical decisions—Who deserves help? How much of the national income should go to the poor? How should this money be collected?—are clouded by empirical confusion. Basic facts are obscured, such as how much the nonpoor actually contribute to the poor, who gets most government money, what employment is available to "welfare" recipients. These confusions are not accidental artifacts of an expanding and therefore complex state, but products of political and ideological conflict in which the "facts" are always constructed by the contestation.

=

This book began with a paradox: Why was ADC, designed by feminists, so bad for women and children? The answer must begin with the understanding that ADC has been constructive as well as destructive; without this understanding, we cannot comprehend the motives of its designers nor why it has lasted. For many women, being able to support themselves and their children was a *sine qua non* for any kind of citizenship and, often, for personal safety and dignity. Women's economic dependence on men not only kept some imprisoned in wretched marriages but also reduced their bargaining positions within marriage, thus discouraging the development of mutually respectful relationships. ADC helped *all* women. ADC produces what some have called the "free rider" effect: Even those who oppose it and resist paying for it benefit from it, because it helped create the possibility of women's independence.

ADC was part of a feminist and welfarist vision—the accomplishment of an impressive women's political force within the federal government. Not only did they help women and children, but they also led in envisioning a commonwealth that could extend full citizenship to the poor. By installing their program within the foundational legislation of the welfare state, they created a basis for its continuation and expansion; a more tenuous program might have collapsed from lack of appropriation or been defeated by conservatives.

Yet even as ADC saved some women and children, it did not advance or foster them. Its history provides evidence that women's power does not always promote all women. If this seems surprising, it is because some commentators have employed the concept of gender as a universal, eternal, opposition of male and female and imagined it as a single determining factor. This look at welfare history employs a more dynamic and relational conception of gender, that is, as a set of social norms about the meanings of femaleness and maleness and about the sexual division of labor; contextual and historically changing; norms that work jointly with many other aspects of individual and group identity and experience. The gendered assumptions that underlie our welfare system were not universal; they expressed a dominant outlook, to be sure, but one that did not fit the needs and understandings of many less privileged citizens. And these gender assumptions did not necessarily express antagonism between men and women but were often shared by both sexes, albeit with different emphases. A shared gender system does not mean the absence of male power over women; it means rather that women struggle to gain power by adapting to their subordination and exploiting the space and means available to them. (For example, women took their social assignment to be child nurturers and used it to build a child welfare movement as a political power base.)

The structure of ADC arose from a maternalism shared by women and men, its practice "assigned" to women. Women welfare reformers, working in this female sphere, accepted a family-wage system. In the nineteenth century and earlier, the poor, women as well as men, had often crusaded for a family wage as a means of rescuing children from labor, lessening women's drudgery, and forcing concessions from capital—as well as confirming men's privileged positions. The family-wage slogan said that only men should earn, but it also said that ten hours' work a day (or eight or twelve) should be enough to support a whole family. But by the early twentieth century the family-wage norm was becoming conservative. It was never a victorious demand, and very few workers dependent on wage labor could ever support families single-handedly; instead poverty sent many wives and children into the wage-labor force, and the stresses of the industrial system seemed to leave more women and children without any male support whatsoever. Responding with anxiety, reformers feared worsening the situation by providing incentives for male irresponsibility and women's overwork. Long after the family wage was doomed, welfare experts tried to contrive a magical assistance program that would somehow shore it up. The result often placed single mothers in a double bind: Already victimized by the failure of the family-wage system, the charity or public assistance system added to their disadvantages—such as low wages and responsibility for children—by emphasizing domesticity as the only maternal virtue.

By the advent of the New Deal, the family-wage norm was a dead weight crushing the imagination of welfare reformers. No feminist leadership challenged the ominous decision to base entitlements to the social insurance programs on wage earning. The majority of women were disenfranchised from social citizenship rights by their very positions in society. While Grace Abbott and her successors were still hoping that ADC would shrink because social insurance would care for men's dependents, the same values and logic led to demands for the expulsion of married women from the labor force. As the family-wage ideal receded in the 1960s and after, and women's economic independence and single mothers became commonplace, the structure of ADC was held in place by the weight of its precedents and the usual administrative investment in continuity. Other anxieties, such as hostility to unwed mothers and to racial minorities, were mobilized to prevent ADC from being raised to the level—in size of stipend and durability of entitlement—of the insurance programs.

Race had been a powerful determinant of ADC from the beginning. In the Progressive Era, welfare reformers concentrated on immigrants, whom they considered racially different. Usually liberal and environmentalist, the reformers were confident that the immigrants could rise as individuals; but they often also perceived many immigrant cultures as inferior and believed that "Americanization" was essential to their welfare agenda. In the New Deal ADC designers intersected with different racial agendas. Social insurance men sought to serve many male immigrants, now disciplined into an industrial working class; FERA people wanted to include agricultural workers, even blacks, under the welfare umbrella. Race was a more potent element than gender in the constriction of Social Security, although racial motives were often indistinguishable from class motives, as an employing class fought to retain its low-wage labor force. The limits set by this opposition were gradually removed as welfare-claiming escalated in later decades and amendments took in formerly excluded groups. But racial consciousness built hostility to public assistance, deepening the stigmatization of its poor and often minority recipients while confirming the respectability of largely white and nonpoor social insurance recipients.

Gender and race interests interacted with professional and state actions. Social workers and social-planning advocates sought individual and collective advancement through building a welfare state. These professional agendas themselves expressed gender and race interests: conflicts and cooperation between women and men and, in the 1930s, between different class perspectives and a characteristically white racial vision. The power structures of Congress and disputes within the executive branch also delimited options and altered the law that materialized—and these structures, too, expressed male and elite patterns of power. Depression social protests produced an emergency atmosphere in which policy makers were bound to consider action urgent and inevitable. The most influential of these mobilizations expressed primarily white and male assumptions about who was needy and deserving.

All these influences carried the past into the present. Progressive Era axioms resisted new information. Both maternalist and social insurance assumptions, operative among Social Security's drafters, denied 1930s realities: growing minority numbers within the northern working class, an irreversible decline of southern agriculture, growing divorce rates, and married women's employment rates, for just a few examples. These holdovers from the past proved powerful because they were not challenged by social movements powerful enough to shift the paradigms. The civil rights movement was not even strong enough to force Roosevelt to condemn lynching, let alone to make the New Deal serve minority Americans equally; and it was itself male dominated, absent the challenge to family-wage assumptions being made by black women. Feminism was at a nadir, and a nonmaternalist vision of welfare was enunciated nowhere except on the Far Left. New Deal political culture, interpreting the threat to the family wage as temporary, glorified the breadwinner-male/domestic-female family.

Dual Social Citizenship

Social Security did not create inequality in social citizenship but solidified it.[1] Most scholars of welfare have noted that the United States has a stratified welfare system.[2] Its superior and inferior "tracks" can be identified variously—social insurance and public assistance, federal and state/local, contributory and noncontributory, contribution or rights-based and needs-based, beneficiaries and dependents, or entitlements and "welfare." The tracks relate obliquely to the old deserving/undeserving distinction: Legally the distinction is made *among* applicants to the inferior programs (because no moral judgements are made at all among those receiving entitlement stipends) and only the "deserving" collect, but in practice the stigma of the inferior programs spreads to all their recipients, and they are frequently all branded as undeserving, while the honor of the entitlement programs imbues all their recipients with honor. Yet another set of tracks distinguishes those "independent" citizens whose benefits (such as tax deductions, home mortgage assistance, public facilities, good schools) come from outside the "welfare" system and are therefore less visible from those "dependents" who collect "welfare."

Recently feminist scholars began to call attention to the gendering and racializing of this system of stratification. The superior programs are disproportionately white and male and they were designed to be so, because that was the dominant image of citizenship in 1935. Workmen's compensation, unemployment insurance, and old-age insurance excluded precisely the kinds of jobs that women and minorities are most likely to have—in small enterprises, for low wages, seasonal and "casual." In 1940, for example, 2.3. million women worked as domestics in private homes (4.4 percent of the entire labor force). Employees of nonprofit enterprises, another group excluded from old-age insurance, were also mainly (61 percent) female. Many of the 2.2 million excluded farm laborers were women.[3] There are no statistics on the numbers of women who were employed but failed to accumulate the continuous employment record required for coverage. Some of these exclusions were corrected in later amendments, but still in 1978–79, white males were 82 percent of the recipients of "primary" programs and women were 60 percent of the recipients of the "secondary," public assistance programs. As late as 1980, 90 percent of AFDC recipients had been employed but were nevertheless excluded from Unemployment Insurance (UI).[4] Moreover, even among the public assistance programs, ADC was the least generous.[5]

Symbolically and practically, welfare differentiation created two arenas of social citizenship: federal and local. White men were usually covered by federal provision, women and minority men by locally controlled programs. The federal programs have higher standards, more generous stipends, a bigger tax base to support them—and dignity. State programs are far more vulnerable to political attacks, declining tax bases and interstate competition. Imagine states trying to rid themselves of elderly residents by lowering Social Security old-age-pension benefits.

This gender analysis only holds if race and class discrimination are added. The exclusions from Social Security programs and the defeat of federal standards were directed at minority and low-wage labor of both sexes. Moreover, many women benefited, and were intended to benefit, from "primary" stream welfare programs, although originally most became eligible as "dependents."[6] Workmen's and unemployment compensation were, of course, a means of providing for the workmen's dependents, and old-age insurance was soon restructured so as to provide benefits for survivors as well as dependents. The treatment of these survivors and dependents varied according to the status of their men. By 1967 the average benefit to a child of a deceased worker under OASI was sixty-two dollars, under AFDC thirty-seven dollars.[7] The main losers were not women and children in general, but those of subordinated race and class.

Entitlement or discretion

The grounds for individual entitlements under Social Security vary, constructed by different streams of welfare thought and political strategy. Social insurance advocates legitimated old-age and unemployment insurance as rights and obligations of government, entitlements which individual citizens could claim in the courts if necessary. In doing so they succeeded in creating a powerful legitimation for a welfare program. They used a legal fiction that contracts had been established between government and citizen, or more specifically between government and worker. The covered worker's entitlement derived from labor—though not, of course, in all jobs—and from a notion that living to old age was ipso facto evidence of a contribution meriting a pension. The single mother's claim derived from need. As Eveline Burns put it in her definitive 1949 description of Social Security, "It is true that since the Social Security Act came into effect, certain groups of public assistance applicants . . . have been granted the right to appeal the agency decision. But because of the very nature of public assistance the 'right' is more apparent than real." As George Bigge of the Social Security Board said of ADC in 1944: "The amount of the payment is related to the need of the individual: that is basic to our conception of public assistance."[8]

In the primary programs the criteria of eligibility were elaborated in detail in the legislation and attendant regulations, affording the government's agent (for example, the worker in the unemployment compensation office) little discretion. In UI it was a matter of length of time at work, definitions of occupation, prescribed evidence that one was seeking work. The duration of the award was fixed, the amount of stipend an unchangeable factor of previous salary and legal maximum. In OAI, one could determine in advance exactly what one would collect.

By contrast, ADC clients faced caseworkers, supervisors, and administrators with discretion regarding who got aid and how much they got. States could define eligibility criteria so long as they did not violate a few federal provisions, and these—even the requirement that the program be statewide—were often evaded by explaining coverage in terms of individual eligibility requirements. The federal government prescribed no level of support. ADC designers preferred a family budgeting system to a flat rate because budgeting required casework in which a social worker would help a mother define the family's particular needs and manage the household economy in the most effective way. In practice the states offered little casework, because it was expensive, but gave "caseworkers" great discretion in setting the stipend, especially in a downward direction. They were encouraged to search for hidden resources within the family or household and to cancel or reduce stipends compensatorily. The budget method kept recipients insecure, encouraged them in dishonesty, and communicated that they were charity cases suspected of defrauding the citizenry.

Supervision

The federal statute did not require but merely permitted ongoing supervision of ADC recipients. But after the Social Security Act was passed, the Social Security Board went further in encouraging supervision and "suitable home" requirements for ADC receipt as part of its campaign to raise the status of the insurance programs. Determining suitability necessitated supervision.

The board encouraged states to supervise and rehabilitate clients. Its 1936 model state bill explained: "This Act affords a unique opportunity to raise the standards of home care. The feature should be stressed in the drafting of this legislation." It called for investigations of the home and periodic reconsiderations of the amount of assistance.[9] Home visits were the norm in casework at this time, and many social workers argued that clients preferred home visits, to protect their privacy against meeting others or being seen by others.[10] The drive to control expenses soon shifted the locus of supervision to offices, which most clients in fact preferred, and surveillance focused more on receipts and budgets and less on housecleaning. But the assumption remained that a public assistance client was in need of counseling and rehabilitation and had fewer privacy rights than others. After World War II social welfare leaders hoped to introduce the new psychiatric casework into ADC. This move represented not so much an expansion of the services offered to clients as another mode of infantilizing and victim blaming. A 1945 Social Security Board manual for public assistance agencies published vignettes that trivialized poverty as a source of clients' problems and blamed them instead on a lack of wisdom or maturity: Mrs. D. "cannot accept a wise plan for medical care" for her husband because "Mr. D. had been the head of the house and . . . Mrs. D. always had been dependent on him and on the approval and disapproval of others." Mrs. K. "showed complicated attitudes about her husband's mental illness" until "one day she brought out her fear that she had been to blame for his mental illness." Mrs. E. "at first placed the total responsibility for her son's delinquent behavior on his bad inheritance from his father and on his associates in the neighborhood. Only gradually, as the mother realized that the worker's interest in the boy's problem stemmed from a wish to help rather than from an impulse to check on and to criticize her, could she begin to admit her long-standing ineptitude . . . and her need for help in understanding him."[11] This psychiatrization never caught on because it would have been so expensive, but the attempt reveals an entirely different concept of a welfare program than that in unemployment compensation or OAI.

Means test and work test

When the Social Security Act was passed, only ADC required that clients be "needy."[12] To establish need a client had to be not only without income but also without resources, including property or services which many at the time considered essential, such as telephones or automobiles or houses, and which might stave off poverty and help a temporarily reduced client regain position. Cash savings were not allowed. Thus in many instances an ADC applicant would have to get rid of useful resources even at a loss, impoverishing herself in order to qualify. The program did not reward thrift. Moreover, in many states close relatives were legally responsible for the support of dependents, and more distant relatives might be pressured to provide. By contrast one could have millions and still collect unemployment compensation or OAI.

The means test was ongoing. If a resource was gained, in kind as well as in cash, it had to be reported and the stipend reduced proportionately. This requirement for continual requalification was a disincentive for upward mobility and "escape" from "welfare." Means tests served to increase the discretion of the caseworker and to decrease the predictability and sense of entitlement of the recipient, in sharp contrast, again, to the social "insurance" programs.

Closely related to the means test was what Joel Handler has called the "work test," which operated in contradictory ways for ADC recipients. Beneficiaries of general relief had either to prove that they were unemployable or be prepared to take virtually any employment, and black women in the South were in this respect treated much like men on relief. But for women elsewhere and for white women in the South, ADC operated a pincers trap. The rules banned paid employment unless the earnings were reported and then deducted from a stipend; but the stipends were beneath subsistence and caseworkers knew that their clients had to supplement their incomes somehow. Luck and skill at dissemblance, not rules, determined who got caught. The system turned workers once intended to be professional social workers into a bureaucratic police, for whom doing their jobs right encouraged clients' silence and cunning. Grace Abbott would have been horrified to hear these agents called caseworkers.

A comparison to the primary stream programs illustrates the ambivalence of ADC in relation to mothers' employment. OAI was intended to get the elderly out of the labor force; UI tried to keep men in the labor force—to preserve their identities as breadwinners. ADC was inconsistent. Its proclaimed mission was to keep mothers at home but its workings producing the opposite effect. No wonder so many have considered ADC simply punitive towards poor women. ADC was trapped in the gendered contradictions of its origins, the family-wage mythology.

Morals test

ADC was unique among all welfare programs in its subjection of applicants to a morals test. The most frequent measurement of a "suitable home" was sexual behavior. The presence of a man in the house, or the birth of an illegitimate child, made the home unsuitable. These provisions also permitted racist policies: For example, black-white relationships were particularly likely to make a child's home declared unsuitable. The search for these "moral" infractions produced intense supervision and violations of privacy. According to a leading ADC expert, writing about the 1940s and 1950s:

> Across the country three levels of surveillance emerged: 1) a home was watched during the day or night or both; 2) two investigators made a surprise visit with one at the front door, the other at the back door, in the hope of apprehending an errant man; or 3) the investigators demanded entry and searched the premises for a man or evidence that a man might be included in the family unit. . . . the "surprise element" of the actual visit was considered to be one of its chief merits.[13]

(The presence of a man could also make the family fail the means test. Through the administrative process recently called "deeming," caseworkers had the discretion to "deem" the income of any adult household members as available for the support of the dependent children.)

No welfare program, not even in the secondary, public assistance stream, investigated and judged men's sexual morality. Social Security, of course, had not invented this double standard. But once incorporated into welfare administration, it took on a new and more powerful life because it was enforced by a devastating penalty: ending subsistence payments for a mother and children.

Ironically in some states the morals test was enforced by making ADC a preferred program and referring those who did not provide "suitable homes" to general relief. There single mothers and their children usually received stipends still lower than those from ADC.[14] This policy derived from the original intent of the mothers' aid proponents, to let these recipients avoid the stigma of charity; this is what Edith Abbott meant when she promised that ADC would support only "nice" families.[15] The problem was that by policing ADC recipients to enforce "nice" behavior, the program became more, not less, stigmatizing.

=

The stratified welfare system produced a variety of deleterious consequences, political as well as economic, and not only for the poor. While universal benefits reinforce social coherence, the U.S. welfare system exacerbates resentments. Over time the resulting politics of resentment weakened the Democratic party. While some analyses of the demise of the Roosevelt political coalition have implicated an overexpansion of the welfare state, particularly "New Society" programs, the limited and fragmented welfare system of the New Deal was at least equally culpable. Social Security, by providing differential benefits, deepened fissures among the Democrats' own electoral constituency and undermined the legitimacy of its own welfare compromises. These may have been unavoidable; nevertheless it is useful to understand what happened.

These most limiting compromises were required not by popular lack of enthusiasm but by Congress. It was the Roosevelt Democratic coalition in Congress, as filtered through congressional committees controlled by southern chairs, that required reducing the economic security offered to low-wage labor. Roosevelt could not and probably would not have threatened to "pack" the congressional committees as he did the Supreme Court. Nevertheless, he had a rare opportunity, if he had found a way to exploit it. The New Deal temporarily transformed the Democratic party into something like a European Labor or a Social Democratic party: It supported unionization, a welfare state, and reintroduced the language of class into mainstream electoral discourse.[16] Accepting this implicit bargain, organized labor broke with the AFL's antipolitical tradition to become a partner of the Democratic party. As early as 1936, the youthful CIO spent nearly $1 million for the Democratic ticket in four industrial states alone. Like other Social Democratic parties, the Democrats also gained support during the Depression from formerly Republican urban liberal professionals and white-collar workers. But the Democratic party, unlike its European counterparts, simultaneously continued as a sectional party of the South, where black disenfranchisement and one-party rule protected it from challenges. The smaller but still-consequential reduction of the northern electorate (as a result of such Progressive Era reforms as voter registration) limited northern electoral support for the party, thus reinforcing its dependence on the South.[17] At first the New Deal seemed to offer the possibility of breaking that southern control. For example, nonsouthern voter turnout increased dramatically in a short time, from 66 percent in 1932 to 73 percent in 1940,[18] and blacks moving north added dramatically to the Democratic vote. The northern New Deal coalition was strengthened by the promise of its welfare program, which was extremely popular.

But the actual operations of Social Security nourished divisions among the Democratic electorate. Most destructive were those between beneficiaries of the primary programs—the upper working class and middle class—and those who got "welfare." As taxes increased, recipients of the secondary programs became scapegoats. Unions and many middle-class liberals imagined in 1936 and 1940 that Social Security was just a beginning; they expected medical insurance, at least, to follow. When, after World War II, an expansion of the welfare state was not forthcoming, middle-class and upper-working-class voters looked less to government for the measures that would guarantee their security and more to the private sector. The rise of private health insurance and pensions lessened their support for a shared social citizenship and further distanced them from those who could not get or could not afford private welfare. In electoral politics this meant that national Democratic politicians had to target the "swing" voters who (erroneously) did not feel dependent on a welfare state; the neglected and maligned poor who did support welfare increasingly became nonvoters, political noncitizens. This became a downward spiral: The more the poor did not vote, the more the Democrats focused their appeals on conservative "swing" voters.

Meanwhile extraordinary changes in the role of women in the 1940s, 1950s, and 1960s made the New Deal welfare structure even more destructive. Its failure to support women workers did not stop women's participation in employment but helped lock them into the worst conditions both at work and at home. Women workers needed federal support for child care, a decent minimum wage, and benefits in women's jobs, parental leave and adequate provision for those mothers who could not or would not enter the labor force. Lacking these, working mothers in particular, both single and married, faced two bad choices—employment or "welfare," both on inferior terms. Those very stresses, combined with women's growing economic independence and self-confidence, contributed to raising the divorce rate and thus the numbers of single mothers. Even as the "feminine mystique," with its romanticization of wifehood and motherhood, flourished in the 1950s, more and more women were actually rejecting domesticity. Divorce, birth control, and "career women" generated sharper differences and even hostilities among women. Some women experienced feminism as an attack on them as well as on men. A contradictory reaction criticized some women for being breadwinners and "welfare mothers" for not being breadwinners—for demanding "welfare" in order not to "work" ("work" now meaning paid employment). By the 1970s attacks on women's nontraditional sexual and public behavior became a prominent theme in conservative backlash movements against New Deal and "Great Society" social programs. Hostility to "welfare" was nourished by a new kind of conservative coalition, which drew on objections to feminism and sexual "permissiveness" as well as to taxes and the increasing militance among the minority poor.

Most demanding of all, the welfare system worsened inequality. With a bit of deliberate exaggeration, one can argue that the Social Security Act helped create today's "underclass" of the hopelessly poor. Certainly public assistance redistributed some resources to the poor. While all Americans paid taxes (even those without income pay sales taxes and higher prices to compensate business for its taxes), the poor usually got more directly than they paid directly. But public assistance is nowhere near as redistributive as it appears. Even during periods defined as prosperous—the 1950s and 1960s—relative indicators for stigmatized groups moved downward. For example, even while black employment and income was growing, the proportion of unemployment suffered by blacks increased. And the numbers of the poor who were marginally employed also increased, notably those who could not get into full-time, major-industry jobs but depended on service-sector, seasonal, temporary employment.

The gains "welfare" offered the poor were undercut by the reverse redistributive effects of the good, non-"welfare" programs. Benefits to middle-class and upper-working-class men and their dependents were greater, absolutely and proportionately, than contributions to the poor. The conservative attack on the welfare state has convinced some people that the conflict is between those who want to increase and those who want to reduce government aid. In fact a better debating point would be how government aid is distributed. By the 1980s, 80 percent of the U.S. social welfare budget went to the nonpoor.[19] Even the War on Poverty contributed more to the nonpoor than to the poor. In the half century since Social Security was passed, these welfare benefits accounted for a larger share of economic improvement, among those who experienced it, than did income. That is, more employed people would have been poor had it not been for government provision.[20] The good Social Security programs got steadily better. OAI benefits were increased, protected against inflation, and extended to more beneficiaries, especially dependents. By contrast the real value of ADC and other public assistance programs fell, and in the 1970s eligibility criteria began to exclude more of the poor.[21]

Social Security's stimulus to inequality was strengthened by the two major omissions—public jobs and medical insurance. People with good jobs increasingly relied on private welfare benefits and lost their political common ground with those who had neither jobs nor benefits.

In saying that Social Security created an "underclass," the claim is not simply that its inequities and exclusions left some people economically disadvantaged, but that the legislation actively contributed to civil, political, and social inequities, exclusions from "the edifice of citizenship."[22] The superior welfare programs as well as hidden non-"welfare" assistance appear as rights and deserved benefits that increase a citizen's self-esteem and feeling of entitlement. Public assistance recipients are daily told that they are parasites. Symbolically and practically, the insurance programs extended the meaning of first-class U.S. citizenship to include an economic shield against impoverishment, creating social citizenship alongside civil and political citizenship.[23] By contrast the public assistance programs embodied a lack of national social citizenship, underlined by sending the poor to the states to get help and forcing the near-poor to become impoverished and humiliated *before* help was forthcoming. Public assistance constructs despair through lack of opportunity—the determining condition of the alleged "underclass."

These inequities of wealth, respect, and rights translated into political inequities. The fact that old-age pensions were not classified as "welfare," for example, then strengthened the lobbying power of the organizations of the elderly (such as the AARP); this strength then helped them maintain benefit levels and further reinforced their identity as citizens collecting entitlements. By contrast ADC recipients, already stigmatized as poor single mothers, grew politically weaker because of their continuing poverty and increasing discouragement. Their indigence and stigmatization in turn undercut their ability to organize to create political pressure, and their lack of organizational strength further weakened the respect they could evoke. Nothing illustrates this better than the fact that when "welfare" clients did organize—as during the late 1960s when the National Welfare Rights Organization was strong—they made substantial gains, which were eroded as that organization weakened in the 1970s.

＝

The National Welfare Rights Organization reminds us of the importance of political actors. The structural determinants of Social Security—gender relations, race relations, the economy, the party system, for example—set constraints on what welfare champions could do. But our welfare system, rudimentary and inadequate as it is, would not exist without the creativity and compassion of an extraordinary group of advocates. Their very compassion, however, indicates their limitations. Compassion arises from pity for the suffering of others. Julia Lathrop's hope that that pity would be transformed into justice was never fully realized, partly because her group did not listen closely enough to what those "others" really wanted. They might have become more critical of their maternalism, of the family-wage system, had they been closer to women for whom the system did not work.

ADC designers made the wrong alliances. Politics is always a matter of the allies you choose. Women welfare activists allied with male social insurance advocates, with the Republican and then the Democratic party, with state welfare administrators and with a network of white middle-class women's organizations. They did not seek out the poor. Indeed to some degree they insulated themselves from the activism of the poor. Continuing a Progressive Era moral-reform legacy, they never entirely shed the belief that something more than lack of money was wrong with the poor, especially poor single mothers. They were convinced that the poor needed casework—counseling and rehabilitation—and they designed ADC to regulate morals and housekeeping. And poor women had no collective presence powerful enough to create an alliance in which they could represent themselves. Nor did the ADC designers seek out African American women reformers, who had created strong organizations, even national ones, as allies. Had they done so they would have met with a useful skepticism about the family-wage norm and a more positive attitude toward women's economic independence. The Children's Bureau network also separated themselves from the labor movement. They neither emphasized the importance of a minimum wage and union power nor struggled with the unions to defend women's right to equal wages and equal work.

They allied instead with the powerful, and this brought them some successes. Indeed, as they moved closer to political power themselves, they may have lost their freedom to seek out more grassroots alliances; such coalitions may have been incompatible with the victories they did get. In that case we are looking at tragedy, not folly. They thought they were being "half-a-loaf girls." But there is a difference between accepting a pay increase in installments for everyone and accepting a wage compromise in which the higher-paid employees get a 5 percent raise as an entitlement and the lower-paid get 2 percent based on proving their need. Social Security's half loaf was of the latter type. In accepting it they weakened themselves by reducing their own constituency and they ended by losing some of their own political power, as ADC was taken from them. They believed that by compromising as they did they could get something now and something more later, but this is not what happened. Rather than bringing one group after another under the protection of federal security programs, they set in train a process of fragmentation that weakened political support for a welfare state altogether. By accepting a program that provided superior benefits for some and inferior ones for others, the Children's Bureau group allowed the division of their political base. In real dollars they got steadily smaller pieces of the loaf as the years went by.

—

Santayana's claim—that those who do not remember their history are condemned to repeat it—does not promise that knowledge will transform, only that lack of it dooms us. But even this cautious proposition gains strength in the case of welfare, where the "lessons" of history are particularly sharp as we contemplate welfare "reform."

It does not pay to try to minimize opposition through niggardly and means-tested welfare provision. One of several paradoxes about welfare is that a bigger welfare state is likely to be a more popular one. One pattern visible even in the 1930s is that those who benefit from welfare, and know that they do, support welfare. Today so many welfare programs are hidden, especially for the nonpoor, that recipients are not always aware of the benefits they receive. Thus welfare stratification has political consequences. We cannot afford to expand the number of programs only for the poor. Means-tested programs set up downward spirals, at once making things worse for recipients *and* more resented by taxpayers. Universal programs will command broader support.

We can resist the ills of the stratification we are already stuck with by transforming our language to make hidden benefits or "entitlement" as visible as welfare. Let politicians and the press refer to Social Security OAI, home mortgage deductions, schools and parks, garbage disposal, and corporate tax breaks as welfare. Of course the taint of the second track derives as much from the low status of those who are served by it—women, single mothers, minorities, the poor. But a vicious cycle operates here in which the stigma of programs and of recipients reinforce each other, and it is possible to break that downward spiral.

These lessons are hard to act on, because so much political inertia inheres in the current system and so much political risk in trying to change it. One lesson may be easier to translate into action today: that maternalism is not adequate to women's and children's needs. For very different reasons feminists and antifeminists now often agree that men's economic responsibility for women is a chimera, that it is acceptable for mothers to be employed out of their homes. Building on this, we can see that welfare programs must help mothers to be wage earners *and* to meet domestic labor obligations. Most women do both most of the time; some women will need or want to do unpaid child raising full-time for some periods. Welfare can only be effective in nurturing children and strengthening mothers if it supports both. Some income support for single parents will be necessary along with measures to help them establish themselves as workers supported by wages—such as day-care centers, medical insurance, parental leave, and good wages. A social policy that encourages men to meet domestic labor obligations would also help. Welfare and jobs policies are inextricably connected.

These lessons, even when they derive from the inadequacies of our welfare system, remind us of the extraordinary debts we owe the visionaries and politicians who began our welfare state. Today's welfare problems were not mainly created by mistakes and certainly not by lack of good intentions. They derive more from historical constraints—on the ability to foresee future social and economic developments and on the range of political possibility—and above all from the political exclusion of those with the greatest need to be included: the poor. Yesterday's welfare advocates accepted many limits because they believed they were creating a beginning. Our task is to continue.

Appendix: Welfare Reform Leaders

These are the individual welfare reformers discussed in chapters 4, 5, and 6. They were selected because they were the leaders of national organizations that campaigned for welfare programs, or government officials responsible for welfare programs who were also important welfare advocates, or nationally prominent builders of private welfare institutions. Each is identified by her or his single most important general area of activism.

White Women Welfare Activists

Name	Main Reform
Abbott, Edith	Social work, academic
Abbott, Grace	Children's Bureau
Addams, Jane	Settlement
Amidon, Beulah Elizabeth	Social work
Anderson, Mary	Women's Bureau
Armstrong, Barbara Nachtrieb	Social Security
Armstrong, Florence Arzelia	Social Security
Beyer, Clara Mortenson	Children's Bureau
Blair, Emily Newell	Democratic Party
Bradford, Cornelia Foster	Settlement

Name	Main Reform
Breckinridge, Sophonisba Preston	Social work, academic
Brown, Josephine Chapin	Social work
Burns, Eveline Mabel	Social Security
Cannon, Ida Maud	Medical social work
Colcord, Joanna	Social work
Coyle, Grace Longwood	Social work, academic
Crane, Caroline Bartlett	Sanitation reform
Deardorff, Neva Ruth	Social work
Dewson, Mary W. (Molly)	Democratic Party
Dinwiddie, Emily Wayland	Housing reform
Dudley, Helena Stuart	Settlement
Dunn, Loula Friend	Social work
Eastman, Crystal (Catherine)	Industrial health
Einstein, Hannah Bachman	Mothers' pensions
Eliot, Martha May	Children's Bureau
Ellickson, Katherine Pollak	Social Security
Elliott, Harriet Wiseman	Democratic Party
Engle, Lavinia Margaret	Social Security
Evans, Elizabeth Glendower	Consumers' League
Fuller, Minnie Ursala	Child welfare
Goldmark, Josephine Clara	Consumers' League
Goldmark, Pauline Dorothea	Consumers' League
Gordon, Jean Margaret	Consumers' League
Hall, Helen	Settlement
Hamilton, (Amy) Gordon	Social work, academic
Hamilton, Alice	Industrial health
Hoey, Jane Margueretta	Social Security
Iams, Lucy Virginia Dorsey	Housing reform
Keller, Helen	Health reform
Kelley, Florence Molthrop	Consumers' League
Kellor, Frances (Alice)	Immigrant welfare
Lathrop, Julia Clifford	Children's Bureau
Lenroot, Katharine Fredrica	Children's Bureau
Loeb, Sophie Irene Simon	Mothers' Pensions
Lundberg, Emma Octavia	Children's Bureau
Maher, Amy	Social Security
Mason, Lucy Randolph	Consumers' League
McDowell, Mary Eliza	Settlement

Name	Main Reform
McMain, Eleanor Laura	Settlement
Miller, Frieda Segelke	Women's Bureau
Moskowitz, Belle Israels	Democratic Party
Newman, Pauline	Women's Bureau
Perkins, Frances	Social Security
Peterson, Agnes L.	Women's Bureau
Pidgeon, Mary Elizabeth	Women's Bureau
Rankin, Jeannette Pickering	Congresswoman
Raushenbush, Elizabeth Brandeis	Unemployment
Regan, Agnes Gertrude	Social work
Richmond, Mary Ellen	Social work
Roche, Josephine Aspinall	Consumers' League
Roosevelt, (Anna) Eleanor	Social work
Schneiderman, Rose	Labor
Sherwin, Belle	Club
Simkhovitch, Mary Kingsbury	Settlement
Springer, Gertrude Hill	Social work
Switzer, Mary Elizabeth	Social work
Taft, (Julia) Jessie	Social work
Thomas, M. Carey	Education
Towle, Charlotte Helen	Social work, academic
Vaile, Gertrude	Social work
Van Kleeck, Mary Abby	Women's Bureau
Wald, Lillian D.	Settlement
White, Sue Shelton	Democratic Party
Wood, Edith Elmer	Housing reform
Woodbury, Helen Laura Sumner	Children's Bureau
Woodward, Ellen Sullivan	Social work

Black Women Welfare Activists

Name	Main Reform
Alexander, Sadie Tanner Mossell	Civil rights
Anthony, Lucille	Health
Barnes, Margaret E.	Education
Barrett, Janie Porter	Education

Name	Main Reform
Bearden, Bessye	Civil rights
Bethune, Mary McLeod	Education
Bowles, Eva Del Vakia	Social work
Brawley, Ruth Merrill	Social work
Brown, Charlotte Hawkins	Education
Brown, Sue M.	Education
Burroughs, Nannie Helen	Education
Callis, Myra Colson	Employment
Carter, Ezella	Education
Cary, Alice Dugged	Child welfare
Cook, Coralie Franklin	Education
Cooper, Anna Julia Haywood	Education
Davis, Belle	Health
Davis, Elizabeth Lindsey	Club
Dickerson, Addie W.	Club
Faulkner, Georgia M. DeBaptiste	Social work
Fauset, Crystal Bird	Civil rights
Ferebee, Dorothy Boulding	Health
Gaines, Irene McCoy	Civil rights
Harris, Judia C. Jackson	Social work
Haynes, Elizabeth Ross	Civil rights
Hedgeman, Anna Arnold	Civil rights
Height, Dorothy I.	Civil rights
Hope, Lugenia Burns	Social work
Hunter, Jane Edna Harris	Social work
Hunton, Addie D. Waites	Civil rights
Jackson, Juanita Elizabeth	Civil rights
Jeffries, Christina Armistead	Civil rights
Johnson, Bertha La Branche	Education
Johnson, Kathryn Magnolia	Civil rights
Jones, Verina Morton	Social work
Laney, Lucy Craft	Education
Lawton, Maria Coles Perkins	Education
Lindsay, Inabel Burns	Education
Lyle, Ethel Hedgeman	Club
Mallory, Arenia Cornelia	Education
Malone, Annie M. Turnbo	Education
Marsh, Vivian Osborne	Club

Name	Main Reform
Matthews, Victoria Earle	Social work
Mays, Sadie Gray	Social work
McCrorey, Mary Jackson	Social work
McDougald, G. Elsie Johnson (Ayer)	Education
McKane, Alice Woodby	Health
Merritt, Emma Frances Grayson	Education
Nelson, Alice Ruth Dunbar	Social work
Pickens, Minnie McAlpin	Civil rights
Randolph, Florence	Club
Ridley, Florida Ruffin	Club
Ruffin, Josephine St. Pierre	Club
Rush, Gertrude E.	Social work
Saddler, Juanita Jane	Civil rights
Snowden, Joanna Cecilia	Social work
Stewart, Sallie Wyatt	Social work
Talbert, Mary Barnett	Civil rights
Taylor, Isabelle Rachel	Social work
Terrell, Mary Eliza Church	Civil rights
Walker, A'Lelia	Social work
Walker, Maggie Lena	Social work
Warren, Sadie	Social work
Washington, Margaret Murray	Education
Wells, Eva Thornton	Social work
Wheatley, Laura Frances	Education
Williams, Fannie Barrier	Social work
Young, Mattie Dover	Social work

White Men Welfare Activists

Name	Occupation
Adler, Felix	Minister
Alexander, Will	Minister
Altmeyer, Arthur	Welfare administrator
Andrews, John	Welfare administrator
Bane, Frank	Welfare administrator

Name	Main Reform
Bigge, George Edmund	Economics professor
Billikopf, Jacob	Social work administrator
Bliss, William Dwight	Minister
Bookman, Clarence Monroe	Welfare administrator
Brandeis, Louis	Judge
Brooks, John Graham	Minister
Bruno, Frank	Social work, academic
Burns, Allen	Educator
Butler, Amos	Penologist
Clague, Ewan	Economist
Cohen, Wilbur	Welfare administrator
Commons, John	Economics professor
Darlington, Thomas	Welfare administrator
Davis, Michael Marks, Jr.	Social work administrator
Dawson, Miles Menander	Lawyer
De Forest, Robert Weeks	Lawyer
Devine, Edward Thomas	Social work administrator
Doten, Carroll Warren	Economist
Ely, Richard Theodore	Economics professor
Epstein, Abraham	Welfare administrator
Ezekiel, Mordecai	Government economist
Falk, Isidore Sydney	Public health professor
Farnam, Henry Walcott	Economics professor
Folks, Homer	Social work administrator
Frankel, Lee Kaufman	Insurance executive
Frankfurter, Felix	Judge
Glenn, John Mark	Foundation executive
Hard, William	Journalist
Hart, Hastings Hornell	Minister
Henderson, Charles Richmond	Sociology professor
Hodson, William	Welfare administrator
Hoffman, Frederick Ludwig	Statistician
Hopkins, Harry	Welfare administrator
Hunter, Robert	Social worker
Ickes, Harold	Lawyer
Kellogg, Paul	Journalist

Name	Main Reform
Kingsbury, John Adams	Foundation executive
Leiserson, William Morris	Government economist
Lindsay, Samuel McCune	Sociology professor
Lindsey, Benjamin	Judge
Lovejoy, Owen	Minister
Lurie, Harry	Social work administrator
Macy, Valentine	Financier
McKelway, Alexander Jeffrey	Minister
Murphy, J. Prentice	Social work administrator
Pink, Louis Heaton	Lawyer
Raushenbush, Paul A.	Social insurance administrator
Reynolds, James Bronson	Lawyer
Riis, Jacob August	Journalist
Robins, Raymond	Lawyer
Rubinow, Isaac	Physician
Ryan, John Augustine	Priest
Seager, Henry Rogers	Economist
Sinai, Nathan	Welfare academic
Stelzle, Charles	Minister
Stokes, Isaac Newton Phelps	Architect
Stokes, James Graham Phelps	Physician
Street, Elwood Vickers	Welfare administrator
Swift, Linton Bishop	Welfare administrator
Sydenstricker, Edgar	Statistician
Taylor, Graham	Minister
Tugwell, Rexford	Economics professor
Veiller, Lawrence Turnure	Welfare administrator
Walling, William	Nonemployed by choice
Weber, Adna Ferrin	Economics professor
West, Walter Mott	Social work administrator
Williams, Aubrey	Welfare administrator
Wines, Frederick Howard	Statistician
Witte, Edwin Edward	Economics professor
Woods, Robert Archey	Social work leader
Youngdahl, Benjamin Emanuel	Welfare administrator

Notes

Sources

The following manuscript collections were used in this book:

Grace Abbott Papers, Regenstein Library, University of Chicago

Arthur Altmeyer Papers, State Historical Society of Wisconsin

Mary Anderson Papers, Schlesinger Library, Radcliffe College

Mary McLeod Bethune Museum and Archives, Washington D.C.

Black Women Oral History Project, Schlesinger Library, Radcliffe College

John Graham Brooks Papers, Schlesinger Library, Radcliffe College

Children's Bureau Papers, National Archives

Wilbur Cohen Papers, State Historical Society of Wisconsin

Oral History Collection, Columbia University

John Commons Papers, State Historical Society of Wisconsin

Anna Julia Cooper Papers, Moorland-Spingarn Collection, Howard University

Mary Dewson Papers, Schlesinger Library, Radcliffe College

Paul Douglas Papers, Chicago Historical Society

Martha Eliot Papers, Schlesinger Library, Radcliffe College

Florence Kelley Papers, Schlesinger Library, Radcliffe College

Julia Lathrop Papers, Rockford College

Moorland-Spingarn Collection, Howard University

National Council of Negro Women Papers, Washington, D.C.

Public Health Service Records, National Archives

Edith Rockwood Papers, Schlesinger Library, Radcliffe College

Lucy Slowe Papers, Moorland-Spingarn Collection, Howard University

Social Security Board Papers, National Archives

Mary Church Terrell Papers, Moorland-Spingarn Collection, Howard University

Edwin Witte Papers, State Historical Society of Wisconsin

Women's Bureau Papers, National Archives

Helen Sumner Woodbury Papers, State Historical Society of Wisconsin

Ellen Woodward Papers, Schlesinger Library, Radcliffe College

Women in Federal Government Project, Schlesinger Library, Radcliffe College

WPA Papers of Alfred E. Smith, Moorland-Spingarn Collection, Howard University

Chapter 1. What Is "Welfare"?

1. Some of the more prominent of these include, in chronological order: Richard Cloward and Frances Fox Piven, *Regulating the Poor: The Functions of Public Welfare* (New York: Random House, 1971); Walter I. Trattner, *From Poor Law to Welfare State* (New York: Free Press, 1974); James T. Patterson, *America's Struggle Against Poverty 1900–1980* (Cambridge, Mass.: Harvard University Press, 1981); John H. Ehrenreich, *The Altruistic Imagination: A History of Social Work and Social Policy in the United States* (Ithaca: Cornell University Press, 1985); Michael B. Katz, *In the Shadow of the Poorhouse: A Social History of Welfare in America* (New York: Basic Books, 1986) and *The Undeserving Poor: From the War on Poverty to the War on Welfare* (New York: Pantheon, 1989); Mimi Abramovitz, *Regulating the Lives of Women: Social Welfare Policy from Colonial Times to the Present* (Boston: South End Press, 1988); Edward D. Berkowitz and Kim McQuaid, *Creating the Welfare State* (Lawrence: University Press of Kansas, 1988); Bruce S. Jansson, *The Reluctant Welfare State* (Belmont, CA: Wadsworth, 1988); Joel Handler and Yeheskel Hasenfeld, *The Moral Construction of Poverty: Welfare Reform in America* (Newbury Park: Sage, 1991); Edward D. Berkowitz, *America's Welfare State from Roosevelt to Reagan* (Baltimore: Johns Hopkins University Press, 1991); Alan Dawley, *Struggles for Justice: Social Responsibility and the Liberal State* (Cambridge, Mass.: Harvard University Press, 1991) and Theda Skocpol, *Protecting Soldiers and Mothers: The Political Origins of Social Policy in the United States* (Cambridge, Mass.: Harvard University Press, 1992); Ann Shola Orloff, *The Politics of Pensions: A Comparative Analysis of Britain, Canada, and the United States, 1880–1940* (Madison: University of Wisconsin Press, 1993).

2. Historical sociologist Barrington Moore, Jr., wrote about the "suppression of historical alternatives" in this spirit. By examining such options he sought to distinguish concrete, possible alternatives from ideas that were outside the realm of historical possibility, and to be able not only to explain what happened as one choice among others but to assess the moral responsibility of historical actors for their choices. (His example was the opportunity German Social-Democrats had in 1918 to make alliances with the Left rather than the Right. His underlying concern was the responsibility for the rise of Nazism.) Barrington Moore, Jr., *Injustice: The Social Bases of Obedience and Revolt* (New York: Sharpe, 1987).

3. Carl Degler, *Out of Our Past: The Forces That Shaped Modern America* (1959; rev. ed., New York: Harper & Row, 1970), p. 379.

4. Arthur A. Ekirch, Jr., *Ideologies and Utopias: The Impact of the New Deal on American Thought* (Chicago: Quadrangle, 1969), p. 107.

5. Nancy F. Cott, *The Grounding of Modern Feminism* (New Haven: Yale University Press, 1987), pp. 4–5.

6. Too many such debates take on a moralistic character, as if using "feminist" as a synonym for "virtuous," and allowing those who disagree about issues to argue instead about who is within and who is without a blessed circle. E.g., "No real feminist would be married to such a man" or "No real feminist would attack other women that way."

7. Michael Ignatieff, *The Needs of Strangers: An Essay on Privacy, Solidarity, and the Politics of Being Human* (New York: Viking, 1985).

8. I am indebted to Allen Hunter's typical perspicacity on this point.

9. Lisa Peattie and Martin Rein, *Women's Claims: A Study in Political Economy* (Oxford: Oxford University Press, 1983).

Chapter 2. Single Mothers: The Facts and the Social Problem

1. Belle Lindner Israels, "Widowed Mothers," *Survey* 22 (Sept. 4, 1909), p. 741.

2. Sophonisba Preston Breckinridge, "Neglected Widowhood in the Juvenile Court," *American Journal of Sociology* 16 (July 1910), p. 87.

3. Zilpha D. Smith, *Deserted Wives and Deserting Husbands: A Study of 234 Families . . . of the Associated Charities of Boston* (Boston: Associated Charities, 1901), p. 16.

4. Beverly Stadum, *Poor Women and Their Families: Hard Working Charity Cases 1900–1930* (Albany, N.Y.: SUNY Press, 1992), pp. 8–9.

5. The distinction between morals and moralism, moral and moralistic, is important. Concern with morality is inevitable and even desirable in any discussion of a topic that involves human suffering, but moralism is problematic. While they are not often clearly distinguished, two different words (and concepts) are in play here. "Moralistic" came from the practice of a moralist, one who teaches or philosophizes about morality; and

it has become a pejorative term, referring to unwanted and for objectionable moral judgments. The attempt to disguise ethical judgments, furthermore, often produces moralism—the presentation of conclusions as scientific, universal, and objective because the moral assumptions on which they rest are dissimulated.

6. After about 1960 single motherhood began to increase significantly. From some 9 percent of families in 1960, single-mother-and-children units became 20 percent of families by 1985. More than half of all children born since 1975 will live in a mother-only family at some point before age eighteen. Larry Bumpass, "Children and Marital Disruption: A Replication and Update," *Demography* 21 (1984), pp. 71–82.

7. The figures are not definitive because the structure of the federal censuses makes it difficult to determine exactly how many there were. In the absence of a belief that single mothers were a significant problem, census takers were not motivated to count them. Many single mothers did not head their own households but lived in households headed by relatives, for example. Census takers did not inquire into family relationships within a household and only listed residents according to their relation to a head. Thus one might know that a man had several daughters and one grandchild in his house, but one could not easily learn who were the parents of the grandchild. Moreover, birth and death registration—which allows the compilation of fertility statistics—was a state, not a federal, matter, and quite incomplete. This was especially true in black rural areas of southern states.

8. Eighty percent in 1900. Linda Gordon and Sara McLanahan, "Single Parenthood in 1900," *Journal of Family History* 16:2 (1991), pp. 97–116. These are likely to be underestimates because the figures are necessarily based on numbers of children, and presumably single mothers on average had fewer children than married ones. All figures on single mothers in 1900 come from this article.

9. Shere L. Bartlett and Daniel C. Kallgren, "The Black Family in the United States: A Reassessment" (typescript, University of Minnesota, 1990). This paper is less detailed because it does not examine single mothers in subfamilies and reports simply the census categories of female- and male-headed households.

10. Data on subfamilies for 1910, 1920, and 1930 are not yet available.

11. Barbara Whalen, "The Beheading of the American Household" (seminar paper, University of Wisconsin, 1991).

12. On this point the findings of the Gordon-McLanahan study are corroborated by other studies, for example, S. Philip Morgan et al., "Racial Differences in Household and Family Structure at the Turn of the Century" (typescript, Population Studies Center, University of Pennsylvania, Feb. 1992).

13. When it was first used, by Emma Lundberg in 1933, it referred only to unmarried mothers. Emma O. Lundberg, *Unmarried Mothers in the Municipal Court of Philadelphia* (Philadelphia: Thomas Skelton Harrison Foundation, 1933).

14. There was no significant race difference here—about three-fourths of black and white single mothers were widows.

15. This is an overestimate for several reasons: It counts only heads of household, the only group for whom this data was available. The proportion of *all* single mothers who were widows was lower, since another 20 percent of children lived with single mothers in subfamilies, and these mothers were less likely to be widows. Moreover it seems likely that women often dissembled about the source of their single motherhood.

16. Only 18 percent of widows, or approximately 846,000, were under forty-five years old in 1930; those older than forty-five were unlikely to have small children. By contrast there were approximately 1,542,000 woman-headed families with children. Isaac M. Rubinow, *The Quest for Security* (New York: Henry Holt, 1934), pp. 478–79; 1930 census. The roughness of these figures comes from the fact that the categories in the 1930 census did not allow the accurate determination of single-parent families. Figures cited for 1900 come from an analysis of a public-use sample of that year's census, and no such sample has yet been made for 1930.

17. Hendrik Hartog, "Marital Exits and Marital Expectations in Nineteenth Century America," *Georgetown Law Journal* 80:1 (Oct. 1991), pp. 95–129.

18. Linda Gordon, *Heroes of Their Own Lives: The History and Politics of Family Violence* (New York: Viking, 1988), chap. 4; Agency for Providing Situations in the Country for Destitute Mothers with Infants, *Annual Report* (1899, 1902, 1905, 1906).

19. Traditional expectations that earning a living was a whole-family responsibility were reflected, for example, in census categories. In Great Britain, censuses up through 1831 inquired as to the occupations of families, not of individuals, assuming that the entire family participated in an economic enterprise; in the United States the 1840 census still proceeded in this way. Economist Nancy Folbre has shown that it was only through a gradual process, completed for the U.S. census by about 1900, that women became officially categorized as dependents. Nancy Folbre, "The Unproductive Housewife: Her Evolution in Nineteenth-Century Economic Thought," *Signs* 16:3 (Spring 1991), pp. 463–84; Nancy Folbre and Marjorie Abel, "Women's Work and Women's Households: Gender Bias in the U.S. Census," *Social Research* 56:3 (Autumn 1989), pp. 545–69.

20. From the Civil War to the Great Depression the divorce rate had grown from 1.2 per thousand in 1860 to 7.7 in 1920, dropping to 6.8 in the early 1930s due to economic hardship; Paul H. Jacobson, *American Marriage and Divorce* (New York: Rinehart, 1969), table 42. For a variety of reasons these census figures are probably underestimates, however. But these are overall rates; divorce was much less frequent among parents of young children. In any case it was not a major concern among those thinking about poor single mothers in the New Deal.

21. Clark E. Vincent, "Illegitimacy," in *International Encyclopedia of the Social Sciences*, ed. David L. Sills (New York: Macmillan Free Press, 1968), vol. 7, pp. 85–90.

22. Thus a Children's Bureau estimate of the illegitimacy rate as 4.6 per thousand in 1915 may have been a distinct understatement. Emma O. Lundberg and Katharine F. Lenroot, *Illegitimacy as a Child-Welfare Problem*, 2 vols. (Washington, D.C.: U.S. Children's Bureau Publication No. 66, 1920), vol. 1, p. 21.

23. This and many of the other generalizations here are corroborated by Mary Odem's "Single Mothers, Delinquent Daughters, and the Juvenile Court in Early 20th Century Los Angeles," *Journal of Social History* 25:1 (Fall 1991), pp. 27–43; and by S.J. Kleinberg, "Widowhood, Poverty, and Economic Survival in the United States in the Progressive Era," typescript.

24. Gwendolyn Salisbury Hughes, *Mothers in Industry: Wage-Earning by Mothers in Philadelphia* (New York: New Republic, 1925), p. 22.

25. Rubinow, *Quest for Security*, p. 481.

26. Mary E. Richmond and Fred Hall, *A Study of Nine Hundred and Eighty-Five Widows Known to Certain Charity Organization Societies in 1910* (New York: Russell Sage Foundation, 1913).

27. Kleinberg, "Widowhood," p. 19.

28. Sheila M. Rothman, "Other People's Children," *The Public Interest* 30 (1973), esp. pp. 13–21; John O'Grady, *Catholic Charities in the United States: History and Problems* (Washington, D.C.: National Conference of Catholic Charities, 1930), pp. 310–17; Linda Gordon, "Black and White Visions of Welfare: Women's Welfare Activism, 1890–1945," *Journal of American History* 78 (Sept. 1991), pp. 559–90; see also chap. 4 in this book.

29. Sonya Michel, "The Limits of Maternalism: Policies toward American Wage-earning Mothers during the Progressive Era," in Seth Koven and Sonya Michel, eds., *Mothers of a New World: Maternalist Politics and the Origins of Welfare States* (New York: Routledge, 1993), pp. 277–320; Emily D. Cahan, *Past Caring: A History of U.S. Preschool Care and Education for the Poor, 1820–1965* (New York: National Center for Children in Poverty, School of Public Health, Columbia University, 1989).

30. Sheila M. Rothman, *Woman's Proper Place: A History of Changing Ideals and Practices, 1870 to the Present* (New York: Basic Books, 1978), pp. 89–90.
31. Gordon, *Heroes*, chap. 4.
32. Commonwealth of Massachusetts, *Report of the Commission on the Support of Dependent Minor Children of Widowed Mothers* (Boston: Wright & Potter, 1913), p. 13.
33. Robert H. Bremner, ed., *Children & Youth in America: A Documentary History* (Cambridge, Mass.: Harvard University Press, 1971), vol. 2, pp. 249–90.
34. Amos Griswold Warner, Stuart Alfred Queen, and Ernest Bouldin Harper, *American Charities and Social Work*, 4th ed. (New York: Thomas Y. Crowell, 1930), p. 124.
35. Kleinberg, "Widowhood," pp. 9–10.
36. Gordon, *Heroes*; this periodization has since been elaborated by Lisa Brush in her dissertation, "Worthy Widows, Welfare Cheats: The Professional Discourse on Single Mothers in the United States, 1900–1988" (Ph.D. dissertation, University of Wisconsin-Madison, 1993). A small selection of references: Smith, *Deserted Wives*; Mary Conyngton, *How to Help: A Manual of Practical Charity* (New York: Macmillan, 1906), pp. 150–51; Helen Foss, "The Genus Deserter: His Singularities and Their Social Consequences—A Study of Local Fact and Interstate Remedies," *Charities* 10 (May 2, 1903), pp. 456–60; Charles Zunser, "Family Desertion (Report on a Study of 423 Cases)," *Annals of the American Academy of Political and Social Science* 145:234 (Sept. 1929), pp. 98–104; Ada Eliot, "Deserted Wives," *Charities Review* 10 (Oct. 1900); Rev. E. P. Savage in National Conference of Charities and Corrections (NCCC), *Proceedings* (1897), pp. 317–28; Maurice B. Hexter, "The Business Cycle, Relief Work, and Desertion," *Jewish Social Service Quarterly* 1 (Feb.–May 1924), pp. 3–33; Joanna Colcord, *Broken Homes: A Study of Family Desertion and Its Social Treatment* (New York: Russell Sage Foundation, 1919); Earle Edward Eubank, *A Study of Family Desertion* (Chicago: Dept. of Public Welfare, 1916).
37. Smith, *Deserted Wives*, p. 3.
38. Ibid.
39. Joseph Logan, "Recreant Husbands," in NCCC, *Proceedings* (1911), p. 402.
40. Quoted in Martha May, "The 'Problem of Duty': The Regulation of Male Breadwinning and Desertion in the Progressive Era," *Social Service Review* 62:1 (Mar. 1988), pp. 40–60; quote p. 43.
41. Charles Zunser, "The National Desertion Bureau," National Conference of Jewish Social Service, *Proceedings* (1923), pp. 386–404,

reprinted in Robert Morris and Michael Freund, eds., *Trends and Issues in Jewish Social Welfare in the United States, 1899–1952* (Philadelphia: Jewish Publication Society, 1966), pp. 66–76; Smith, *Deserted Wives*; Lilian Brandt, *Five Hundred and Seventy-Four Deserters and Their Families* (New York: Charity Organization Society, 1905).

42. Eliot, "Deserted Wives."
43. Logan, "Recreant Husbands."
44. For examples, see ibid.; William Baldwin, "Making the Deserter Pay the Piper," *Survey* 23 (Nov. 20, 1902), pp. 249–52.
45. May, "The 'Problem of Duty,'" pp. 43–44.
46. Walter E. Weyl, "The Deserter," *Charities and the Commons* 21 (Dec. 5, 1908), p. 389.
47. Smith, *Deserted Wives*, for example, p. 9; Brandt, *Five Hundred and Seventy-Four Deserters*, for example, pp. 41–42.
48. Quoted in Eubank, *Study of Family Desertion*, p. 19.
49. Colcord, *Broken Homes*, p. 8.
50. Gordon, *Heroes*, chap. 4.
51. Baldwin, "Making the Deserter Pay"; Weyl, "The Deserter"; Foss, "The Genus Deserter"; Abigail S. Moore, "Marital Desertion among New York Jews"(paper presented at the Annual Meeting of the Organization of American Historians), 1980.
52. Stuart Alfred Queen and Delbert Martin Mann, *Social Pathology* (New York: Thomas Y. Crowell, 1925), p. 80.
53. Eubank, *Study of Family Desertion*, p. 13.
54. For example, Massachusetts Commission on the Support of Dependent Minor Children of Widowed Mothers, *Report* (Boston, 1913).
55. For example, Breckinridge, "Neglected Widowhood"; *Report of the New York State Commission on Relief for Widowed Mothers* (Albany: J.B. Lyon 1914; reprint, New York: Arno, 1974).
56. *Report of the New York State Commission*, p. 62; Gordon, *Heroes*.
57. *Report of the New York State Commission*, pp. 7, 17.
58. Ibid., p. 7; Breckinridge, "Neglected Widowhood." When Isaac Rubinow spoke of widowhood or "orphaned families," he admitted, some were widows "in the economic if not statistical sense, deserted women, divorced women, wives of tubercular husbands, wives whose husbands are alcoholics or inmates of state institutions for mental diseases." Rubinow, *Quest for Security*, chap. 34, esp. pp. 477 and 479.
59. Abraham Epstein, *Insecurity—A Challenge to America: A Study of Social Insurance in the United States and Abroad* (New York: Random House, 1933, 1936, and 1938), reissued with introduction by Paul Douglas (New York: Agathon Press, 1968), chaps. 33–34; Rubinow, *Quest for Security*, chap. 33, esp. p. 479.

60. Lundberg and Lenroot, *Illegitimacy*; Regina G. Kunzel, "The Professionalization of Benevolence: Evangelicals and Social Workers in the Florence Crittenton Homes, 1915 to 1945," *Journal of Social History* 22:1 (Fall 1988), pp. 21–43.

61. Charlotte Lowe, "The Intelligence and Social Background of the Unmarried Mother," *Mental Hygiene* 11:4 (Oct. 1927), p. 793. I am indebted to Lisa Brush for this reference. Diagnoses of "feeblemindedness" in unwed mothers were common.

62. Lundberg and Lenroot, *Illegitimacy*; Ida Parker, *A Follow-up Study of 550 Illegitimacy Applications* (Boston: Research Bureau on Social Case Work, 1924); Ruth Reed, *The Illegitimate Family in New York City: Its Treatment by Social and Health Agencies* (New York: Welfare Council of New York City, 1933); Mabel Higgins Mattingly, "The Unmarried Mother and Her Child: A Fact Finding Study of Fifty-three Cases of Unmarried Mothers Who Kept Their Children" (M.S. thesis, Western Reserve University, 1928), cited by Brush, "Worthy Widows."

63. Brush, "Worthy Widows."

64. Lundberg and Lenroot, *Illegitimacy*, vol. 2, passim, esp. table 5, p. 89; Commonwealth of Massachusetts, Special Commission Established to Investigate Laws Relative to Dependent . . . Children, *Report* (Boston, 1931), appendix G. Of course the major cause of infant mortality was poverty—and "illegitimate" children were more likely to be poor.

65. Children's Bureau Mss., Box 240, 10-13-0, 10-13-2, and 10-13-2-3; Lundberg and Lenroot, *Illegitimacy*.

66. Agency for Assisting and Providing Situations in the Country for Destitute Mothers with Infants, *Annual Report* (New York, 1904), p. 13.

67. Ibid., p. 12.

68. Corinne Sherman, "Racial Factors in Desertion," *The Family* 3:6–9 (Nov. 1922), quote from no. 7, p. 169.

69. Gordon, *Heroes*, chaps. 4 and 5, passim. However, some early studies already provided evidence against linking delinquency with single mothers, as the Massachusetts Commission on the Support of Dependent Minor Children of Widowed Mothers, *Report* (Boston: Wright & Potter, 1913), pp. 162–63.

70. Gordon, *Heroes*, chap. 4; Breckinridge, "Neglected Widowhood."

71. This term was coined by William O'Neill in his *Everyone Was Brave: The Rise and Fall of Feminism in America*, to refer to the women's social reform network active in the Progressive Era, many of whom had come from the women's rights movement, and the label has stuck. The women themselves, however, did not call themselves feminists and even used this word pejoratively, to describe those who insisted on formally identical treatment of women and men.

72. Gordon, *Heroes*.

73. Hughes, *Mothers in Industry.*
74. Susan Traverso in her Ph.D. dissertation, "The Politics of Welfare: Boston, 1910–1945" (University of Wisconsin-Madison in progress), also found a silence about single mothers in the 1930s, 1940s, and 1950s.
75. Charles Johnson, *Shadow of the Plantation* (Chicago: University of Chicago Press, 1934), p. 100; Irene Graham, "The Negro Family in a Northern City," *Opportunity* 8:2 (Feb. 1930), pp. 48–51, based on 1920 census; Allison Davis and John Dollard, *Children of Bondage: The Personality Development of Negro Youth in the Urban South* (Washington, D.C.: American Council on Education, 1940), pp. xxi–xxii; Hortense Powdermaker, *After Freedom: A Cultural Study of the Deep South* (New York: Atheneum, 1939), p. 143; John Dollard, *Caste and Class in a Southern Town* (New Haven, Conn.: Yale University Press for the Institute of Human Relations, 1937), p. 414, quoted by James T. Patterson, *America's Struggle Against Poverty 1900–1980* (Cambridge, Mass.: Harvard University Press, 1981), p. 39.
76. Ultimately it may be impossible to retain this distinction, to separate cultural from economic factors in the history of black family structure in the United States. Cultures are, after all, affected by large-scale economic conditions.

Chapter 3. State Caretakers: Maternalism, Mothers' Pensions, and the Family Wage

1. My interpretation of mothers' aid, or mothers' pensions as the program was often popularly known, has been primarily influenced by that of Molly Ladd-Taylor, who has been kind enough to share her work with me over the years that I have been working on welfare, and I am extremely grateful. More recently I have benefited from Michel, "The Limits of Maternalism," pp. 277–320; Robyn Muncy, *Creating a Female Dominion in American Reform, 1890–1935* (New York: Oxford University Press, 1991); Joanne Goodwin, "An American Experiment in Paid Motherhood: The Implementation of Mothers' Pensions in Early Twentieth Century Chicago," *Gender and History* 4:3 (Autumn 1992), pp. 323–42.
2. Women's historians and welfare scholars are engaged in a lively debate about maternalism. Most scholars oppose maternalism to feminism, either because they prefer a narrower definition of feminism, referring exclusively to new currents of thought that sought complete equality and similar treatment for men and women—following Nancy Cott here; or because they want to emphasize the conservative aspects of

maternalism—as in the work of Sonya Michel. I prefer a broader definition of feminism, one closer to today's usage and one that can be used to indicate the continuity among various strands of women's movements; and I think it vital to recognize that there has been maternalist feminism (while there has also, of course, been maternalist antifeminism). Maternalist feminists, in my definition, sought to use women's assigned sphere of activity, and particularly their social identities as mothers, as a route to greater power. For references, see note 78 below.

3. Barbara J. Nelson, "Mothers' Aid, Pauper Laws, and Woman Suffrage: The Intersection of the Welfare State and Democratic Participation, 1913–1935" (unpublished paper, 1989).

4. Mary F. Bogue, *Administration of Mothers' Aid in Ten Localities* (Washington, D.C.: U.S. Children's Bureau Publication No. 184, 1928), p. 5.

5. Gordon, *Heroes*.

6. Lori D. Ginzburg, "'Moral Suasion is Moral Balderdash': Women, Politics, and Social Activism in the 1850s," *Journal of American History* 73:3 (Dec. 1986), pp. 601–22.

7. Farm and domestic labor seemed more acceptable to them than industrial or street labor, and reformers wanted to move upward the minimum age for children's leaving school.

8. Kleinberg, "Widowhood," p. 14; on Pittsburgh see S. J. Kleinberg, *The Shadow of the Mills: Working Class Families in Pittsburgh, 1870–1917* (Pittsburgh: Pittsburgh University Press, 1989), p. 127. Progressive welfare reformers wanted children in school, and they understood that resistance to schooling came less from children than from their needy parents and that single mothers were particularly dependent on children's income.

9. For example, Sophie Irene Loeb, "Johnny Doe, His Mother and the State," *Harper's Weekly* 58 (Jan. 13, 1914), p. 24.

10. For example, Israels, "Widowed Mothers," pp. 741–42.

11. Edith Abbott and Sophonisba Breckinridge, *The Administration of the Aid-to-Mothers Law in Illinois* (Washington, D.C.: U.S. Children's Bureau Publication No. 82, 1921); Bogue, *Administration of Mothers' Aid*.

12. The arguments of the opposition are reviewed in Gordon, *Heroes*, chap. 4; Grace Abbott, "Mothers' Aid in the Modern Public Assistance Program," in her *From Relief to Social Security: The Development of the New Public Welfare Services and Their Administration* (New York: Russell & Russell, 1966), pp. 265 ff.; Ann Vandepol, "Dependent Children, Child Custody, and the Mothers' Pensions: The Transformation of State-Family Relations in the Early 20th Century," *Social Problems* 29:3 (Feb. 1982), pp. 221–35; Barbara Nelson, "The Origins of

326 Notes to pages 41–43

the Two-Channel Welfare State: Workmen's Compensation and Mothers' Aid," in Linda Gordon, ed., *Women, the State, and Welfare* (Madison: University of Wisconsin Press, 1990); Mark H. Leff, "Consensus for Reform: The Mothers' Pension Movement in the Progressive Era," *Social Service Review* 47 (Sept. 1973), pp. 397–417.

13. NCCC, *Proceedings* (for example, 1902), pp. 378–83 passim. A prominent economist even opposed higher wages for women on the grounds that they might thus be tempted to neglect home duties; Alice Kessler-Harris, *A Woman's Wage: Historical Meanings & Social Consequences* (Lexington: University Press of Kentucky, 1990), pp. 19–20.

14. Edward T. Devine, "Pensions for Mothers," in *American Labor Legislation Review* 3 (June 1913), pp. 191–201, quote p. 193; Otto T. Bannard in *Report of the New York State Commission on Relief for Widowed Mothers* (1914; reprint, New York: Arno, 1974), p. 132.

15. NCCC, *Proceedings* (1912), p. 479.

16. *Report of the New York State Commission*, p. 7.

17. Muriel W. Pumphrey and Ralph E. Pumphrey, "The Widows' Pension Movement, 1900–1930: Preventive Child-Saving or Social Control?" in Walter I. Trattner, ed., *Social Welfare or Social Control? Some Historical Reflections on "Regulating the Poor"* (Knoxville: University of Tennessee Press, 1983), pp. 51–66; Eve P. Smith, "The Failure of the Destitute Mothers' Bill: The Use of Political Power in Social Welfare," *Journal of Sociology and Social Welfare* 14:2 (June 1987), pp. 63–87; Barbara Randall Joseph, "The Discovery of Need, 1880–1914," (Ph.D. dissertation, Columbia University, 1986), pp. 108–10.

18. Editorial in *The Outlook* (108 [Dec. 9, 1914], p. 809) endorsing home scholarships for fatherless children; John Clayton Drew, "Child Labor and Child Welfare: The Origins and Uneven Development of the American Welfare State" (Ph.D. dissertation, Cornell University, 1987), pp. 101–7.

19. New York City Municipal Archives, Mayors' Papers, 90-SWL-37, May 3, 1897. Other letters are in SWL-36 and SML-6. Cited in Maureen Fitzgerald, "Irish-Catholic Nuns and the Development of New York City's Welfare System, 1840–1900" (Ph.D. dissertation, University of Wisconsin, 1992), pp. 599–600.

20. Gordon, *Heroes*, chap. 4.

21. Kleinberg, "Widowhood," p. 33.

22. Molly Ladd-Taylor, *Raising a Baby the Government Way: Mothers' Letters to the Children's Bureau 1915–1932* (New Brunswick, N.J.: Rutgers University Press, 1986), pp. 139, 149, 151, 158, 159, 160.

23. Skocpol, *Protecting Soldiers and Mothers*, chaps. 6 and 8; Molly Ladd-Taylor, *Mother-Work: Women, Child Welfare and the State, 1890–1930* (Urbana and Chicago: University of Illinois Press, 1994).

24. It was also relevant that ERA opponents had a sense of investment in the protective legislation they had worked so hard to get for women and children, and which they believed would be overturned by an ERA; and of course personality clashes and strategic/tactical disagreements heightened distrust and masked considerable commonality. Wendy Sarvasy, "Beyond the Difference versus Equality Policy Debate: Postsuffrage Feminism, Citizenship, and the Quest for a Feminist Welfare State," *Signs* 17:2 (Winter 1992), pp. 329–62.
25. See editorials in *Equal Rights*, such as "Regarding Mothers' Pensions," Sept. 1, 1923, p. 28, and "Mothers' Pensions and the Amendment," May 3, 1924, p. 92; Eleanor Taylor Marsh, "Equal Rights and Mothers' Pensions," *Equal Rights* (Jan. 19, 1924), p. 390; Eleanor Taylor, "Wages for Mothers," *The Suffragist* (Nov. 1920), pp. 273–75. I am indebted to Ellen DuBois for these references. For a stronger version of this interpretation, strongly emphasizing this interest in gender-neutral legislation, see Sarvasy, "Beyond the Difference."
26. Gordon, *Heroes*; Anthony M. Platt, *The Child Savers: The Invention of Delinquency* (Chicago: University of Chicago Press, 1969); Barbara M. Brenzel, *Daughters of the State: A Social Portrait of the First Reform School for Girls in North America, 1856–1905* (Cambridge, Mass.: MIT Press, 1983); Ellen Ryerson, *The Best-Laid Plans: America's Juvenile Court Experiment* (New York: Hill and Wang, 1978).
27. Ladd-Taylor, *Raising a Baby*, p. 142.
28. Molly Ladd-Taylor, "Mothers Pensions" typescript, p. 9.
29. Ibid., pp. 8–9. See chap. 4 for more on black women.
30. On women's motivations, see Muncy, *Creating a Female Dominion*, esp. chaps. 1 and 3.
31. Emma Octavia Lundberg, *Unto the Least of These: Social Services for Children* (New York: Appleton-Century-Crofts, 1947), pp. 131–32; Gordon, *Heroes*, chap. 4; Handler and Hasenfeld, *The Moral Construction of Poverty*, p. 67; Roy Lubove, *The Struggle for Social Security, 1900–1935* (Cambridge, Mass.: Harvard University Press, 1968).
32. Winifred Bell, *Aid to Dependent Children* (New York: Columbia University Press, 1965), p. 29; Bogue, *Administration of Mothers' Aid*.
33. Michael M. Cenci, "Day Care as a Form of Indoor Relief," in June Axinn et al., *The Century of the Child: Progress and Retreat*, eds., (Philadelphia: University of Pennsylvania School of Social Work, 1973), quoting Pennsylvania Mothers' Assistance Fund, 1913 and 1916 annual reports, p. 47.
34. For many other examples of standards for "suitable homes," see Gordon, *Heroes*; and Elizabeth Ewen, *Immigrant Women in the Land of Dollars: Life and Culture on the Lower East Side, 1890–1925* (New York: Monthly Review Press, 1985).

35. The stipend was to provide "opportunity for instruction in food values, buying, and household management . . ." according to the *Proceedings of Conference on Mothers' Pensions* (Washington, D.C.: U.S. Children's Bureau Publication No. 109, 1922), p. 4. See also Abbott and Breckinridge, *Administration of the Aid-to-Mothers Law in Illinois*; Elizabeth L. Hall, *Mothers' Assistance in Philadelphia: Actual and Potential Costs, A Study of 1010 Families* (Hanover, N.H.: Sociological Press, 1933), pp. 27–29; Emma O. Lundberg, "Aid to Mothers with Dependent Children," *Annals of the American Academy of Political and Social Science*, 98:187 (Nov. 1921), pp. 97–105; Florence Nesbitt, *Standards of Public Aid to Children in Their Own Homes* (Washington, D.C.: U.S. Children's Bureau Publication No. 118, 1923); Bogue, *Administration of Mothers' Aid*, to cite but a few of the many sources for these Americanizing purposes of mothers' aid.
36. *Proceedings of Conference on Mothers' Pensions*, p. 4.
37. Constance McLaughlin Green, *The Secret City: A History of Race Relations in the Nation's Capital* (Princeton, N.J.: Princeton University Press, 1967), p. 223.
38. Goodwin, "An American Experiment," table 1, p. 339.
39. Odem, "Single Mothers, Delinquent Daughters," p. 29.
40. Two examples: Some Baltimoreans explicitly opposed mothers' aid because they did not wish public funds to be used for blacks; a U.S. Children's Bureau divisional director considered the disinclination to aid blacks to be the main reason that six southern states had no programs. Emma Lundberg to Mrs. Walter S. Ufford, n.d., Children's Bureau Mss., National Archives, Box 209, quoted by Kleinberg, "Widowhood," p. 35., n.d.
41. U.S. Children's Bureau, *Mothers' Aid 1931* (Washington, D.C.: U.S. Children's Bureau Publication No. 220, 1931), pp. 13–14.
42. In Emma Lundberg's and Katharine Lenroot's massive study done for the Children's Bureau, race was not used as a variable. *Illegitimacy as a Child-Welfare Problem*.
43. Hall, *Mothers' Assistance in Philadelphia*.
44. Gwendolyn Mink, *The Wages of Motherhood: Maternalist Social Policy and Women's Inequality in the Welfare State, 1917–1942* (Ithaca, N.Y.: Cornell University Press, forthcoming), p. 44; see also her "The Lady and the Tramp: Gender, Race, and the Origins of the American Welfare State," in Linda Gordon, ed., *Women, the State, and Welfare* (Madison: University of Wisconsin Press, 1990), pp. 92–122.
45. Julia Lathrop, "Discussion," NCCC, *Proceedings* (1912), 487–88.
46. The influential *Report of the New York State Commission* demonstrated the appalling lack of help available to them.
47. Devine, "Pensions for Mothers"; Kleinberg, "Widowhood."

48. Odem, "Single Mothers," p. 30.
49. Pumphrey and Pumphrey, "The Widows' Pension Movement, 1900–1930."
50. James D. Marver and Meredith A. Larson, "Public Policy Toward Child Care in America: A Historical Perspective," in Philip K. Robins and Samuel Weiner, eds., *Child Care and Public Policy: Studies of the Economic Issues* (Lexington, Mass.: Lexington Books, 1978), p. 31.
51. One socialist-leaning advocate of more widespread welfare provision pointed out that the class difference ought to be the other way around: Isaac Rubinow thought that mothers' employment ought to be more encouraged "in the middle classes, where the earning capacity of the professional woman is sufficiently high to allow for employment of help," in *Survey* 52 (May 15, 1924), p. 235, quoted in Mink, *Wages of Motherhood*, chap. 2, p. 13.
52. Folbre and Abel, "Women's Work and Women's Households," pp. 545–69; Goodwin, "An American Experiment"; FERA, *An Analysis of the "Unemployable" Families and Non-Family Persons on Urban Relief Rolls, December 1934* (Research Bulletin D-6, Feb. 5, 1935), n.p.
53. Caroline Manning, *The Immigrant Woman and Her Job* (Washington, D.C.: U.S. Women's Bureau Bulletin No. 74, 1930), p. 57.
54. Abbott and Breckinridge, *The Administration of the Aid-to-Mothers Law in Illinois*, pp. 35, 64; Ladd-Taylor, *Mother-Work*, pp. 268–69; Sara McLanahan and Irwin Garfinkel, "Single Mothers, The Underclass, and Social Policy," *Annals of the American Academy of Political and Social Science* 501 (Jan. 1989), p. 99; the example of Mrs. C. is taken from Joanne Goodwin, "Women on Welfare: The State and Single Motherhood, Chicago, 1900–1930" (paper presented at the Social Science History Association conference, 1989), pp. 8–9.
55. Alice L. Higgins and Florence Windom of Boston Associated Charities, "Helping Widows to Bring Up Citizens," NCCC, *Proceedings* (1910), pp. 138–44; Cenci, "Day Care as a Form of Indoor Relief," p. 47, quoting Pennsylvania Mothers' Assistance Fund, 1913, 1916, and 1918 reports.
56. Rabbi Rudolph I. Coffee, for example, "Why Pennsylvania Needs a Widows' Pension Law," in William H. Slingerland, ed., *Child Welfare Work in Pennsylvania: A Co-operative Study of Child-Helping Agencies and Institutions* (New York: Russell Sage Foundation, 1915), pp. 131–34; Lubove, *The Struggle for Social Security*; Leff, "Consensus for Reform."
57. Skocpol, *Protecting Soldiers and Mothers*, p. 426.
58. Ibid., p. 468.
59. Ibid., pp. 477–78.
60. Quoted in Jane Addams, *My Friend Julia Lathrop* (New York: Macmillan, 1935), p. 123.

61. Quoted by Cenci, "Day Care as a Form of Indoor Relief," p. 47, from Pennsylvania Mothers' Assistance Fund, 1916 annual report, pp. 7–11.

62. Evalyn T. Cavin, head of the Mothers' Assistance Fund for Philadelphia, in 1924, quoted in Mink, *Wages of Motherhood*, p. 16.

63. John Lewis Gillin, *Poverty and Dependency: Their Relief and Prevention* 3rd. ed. (New York: D. Appleton-Century, 1937), p. 411.

64. Gordon, *Heroes*.

65. Sheila M. Rothman, "Other People's Children," *The Public Interest* 30 (1973), pp. 15–16.

66. Cahan, *Past Caring*, p. 22.

67. Rothman, "Other People's Children," p. 16.

68. Grace Abbott, *The Child and the State* (Chicago: The University of Chicago Press, 1938), p. 230.

69. Cenci, "Day Care as a Form of Indoor Relief."

70. Kessler-Harris, *A Woman's Wage*, pp. 9–10.

71. Hughes, *Mothers in Industry*, chap. 1; Residents of Hull-House, *Hull-House Maps and Papers* (New York: Thomas Y. Crowell, 1895), p. 21; Folbre and Abel, "Women's Work and Women's Households"; Sophonisba P. Breckinridge, "The Home Responsibilities of Women Workers and the 'Equal Wage'" *Journal of Political Economy* 31 (1928), p. 537; Dorothy Wolf Douglas, "The Cost of Living for Working Women: A Criticism of Current Theories," *Quarterly Journal of Economics* 34 (1920), pp. 225–59.

72. Residents of Hull-House, *Hull-House Maps and Papers*, p. 21.

73. Breckinridge, "Home Responsibilities."

74. This controversy is discussed by both Beatrix Hoffman, "Insuring Maternity: The Campaign for Health Insurance" (paper presented at the Berkshire Conference on Women's History, 1993) and Mink, *Wages of Motherhood*, chap. 3, p. 11, and chap. 2, p. 24.

75. Charlotte Perkins Gilman, "Maternity Benefits and Reformers," *The Forerunner* 7 (Mar. 1916), pp. 65–66, anthologized in Larry Ceplair, ed., *Charlotte Perkins Gilman: A Nonfiction Reader* (New York: Columbia University Press, 1991), p. 258.

76. This was the only group called "feminist" at the time, and indeed their principled stand for women's economic independence was at the core of what "feminism" meant in the early twentieth century.

77. This was the attitude of Florence Kelley, at the radical edge of this group; see for example her "Minimum-Wage Laws," *Journal of Political Economy* 20:10 (Dec. 1912), p. 1003. There were in fact NWP people arguing for women's economic independence who did have poor women in mind, such as Alice Beal Parsons, *Woman's Dilemma* (New York: Thomas Y. Crowell, 1926), part 2, chap. 5, pp. 273, 292–93, 298.

78. Maternalism is used as an explanatory concept but not defined by Skocpol, *Protecting Soldiers and Mothers*. Excellent examples of the

use of the concept can be found in Koven and Michel, eds., *Mothers of a New World*; Sonya Michel and Seth Koven, "Womanly Duties: Maternalist Politics and the Origins of the Welfare State in France, Great Britain and the United States, 1880–1920," *American Historical Review* 95 (Oct. 1990), pp. 1076–1108; Eileen Boris, "Regulating Industrial Homework: The Triumph of 'Sacred Motherhood,'" *Journal of American History* 71 (Mar. 1985), pp. 745–63; Gisela Bock and Pat Thane, eds., *Maternity and Gender Policies: Women and the Rise of the European Welfare States, 1880s–1950s* (London: Routledge, 1991); Carolyn Strange, "Mothers on the March: Maternalism in Women's Protest for Peace in North America and Western Europe, 1900–1935," in Guida West and Rhoda Lois Blumberg, eds., *Women and Social Protest* (New York: Oxford University Press, 1990), pp. 209–24.

For critical considerations of the concept see Linda Gordon and Theda Skocpol, "Gender, State and Society: A Debate," *Contention* 2:3 (Spring 1993), pp. 139–89; "Maternalism as a Paradigm," a symposium in *Journal of Women's History* 5:2 (Fall 1993), pp. 95–131; Karen Offen, "Defining Feminism: A Comparative Historical Approach," *Signs* 14 (Autumn 1988), pp. 119–157; Eileen Yeo, "Social Motherhood and the Sexual Communion of Labor in British Social Science, 1850–1950," *Women's History Review* 1:1 (1992), pp. 63–87. A critique of the consequences of maternalist policies is in Mary Frances Berry, *The Politics of Parenthood: Child Care, Women's Rights, and the Myth of the Good Mother* (New York: Viking, 1993).

79. Charlotte Perkins Gilman, "On Ellen Key and the Woman Movement," *The Forerunner* 4 (Feb. 1913), pp. 35–38, anthologized in Ceplair, ed., *Charlotte Perkins Gilman*, p. 235.
80. Sarvasy, "Beyond the Difference."
81. Ladd-Taylor, *Mother-Work*, p. 368.
82. Theresa Malkiel, "The Lowest Paid Workers," *Socialist Woman* (Sept. 1908).
83. Reported in Arthur W. Towne, "New York State Conference," *Survey* 25 (Nov. 26, 1910), pp. 321–24.
84. Charlotte Perkins Gilman, "Paid Motherhood," *The Independent* 62 (Jan. 10, 1907), pp. 75–78.
85. William Hard, "Discussion," *American Labor Legislation Review* 3 (June 1913), pp. 229–34, quote p. 233.
86. William Hard, "The Moral Necessity of 'State Funds to Mothers,'" *Survey* 29 (Mar. 1, 1913), pp. 769–73.
87. See Hard's series on women's legal status in *The Delineator*, "With All My Worldly Goods I Thee Endow" (1911–12); Sarvasy, "Beyond the Difference."
88. Homer Folks, "Discussion," NCCC, *Proceedings* (1912), pp. 485–87; Devine, "Pensions for Mothers."

89. Anna Martin, *The Mother and Social Reform* (National Union of Women's Suffrage Societies, 1913), pp. 1063–65, quoted in John Clarke, Allan Cochrane, and Carol Smart, eds., *Ideologies of Welfare: From Dreams to Disillusion* (London: Hutchinson, 1987), pp. 63–64.

90. Carol Dyhouse, *Feminism and the Family in England 1880–1939* (London: Basil Blackwell, 1989), pp. 92–104; Eleanor Rathbone, *The Disinherited Family* (London: George Allen and Unwin, 1924).

91. Dyhouse, *Feminism and the Family*, p. 94.

92. Vivien Hart, "Watch What We Do: Women Administrators and the Implementation of Minimum Wage Policy, Washington, D.C., 1918–1923" (paper presented at the Berkshire Conference on Women's History, 1990), p. 2; Taylor, "Wages for Mothers"; Breckinridge, "Home Responsibilities."

93. Harriot Stanton Blatch and Alma Lutz, *Challenging Years: The Memoirs of Harriot Stanton Blatch* (New York: G. P. Putnam's Sons, 1940), chap. 5, "Women and the World's Work," quote p. 324.

94. Crystal Eastman, "Now We Can Begin," *The Liberator* (Dec. 1920), from Blanche Wiesen Cook, ed., *Crystal Eastman on Women & Revolution* (New York: Oxford University Press, 1978), p. 57.

95. Katharine Anthony, *The Endowment of Motherhood* (New York: B. W. Huebsch, 1920), pp. vii, 3.

96. Rathbone, *The Disinherited Family*, p. 15.

97. For example, Breckinridge, "Home Responsibilities."

98. Folbre and Abel, "Women's Work and Women's Households," p. 22.

99. Ibid.; Paul H. Douglas, *In the Fullness of Time: The Memoirs of Paul H. Douglas* (New York: Harcourt Brace Jovanovich, 1971), pp. 66–67.

100. Conspicuously missing from the scholarship about women's activities in this period is an attempt to identify and compare the perspectives of the more prominent women's groups, such as the General Federation of Women's Clubs and its affiliates, the National Congress of Mothers, the Women's Christian Temperance Union, the Consumers' Leagues, and so on.

101. See examples in Grace Abbott, "Mothers' Aid and Public Assistance," 1938, in *From Relief to Social Security*, p. 267; and Mary E. Richmond, "'Pensions' and the Social Worker," *Survey* 29 (Feb. 15, 1913), pp. 665–66. There was never a firm division between the entitlement and the charity/casework vision of mothers' aid; the difference was more one of emphasis. Nor did all analyze the alternatives dichotomously. Wiley Swift, for example, writing for a National Child Labor Committee publication in 1921, supported pensions for mothers—"If a soldier is to be paid for depopulating other countries . . . mothers ought to be paid for populating our own"—but denied that this was the best way to provide for children. Swift was, more-

over, like many who supported the concept of pensions but was nevertheless convinced that they had to be supervised by experts: "Every case must be studied and the proper solution worked out. . . . Sometimes it will not be wise to undertake to keep the family intact." Wiley H. Swift, "Pensions for Mothers or Aids for Children?" *The American Child* 3:1 (May 1921), pp. 24–26.

102. In the big cities in the early twentieth century, working-class working "girls" were often well organized and militant in workplace struggles, but working-class mothers were less able to make their voices heard publicly.

103. Richmond, "Pensions and the Social Worker," quote p. 666; Miriam Cohen and Michael Hanagan, "The Politics of Gender and the Making of the Welfare State, 1900–1940," *Journal of Social History* 24:3 (Spring 1991), pp. 473, 475.

104. Gertrude Vaile, "Public Relief," in *College Women and the Social Sciences: Essays by Herbert Elmer Mills and his Former Students* (New York: John Day Company, 1934), p. 33.

105. Lathrop to Marie L. Obenauer of Los Angeles, Oct. 15, 1915, Children's Bureau Mss., Box 122, Folder 10,481.

106. Vaile, "Public Relief," p. 33.

107. Breckinridge, "Home Responsibilities," pp. 533–34, 543; see also, for example, Hughes, *Mothers in Industry*, chap. 1.

108. For example, NCCC, *Proceedings* (1912), pp. 479, 481–87, 492.

109. Nelson, "The Origins of the Two-Channel Welfare State;" Orloff, "Gender and Early U.S. Social Policy," *Journal of Policy History* 3 (1991), pp. 249–81; Handler and Hasenfeld, *Moral Construction of Poverty*, p. 45; Skocpol, *Protecting Soldiers and Mothers*.

110. Edith Abbott, "The Experimental Period of Widows' Pension Legislation," NCSW, *Proceedings* 44 (1917), p. 154–64, quote pp. 154–55.

111. Goodwin, "An American Experiment," p. 338.

112. Ladd-Taylor, *Mother-Work*, pp. 283–84; *Raising a Baby*, p. 161.

113. I cannot resist a digression here into an epistemological debate among historians about the usefulness of poststructuralism. The use of the phrase "mothers' pensions" is a clear example of a disjuncture between language and non-linguistic reality. In this case an interesting victory won by the women's social-work-reform network brought into usage a word—"pensions"—that marked not only a legitimization of aid to some groups of single mothers but also, by analogy, an association of that aid with the hallowed veterans' pensions dating from the Civil War and therefore a destigmatization of this form of relief. By contrast, the material policy indicated by the notion of pensions was decisively defeated.

114. Grace Abbott, "Mothers' Aid and Public Assistance," p. 267.

115. Changing definitions of single mothers in these various waves of concern are being studied by Brush, "Worthy Widows."

Chapter 4. "Pity Is a Rebel Passion": The Women's Social Work Perspective

1. The subjects of this chapter have been intensely and extensively studied by women's historians, and many of the judgments in this chapter are in some ways collective products—both because we have learned from each other specifically and also because we have been part of a collective experience of developing the questions, methods, and analytic perspectives of a new women's history. I feel particularly influenced by Lela Costin, Ellen Fitzpatrick, Alice Kessler-Harris, Molly Ladd-Taylor, Gwendolyn Mink, Robyn Muncy, Barbara Sicherman, and Kathryn Sklar. There are differences of interpretation among us, within a remarkably large field of agreement. The differences may result primarily from the different questions that animate our research: My key questions have to do with the influences on ADC.
2. Quoted in Jane Addams, *My Friend Julia Lathrop* (New York: Macmillan, 1935), p. 118.
3. See correspondence in Lathrop Mss., Correspondence 1920 Folder, Lathrop to Senator La Follette, July 20, 1920, and his response July 23, 1920; Lathrop to Mrs. Medill McCormick, Sept. 7, 1920, and the response from Senator McCormick, Sept. 28, 1920.
4. Quoted in Lela B. Costin, *Two Sisters for Social Justice: A Biography of Grace and Edith Abbott* (Urbana: University of Illinois Press, 1983), p. 100.
5. This network has been differently named by historians who approached it from varied perspectives. William O'Neill labeled these women "social feminists," helping to distinguish them from suffragists because of their primary concentration on helping the poor. Women's historians of the Progressive Era have spoken of a "women's political culture" and "female dominion." Some have objected to the term "social feminism"; while it is surely imprecise, there is no better one.
6. Addams, *My Friend Julia Lathrop*, p. 178.
7. This national leadership network was not necessarily representative of local activists and leadership.
8. Nancy Pottisham Weiss, "Save the Children: A History of the Children's Bureau, 1903–1918" (Ph.D. dissertation, UCLA, 1974), pp. 64–65.
9. I came to perceive the existence of this alternative gender system by asking questions arising from the feminist notion that "the personal is political." In the case of this network, their friendships and political alliances were one and the same and their personal experience affected their political vision. This might be described as a *modified* version of "standpoint theory," as articulated by Nancy Hartsock in "The Feminist Standpoint: Developing the Ground for a Specifically Feminist Historical Materialism," or of a "situated knowledges" approach as advocated by Dorothy Smith in "Women's Perspective as a Radical Critique of

Sociology," both in Sandra Harding, ed., *Feminism and Methodology* (Bloomington: Indiana University Press, 1987), pp. 157–80 and 84–96, among other attempts to specify the relation between social being and social consciousness. I share the position that political visions are not disconnected from social position but that there are no determined causal relations or predictability in their relations.

10. I was stimulated to the "collective biography" approach by Susan Ware, *Beyond Suffrage: Women and the New Deal* (Cambridge, Mass.: Harvard University Press, 1981); Allen F. Davis, *Spearheads for Reform: The Social Settlements and the Progressive Movement, 1890–1914* (New York: Oxford University Press, 1967); and Judith Ann Trolander, *Professionalism and Social Change: From the Settlement House Movement to Neighborhood Centers, 1886 to the Present* (New York: Columbia University Press, 1987). Stephen Kalbert apparently did something similar in "The Commitment to Career Reform: The Settlement Movement Leaders," *Social Service Review* 49 (Dec. 1975), pp. 608–28, but ignored gender to the extent of not even mentioning whether he included men or women or both. Starting with the work of those who actually wrote ADC, I tracked down their network by noting who their correspondents were, whom they worked with in organizations, whom they mentioned. I make no claims that this group is inclusive or representative, and I may inadvertently have excluded many who belong. But I believe that the generalizations I base on this sample will not be much altered by the addition of others, provided one bears in mind that I am examining a national leadership, not local activists. My collection includes seventy-six women—national leaders in the key civic organizations campaigning for public welfare, such as the settlements, the NCL, the National Child Labor Committee, the American Association for Labor Legislation, and women who held state or federal welfare-related public office.

11. Of the ten women who were divorced, widowed, or separated, only four were employed.

12. Barbara Miller Solomon, *In the Company of Educated Women: A History of Women and Higher Education in America* (New Haven, Conn.: Yale University Press, 1985), p. 63.

13. Seventy-eight percent had been social workers at one time in their lives; 68 percent had social work as their major reform area. I checked to see if the social work background could have been characteristic particularly of the less prominent women in this network, but such was not the case. The most prominent two-thirds of the group were even more frequently social workers—84 percent.

14. This pattern is also noted by Stanley Wenocur and Michael Reisch, *From Charity to Enterprise: The Development of American Social Work in a Market Economy* (Urbana: University of Illinois Press, 1989), p. 33.

15. Jill Conway in her "Women Reformers and American Culture, 1870–1930," saw this break as constructing two fundamental types of reformer: the "sage" or "prophetess," who used feminine qualities such as insight and intuition to justify her activities, and the "expert."

16. Some examples of the uses of "social work" in the 1930s: U.S. Congressman Fred Vinson, complaining about Frances Perkins and her Department of Labor staff, insisted, "No damned social workers are going to come into my State to tell our people whom they shall hire." Quoted in George Martin, *Madame Secretary Frances Perkins: A Biography of America's First Woman Cabinet Member* (Boston: Houghton Mifflin, 1976), p. 355. When Lavinia Engle was asked to work for the Social Security Board, her first response was that because she wasn't a social worker, she wasn't qualified; see "The Reminiscences of Lavinia Engle" (1967), p. 29, in the Oral History Collection of Columbia University. Frances Perkins continued to use "social work" in this broad way in her oral history; see "The Reminiscences of Frances Perkins" (1955), pp. 21, 58–59, 65–67, 185, 443, in the Oral History Collection of Columbia University. According to *Encyclopedia of the Social Sciences*, "Organized welfare, or social, work, as conducted under the auspices of privately controlled philanthropic agencies, is distinguished from public welfare, which may be called public social work." Edward Lindeman, "Public Welfare," in *Encyclopedia of the Social Sciences*, vol. 12 (New York: Macmillan, 1934), p. 687.

17. Maher to Dewson, Sept. 6, 1931? Dewson Mss., Box 2, Folder 17. ("Sept. 6" is in Maher's writing, and "1931?" was added later, probably by Dewson going through her own papers.)

18. It is possible that at a later period, in the Great Depression, New York City also came to play an important role for black welfare activists. Several worked for the YWCA or various welfare programs in the city, and Dorothy Height's interview offers evidence of the importance of welfare jobs for black women, providing a relative openness to their advancement that was unavailable to them elsewhere. See "Interview with Dorothy I. Height," conducted by Polly Cowan (1974–76), p. 9, in Black Women Oral History Project, Schlesinger Library.

19. "The Reminiscences of Isidore Sydney Falk" (1968), pp. 7–8, in the Oral History collection of Columbia University; Ladd-Taylor, *Mother-Work*, 305 ff; Clara Beyer, *History of Labor Legislation for Women in Three States* (Washington, D.C.: Women's Bureau Bulletin No. 66, 1932), Part 1, pp. 5–8, and chap. 3; William W. Bremer, *Depression Winters: New York Social Workers and the New Deal* (Philadelphia: Temple University Press, 1984).

20. R. L. Duffus, *Lillian Wald: Neighbor and Crusader* (New York: Macmillan, 1938), pp. 200 ff.; Lillian Wald, *Windows on Henry Street*

(Boston: Little, Brown, 1934); Mary Kingsbury Simkhovitch, *Neighborhood: My Story of Greenwich House* (New York: W.W. Norton, 1938); Bremer, *Depression Winters*.

21. Martin, *Madame Secretary*, pp. 134–35; Elisabeth Israels Perry, "Training for Public Life: ER and Women's Political Networks in the 1920s," in Joan Hoff-Wilson and Marjorie Lightman, eds., *Without Precedent: The Life and Career of Eleanor Roosevelt* (Bloomington: Indiana University Press, 1984), p. 30.

22. Elizabeth Israels Perry, *Belle Moskowitz: Feminine Politics and the Exercise of Power in the Age of Alfred E. Smith* (New York: Oxford University Press, 1987), pp. 76–77; Walter Trattner, "Theodore Roosevelt, Social Workers, and the Election of 1912: A Note," *Mid-America* 50 (Jan. 1968), pp. 64–69. On pre-woman suffrage women's electoral participation, see, for example, S. Sara Monoson, "The Lady and the Tiger: Women's Electoral Activism in New York City Before Suffrage," *Journal of Women's History* 2 (Fall 1990), pp. 100–35.

23. On settlement relationships, see Virginia Kemp Fish, "The Hull House Circle: Women's Friendships and Achievements," in Janet Sharistanian, ed., *Gender, Ideology and Action: Historical Perspectives on Women's Public Lives* (Westport, Conn.: Greenwood Press, 1986); Kathryn Kish Sklar, "Hull House in the 1890s: A Community of Women Reformers," *Signs* 10 (Summer 1985), pp. 658–77; Mina Carson, *Settlement Folk: Social Thought and the American Settlement Movement, 1885–1930* (Chicago: University of Chicago Press, 1990).

24. Costin, *Two Sisters for Social Justice*, pp. 38–40; Martin, *Madame Secretary*, p. 233; Lathrop Mss., Correspondence Folders.

25. Tracey B. Strong and Helene Keyssar, *Right in Her Soul: The Life of Anna Louise Strong* (New York: Random House, 1983), p. 62.

26. For example, Sara T. Arneill, chairman, Colorado Child Welfare Department, to Grace Meigs of the CB, May 28, 1918, in Children's Bureau Mss., Box 51, Folder 6011.

27. For example, Ethel Erickson to Anderson, July 14, 1938; Anderson to Erickson, Aug. 4, 1938; Erickson to Anderson, July 29, 1942; Anderson to Erickson, Aug. 1, 1942; in Women's Bureau Mss., Box 1263.

28. Beyer was one of the exceptional members of this network in that she was married, and could not arrange her life to work full-time. Hart, "Watch What We Do," p. 14.

29. We see here the conviction that motherhood rendered a woman unfit for serious employment, at least until the children were grown; this will be discussed further below.

30. Undated letters in Lathrop Mss., Correspondence 1922 Folder.

31. Grace Abbott to Julia Lathrop (emphasis in original), n.d. but probably

November 1921, in Lathrop Mss., Correspondence 1921 Folder. Abbott meant the Women's Joint Congressional Committee, established in 1921.

32. Julia Lathrop, "The Children's Bureau," in NCCC, *Proceedings* (1912), pp. 30–33.

33. Anne Firor Scott, *Natural Allies: Women's Associations in American History* (Urbana: University of Illinois Press, 1991), pp. 155–56. In fact, Anne Scott suggested to me in a private conversation that the lack of separation between professionals and amateur reformers constituted a unique strength of the United States, as opposed, for example, to the European, women's social reform movement in this period. See also Nancy Cott, *Grounding of Modern Feminism*, p. 90.

34. Julia Lathrop to Glenn, Apr. 24, 1912, Abbott Mss., Box 57, Regenstein Library.

35. While nonemployed during the 1920s, Clara Beyer, when asked in an interview what she was doing, said not that she was raising children but that her "task" was "to build up organizational support through the Children's Bureau for the Child Labor Amendment." Meg McGavran Murray, "The Work Got Done: An Interview with Clara Mortenson Beyer," in *Face to Face: Fathers, Mothers, Masters, Monsters—Essays for a Nonsexist Future* (Westport, Conn.: Greenwood Press, 1983), pp. 216–17.

36. Florence Kelley to Mary Anderson, June 28, 1920, Anderson to Mary Dewson, Aug. 23, 1920, Anderson to Dewson, Oct. 23, 1922, Dewson to Anderson, June 1, 1923, Women's Bureau Mss., Box 843. There are literally hundreds of other examples in Children's Bureau Mss.

37. Grace Abbott to Julia Lathrop, n.d., Lathrop Mss., Correspondence 1923 Folder. Private funding of particular government projects was a continuing pattern in the welfare field.

38. Mary Anderson to Mary van Kleeck, Jan. 8, 1937, Anderson Mss., Box 1, Folder 22; Judith Sealander, "Feminist Against Feminist: The First Phase of the Equal Rights Amendment Debate, 1923–1963," *South Atlantic Quarterly* 81 (Spring 1982), pp. 154–56. Mary Beard participated in the early meeting but did not, ultimately, sign the charter; thanks to Nancy Cott for clarification on this point.

39. Gertrude Gogin to Lathrop, Oct. 14, 1918, Children's Bureau Mss., Box 51, Folder 6011.

40. Alice Hamilton to Grace Abbott, Nov. 17, 1932, Abbott Mss., Box 36, Folder 12; several such letters by Julia Lathrop in Lathrop Mss., Correspondence Folders.

41. Grace Abbott to Julia Lathrop, Aug. 3, 1922, Lathrop Mss., Correspondence 1922 Folder.

42. Grace Abbott to Katharine Lenroot, Apr. 9, 1936, Abbott Mss., Box 61, Folder 6.

43. Mary M. W. to Helen Sumner (Woodbury), Nov. 13, 1915, in Wood-bury Mss., Box 1, Folder 6. The woman being recommended was Mrs. William Lowell Putnam.
44. Their singleness was characteristic of other women of their race, class, and education in this period. In 1890, for example, over half of all women doctors were single; of those earning Ph.D.'s between 1877 and 1924, three-fourths remained single. As late as 1920 only 12 per-cent of all professional women were married. See, for example, Carl Degler, *At Odds: Women and the Family in America from the Revolu-tion to the Present* (New York: Oxford University Press, 1980), p. 385. Darlene Rebecca Roth in "Matronage: Patterns in Women's Organiza-tions, Atlanta, Georgia, 1890–1940" (Ph.D. dissertation, George Washington University, 1978), p. 182, corroborates the significance of marital breaks in the lives of activists, finding that civically active white women in Atlanta in this period were more likely to be widows. The particular strength of this network of unmarried women is also dis-cussed by Wendy Beth Posner, "Charlotte Towle: A Biography" (Ph.D. dissertation, University of Chicago School of Social Service Adminis-tration, 1986), pp. 47, 77–87.
45. Scott, *Natural Allies*, esp. chaps. 5–7.
46. Thanks to Alice Kessler-Harris for this insight.
47. Most of their acquaintances, outside their circles of intimates, were probably unaware of the possibility that they had sexual relations with other women. Some of their conservative opponents, however, insinu-ated attacks on their personal lives, particularly on the grounds that their childlessness unfitted them for child welfare responsibility.
48. On "Boston marriages" see Micaela di Leonardo, "Warrior Virgins and Boston Marriages: Spinsterhood in History and Culture," *Feminist Issues* 5 (Fall 1985), pp. 47–68.
49. Memoir by Mrs. Tilden Frank Phillips (sister of Edith Rockwood), written Feb. 22 and Feb. 26, 1953, Folder 22; and the will of Edith Rockwood, Folder 20, in Edith Rockwood Mss.
50. Blanche Wiesen Cook, *Eleanor Roosevelt, I: 1884–1933* (New York: Viking, 1992).
51. Blanche Wiesen Cook, "The Historical Denial of Lesbianism," *Radical History Review* 20 (Spring/Summer 1979), pp. 60–65; for quotations from a (hostile) contemporary source, see James Johnson, "The Role of Women in the Founding of the United States Children's Bureau," in Carol V. R. George, ed., *"Remember the Ladies": New Perspectives on Women in American History: Essays in Honor of Nelson Manfred Blake* (Syracuse: Syracuse University Press, 1975), p. 191.
52. When lesbian history was initially being written, these relationships with other women were seen, first, in exclusively private and individual terms, and, second, as a lifestyle that isolated them from the heterosexual social

and cultural mainstream. Recently Estelle Freedman and Blanche Wiesen Cook have helped change that paradigm. Cook, "Historical Denial"; Cook, "Female Support Networks and Political Activism: Lillian Wald, Crystal Eastman, Emma Goldman," in Nancy F. Cott and Elizabeth H. Pleck, eds., *A Heritage of Her Own: Toward a New Social History of American Women* (New York: Simon and Schuster, 1979), pp. 412–44; Cook, *Eleanor Roosevelt*; Estelle Freedman, "Separatism as Strategy: Female Institution Building and American Feminism, 1870–1930," *Feminist Studies* 5 (Fall 1979), pp. 512–29.

53. For example, Florence Kelley to Julia Lathrop, Sept. 27, 1922, in Lathrop Mss., NCL folder. On nuns see Maureen Fitzgerald, "Irish-Catholic Nuns and the Development of New York City's Welfare System, 1840–1900" (Ph.D. Dissertation: University of Wisconsin-Madison, 1992). The similarity is, of course, limited because nuns were ultimately subordinated to a patriarchal authority system, while the women of this welfare-reform community were, of course, trying to escape and resist patriarchal authority.

54. Posner, "Charlotte Towle," p. 78.

55. Dewson to Clara Mortenson [later Beyer], Aug. 10, 1920, in Beyer Mss., Box 2, Folder 38.

56. Susan B. Anthony, "Homes of Single Women" (October 1877), in Ellen Carol DuBois, ed., *Elizabeth Cady Stanton, Susan B. Anthony: Correspondence, Writings, Speeches* (New York: Schocken, 1981), pp. 146–51, emphasis in original.

57. Quoted from the *Congressional Record* in Costin, *Two Sisters for Social Justice*, pp. 141–42.

58. Julia Lathrop to Judge Ben Lindsey, Dec. 7, 1927 in Lathrop Mss., Correspondence July–December 1927 Folder.

59. Mary Dewson to Clara Beyer, Oct. 12, 1931, in Beyer Mss., Box 2, Folder 40; "Interview with Caroline Ware," conducted by Susan Ware, pp. 40–42, in the Women in Federal Government Project, Schlesinger Library; Janice Andrews, "Role of Female Social Workers in the Second Generation: Leaders or Followers" (typescript, 1989). The possibility of combining marriage and career had been debated intensely starting in the 1920s, but it was in the following decade that the change began to be evident. See Lois Scharf, *To Work and to Wed: Female Employment, Feminism, and the Great Depression* (Westport, Conn.: Greenwood, 1980); and Margaret W. Rossiter, "Outmaneuvered Again—The Collapse of Academic Women's Strategy of Celibate Overachievement" (paper presented at the Berkshire Conference on Women's History, 1993).

60. Beyer to Eastman, Apr. 10, 1930, in Beyer Mss., Box 2, Folder 39.

61. Beyer to Molly Dewson, Oct. 9, 1931, in ibid., Box 2, Folder 40.

62. Beyer to Abbott, Jan. 28, 1932, and undated response, in ibid., Box 5, Folder 41.

63. Historian Susan Ware computed, about a different and smaller but overlapping sample of New Deal women, that almost 50 percent (thirteen of twenty-eight) were from political families. Ware, *Beyond Suffrage*, appendix C.

64. Hart, "Watch What We Do," p. 31.

65. Julia Lathrop to Medill McCormick, Sept. 7, 1920; response from Senator McCormick, Sept. 28, 1920, in Lathrop Mss., Correspondence 1920 Folder.

66. Hart, "Watch What We Do," p. 5; Sklar, "Hull House"; Clement E. Vose, "The National Consumers' League and the Brandeis Brief," *Midwest Journal of Political Science* 1:3–4 (Nov. 1957), pp. 267–90.

67. "The Reminiscences of Felix Frankfurter," (1955), pp. 157–58, 159, and 177, in the Oral History Collection of Columbia University.

68. Paul H. Douglas, *In the Fullness of Time: The Memoirs of Paul H. Douglas* (New York: Harcourt Brace Jovanovich, 1971), p. 45.

69. Florence Kelley to John Graham Brooks, Aug. 13, 1913, Brooks Mss., Box 1, Folder 18.

70. Linda Gordon, *Woman's Body, Woman's Right: Birth Control in America* (New York: Viking, 1976), chaps. 6 and 7.

71. Gordon, *Heroes*.

72. John Patrick McDowell, *The Social Gospel in the South: The Woman's Home Mission Movement in the Methodist Episcopal Church, South, 1886–1939* (Baton Rouge: Louisiana State University Press, 1982), pp. 60–72.

73. Grace Abbott to Julia Lathrop, Jan. 18, 1921, Lathrop Mss., Correspondence 1921 folder.

74. For example, Beth S. Wenger, "Jewish Women of the Club: The Changing Public Role of Atlanta's Jewish Women (1870–1930)," *American Jewish History* 76:3, March 1987, pp. 311–333; Faith Rogow, "'Gone to Another Meeting': A History of the National Council of Jewish Women" (Ph.D. Dissertation, SUNY-Binghamton, 1989).

75. Simkhovitch, *Neighborhood*, p. 64.

76. Florence Kelley to John Graham Brooks, Aug. 13, 1913, John Graham Brooks Mss., Box 1, Folder 18.

77. Arthur Kellogg to Julia Lathrop, July 18, 1927, Graham Romeyn Taylor to Lathrop, July 22, 1927, and Florence Kelley to Lathrop, July 21, 1927, all in Lathrop Mss., Correspondence July–December 1927 Folder.

78. On Hispanics, see Sandra Schackel, *Social Housekeepers: Women Shaping Public Policy in New Mexico 1920–1940* (Albuquerque: University of New Mexico, Press, 1992), p. 42.

79. Florence Kelley, "The Sterling Discrimination Bill," *Crisis* 26:6 (Oct. 1923), pp. 252–55; Mink, *Wages of Motherhood*, chap. 5, pp. 16–17.

80. Jacqueline Anne Rouse, *Lugenia Burns Hope: Black Southern Reformer* (Athens: University of Georgia Press, 1989), p. 17. See chap. 5 for more on Hope.

81. Davis, *Spearheads for Reform*, pp. 94–102.

82. Elisabeth Lasch, "Female Vanguard in Race Relations: 'Mother Power' and Blacks in the American Settlement House Movement" (paper presented at the Berkshire Conference on Women's History, 1990).

83. The story of white feminist racism is well told by Paula Giddings, *When and Where I Enter: The Impact of Black Women on Race and Sex in America* (New York: William Morrow, 1984), pp. 123–30; on the WCTU see Constance Green, *The Secret City*, p. 164.

84. Cited by Beatrix Hoffman, "Insuring Maternity" (paper presented at the Berkshire Conference on Women's History, 1993), p. 5.

85. Molly Ladd-Taylor, "'Grannies' and 'Spinsters': Midwife Education Under the Sheppard-Towner Act," *Journal of Social History* 22:2 (1988), pp. 255–75.

86. For example, Grace Abbott to Julia Lathrop, Jan. 26, 1922 in Lathrop Mss., Correspondence 1921 Folder.

87. Secretary of the Interior Dr. Ray Lyman Wilbur, head of the conference, insultingly attributed this gain to advances in the qualifications of blacks, blaming their previous lack of representation on their lack of expertise; Ray Lyman Wilbur, "Negro Cooperation in the White House Conference," *Opportunity* 8:11 (Nov. 1930), pp. 328–29, 344.

88. Nancy J. Weiss, *Farewell to the Party of Lincoln: Black Politics in the Age of FDR* (Princeton, N.J.: Princeton University Press, 1983), p. 49.

89. Ibid., p. 59.

90. Brenda Clegg Gray, *Black Female Domestics During the Depression in New York City, 1930–1940* (New York: Garland, 1993), p. 97.

91. Gordon, *Heroes*.

92. Louis J. Covotsos, "Child Welfare and Social Progress: A History of the United States Children's Bureau, 1912–1935" (Ph.D. Dissertation, University of Chicago, 1976), p. 53. He saw the CB's constant extragovernmental consultation, as Judith Sealander saw that of the Women's Bureau, as a sign of weakness and marginality, but the record suggests otherwise; a better interpretation is in Ladd-Taylor. Thanks to Landon Storrs for noticing Sealander's position on this.

93. I am indebted to Alice Kessler-Harris for noting this irony.

94. Lillian Wald, "The Idea of the Children's Bureau," National Conference of Social Work (NCSW) *Proceedings* (Philadelphia, 1932), pp. 33–35; Lillian D. Wald, *The House on Henry Street* (New York: Henry Holt, 1915), pp. 164–65; Duffus, *Lillian Wald*, pp. 93–95; Dorothy E. Bradbury, *Five Decades of Action for Children: A History of the Children's Bureau* (Washington, D.C.: U.S. Department of HEW, Social Security Administration, Children's Bureau, 1962), p. 1.

95. Florence Kelly recollects the campaign in a letter to Julia Lathrop, Election Day, 1930, in Lathrop Mss., Correspondence 1930 Folder. See also Robyn Muncy, *Creating a Female Dominion in American Reform, 1890–1935* (New York: Oxford University Press, 1991), pp. 101 ff.

96. On Women's Bureau perspective, see Sophonisba Breckinridge, "The Home Responsibilities of Women Workers and the 'Equal Wage,'" *Journal of Political Economy* 31 (1928), p. 524; Dorothy Wolf Douglas, "The Cost of Living for Working Women: A Criticism of Current Theories," *Quarterly Journal of Economics* 34 (1920), p. 233.

97. Mary Dewson to Clara Beyer, July 7, 1934, Beyer Mss., Box 3, Folder 45.

98. Emma Duke, Director, Industrial Division, Children's Bureau, to Rev. J.C. Cunningham of Buffalo, South Carolina, July 12, 1919, Children's Bureau Mss., Box 152, Folder 13-1-4.

99. Robert C. Reinders, *American Social Workers in the Years of the Locust, 1929–1933* (Buffalo, N.Y.: Catalyst, [197-?]), p. 29.

100. Children's Bureau Mss., for example, Box 476, Folder 0-2-3. These letters were usually answered by Agnes K. Hanna, Chief, Social Service Division.

101. Sara T. Arneill of Woman's Council of Defense for Colorado, Denver, to Grace Meigs, Children's Bureau, May 28, 1918, Children's Bureau Mss., Box 51, Folder 6011.

102. Sarah Bluymenthal Schaar, Jewish Social Service Bureau of Chicago, to Grace Abbott, Oct. 5, 1922, Children's Bureau Mss., Box 162.

103. John B. Andrews to Grace Abbott, May 7, 1926, in Abbott Mss., Box 28, Folder 3.

104. John Hall to Grace Abbott, Aug. 27, 1924, in ibid., Box 36, F-3.

105. Of course, they were not the only politicians to understand the advantages of inclusion, but they were noted for their expertise at this practice. Historian William Bremer attributes the New Deal's "conference" method to these women, especially to Frances Perkins as secretary of labor, who had learned it in her work in the New York Consumers' League; Bremer, *Depression Winters*, p. 158.

106. Norman Hapgood, ed., *Professional Patriots* (New York: Albert & Charles Boni, 1927), appendix.

107. *Congressional Record* (69th Congress, 1st Session, 1926), pp. 12946–67, quoted by Allen Davis, *American Heroine: The Life and Legend of Jane Addams* (London: Oxford University Press, 1973), p. 266.

108. Grace Abbott to Julia Lathrop, summer 1922 but n.d., in Lathrop Mss., Correspondence 1922 Folder.

109. Lathrop Mss., Correspondence 1926 Folder.

110. Hearings of House Comm. on Interstate and Foreign Commerce on H.R. 10925 (early version of Sheppard-Towner), 66th Cong., 3rd sess., Dec. 1920, p. 46.

111. Grace Abbott to Julia Lathrop, Jan. 18, 1921, Lathrop Mss., Correspondence 1921 Folder.
112. White House Conference on Child Health and Protection, *Report of the Committee on Public Health Organization, Section II: Public Health Service and Administration* (New York: Century Co., 1932); *The Seven Years of the Maternity and Infancy Act* (Washington, D.C.: U.S. Children's Bureau Publication No. 203, 1931).
113. Muncy, *Creating a Female Dominion*, chap. 4.
114. Sheppard-Towner was repealed in 1927 but given a final two years of funding, so that it remained in operation until 1929. On the opposition, see Dorothy E. Johnson, "Organized Women as Lobbyists in the 1920s," *Capitol Studies* 1:1 (1972).
115. Muncy, *Creating a Female Dominion*, p. 148.
116. "The Reminiscences of Martha May Eliot" (1966, 1974), in the Oral History Collection of Columbia University; Grace Abbott, "Minority Report from White House Conference," 1930, in Eliot Mss., Box 18, Folder 250; Covotsos, "Child Welfare."
117. William R. Brock, *Welfare, Democracy, and the New Deal* (Cambridge: Cambridge University Press, 1988), p. 32.
118. *The Promotion of the Welfare and Hygiene of Maternity and Infancy . . . Fiscal Year Ended June 30, 1929* (Washington, D.C.: U.S. Children's Bureau Publication No. 203, 1931); "The Reminiscences of Martha May Eliot," for example, p. 11.
119. This was acknowledged even by an FERA employee, quite critical of the CB; see Josephine Chapin Brown, *Public Relief 1929–1939* (New York: Henry Holt, 1940), p. 52.
120. To cite but a few examples: Katharine Lenroot to Thomas Mimms of the Georgia State Department of Public Welfare, thanking him for telegraphing Senator Walter George to encourage the Senate Appropriations Committee to restore a cut in the Children's Bureau budget, Aug. 24, 1935; Katharine Lenroot to Emma Puschner, Director of National Child Welfare Division of American Legion, asking if the American Legion in Texas could influence Congressman James Buchanan, chairman of the House Appropriations Committee, regarding the Deficient Appropriation expected in January 1936, Sept. 6, 1935; both in Eliot Mss., Box 21, Folder 305.
121. David Ward, *Poverty, Ethnicity, and the American City, 1840–1925: Changing Conceptions of the Slum and the Ghetto* (Cambridge, England: Cambridge University Press, 1989). Ward contrasts the U.S. outcome to the British, where local councils were so important in social provision.
122. For example, Edith Abbott, "Public Welfare and Politics," in NCSW, *Proceedings* 63 (1936), pp. 27–45.
123. Covotsos, "Child Welfare."

124. Abbott, *From Relief to Social Security,* passim.

125. Mrs. Henry Moskowitz, "How Far Have Social Welfare Considerations Entered into State, National, and Local Elections," NCSW, *Proceedings* 50 (1923), pp. 465–69.

126. For example, Robert W. Kelso, "Is There a Dividing Line," NCSW *Proceedings* (1921), pp. 215–18.

127. Brock, *Welfare, Democracy,* pp. 41–43.

128. Gertrude Vaile, "Some Significant Trends Since Cleveland, 1912," NCSW, *Proceedings* (1926), pp. 3–11.

129. Hart, interview with Beyer, in "Watch What We Do," p. 1.

130. Cott, *Grounding of Modern Feminism,* pp. 140, 191, 206, quote p. 205.

131. Sybil Lipschultz, "Social Feminism and Legal Discourse: 1908–1923," *Yale Journal of Law and Feminism* 2:1 (Fall 1989), pp. 131–60; Joan G. Zimmerman, "The Jurisprudence of Equality: The Women's Minimum Wage, the First Equal Rights Amendment, and *Adkins v. Children's Hospital,* 1905–1923," *Journal of American History* 78 (June 1991), pp. 188–225.

132. Linda Gordon, "Putting Children First: Women, Maternalism and Welfare in the 20th Century," forthcoming in *Transforming U.S. History: New Feminist Essays,* Linda Kerber et al., eds. (Chapel Hill: University of North Carolina Press, 1995).

133. Gordon, "Putting Children First."

134. Esther Lucille Brown, *Social Work as a Profession* (1935; reprint, New York, 1942), pp. 142–43.

135. Ruth Hutchinson Crocker, *Social Work and Social Order: The Settlement Movement in Two Industrial Cities, 1889–1930* (Urbana: University of Illinois Press, 1992).

136. In failing to recognize this social work continuum, Donald Brieland in "The Hull-House Tradition and the Contemporary Social Worker: Was Jane Addams Really a Social Worker?" *Social Work* 35:2 (Mar. 1990), pp. 134–38, is mistaken in his denial that Adams was a "social worker."

137. Grace Abbott to Perkins, Feb. 23, 1934, in Abbott Mss., Box 37.

138. Throughout the New Deal the people close to the Children's Bureau were to insist on joint state/federal funding and administration and to oppose direct federal administration resolutely. They were more favorable to county than to city programs, because they feared the neglect of the rural poor. Grace Abbott to Edwin Embree, Oct. 12, 1929, in Abbott Mss., Box 36, Folder 9; Abbott to Perkins, Feb. 23, 1934, in ibid., Box 37; Abbott, "The County Versus the Community As an Administrative Unit" (1929), in *From Relief to Social Security,* pp. 370–78.

139. Grace Abbott memo to Frances Perkins, Feb. 23, 1934, in Eliot Mss., Box 21, Folder 305; Grace Abbott's testimony to House Ways and Means Committee on H.R. 4120, 74th Cong., 1st sess., pp. 493–99;

346 Notes to pages 101–105

Katharine Lenroot's testimony to Senate Finance Committee on S. 1130, 74th Cong., 1st sess., pp. 337–369; "The Reminiscences of Katharine Fredrica Lenroot" (1965), pp. 96–97, in the Oral History Collection of Columbia University; Katharine Lenroot to Frances Perkins, Sept. 21, 1936 and Katharine Lenroot to Grace Abbott, Oct. 22, 1936, in Abbott Mss., Box 61, Folder 6.

140. Abbott, "Public Welfare and Politics," pp. 27–45. Skocpol, *Protecting Soldiers and Mothers.*

141. Grace Abbott's statement to 20th Century Fund Commission on Old Age Security, 1936, in Abbott Mss., Box 72, Folders 1–6.

142. Muncy, *Creating a Female Dominion*, pp. 76 ff.; Ellen Fitzpatrick, *Endless Crusade: Women Social Scientists and Progressive Reform* (New York: Oxford University Press, 1990), p. 212.

143. Grace Abbott, "What About Mothers' Pensions Now?", *Survey* 70:3 (Mar. 19, 1934), pp. 80–81. Alice Kessler-Harris has shown that the same "budget," needs-based approach was being applied to determining women's wages; *A Woman's Wage*, chap. 1 passim, pp. 89 ff.

144. "The Reminiscences of Frank Bane" (1963), p. 14, in the Oral History Collection of Columbia University.

145. "The Reminiscences of Katharine Fredrica Lenroot," p. 26.

146. Sonya Michel and Robyn Rosen, "The Paradox of Maternalism: Elizabeth Lowell Putnam and the American Welfare State," *Gender and History* 4:3 (Autumn 1992), pp. 364–86.

147. Lundberg, *Unto the Least of These*; Abbott, *From Relief to Social Security.*

148. *Mothers' Aid, 1931* (Washington, D.C.: U.S. Children's Bureau Publication No. 220, 1933), pp. 20–21.

149. For example, correspondence between Julia Lathrop and John B. Andrews, secretary of the AALL, 1915–1917, in Children's Bureau Mss., Box 122, Folder 10, 481; correspondence between Martha Eliot and John Kingsbury of Milbank Fund, in Eliot Mss., Box 21; Grace Abbott to Frances Perkins, Feb. 23, 1934, in Abbott Mss., Box 36, Folder 15. The Children's Bureau repeated this gambit twenty-five years later, using World War II as an argument for public medical insurance.

150. Breckinridge to Julia Lathrop, Nov. 1, 1915, in Children's Bureau Mss., Box 151, Folder 13-1-1; Katharine Felton to Jessica Peixotto, Feb. 27, 1918, in ibid., Box 122, Folder 10,481.

151. Quoted in Costin, *Two Sisters for Justice*, p. 205.

152. Blanche Coll, "Public Assistance: Reviving the Original Comprehensive Concept of Social Security," in Gerald D. Nash, Noel H. Pugach, and Richard F. Romasson, eds., *Social Security: the First Half Century* (Albuquerque: University of New Mexico Press, 1988), pp. 230–31.

153. Grace Abbott, "Mothers' Aid and Public Assistance," in *From Relief to Social Security*, pp. 286–89; "The Reminiscences of Katharine Fredrica Lenroot," pp. 50–53; Coll, "Public Assistance," pp. 221–41.

154. Jacob Fisher, *The Response of Social Work to the Depression* (Boston: G. K. Hall, 1980), pp. 148–49.

155. Florence Kelley to Julia Lathrop, Apr. 21, 1923, in Lathrop Mss., NCL Folder.

156. Grace Abbott, n.d., typewritten note in Abbott Mss., Box 25, F-9. See also Grace Abbott to Julia Lathrop, n.d. 1924, in Lathrop Mss., Correspondence Jan.–June 1924 folder.

157. Martin, *Madame Secretary*, pp. 284, 211.

158. Jane Addams, "The Modern City and the Municipal Franchise for Women," 1906, Warren, Ohio, in *History of Women*, microfilm collection (New Haven, Conn.: Research Publications, 1975).

159. For example, Eleanor Roosevelt called a White House Conference on the Emergency Needs of Unemployed Women in 1933; administrators Ellen Woodward of the FERA and Hilda Worthington Smith of WPA set up separate programs for women. Susan Ware, "Women and the New Deal," in Harvard Sitkoff, ed., *Fifty Years Later: The New Deal Reexamined* (Philadelphia: Temple University Press, 1985), pp. 119–20.

160. For a correspondence about what to do with a meeting in which there would be one man among numerous women, see Louise E. Schutz of the Association of Governmental Labor Officials to E.N. Mathews, Director of the Industrial Division for the Children's Bureau, Feb. 6, 1926, and Mathews to Schutz, Mar. 22, 1926, in Children's Bureau Mss., Box 1025, File 6-1-5-4.

161. We will meet some of these women—for example, Eveline Burns and Jane Hoey—in chap. 9.

162. Grace Abbott to S. K. Ratcliffe, Oct. 5, 1926, in Abbott Mss., Box 36, Folder 5, Julia Lathrop to Judge Ben Lindsey, Dec. 7, 1927, and response from Lindsey, Dec. 18, 1927 in Lathrop Mss., Correspondence July–December 1927 Folder.

163. Children's Bureau Mss., Box 830, Folders 13-1-0-2 and 13-1-0-3.

Chapter 5. "Don't Wait for Deliverers": Black Women's Welfare Thought

1. Nineteenth-century black nationalists, such as Alexander Crummell and Martin Delany, sought black progress through patriarchal authority. See Wilson Jeremiah Moses, *Alexander Crummell: A Study of Civilization and Discontent* (New York: Oxford University Press, 1989), pp. 218–20.

2. A black male welfare vision in the early twentieth century also needs study. It seems possible that black men were more drawn to materialist, even Marxist, analyses and labor-based strategies than were women—although here, as among whites, the differences should not be overstated.

3. Schackel's *Social Housekeepers* shows, for example, that Hispanic and Indian women's voluntarism was less formally organized because it was built into family, community, and religion, while black middle-class women's voluntarism, like whites', reached into the public and created formal organizations; pp. 95 ff.

4. African American women's welfare activism has been excluded from most welfare histories. Katz, *In the Shadow of the Poorhouse*; Patterson, *America's Struggle Against Poverty*; Trattner, *From Poor Law to Welfare State*; Berkowitz, *America's Welfare State*; Anthony M. Platt, *E. Franklin Frazier Reconsidered* (New Brunswick: Rutgers University Press, 1991), pp. 69–70. Even women could be guilty of this neglect: One of the subjects of this study, Inabel Burns Lindsay, former dean of the Howard University School of Social Work, herself wrote a dissertation on this topic at the University of Pittsburgh (1952), and published "Some Contributions of Negroes to Welfare Services, 1865–1900," *Journal of Negro Education* 25 (Winter 1956), pp. 15–24. Her publication did not spark others, however. Edyth L. Ross, comp. and ed., *Black Heritage in Social Welfare, 1860–1930* (Metuchen, N.J., Scarecrow Press, 1978), is a valuable collection of documents. Neither publication considers the particular role of women.

5. Charles L. Coon, "Public Taxation and Negro Schools," quoted in W. E. B. Du Bois, ed., *Efforts for Social Betterment among Negro Americans* (Atlanta University Publication No. 14, 1909), p. 29. The tax money spent on black schools was, of course, proportionally and absolutely far less than that spent on white.

6. Quoted in Cynthia Neverdon-Morton, *Afro-American Women of the South and the Advancement of the Race, 1895–1925* (Knoxville, Tenn., University of Tennessee Press, 1989), p. 79.

7. Dorothy C. Salem, *To Better Our World: Black Women in Organized Reform, 1890–1920* (Brooklyn, N.Y.: Carlson, 1990), p. 67.

8. Louie D. Shivery, "The History of the Gate City Free Kindergarten Association," from "The History of Organized Social Work Among

Atlanta Negroes, 1890–1935" (M.A. thesis, Atlanta University, 1936), pp. 4–11, quoted in Ross, *Black Heritage in Social Welfare*, pp. 261–62. For an equally poignant example of struggles to raise money in the North, see Alice Dunbar's (later Alice Dunbar Nelson's) story of a New York City day-nursery project, "A Kindergarten Club," *Southern Workman* 32:8 (Aug. 1903), pp. 386–90.

9. Tera Hunter, "'The Correct Thing': Charlotte Hawkins Brown and the Palmer Institute," *Southern Exposure* 11 (Sept./Oct. 1983), pp. 37–43; Sandra N. Smith and Earle H. West, "Charlotte Hawkins Brown," *Journal of Negro Education* 51:3 (1982), pp. 191–206.

10. Darlene Clark Hine, "'We Specialize in the Wholly Impossible': The Philanthropic Work of Black Women," in Kathleen D. McCarthy, ed. *Lady Bountiful Revisited: Women, Philanthropy, and Power* (New Brunswick, N.J.: Rutgers University Press, 1990), p. 84.

11. Women in all three types of groups were often religious, but in the secular groups they organized across the lines of different denominations and without a religious umbrella. Evelyn Brooks Higginbotham, *Righteous Discontent: The Women's Movement in the Black Baptist Church, 1880–1920* (Cambridge, Mass.: Harvard University Press, 1993), p. 183; Lindsay, "Some Contributions of Negroes to Welfare"; David T. Beito, "Mutual Aid, State Welfare, and Organized Charity: Fraternal Societies and the 'Deserving' and 'Undeserving' Poor, 1890–1930," typescript 1992, author's possession.

12. Female benevolent societies among African Americans date back to the late eighteenth century. Anne Firor Scott, "Most Invisible of All: Black Women's Voluntary Associations," *Journal of Southern History* 56 (Feb. 1990), p. 6; Gerda Lerner, *Black Women in White America: A Documentary History* (New York: Pantheon, 1972), pp. 437–40; "African-American Philanthropy Has a Long, Rich History," *Philanthropy Matters* (Indiana University Center on Philanthropy), Summer 1993, pp. 2–5.

13. Beito, "Mutual Aid, State Welfare."

14. Higginbotham, *Righteous Discontent*, p. 161.

15. Erlene Stetson, "Black Feminism in Indiana, 1893–1933," *Phylon* 44:4 (Dec. 1983), p. 293; Eleanor Flexner, *Century of Struggle: The Woman's Rights Movement in the United States* (Cambridge, Mass.: Harvard University Press, 1959), p. 191. The white women made excuses, asserting that the rebuff occurred because the black women had no national organization. But in the following year some of the very same women spurned Fannie Barrier Williams when she applied for membership in the Chicago Women's Club.

16. Ida B. Wells, *Crusade for Justice: The Autobiography of Ida B. Wells*, ed. Alfreda M. Duster (Chicago: University of Chicago Press, 1970).

17. Lerner, *Black Women*, pp. 448–50.

18. Davis, *Spearheads for Reform*, p. 95.
19. *The Colored People of Chicago: An Investigation Made for the Juvenile Protective Association* by A. P. Drucker, Sophia Boaz, A. L. Harris, and Miriam Schaffner, text by Louise De Koven Bowen, pamphlet, 1913, no page numbers; copy in Lathrop Mss., Folder Correspondence 1913.
20. Only a few of the sixty-eight black women on whom this chapter is based held what might be called governmental positions: Bethune was director of the Division of Negro Affairs at the National Youth Administration under FDR; Alice Cary was a "traveling advisor" to the Labor Department during World War I; Crystal Fauset was a state legislator from Philadelphia and race relations advisor to the WPA during the New Deal; Anna Hedgeman was assistant to the New York City Commissioner of Welfare in 1934 (later she became the first black woman in a New York City mayoral "cabinet"). By contrast, 53 percent of the white women held federal government positions and 58 percent held state positions.
21. Yet it must be emphasized that these white reformers were not more racist, and often less, than the men engaged in similar activity. Eight white women from this sample were among the founding members of the NAACP: Jane Addams, Florence Kelley, Julia Lathrop, Sophonisba Breckinridge, Mary McDowell, Lillian Wald, and Edith and Grace Abbott. Some white women were singled out by black leaders for praise for their work on behalf of African Americans. W. E. B. Du Bois eulogized Florence Kelley on her death in 1932 for her courage and commitment. Segregation and the racism that lay behind it was endemic in the United States, and that these white women did not usually transcend it must be considered historically. Indeed Du Bois and Butler R. Wilson at Kelley's funeral spoke honestly of the limitations of the white reformers in this area and of Kelley's personal transcendence of her initial fears: When at first the NAACP's journal *The Crisis* called for social as well as economic and political equality between the races, Kelley "was aghast" and considered resigning from her honorary position on the board; but she persevered and later, in Du Bois's words, "acknowledged that this was a plain and temperate statement of a perfectly obvious truth." Butler R. Wilson, statement at Kelley's funeral, in Kelley Mss., Folder 2, Schlesinger Library; see also Herbert Aptheker, ed., "Du Bois on Florence Kelley," *Social Work* 11 (Oct. 1966), p. 100, and Louis L. Athey, "Florence Kelley and the Quest for Negro Equality," *Journal of Negro History* 56 (Oct. 1971), pp. 249–61.
22. Higginbotham, *Righteous Discontent*, p. 97; Steven J. Diner, "Chicago Social Workers and Blacks in the Progressive Era," *Social Service*

Review 44 (Dec. 1970), pp. 393–410; Sandra M. Stehno, "Public Responsibility for Dependent Black Children: The Advocacy of Edith Abbott and Sophonisba Breckinridge," *Social Service Review* 62 (Sept. 1988), pp. 485–503; Lerner, *Black Women in White America*, p. 459; Salem, *To Better Our World*, pp. 248–50; Jacquelyn Dowd Hall, *Revolt Against Chivalry: Jessie Daniel Ames and the Women's Campaign Against Lynching* (New York: Columbia University Press, 1979), p. 66. Black women participated in the conflict-ridden 1930 White House Conference on Children. Wilbur, "Negro Cooperation in the White House Conference."

23. Neverdon-Morton, *Afro-American Women of the South*, pp. 191–236; Rosalyn Terborg-Penn, "Discrimination Against Afro-American Women in the Woman's Movement, 1830–1920," in Sharon Harley and Rosalyn Terborg-Penn, eds., *The Afro-American Woman: Struggles and Images* (Port Washington, N.Y.: National University Publications, 1978), pp. 17–27.

24. Tullia Brown Hamilton, "The National Association of Colored Women, 1896–1920" (Ph.D. Dissertation, Emory University, 1978), p. 62.

25. Philip Jackson, "Black Charity in Progressive Era Chicago," *Social Service Review* 52:3 (Sept. 1978), pp. 400–17; Allan H. Spear, *Black Chicago: The Making of a Negro Ghetto, 1890–1920* (Chicago: University of Chicago Press, 1967).

26. Ena Farley, "Caring and Sharing Since World War I: The League of Women for Community Service—A Black Volunteer Organization in Boston," *Umoja: A Scholarly Journal of Black Studies* 1 (Summer 1977), pp. 1–12, reprinted in vol. 5 of Darlene Clark Hine, ed., *Black Women in American History* 16 vols. (Brooklyn, N.Y.: Carlson, 1990).

27. Quoted in Sharon Harley, "Mary Church Terrell: Genteel Militant," in Leon Litwack and August Meier, eds., *Black Leaders of the Nineteenth Century* (Urbana: University of Illinois Press, 1988), pp. 306–21, quotation p. 311.

28. *The Woman's Era* (Nov. 1895). Quoted in Wilson Jeremiah Moses, "Domestic Feminism, Conservatism, Sex Roles, and Black Women's Clubs 1893–1896," *Journal of Social and Behavioral Sciences* 24:4 (Fall 1978), p. 174.

29. Black women's activism has been doubly neglected, not only by white welfare histories but also by male civil rights histories. Thus the NAACP, founded in 1909, is frequently cited as the first national black organization.

30. I am in sympathy with Nancy Cott's critique of use of the concept "social feminism," in Nancy Cott, "What's in a Name? The Limits of 'Social Feminism': or, Expanding the Vocabulary of Women's History,"

Journal of American History, 76 (December 1989), pp. 809–29, but it remains descriptive of a widely understood phenomenon and we have as yet no term to substitute.

31. *The Woman's Era* was the name of a black Boston journal, founded by Josephine St. Pierre Ruffin.

32. Fannie Barrier Williams, "Opportunities and Responsibilities of Colored Women," speech delivered at Memphis, 1896, in James T. Haley, ed., *Afro-American Encyclopaedia* (Nashville: Haley & Florida, 1896), p. 148.

33. To examine their collective experience, I identified black women who were national leaders in welfare reform and used them as a sample. I included women who were national leaders in efforts to build institutions or provide services of social provision—schools, health care projects, settlements, for example. The group I assembled is listed in the appendix. It proved considerably more difficult to find "personal" information about the black than the white women, partly because black women never had the prominence of the white and their lives were therefore less well documented. However, reticence in writing about personal matters was also characteristic of black women, who were understandably circumspect because of the traditional public stigmatizing of black "morals." See Darlene Clark Hine, "Rape and the Inner Lives of Black Women in the Middle West: Preliminary Thoughts on the Culture of Dissemblance," in *Unequal Sisters: A Multicultural Reader in U.S. Women's History*, Ellen Carol DuBois and Vicki L. Ruiz, eds. (New York: Routledge, 1990), pp. 292–97; Deborah Gray White, "'Too Heavy a Load': Ideas of Race, Class, and Gender in Black Women's Associational Life, 1896–1980" (New York: Norton, forthcoming), for example, pp. 81–82.

34. Jacqueline Rouse, biographer of Lugenia Burns Hope of Atlanta, also discussed a "network," listing other black activists who formed with Hope a close southern group by about 1910: Bethune in Florida, Nettie Napier and M. L. Crosthwait of Tennessee, Jennie Moton and Margaret Washington of Alabama, Maggie Lena Walker and Janie Porter Barrett of Virginia, Charlotte Hawkins Brown and Mary Jackson McCrorey of North Carolina, and Lucy Laney and Florence Hunt also in Georgia. (Nannie Burroughs, who had done her first work in Kentucky, was by this time in Washington, D. C.) Rouse also identifies an overlapping group of black southern educators—Hope, Hunt, McCrorey, Washington, Moton, Bethune, with the addition of Marion B. Wilkinson of South Carolina State College; Julia A. Fountain of Morris Brown College in Atlanta; and A. Vera Davage of Clark College in Atlanta; Jacqueline Rouse, *Lugenia Burns Hope: Black Southern Reformer* (Athens: University of Georgia Press, 1989), pp. 5, 55.

35. Paula Giddings, *In Search of Sisterhood: Delta Sigma Theta and the Challenge of the Black Sorority Movement* (New York: Morrow, 1988). Darlene Rebecca Roth in "Matronage: Patterns in Women's Organizations, Atlanta, Georgia, 1890–1940" (Ph.D. dissertation, George Washington University, 1978), found that black club women retained closer ties with their schools than did white club women, p. 183.

36. Hine, "'We Specialize in the Wholly Impossible'," pp. 70–93.

37. Nancy M. Robertson computed this proportion from my list in her "'In the Minds of Privileged White Women': The Image of African-American Women in the YWCA in the Early Twentieth Century" (paper presented at the Berkshire Conference on Women's History, 1993), p. 7 n. 25. Victoria Matthews's Black Rose Home influenced the YWCA, through its leader Grace Dodge, to bring black women onto its staff, which experience groomed many black women leaders. The YWCA remained segregated and these activists fought that segregation. Nevertheless, as Dorothy Height points out forcefully in her interview, "it was unmatched by any other major group drawn from the major white population" in the opportunities it offered to black women; "Interview with Dorothy I. Height," conducted by Polly Cowan (1974–76), p. 173, in Black Women Oral History Project, Schlesinger Library. See also descriptions of YWCA opportunities in "Interview with Frankie V. Adams," conducted by Gay Francine Banks (1977), p. 9, in ibid.; Salem, *To Better Our World*, p. 46.

38. For example, when Fannie Barrier Williams spoke in Memphis in 1896, she had never been in the South before, having been raised in upstate New York and settled in Chicago. Williams, "Opportunities and Responsibilities of Colored Women," pp. 146–61.

39. I could not identify birthplaces for all the women, and those with missing information include some likely to have been southern-born.

40. Mary McLeod Bethune urged Slowe to be "steadfast." Slowe Mss., Box 90-3, Folder 59, Moorland-Spingarn Collection; see also Slowe Mss. Box 90-4, Folder 100, esp. June 9, 1933 to Slowe from a group of six women alumnae and Aug. 23, 1933 to Slowe from Clayda J. Williams in NYC; Slowe Mss., Box 90-2, Folder 28, Mary McLeod Bethune to Slowe, Nov. 23, 1933. Howard was notorious for its discriminatory treatment of women, backward even in relation to other colleges at the time. On Howard see Giddings, *In Search of Sisterhood*, p. 43.

41. White, "'Too Heavy a Load.'"

42. Compared to 34 percent of the whites.

43. Others have reached similar conclusions: see Marilyn Dell Brady, "Kansas Federation of Colored Women's Clubs, 1900–1930," *Kansas History: A Journal of the Central Plains* 9 (Spring 1986), pp. 19–30;

Linda Marie Perkins, "Black Feminism and 'Race Uplift,' 1890–1900" (working paper, Bunting Institute, Radcliffe College, Cambridge, Mass., 1981), p. 4; Salem, *To Better Our World*, p. 67. Hamilton's "The National Association of Colored Women" corroborates this as well as many other of my biographical findings about black women leaders.

44. Twenty percent of the married women were widowed, divorced, or separated. There may have been a trend over time away from women benefiting from their husbands' positions, but my information did not allow me to measure it. Higginbotham reports that early female church leaders were often wives of prominent ministers, while this was less often the case later on; *Righteous Discontent*, p. 62.

45. This proportion was characteristic of the whole U.S. black population in the second half of the period studied. In the black population in general, 7% of all married women born 1840–59 were childless, and 28 percent of those born 1900–19 were childless. Figures from Department of Commerce, Bureau of the Census, *Historical Statistics of the U.S.: Colonial Times to 1970*, part 1 (Washington, D.C.: U.S. Government Printing Office, 1975), p. 53. There were no unmarried mothers.

46. It is true that black women's overall fertility was declining rapidly in this period, falling by one-third between 1880 and 1910; that southern black women had fewer children than southern white women; and that some of this low fertility was attributable to poor health and nutrition. Moreover, the women in this network were virtually all urban, and urban blacks' fertility was only half that of rural blacks. See Jacqueline Jones, *Labor of Love, Labor of Sorrow: Black Women, Work, and the Family from Slavery to the Present* (New York: Basic Books, 1985), pp. 122–23. Supporting my guess that such black women were using birth control, see Jessie M. Rodrique, "The Black Community and the Birth-Control Movement," in Kathy Peiss and Christina Simmons, eds., *Passion and Power: Sexuality in History* (Philadelphia, Temple University Press, 1989), pp. 138–54. (This article offers a convincing criticism of my own earlier work, which overstated black hostility to birth control campaigns because of their genocidal implications.) See also Darlene Clark Hine, "Black Migration to the Urban Midwest: The Gender Dimension, 1915–1945," in Joe William Trotter, ed., *The Great Migration in Historical Perspective: New Dimensions of Race, Class and Gender* (Bloomington: Indiana University Press, 1991). I also learned from Elizabeth Lasch's unpublished paper, "Female Vanguard in Race Relations," p. 4, that Margaret Murray Washington's settlement at Tuskegee offered a course of study on "sex hygiene" that included birth control; this suggests the need for further research on black women's advocacy of birth control.

47. I was able to identify 25 percent (seventeen) with prosperous parents. On the black elite, see Willard B. Gatewood, *Aristocrats of Color: The Black Elite, 1880–1920* (Bloomington: Indiana University Press, 1990).

48. Brady found the same marital patterns in her local study, "Kansas Federation of Colored Women's Clubs." The major figures she studied were married and supported by their husbands.

49. "Interview with Alfreda Duster," conducted by Marcia Greenlee (1978), p. 9, in Black Women Oral History Project; Anna Arnold Hedgeman, *The Trumpet Sounds: A Memoir of Negro Leadership* (New York: Holt, 1964), pp. 3–28.

50. The fact that about 40 percent were born outside the South provides further evidence of their high status, since the evidence suggests that the earlier northward migrants were the more upwardly mobile; Hamilton, "The National Association of Colored Women," p. 41; Paula Giddings, *When and Where I Enter: The Impact of Black Women on Race and Sex in America* (New York: Morrow, 1984), p. 108; Kathleen C. Berkeley, "'Colored Ladies Also Contributed': Black Women's Activities from Benevolence to Social Welfare, 1866–1896," in Walter J. Fraser, Jr., R. Frank Saunders, Jr., and Jon L. Wakelyn, eds., *The Web of Southern Social Relations: Women, Family and Education* (Athens: University of Georgia Press, 1985), pp. 185–86. For a personal description of class distinctions among Afro-Americans, see, for one example, Hedgeman, *The Trumpet Sounds*, pp. 25, 74. On Boston black snobbishness, see Farley, "Caring and Sharing Since World War I," pp. 317–27. On Chicago black clubwomen's elite status, see Jackson, "Black Charity," p. 404.

51. For corroboration on the employment of well-to-do black women, see Roth, "Matronage," pp. 180–81, and Charles Pete T. Banner-Haley, *To Do Good and To Do Well: Middle-Class Blacks and the Depression, Philadelphia, 1929–1941* (New York: Garland, 1993), pp. 61 ff.; on black women's socialization toward employment, see "Interview with Inabel Burns Lindsay," conducted by Marcia Greenlee (1977), pp. 4, 40, in Black Women Oral History Project. For an indicative compilation of biographies of local activists, see Charlotte K. Mock, *Bridges: New Mexican Black Women, 1900–1950* (Albuquerque: New Mexico Commission on the Status of Women, 1985).

52. Higginbotham, *Righteous Discontent*, p. 41.

53. For an early study about this, see E. Wilbur Bock, "Farmer's Daughter Effect: The Case of the Negro Female Professionals," *Phylon* (Spring 1969), pp. 17–26. For an early example: Around 1910 among the graduates of Washington, D.C.'s leading black high school, Dunbar, girls outnumbered boys two-to-one. This does not mean that girls were

treated preferentially; on the contrary. Dunbar's girl graduates mainly went on to D.C.'s free Miner Teacher's College, while boys tended to go to a variety of colleges, often with scholarships. See Melinda Chateauvert, "The Third Step: Anna Julia Cooper and Black Education in the District of Columbia," *Sage: A Scholarly Journal on Black Women* (Student Supplement 1988), pp. 7–13.

54. Charles S. Johnson, *The Negro College Graduate* (Chapel Hill: University of North Carolina Press, 1938), pp. 18–20; Bureau of the Census, *The Social and Economic Status of the Black Population in the United States: An Historical View, 1790–1978* (Washington, D.C.: Current Population Reports, Special Studies Series P-23, No. 80, 1979), p. 93.

55. On black discrimination against darker-skinned women, see, for example, Nannie Burroughs, "Not Color But Character," *The Voice of the Negro: An Illustrated Monthly* (Atlanta) 1 (July 1904), pp. 277–79; "Interview with Duster," p. 52; Paula Giddings, *In Search of Sisterhood*, p. 105; Perkins, "Black Feminism," p. 4; Nancy J. Weiss, *Farewell to the Party of Lincoln: Black Politics in the Age of FDR* (Princeton, N.J.: Princeton University Press, 1983), p. 139. In "'Colored Ladies Also Contributed'," Berkeley argues against the importance of class differences in the NACW, but I found them substantial. On class development among blacks in this period see August Meier and David Lewis, "History of the Negro Upper Class in Atlanta, Georgia, 1890–1958," *Journal of Negro Education* 28 (Spring 1959), pp. 128–39.

56. Giddings, *When and Where I Enter*, pp. 178–79 on Charlotte Hawkins Brown; Perkins, "Black Feminism," p. 4; Green, *The Secret City*; White, "'Too Heavy a Load,'" pp. 93 ff.; Burroughs, "Not Color But Character."

57. In these comments on the class attitudes of black women welfare reformers I am mainly indebted to the interpretations of Deborah Gray White, "'Too Heavy a Load.'"

58. "Interview with Duster," p. 37; "Interview with Lindsay," p. 49.

59. Banner-Haley, *To Do Good and To Do Well*, p. 48; Paula Giddings, *In Search of Sisterhood*.

60. Hedgeman, *The Trumpet Sounds*, pp. 1–28.

61. Chateauvert, "The Third Step"; "Interview with Height," p. 40; "Interview with Caroline Ware," conducted by Susan Ware, p. 94, in Women in Federal Government Project.

62. This narrow definition reflects a historical usage specific to the United States rather than a logical distinction; in some countries, schools are considered part of the welfare state, for example.

63. Hamilton also found this predominance of focus on education in "The National Association of Colored Women," pp. 45–46. Similarly Roth found that even among Atlanta's most elite organization of black

women, the Chautauqua Circle, all had been employed as teachers; in "Matronage," p. 181. Carole O. Perkins draws the same conclusion in "The Pragmatic Idealism of Mary McLeod Bethune," *Sage* 5 (Fall 1988), pp. 30–36.

64. In his 1907 report on economic cooperation among African Americans, for example, Du Bois counted 151 church-connected and another 161 nonsectarian private Negro schools. W. E. B. Du Bois, ed., *Economic Cooperation among Negro Americans* (Atlanta University Publication No. 12, 1907), pp. 80–88. Although he did not discuss the labor of founding and maintaining these institutions, we can guess that women contributed disproportionately.

65. Mary Terrell, "What the National Association Has Meant to Colored Women," Terrell Mss., Box 102-3, Folder 127, n.d. but approx. 1926; Brady, "Kansas Federation of Colored Women's Clubs," pp. 19–30; Farley, "Caring and Sharing Since World War I," p. 326.

66. Sarah Collins Fernandis, "Neighborhood Interpretations of a Social Settlement," *Southern Workman* 35:1 (Jan. 1906), p. 48.

67. Du Bois, *Efforts for Social Betterment*, pp 65–77; Russell H. Davis, *Black Americans in Cleveland: From George Peake to Carl B. Stokes, 1796–1969* (Washington, D.C.: Associated Publishers, 1972), p. 192; Iris Carlton-LaNey, "Old Folks' Homes for Blacks During the Progressive Era," *Journal of Sociology and Social Welfare* 16:3 (Sept. 1990), pp. 43–60. There were one hundred black institutions for the elderly and orphans in Chicago by 1913. Jackson, "Black Charity," pp. 403–4.

68. Darlene Clark Hine, *Black Women in White: Racial Conflict and Cooperation in the Nursing Profession, 1890–1950* (Bloomington: University of Indiana Press, 1989), p. xvii; Edward H. Beardsley, *A History of Neglect: Health Care for Blacks and Mill Workers in the Twentieth-Century South* (Knoxville: University of Tennessee Press, 1987), p. 101; Salem, *To Better Our World*, p. 74; Du Bois, *Economic Cooperation*, pp. 92–103; Du Bois, *Efforts for Social Betterment*, pp. 17–22; Scott, "Most Invisible of All," p. 6; Claude F. Jacobs, "Benevolent Societies of New Orleans Blacks During the Late Nineteenth and Early Twentieth Centuries," *Louisiana History* 29 (Winter 1988), pp. 21–33; Berkeley, "'Colored Ladies Also Contributed,'" pp. 181–203; Jackson, "Black Charity," p. 406; Susan Lynn Smith, "'Sick and Tired of Being Sick and Tired:' Black Women and the National Negro Health Movement, 1915–1950" (Ph.D. dissertation, University of Wisconsin, 1991); Susan Lynn Smith, "Black Activism in Health Care, 1890–1950" (paper presented at the Black Health Conference, University of Wisconsin, Madison, April 1990); Schackel, *Social Housekeepers*.

69. Earline Rae Ferguson, "The Woman's Improvement Club of Indianapolis:

Black Women Pioneers in Tuberculosis Work, 1903–1938," *Indiana Magazine of History* 84 (Sept. 1988), pp. 237–61; Darlene Clark Hine, *When the Truth Is Told: A History of Black Women's Culture and Community in Indiana, 1875–1950* (Indianapolis: National Council of Negro Women, Indianapolis Section, 1981). The Atlanta Neighborhood Union also worked against TB; see Cynthia Neverdon-Morton, "Self-Help Programs as Educative Activities of Black Women in the South, 1895–1925: Focus on Four Key Areas," *Journal of Negro Education* 51 (Summer 1982), pp. 207–21; and Walter R. Chivers, "Neighborhood Union: An Effort of Community Organization," *Opportunity* (June 1925), pp. 178–79.

70. Beardsley, *A History of Neglect*, pp. 104–5.
71. Barbara A. Woods, "Modjeska Simkins and the South Carolina Conference of the NAACP, 1939–1957," in Vicki L. Crawford, Jacqueline Anne Rouse, and Barbara Woods, eds., *Women in the Civil Rights Movement: Trailblazers and Torchbearers, 1941–1965* vol. 16 in Darlene Clark Hine, ed., *Black Women in United States History* (Brooklyn, N.Y.: Carlson Publishing, 1990), pp. 99–120. Simkins's work is also briefly summarized in Beardsley, *A History of Neglect*, pp. 108–12.
72. Smith, "'Sick and Tired,'" chap. 6; quotation from a report by Dr. Dorothy Ferebee, director of the AKA project, quoted in Smith, "'Sick and Tired,'" p. 323. The AKA project was inspired by Arenia Mallory, one of the welfare leaders discussed in this chapter.
73. For a similar perspective, see Eileen Boris, "The Power of Motherhood: Black and White Activist Women Redefine the 'Political,'" in Koven and Michel, *Mothers of a New World*, pp. 213–245.
74. Quoted in Hamilton, "The National Association of Colored Women," p. 99.
75. Frances R. Bartholomew, "A Northern Social Settlement for Negroes," *Southern Workman* 32:2 (Feb. 1903), p. 101.
76. Williams, "Opportunities and Responsibilities," p. 150; H. F. Kletzing and W. H. Crogman, *Progress of a Race, or, the Remarkable Advancement of the Afro-American . . .* (Atlanta: J. L. Nichols & Co., 1897), statements by Lucy Laney, p. 214; Fannie Barrier Williams, p. 204; Frances E. W. Harper, pp. 215–16.
77. Mary Terrell, "What the National Association Has Meant to Colored Women."
78. Jane Edna Hunter, *A Nickel and a Prayer* (Cleveland: n.p., 1940), p. 50, for example.
79. *The Story of the Illinois Federation of Colored Women's Clubs* (pamphlet, n.d. but probably 1922), p. 3; Terrell quoted in Boris, "The Power of Motherhood," p. 221.

80. Quoted in Boris, "The Power of Motherhood," p. 221.
81. Alice T. Miller, "The Woman's Era Club," NACW Mss., quoted in Hamilton, "The National Association of Colored Women," p. 99.
82. Williams, "Opportunities and Responsibilities," p. 155. On criticism of ministers see also White, "'Too Heavy a Load,'" pp. 62–63.
83. *The Story of the Illinois Federation*, p. 4.
84. White, "'Too Heavy a Load,'" pp. 18 ff.
85. Smith and West, "Charlotte Hawkins Brown," p. 199.
86. Anna Julia Cooper, *A Voice from the South* (1892; reprint, New York: Negro University Press, 1969), p. 31
87. Joe William Trotter, Jr., "Blacks in the Urban North: The 'Underclass Question' in Historical Perspective," in Michael B. Katz, ed., *The "Underclass" Debate: Views from History* (Princeton, N.J.: Princeton University Press, 1993), p. 56.
88. Beito, "Mutual Aid, State Welfare."
89. Carlton-LaNey, "Old Folks' Homes," for example.
90. Quoted in Lerner, *Black Women in White America*, p. 576, from Fannie Barrier Williams, "Club Movement Among Colored Women of America," probably 1900.
91. Much has been written about the arrogance and condescension shown by these privileged "social workers" toward their immigrant "clients." Little has been studied about the impact of the immigrant population on the reformers' own ideas.
92. Gordon, "What Does Welfare Regulate?" *Social Research* 55 (Winter 1988), pp. 609–30; Barbara Nelson, "The Origins of the Two-Channel Welfare State: Workmen's Compensation and Mothers' Aid," in Gordon, ed., *Women, the State, and Welfare*, pp. 123–57.
93. Brady, "Kansas Federation of Colored Women's Clubs;" Inabel Burns Lindsay, "Some Contributions of Negroes to Welfare Services, 1865–1900," *Journal of Negro Education* 25 (Winter 1956), pp. 15–24; Green, *The Secret City*, pp. 144–46; Cynthia Neverdon-Morton, *Afro-American Women of the South* and "Self-Help Programs as Educative Activities of Black Women in the South, 1895–1925: Focus on Four Key Areas," *Journal of Negro Education* 51 (Summer 1982), pp. 207–21.
94. Mary Church Terrell, "Club Work Among Women," *The New York Age*, Jan. 4, 1900, p. 1, from Terrell Mss., Box 102-4, Folder 132. Although this speech was given in 1900, another given in 1928 uses virtually the same rhetoric: "Progress and Problems of Colored Women," in *Boston Evening Transcript*, Dec. 15, 1928, Terrell Mss., Box 102-4, Folder 132.
95. White, "'Too Heavy a Load,'" p. 58.
96. Williams, "Opportunities and Responsibilities," p. 150.

97. For just a few examples: Elsie Johnson McDougald [her name is misspelled in this book as Elise], "The Task of Negro Womanhood," in Alain Locke, ed., *The New Negro: An Interpretation* (New York: Albert & Charles Boni, 1925), pp. 369–84; Mary Church Terrell, "Up-To-Date" (a column she wrote regularly for several newspapers), *Norfolk Journal and Guide*, Nov. 3, 1927, in Terrell Mss., Box 102-2, Folder W; Williams, "Opportunities and Responsibilities"; Lucy Slowe in many speeches, Slowe Mss., Box 90-6. See Perkins, "Black Feminism."

98. Du Bois, *The Negro American Family* (Atlanta University Publication No. 13, 1908; reprints, New York: Arno Press, 1968), p. 41.

99. For example, Jackson, "Black Charity"; Moses, "Domestic Feminism, Conservatism."

100. Paula Giddings, "Highlights of the History of Black Women, 1910–1980," *The Crisis* 87 (Dec. 1980), p. 540.

101. Deborah Gray White, "Fettered Sisterhood: Class and Classism in Early Twentieth Century Black Women's History" (paper presented at the American Studies Association Conference, 1989); Hine, "Rape and the Inner Lives of Black Women." White reformers' rhetoric about protecting women named prostitution, not rape, as the problem. See Ellen DuBois and Linda Gordon, "Seeking Ecstasy on the Battlefield: Nineteenth-Century Feminist Views of Sexuality," *Feminist Studies* 9 (Spring 1983), pp. 7–25; Lillian Wald, "The Immigrant Young Girl," NCCC, *Proceedings* (1909), pp. 261–65.

102. For an example of such a folkloric repetition, *The Story of the Illinois Federation* begins its history thus: "In 1895 an obscure man in an obscure Missouri town sent a letter broad-cast over this country and England, reflecting upon the character and morals of our Women. So utterly false were the vile statements, that the women were aroused as never before." p. 1.

103. Smith, "'Sick and Tired,'" pp. 51 ff.

104. McDougald, "The Task of Negro Womanhood," pp. 379–82.

105. White, "'Too Heavy a Load,'" pp. 41 ff.

106. Lucy Laney, "Address," Women's Meeting, 2nd Annual Atlanta University Conference, *Proceedings* (Atlanta: Atlanta University Press, 1898), p. 56. Historian Darlene Clark Hine suggests that efforts to build recreational programs for boys also reflected women's strategies for protecting girls from assault.

107. Mary Terrell, "Club Work of Colored Women," *Southern Workman* 30 (1901), p. 438; Mary Terrell, "What the National Association Has Meant to Colored Women."

108. Wells, *Crusade for Justice*, pp. 42–45; Burroughs, "Not Color But

Character," p. 277; Burroughs and Williams quoted in Hamilton, "The National Association of Colored Women," pp. 108–9.

109. Jackson, "Black Charity," p. 408. The Kansas Federation of Colored Women's Clubs supported a Florence Crittenton Home for Colored Girls in Topeka because no other Crittentons would accept Blacks. Brady, "Kansas Federation of Colored Women's Clubs," pp. 19–30.

110. Phyllis Wheatley Women's Club, n.d., apparently 1906–8, quoted in Jackson, "Black Charity," p. 408. In Los Angeles the Sojourner Truth Industrial Club (the name expresses its consciousness of new urban problems) built a home for orphans and unwed mothers, training them for domestic service but also in "intellectual and moral culture." Lawrence B. de Graaf, "Race, Sex, and Region: Black Women in the American West, 1850–1920," *Pacific Historical Review* 49:2 (May 1980), pp. 285–313.

111. Lynda F. Dickson, "Toward a Broader Angle of Vision in Uncovering Women's History: Black Women's Clubs Revisited," *Frontiers* 9:2 (1987), p. 64.

112. Hunter, *A Nickel and a Prayer*, p. 128.

113. Ibid.; Adrienne Lash Jones, *Jane Edna Hunter: A Case Study of Black Leadership, 1910–1950* (Brooklyn, N.Y.: Carlson Publishing, 1990); Marilyn Dell Brady, "Organizing Afro-American Girls' Clubs in Kansas in the 1920s," *Frontiers* 9:2 (1987), pp. 69–73; Green, *The Secret City*, pp. 144–46; Salem, *To Better Our World*, pp. 44–46; Scott, "Most Invisible of All," p. 15; Monroe N. Work, "Problems of Negro Urban Welfare," *Southern Workman* (Jan. 1924), reprinted in Ross, *Black Heritage in Social Welfare*, pp. 383–84; *Bulletin of National League on Urban Conditions Among Negroes* (Report 1912–13), Foreword, reprinted in ibid., p. 241; Guichard Parris and Lester Brooks, *Blacks in the City: A History of the National Urban League* (Boston: Little, Brown, 1971), chap. 1; Hine, "'We Specialize in the Wholly Impossible,'" p. 73; Lucy Slowe, "Some Problems of Colored Women and Girls in the Urban Process," handwritten draft ms., Box 90-6, Folder 143, Slowe Mss., Moorland-Spingarn Collection; Brady, "Kansas Federation of Colored Women's Clubs," pp. 19–30.

114. Hunter, *A Nickel and a Prayer*, pp. 67–68, 90–91.

115. Evelyn Brooks, "Religion, Politics, and Gender: The Leadership of Nannie Helen Burroughs," *Journal of Religious Thought* 44 (Winter/Spring 1988), pp. 7–22, reprinted in Hine, *Black Women in United States History*, vol. 5, pp. 153–22; Cheryl Townsend Gilkes, "Building in Many Places: Multiple Commitments and Ideologies in Black Women's Community Work," in Ann Bookman and Sandra Morgen, eds., *Women and the Politics of Empowerment* (Philadelphia: Temple University Press, 1988), pp. 53–76.

116. Mrs. N. F. Mossell, *The Work of the Afro-American Woman* (1894; reprint, Freeport, N.Y.: 1971), p. 32.

117. Quoted in Jackson, "Black Charity," p. 410.

118. Ida Wells-Barnett is of course the woman most associated with this challenge, but she was not included in this sample because I had to define her as primarily a civil rights rather than a welfare activist. On Cooper see Sharon Harley, "Anna J. Cooper: A Voice for Black Women," in Harley and Terborg-Penn, eds., *The Afro-American Woman*, pp. 87–96; Louise Daniel Hutchinson, *Anna J. Cooper: A Voice from the South* (Washington, D.C.: Smithsonian Institution Press, 1981). On Terrell see Dorothy Sterling, *Black Foremothers* (New York: Feminist Press, 1979); Elliott Rudwick, *W. E. B. Du Bois: Voice of the Black Protest Movement* (1960; reprint, Urbana, 1982,), pp. 129–30. On struggle in the NACW, see Hamilton, "The National Association of Colored Women," p. 62.

119. Higginbotham, *Righteous Discontent*, pp. 213 ff.; Lucy D. Slowe, "Higher Education of Negro Women," *Journal of Negro Education* 2:3 (July 1933), pp. 352–58.

120. Evelyn Brooks Barnett, "Nannie Burroughs and the Education of Black Women," in Harley and Terborg-Penn, *The Afro-American Woman: Struggles and Images*, pp. 97–108; Evelyn Brooks, "Religion, Politics, and Gender: The Leadership of Nannie Helen Burroughs," *Journal of Religious Thought* 44 (Winter/Spring 1988), p. 12, reprinted in Hine, *Black Women in American History*, vol. 5.

121. Burroughs, speech before two thousand at Bethel AME Church in Baltimore, reported in clipping, n.d.; "Baptists May Oust Nannie H. Burroughs," *Chicago Defender*, Sept. 9, 1939; "Nannie Burroughs Refuses to Speak on National Christian Mission," *Pittsburgh Courier*, Feb. 1, 1941, in Burroughs Vertical File, Moorland-Spingarn Collection.

122. Burroughs in *Louisiana Weekly*, Dec. 23, 1943, quoted in Lerner, *Black Women*, p 552. The best discussion of Burroughs is in Brooks, "Religion, Politics, and Gender."

123. Nannie H. Burroughs, "A New Day Dawns: Domestic Workers Will Get a Break," *Afro-American*, June 11, 1938.

124. "Interview with Lucy Miller Mitchell," conducted by Cheryl Townsend Gilkes (1977), p. 12, in the Black Women Oral History Project, Schlesinger Library.

125. Williams, "Opportunities and Responsibilities," p. 157.

126. Lerner, *Black Women*, pp. 477–97; Robertson, "'In the Minds of Privileged White Women.'" Robertson has found a "colored" YWCA branch as early as 1889; personal communication, June 22, 1993.

127. Story told in Lerner, *Black Women*, pp. 375–76. On the complexity of Brown's attitudes, see Hunter, "'The Correct Thing,'" and Smith and West, "Charlotte Hawkins Brown."

128. Cooper to A. G. Comings, Oct. 1, 1928, Cooper Mss., Box 32-1, Folder 5, Moorland-Spingarn Collection. Cooper was another one of those figures who tirelessly challenged racism even in its apparently "small" or accidental varieties. For example, she wrote to the *Atlantic Monthly* complaining about an article mentioning a poor Negro with lice; *Atlantic* editors (no name signed) to Cooper, Jan. 31, 1935, Cooper Mss., Box 23-1, Folder 5.

129. Slowe, "Some Problems of Colored Women and Girls in the Urban Process," handwritten draft ms., n.d. but probably 1930s, Slowe Mss., Box 90-6, Folder 143.

130. "Interview with Ardie Clark Halyard," conducted by Marcia Greenlee (1978), p. 15, in the Black Women Oral History Project, Schlesinger Library.

131. "Interview with Dorothy Boulding Ferebee," conducted by Merze Tate (1979), p. 9, in ibid.

132. "Interview with Lindsay," pp. 4–5.

133. Sharon Harley, "For the Good of Family and Race: Gender, Work, and Domestic Roles in the Black Community, 1880–1930," *Signs* 15 (Winter 1990), pp. 336–49; Elizabeth Higginbotham and Lynn Weber, "Moving Up with Kin and Community: Upward Social Mobility for Black and White Women," *Gender and Society* 6:3 (Sept. 1992), pp. 416–40.

134. Barnett, "Nannie Burroughs," pp. 101–2.

135. Helen A. Cook, "The Work of the Woman's League, Washington, D.C.," in W. E. B. Du Bois, ed., *Some Efforts of American Negroes for Their Own Social Betterment* (Atlanta: Atlanta University Press, 1898), p. 57; Du Bois, *Efforts for Social Betterment*, pp. 119–20, 126–27; Ross, *Black Heritage in Social Welfare*, pp. 233–34; Perkins, "Black Feminism," pp. 7–8; Terrell, untitled speech, n.d. but approx. 1926, in Terrell Mss., Box 102-3, Folder 127; Beverly Washington Jones, *Quest for Equality: The Life and Writings of Mary Eliza Church Terrell, 1863–1954* (Brooklyn, N.Y.: Carlson, 1990), pp. 22–29; *The Story of the Illinois Federation*, p. 3; Stehno, "Public Responsibility for Dependent Black Children"; Rouse, *Lugenia Burns Hope*, p. 28; Davis, *Black Americans in Cleveland*, p. 195; Sharon Harley, "Beyond the Classroom: The Organizational Lives of Black Female Educators in the District of Columbia, 1890–1930," *Journal of Negro Education* 51:3 (1982), pp. 254–65; Erlene Stetson, "Black Feminism in Indiana"; Green, *The Secret City*, pp. 144–46; Boris, "The Power of Motherhood."

136. Mary Church Terrell, *A Colored Woman in a White World* (Washington, D.C., 1940), p. 153.

137. The white reformers in the first decades of the twentieth century were campaigning hard for mothers' pensions and feared that day

child care would be presented as an alternative, forcing mothers out into poor jobs. But they also continued to see mothers' employment as a misfortune. For example, Florence Kelley in 1909 argued that day nurseries should be acceptable only for temporary emergencies, that the social cost of mothers' employment was always too high. "A friend of mine has conceived the monstrous idea of having a night nursery to which women so employed might send their children. And this idea was seriously described in so modern [*sic*] a publication as Charities and the Commons . . . without a word of editorial denunciation." Florence Kelley, "The Family and the Woman's Wage," NCCC, *Proceedings* (1909), pp. 118–21. On race difference in attitudes towards child care, see Crocker, *Social Work and Social Order*.

138. Quoted in Giddings, *When and Where I Enter*, 205.
139. Barnett, "Nannie Burroughs."
140. Elizabeth Ross Haynes, "Two Million Negro Women at Work," *Southern Workman* 51 (Feb. 1922), pp. 64–72, quoted in Lerner, *Black Women*, p. 260.
141. Quoted in Giddings, *When and Where I Enter*, p. 196. See also Glenda Elizabeth Gilmore, "Gender and Jim Crow: Sarah Dudley Pettey's Vision of the New South," *North Carolina Historical Review* 68:3 (July 1991), pp. 261–85. This view, incidentally, was generally supported by Du Bois.
142. My discussion of Walker is indebted to Elsa Barkley Brown, "Womanist Consciousness: Maggie Lena Walker and the Independent Order of Saint Luke," *Signs* 14 (Spring 1989), pp. 610–33. On the significance of black banks and other businesses, see also Du Bois, *Economic Cooperation*, pp. 103–81.
143. Hedgeman, *The Trumpet Sounds*, pp. 47–48; *Who's Who in Colored America*, 1927, p. 209; Kathryn M. Johnson, *What a Spelman Graduate Accomplished: Ezella Mathis Carter: A Biography and an Appeal* (Chicago: Pyramid Publications, 1935).
144. Hine, "'We Specialize in the Wholly Impossible,'" p. 86; Hine, *When the Truth Is Told*, p. 51.
145. A qualification must be repeated here: While a high proportion of the African-American women leaders were legally married, it does not necessarily follow that their daily lives were lived in close partnerships with their husbands or carried a great deal of domestic labor responsibility.
146. Eileen Boris has identified one paradoxical race difference that resulted from this discrimination: White social feminists campaigned hard against home work because it was so difficult to regulate and often resulted in heightened exploitation, unsafe working conditions, and child labor. By contrast some black leaders favored home work. The

white WTUL adopted as a key image of the ills of the industrial system a portrait of a mother running a pedal sewing machine in a tenement while nursing a baby. Boris, "The Power of Motherhood," p. 44. For black women this image did not have the same meanings; for many of them it would have been a privilege to work while tending their own babies instead of someone else's.

147. Mrs. C. A. VerNooy to FDR, Mar. 2, 1933, Children's Bureau Mss., Box 462.
148. White, "'Too Heavy a Load'"; Sadie T. M. Alexander, "Negro Women in Our Economic Life, *Opportunity* 8:7 (July 1930), pp. 201–3.
149. See chap. 7 on New Deal relief programs. In the lobbying strategy Bethune and her allies did not desert the NACW but rather included it. For example, she tried to get a $2 million appropriation for an NACW exhibition; "Mrs. Bethune Asks 2 Million from Senate," *Afro-American,* May 9, 1936.
150. Hallie Q. Brown, M. C. Lawton, and Myrtle Foster Cook to Coolidge, May 6, 1925, and response, in Records of the Secretary of Agriculture, Correspondence, Box 2, 1924–39, Negroes Folder 1925, National Archives. I am indebted to Susan Smith for this reference. See also Evelyn Brooks Higginbotham, "In Politics to Stay: Black Women Leaders and Party Politics in the 1920s," in Louise A. Tilly and Patricia Gurin, eds., *Women, Politics and Change* (New York: Russell Sage Foundation, 1990), pp. 199–220.
151. Ray Lyman Wilbur, "Negro Cooperation in the White House Conference," *Opportunity"* 8:11 (Nov. 1930), pp. 328–29, 344; White, "'Too Heavy a Load,'" pp. 174–77.
152. See chap. 8 for examples.
153. Smith, "'Sick and Tired,'" pp. 325–27.
154. Kevin Gaines, "De-Naturalizing Race and Patriarchy: Black Women and Black Middle-Class 'Uplift' Ideology" (paper presented at the Berkshire Conference on Women's History, 1993).
155. White, "'Too Heavy a Load'"; Gaines, "De-Naturalizing Race and Patriarchy."
156. In the Roosevelt administration, network members under Bethune's tutelage simultaneously protested discrimination against black job applicants and stressed that blacks needed to improve themselves in order to advance. Corinne Robinson of the Federal Public Housing Authority organized a skit entitled "Lazy Daisy," which called black government workers to shed slothful habits. Robinson to Jeanetta Welch Brown, executive secretary of National Council of Negro Women (NCNW), Sept. 22, 1943, enclosing typescript of "Lazy Daisy," NCNW Mss., Series 5, Box 17, Folder 274.

157. "Interview with Mitchell," introduction, pp. ii–v.
158. Perhaps in part because education was so important a part of the black women's program, and because education developed for whites in the United States as a universal public service, blacks' vision of welfare provision followed that model.
159. This orientation was evident despite the southern state governments' relatively smaller size, and it casts some doubt on "state capacity" explanations for reformers' strategies.
160. Nancy Fraser and Linda Gordon, "Civil Citizenship Against Social Citizenship? On the Ideology of Contract-versus-Charity," in *The Quality of Citizenship*, Bart van Steenbergen, ed. (London: Sage, 1994), pp. 90–107; idem, "Contract versus Charity: Why is There No Social Citizenship in the United States?" *Socialist Review* 22:3 (July–Sept. 1992), pp. 45–68.

Chapter 6. Prevention Before Charity: Social Insurance and the Sexual Division of Labor

1. John Graham Brooks, *Fourth Special Report of the Commissioner of Labor, Compulsory Insurance in Germany* (Washington, D.C.: 1893); John Graham Brooks, "Insurance of the Unemployed," *Quarterly Journal of Economics* 10 (Apr. 1896), pp. 341–48; Frank J. Bruno, *Trends in Social Work, 1874–1956* (New York: Columbia University Press, 1948), p. 258.
2. John R. Commons, *Myself: The Autobiography of John R. Commons* (New York: Macmillan, 1934).
3. See chap. 9.
4. This kind of contribution of academic experts to lawmaking became known as the "Wisconsin Idea."
5. Epstein worked hard to get key members of the women's welfare network to endorse his association, and he succeeded with its more Left-associated members but not with the Children's Bureau leaders. American Association for Old Age Security brochure and misc. correspondence in Lathrop Mss., Correspondence Jan.–June 1927 Folder.
6. Lubove, *The Struggle for Social Security*, pp. 128–43, 172–78; Edwin Witte, *The Development of the Social Security Act* (Madison: University of Wisconsin Press, 1963), pp. 82–83; J. Lee Kreader, "America's Prophet for Social Security: A Biography of Isaac Max Rubinow" (Ph.D. dissertation, University of Chicago, 1988), passim; Louis Leotta, "Abraham Epstein and the Movement for Old Age Security," *Labor History* 16 (Summer 1975), pp. 359–77.
7. In fact advocates used different terminology—"compulsory insurance," "workingmen's insurance," "industrial insurance, and "social insurance."

Skocpol, *Protecting Soldiers and Mothers*, p. 171. They also differed about what eventualities should be covered, which sorts of coverage would be undertaken first, and who should contribute and in what amounts.

8. Paul Douglas, draft article "Social Security for Today: The Need for Unemployment Insurance," 1934, in Douglas Mss., Box 335, "Articles Undated" Folder, Chicago Historical Society. Thanks to Sarah Marcus for this reference. Royal Meeker, U.S. Commissioner of Labor Statistics at the time, defined it as "mutual risk bearing from which the elements of competitive costs and private profits are excluded." Royal Meeker, "Social Insurance in the United States," NCSW, *Proceedings* (1917), p. 528.

9. Bruno, *Trends in Social Work*, p. 261.

10. John R. Commons and A. J. Altmeyer, "Special Report XVI. The Health Insurance Movement in the United States" (1919), in Altmeyer Mss., Box 15, vol. 8, p. 1.

11. For example, Charles Richmond Henderson, "The Logic of Social Insurance," *Annals of the American Academy of Political and Social Science* 33 (Mar. 1909), pp. 265–77. There were, to be sure, significant differences among advocates here: Louis Brandeis's arguments focused more on the poor and on social justice, Charles Henderson's and John Commons's less. Louis D. Brandeis, "The Greatest Life Insurance Wrong," *The Independent* 61 (Dec. 20, 1906), pp. 1475–80, in Edna D. Bullock, ed., *Selected Articles on Compulsory Insurance* (Minneapolis: H. W. Wilson Co. [Debaters' Handbook Series], 1912). Henderson also argued the benefits of health insurance to doctors—they would no longer be obliged to treat "dead beats" without payment—in his "Logic of Social Insurance," 1909, in Bullock, *Compulsory Insurance*, p. 16.

12. Bullock, *Compulsory Insurance*.

13. Alan Dawley, *Struggles for Justice: Social Responsibility and the Liberal State* (Cambridge, Mass.: Harvard University Press, 1991), esp. part 2 and chap. 8; Cynthia Hamilton, "Work and Welfare: How Industrialists Shaped Government Social Service During the Progressive Era," *Journal of Sociology and Social Welfare* 16:2 (June 1989), pp. 67–86.

14. For a clear statement of this by a contemporary, see Meeker "Social Insurance in the United States," pp. 528–29; by a historian, see LaFayette G. Harter, Jr., "John R. Commons: Conservative or Liberal," *Western Economic Journal* 1:3 (Summer 1963), pp. 226–32.

15. *Report of the New York State Commission*, p. 15.

16. See chap. 8 for a discussion of this group.

17. Ninety-six percent of the men had a college education and 84 percent had been to graduate school; among women the figures are 86 and 66 percent. Ratios of male:female college degrees throughout this period

are as follows, computed from *Historical Statistics of the United States* (Washington, D.C.: Bureau of the Census, 1975), part 1, p. 386:

Year	Ratio
1890	100:23
1900	100:23
1910	100:28
1920	100:51
1930	100:66
1940	100:70

However, even when women and men had the same quantity of education, the men's was qualitatively different because of the mentoring they received; women in big universities were treated, at best, with benign neglect. The men in this network groomed and mentored each other just as the women did, but their mentors were usually more influential. Quite a few of the younger men, for example, were students of John Commons—Altmeyer, Andrews, Cohen, Leiserson, Raushenbush, Witte.

18. I considered as elite those of substantial wealth and/or high professional position; the exact figures were 69 percent of women and 34 percent of men.

19. Thirteen percent of the men were foreign born, only 8 percent of women.

20. Muncy, *Creating a Female Dominion*, pp. 72–73. Muncy argues that Edith Abbott's main motivation was careerist and that she was forced into reform by the lack of professional opportunity for women. While this is true, it is also true that Abbott united career and social goals beyond separability. Even had her primary motivation been careerist, she was disciplined into a reform orientation by the women's political culture in which she lived.

21. Of the younger cohort, 70 percent were academics. The men born before 1880 were most commonly lawyers, ministers, or economists/statisticians; the younger men were most often administrators or academics. In other words they made a transition characteristic of all educated men from being self-employed to being salaried workers. Wilbur Cohen, recalling this history many years later, thought that social insurance ideas started in "key colleges and universities." "The Reminiscences of Wilbur J. Cohen" (1974), p. 35, in the Oral History Collection of Columbia University.

22. Although not all of these spent most of their working lives as academics, all had been professors and felt confident and comfortable in academic communities, unlike most of the women. I am indebted to Edward D. Berkowitz for pushing me to clarification on this point.

23. By contrast, the minority of women who were academic were usually only marginally so. Of the ten women welfare activists who were academics, five taught social work, one was the president of a "Seven Sisters" women's college, and only four taught traditionally academic subjects.

24. Occupational comparisons between the men and the women are of limited significance, since virtually all men of their class grew up assuming that they would find a career, and virtually all these men had found a way to integrate welfare advocacy and salaried jobs. The women often worked as volunteers, although the proportion that was employed—61 percent—was far beyond the national average, which moved from 18 to 25 percent between 1890 and 1935. Allowing for these gender differences, a significant occupational difference remained.

25. Fitzpatrick, *Endless Crusade*, p. 176, remarks on this in relation to the small group she studied.

26. Isaac Rubinow, *Social Insurance, with Special Reference to American Conditions* (New York: Henry Holt, 1913), p. 20.

27. Arthur Mann, "British Social Thought and American Reformers of the Progressive Era," *Mississippi Valley Historical Review* 42:4 (Mar. 1956), pp. 672–92; Roy Lubove, "Economic Security and Social Conflict in America: The Early Twentieth Century," *Journal of Social History* 1:1 and 4 (1967–68), pp. 61–87 and 325–50.

28. Mary O. Furner, *Advocacy and Objectivity: A Crisis in the Professionalization of American Social Science, 1865–1905* (Lexington: University Press of Kentucky, 1975), p. 49.

29. Brooks, *Compulsory Insurance in Germany* and "Insurance of the Unemployed"; Frank J. Bruno, *Trends in Social Work*, pp. 157 ff.; John R. Commons and A. J. Altmeyer, "Special Report XVI. The Health Insurance Movement in the United States," 1919 typescript, copies in Altmeyer Mss., Box 15, vol. 8, and Cohen Mss., Box 33; Lee K. Frankel and Miles M. Dawson, with the cooperation of Louis I. Dublin, *Workingmen's Insurance in Europe* (New York: Charities Publication Committee, 1910); Isaac Rubinow, "Studies in Workmen's Insurance: Italy, Russia, and Spain," in 24th annual report of the U.S. Commissioner of Labor on Workmen's Insurance and Compensation Systems in Europe, New York, 1911.

30. Brooks, *Compulsory Insurance in Germany*; Frank J. Bruno, *Trends in Social Work*, pp. 157 ff.; Commons and Altmeyer, "The Health Insurance Movement in the United States."

31. Ronald L. Numbers, *Almost Persuaded: American Physicians and Compulsory Health Insurance, 1912–1920* (Baltimore: Johns Hopkins University Press, 1978).

32. Historian Kathryn Sklar has insightfully referred to gender serving as a surrogate for class power in "The Historical Foundations of Women's Power in the Creation of the American Welfare State, 1830–1930," in Koven and Michel, eds., *Mothers of a New World*, pp. 42–93.

33. W. F. Kennedy, "John R. Commons, Conservative Reformer," *Western Economic Journal* 1 (Fall 1962), pp. 29–42.

34. He once defined social insurance as "a well-defined effort of the organized state to come to the assistance of the wage-earner and furnish him something he individually is quite unable to obtain for himself;" Rubinow, *Social Insurance*, p. 11, quoted in J. Lee Kreader, "Isaac Max Rubinow: Pioneering Specialist in Social Insurance," *Social Service Review* 50 (Sept. 1976), pp. 402–25, also in Frank R. Breul and Steven J. Diner, eds., *Compassion and Responsibility: Readings in the History of Social Welfare Policy in the United States* (Chicago: University of Chicago Press, 1980), p. 295. Abraham Epstein and Paul Douglas had similar views; see Daniel Nelson, *Unemployment Insurance: The American Experience, 1915–1935* (Madison: University of Wisconsin Press, 1969), pp. 195–96.

35. See chap. 4.

36. My research assistant, Lisa Brush, calculated that women used individual stories or vignettes twice as often as men.

37. Lathrop to Grace Abbott, June 24, 1923, Abbott Mss., Box 57, Folder 9, quoted by Muncy, *Creating a Female Dominion*, p. 132.

38. "The Reminiscences of Martha May Eliot" (1966), pp. 46–48, in the Oral History Collection of Columbia University.

39. For example, Paul Douglas, "Family Allowance System as a Protector of Children," *Annals of the American Academy of Political and Social Science*, vol. 121 (Sept. 1925), pp. 16–24; Epstein, *Insecurity*; Abraham Epstein, *The Challenge of the Aged*, rev. 2nd ed. (New York: Macy-Masius: Vanguard Press, 1928); Rubinow, *Social Insurance*; Isaac Rubinow, ed., *The Care of the Aged: Proceedings of the Deutsch Foundation Conference* (Chicago: University of Chicago Press, 1931); Rubinow, *Quest for Security*.

40. Epstein, *Insecurity*, p. 168.

41. William Hard, "Pensioners of Peace," in Bullock, ed., *Compulsory Insurance*, pp. 118–41. It is of course possible that "Smith" was the pseudonym for a real person, but if so my point still holds, for Hard was not interested in the actual facts of his life but only in the hypothetical situation he would have been in had there been public insurance.

42. Lubove, "Economic Security and Social Conflict in America," p. 85.

43. Maurice Taylor, *The Social Cost of Industrial Insurance* (New York: Alfred & Knopf, 1933), quoted in "Burial Insurance," unsigned note in *American Labor Legislation Review* 24:1 (Mar. 1934), p. 43; see also

Eveline Burns, "Social Insurance in Evolution," *American Economic Review* 34 (Mar. 1944, supplement), point 2, p. 199.

44. Brandeis, "The Greatest Life Insurance Wrong."

45. Epstein, *Insecurity*, p. 627.

46. Sklar, "The Historical Foundations of Women's Power," p. 75.

47. Ibid. See also Skocpol: "[The AALL] never gave up its original view of the policymaking process as a set of rational discussions among experts, officials, and organizational leaders," *Protecting Soldiers and Mothers*, p. 179.

48. Eveline Burns categorized principles of entitlement somewhat differently in 1956: needs, contributions, previous earnings. Her categories are actually quite compatible with mine, except that she was focusing on the mechanics of how benefits would be computed. Eveline M. Burns, *Social Security and Public Policy* (New York: McGraw-Hill, 1956), chaps. 1–3.

49. Frederick Wines, "Laws of Settlement and the Right to Public Relief," NCCC, *Proceedings* (1898), p. 223.

50. Arthur James Todd, *The Scientific Spirit and Social Work* (New York: Macmillan, 1920), p. 2.

51. Todd, *The Scientific Spirit and Social Work*, pp. 9–14.

52. Florence Kelley, *Some Ethical Gains through Legislation* (New York: Macmillan, 1905), p. 3. Kelley's rights discourse must be understood in the light of her Marxist education, for she used the concept of exploitation a great deal and in general could be said to be postulating a right to freedom from exploitation. See also Joan G. Zimmerman, "The Jurisprudence of Equality: The Women's Minimum Wage, the First Equal Rights Amendment, and *Adkins v. Children's Hospital*, 1905–1923," *Journal of American History* 78 (June 1991), pp. 195–197, 219.

53. Despite, ironically, the socialist affiliations of several prominent social insurance advocates.

54. In the discussion of needs talk, I am indebted to the work of Nancy Fraser and Barbara Joseph.

55. Homer Folks, "The Child and the Family," in NCCC *Proceedings* (1892), p. 419.

56. Henry S. Curtis, "The Playground"; R. R. Reeder, "Study of the Child from the Institutional Standpoint"; Graham Taylor, "Discussion of Playgrounds and Fresh Air Movement," all in NCCC, *Proceedings* (1907), pp. 278–86; 265–73; 294–95, 298; Owen R. Lovejoy, "The National Child Labor Movement," in NCCC, *Proceedings* (1910), pp. 232–35. An interesting example of the move from rights to needs is in Ora Pendleton's "A Decade of Experience in Adoption," *Annals of the American Academy of Political and Social Science* 212 (1940), p. 193,

referring to the conflict between the "right" to confidentiality and the "need" of the adopted for knowledge about their birth parents. Sophonisba Breckinridge and Edith Abbott postulated such needs in their study *The Delinquent Child and the Home* (New York: Russell Sage Foundation, 1912). Another historian of this women's network, Molly Ladd-Taylor, also observed women's infrequent use of rights rhetoric, in her *Mother-Work: Women, Child Welfare and the State, 1890–1930* (Urbana: University of Illinois Press, 1994) chap. 4.

57. A vivid social work example of the construction of a new need can be seen in the conflict about adoption records in the 1930s and 1940s. In traditional adoptions, which were usually informal, there were no secrets; with the establishment of full legal adoption in the last century, creating parental rights formally identical with those of biological parents, records of an adopted child's birth parents were often sealed, as if to annul the original birth, and new birth certificates were created. Then a new psychology created a discourse about adopted persons' "need for knowledge about . . . their own parents," and assertions that frustrating such needs would create maladjustment. These needs were increasingly deemed more important than any parent's rights. Pendleton, "A Decade of Experience in Adoption," p. 193.

58. For example, see Alexander Johnson, "The Mother-state and Her Weaker Children," President's Address, NCCC, *Proceedings* (1897), p. 5.

59. Quoted in Bruno, *Trends in Social Work*, p. 278.

60. Bertha Reynolds, *An Uncharted Journey: Fifty Years of Growth in Social Work* (New York: Citadel Press, 1963), p. 146.

61. Sidney E. Zimbalist, *Historic Themes and Landmarks in Social Welfare Research* (New York: Harper & Row, 1977), chap. 4.

62. Helen Hart, quoted in Bruno, *Trends in Social Work*, p. 272.

63. David O'Brien, *American Catholics and Social Reform* (New York: Oxford University Press, 1968), pp. 126, 132.

64. This formulation was drawn from an NCCC report. Joseph, "The Discovery of Need 1880–1914," p. 270.

65. William H. Simon, "The Invention and Reinvention of Welfare Rights," *Maryland Law Review* 44:1 (1985), pp. 1–37; and "Rights and Redistribution in the Welfare System," *Stanford Law Review* 38 (July 1986), pp. 1430–1516.

66. U.S. Children's Bureau, *White House Conference on Children in a Democracy*, 1940, p. 117.

67. Charlotte Towle, *Common Human Needs: An Interpretation for Staff in Public Assistance Agencies* (Washington, D.C.: Social Security Board, Public Assistance Report No. 8, 1945), pp. vii, 1–2. When this was published, the ascendancy of the social insurance programs within the Social Security Act already threatened to make casework stigmatizing and inferior.

68. For example, Louise Bolard More, *Wage-Earners' Budgets* (New York: Henry Holt, 1907).

69. The social work appropriation of Freud often suppressed not only the discipline of nondirective, listening therapy that the orthodox psychoanalysts used, but also the critique of "adjustment"—that is, conformity—that Freudian thought contains. Agnes Heller discusses this problem in several places, notably in "Can 'True' and 'False' Needs be Posited?" in her *The Power of Shame: A Rational Perspective* (London: Routledge & Kegan Paul, 1985). See also Russell Jacoby, *Social Amnesia: A Critique of Conformist Psychology from Adler to Laing* (Boston: Beacon Press, 1975).

70. Hannah Arendt, *The Human Condition. A Study of the Central Dilemmas Facing Modern Man* (Chicago: University of Chicago, 1958), especially chap. 2, sec. 9, "The Social and the Private."

71. Michael Ignatieff, *The Needs of Strangers* (New York: Viking, 1985), p. 11.

72. Julia Lathrop, "Hull House as a Laboratory of Sociological Investigation," NCCC, *Proceedings* (1894), pp. 313–19; Lillian Wald, "Nurses in 'Settlement' Work," NCCC, *Proceedings* (1895), pp. 264–65.

73. Mary McDowell, "Friendly Visiting," in NCCC, *Proceedings* (1896), p. 254.

74. Jane Addams, *Twenty Years at Hull-House* (1910; reprint, New York: Macmillan, 1961), p. 103.

75. Grace L. Coyle, "Social Workers and Social Action," *Survey* 73:5 (May 1937), pp. 138–39; a few other examples among many include Bertha Reynolds, "Whom Do Social Workers Serve?," *Social Work Today* 2:6 (May 1935), pp. 5–7, 34; "Case Work Notebook," *Social Work Today* 6:5 (Feb. 1939), pp. 21–22.

76. To appreciate properly the progressive content of their family-wage position, it is useful to distinguish their version of the family-wage system—that women should be free to choose between family and public life—and the conservative version, which insisted that all women belonged in the home.

77. Nancy Fraser, "Struggle Over Needs: Outline of a Socialist-Feminist Critical Theory of Late-Capitalist Political Culture," in Gordon, ed., *Women, the State and Welfare*, p. 223, n. 12.

78. This essay, "The Subjective Necessity of Social Settlements," originally from 1892, was reprinted in Addams's *Twenty Years at Hull-House*, esp. p. 69.

79. Carole Pateman, *The Disorder of Women* (Stanford, Calif.: Stanford University Press, 1989).

80. Susan Sterett, "Constitutionalism and Social Spending: Public Pensions, 1860s–1930s" (typescript, 1993).

81. I am here indebted to the work of Lisa Peattie and Martin Rein,

Women's Claims: A Study in Political Economy (New York: Oxford University Press, 1983).

82. Many of them had gone to the best schools, performed brilliantly, and continued their interest in scholarship after graduation. This was an academically ambitious generation: Nearly one-third of women earning college degrees between 1868 and 1898 went on to do graduate work; eight times as many women earned Ph.D.s in the 1890s as in the whole history of the United States before. However, of nine women who earned Ph.D.s in the social sciences during the University of Chicago's first fifteen years, none got a faculty appointment, while two-thirds of the male Ph.D.s did. Fitzpatrick, *Endless Crusade*, pp. 13, 72–75.

83. Sanborn, quoted by William Leach, *True Love and Perfect Union: The Feminist Reform of Sex and Society* (New York: Basic Books, 1980), p. 316; and by Thomas Haskell, *The Emergence of Professional Social Science: The American Social Science Association and the Nineteenth-Century Crisis of Authority* (Urbana: University of Illinois, 1977), p. 137.

84. Jane Addams, *The Spirit of Youth and the City Streets* (New York: Macmillan, 1909), p. 6. On Addams's scientific method, see Donna L. Franklin, "Mary Richmond and Jane Addams: From Moral Certainty to Rational Inquiry in Social Work Practice," *Social Service Review* 60:4 (Dec. 1986), pp. 504–25.

85. Helen Woodbury, "A Political Engineer," in Woodbury Mss., Box 5, Folder 3 (n.d., probably 1918).

86. Towle, *Common Human Needs*, p. 3.

87. Lubove's characterization of this women's tradition as quintessentially voluntarist is misleading on this point. "Economic Security and Social Conflict in America."

88. On patronage, see Muncy, *Creating a Female Dominion*, pp. 49–51.

89. Anthony R. Oberschall, "The Institutionalization of American Sociology," in *The Establishment of Empirical Sociology: Studies in Continuity, Discontinuity and Institutionalization*, Oberschall, ed. (New York: Harper and Row, 1972), p. 207.

90. Abraham Flexner, "Is Social Work a Profession?" NCCC, *Proceedings*, (1915), pp. 576–90; Maurice J. Karpf, *The Scientific Basis of Social Work: A Study in Family Case Work* (New York: Columbia University Press, 1931), p. 353.

91. Nina Toren, *Social Work: The Case of a Semi-Profession* (Beverly Hills, Calif.: Sage, 1972).

92. Furner, *Advocacy and Objectivity*, pp. 305, 310; Lester Ward, "Contemporary Sociology," *American Journal of Sociology* 7 (1901–2), p. 477, quoted in Oberschall, "The Institutionalization of American Sociology," pp. 209–10. The mainstream of social work, however, as represented by Mary Richmond, resisted the academic aspirations of social workers and valued casework experience over social data.

93. The Brookings Institution at that time ran the Brookings Graduate School of Economics and Government.

94. "Interview with Ida Merriam," p. 18 in Women in Federal Government Project. On women's exclusion from academic jobs, see also Rosalind Rosenberg, *Beyond Separate Spheres: Intellectual Roots of Modern Feminism* (New Haven: Yale University Press, 1982), p. 239.

95. Witte to Wilson, Jan. 18, 1935, Witte Mss., Box 33. The same pattern prevailed well into the 1920s. For example, a major University of Chicago study of Chicago employed 128 research assistants, seventy-nine men and 49 women. Of these, fifty men and five women went on to academic jobs, while twenty women and seven men went into social work. T. V. Smith and Leonard D. White, eds., *Chicago: An Experiment in Social Science Research* (Chicago: University of Chicago Press, 1929; reprint ed., Westport, Conn.: Greenwood, 1968), app. II, pp. 258–65.

96. Martin Bulmer, *The Chicago School of Sociology: Institutionalization, Diversity, and the Rise of Sociological Research* (Chicago: University of Chicago Press, 1984), pp. 39, 68; Fitzpatrick, *Endless Crusade*, p. 212; Muncy, *Creating a Female Dominion*, pp. 66 ff.

97. This fact has been consistently suppressed in many histories. For example, Pauline V. Young, *Scientific Social Surveys and Research*, 4th ed. (New York, Prentice-Hall, 1966), p. 44. Women's contribution was also neglected by Leon Fink, "'Intellectuals' versus 'Workers': Academic Requirements and the Creation of Labor History," *American Historical Review* 96:2 (Apr. 1991), p. 406. Ellen Fitzpatrick pointed out in her rejoinder that he neglected women because they weren't in academia; Fitzpatrick, "Rethinking the Intellectual Origins of American Labor History," in ibid., p. 427.

98. Oberschall, "The Institutionalization of American Sociology," pp. 215–16; Zimbalist, *Historic Themes and Landmarks*, chaps. 2–5.

99. Leach, *True Love and Perfect Union*, p. 300.

100. Folbre and Abel, "Women's Work and Women's Households."

101. Wright supported Annie Howes's study of the health of women college graduates in the early 1880s, published *The Working Girls of Boston*, from the 15th Annual Report of the Massachusetts Bureau of Statistics of Labor, 1884 (Boston: Wright and Potter, 1889), and sponsored a national study of working women in 1888. Women's contributions in this field were further marked by Helen Campbell's quantitative monograph on *Women Wage-Earners: Their Past, Their Present, Their Future* (Boston: Roberts Bros., 1893), and Lucy Maynard Salmon's study of domestic servants in 1892 in the *Journal of the American Statistical Association*.

102. On Wright and the whole history of social surveys, see David Ward,

Poverty, Ethnicity, and the American City, 1840–1925: Changing Conceptions of the Slum and the Ghetto (Cambridge, England: Cambridge University Press, 1989), pp. 53 ff., 123–28; Margo Anderson, "The History of Women and the History of Statistics" (paper presented at Berkshire Conference on Women's History, 1990), pp. 24 ff.; Mary O. Furner, "Knowing Capitalism: Public Investigation and the Labor Question in the Long Progressive Era," in Mary O. Furner and Barry Supple, eds., *The State and Economic Knowledge: The American and British Experiences* (Cambridge, England: Cambridge University Press, 1990), pp. 255–56.

103. Residents of Hull-House, *Hull-House Maps and Papers*, p. 51.

104. Not understanding the importance of the graphic and tabular material, Ely wanted to cut them because of their expense; Kelley refused publication under those circumstances and Ely was forced to back down, although grumbling that he did not have to "take" being handed an ultimatum. Mary Jo Deegan, *Jane Addams and the Men of the Chicago School, 1892–1918* (New Brunswick, N.J.: Transaction Books, 1988), pp. 57–58.

105. *Hull-House Maps and Papers* was published in a series edited by pro-labor economist Richard Ely of the University of Wisconsin. He had first discovered Kelley as the translator of Engels and an important New York socialist intellectual before she came to Chicago. Oberschall also sees *Hull-House Maps and Papers* as the originating work of the American social survey, in "Institutionalization of American Sociology," p. 216, as does Michael Gordon, "The Social Survey Movement and Sociology in the U.S.," *Social Problems* 21 (1973), p. 290; and Robert E. Park, "The City as a Social Laboratory," in Smith and White, eds., *Chicago*, p. 4. The Pittsburgh Survey was stimulated by Mrs. Alice B. Montgomery, chief probation officer of Allegheny, Pennsylvania, Juvenile Court; having read a report on social conditions in Washington, D.C., she wrote to Paul Kellogg, asking for a similar study of Pittsburgh; Gordon, "The Social Survey Movement," p. 291. Margaret Byington, Crystal Eastman, Elizabeth Butler, and Florence Lattimore did four of the six parts of the Pittsburgh Survey.

106. Margaret Sage was not only the foremost female philanthropist of her age but also, through her wealth, a member of women's reform networks in New York. She gave millions to women's and black colleges, child welfare, women's health, and charity organization work. Figures in Sheila Slaughter and Edward T. Silva, "Looking Backwards: How Foundations Formulated Ideology in the Progressive Era," in Robert F. Arnove, ed., *Philanthropy and Cultural Imperialism: The Foundations at Home and Abroad* (Boston: G. K. Hall, 1980), p. 59.

107. Shelby M. Harrison, *The Social Survey* (New York: Russell Sage

Foundation, 1931), p. 31. Although he marginalizes women's contributions, Thomas Haskell's interpretation of the development of professional social science is consonant with mine on this point. He identifies professionalism as "a major cultural *reform*, a means of establishing authority so securely that the truth and its proponents might win the deference even of a mass public." Haskell, *The Emergence of Professional Social Science*, p. 65.

108. Allen Eaton and Shelby M. Harrison, *A Bibliography of Social Surveys* (New York: Russell Sage Foundation, 1930).

109. Slaughter and Silva, "Looking Backwards," p. 59.

110. The early (1890–1930) social surveys were not exactly statistics in the modern sense: They did not use probability sampling, and they did little if any analysis of their data. These techniques developed in survey research only in the late 1930s. See Bulmer, *The Chicago School of Sociology*. Nevertheless, the term "statistics" is loosely used and was regularly applied to this early work. I have refrained from calling it statistical unless I am quoting, reserving the appellation "quantitative" for this early work, which was mainly descriptive.

111. Zimbalist, *Historic Themes and Landmarks*, pp. 193–95. For an example of the Children's Bureau's self-consciousness about this role, see Grace Abbott to Frances Perkins, Memo, March 23, 1933, in Abbott Mss., Box 36, Folder 13.

112. Muncy, *Creating a Female Dominion*, p. 91.

113. Steven J. Diner, "Department and Discipline: The Department of Sociology at the University of Chicago, 1892–1920," *Minerva* 13:4 (Winter 1975), pp. 514–53; Albert Hunter "Why Chicago?" *American Behavioral Scientist* 24 (Nov.–Dec. 1980).

114. Rosenberg, *Beyond Separate Spheres*, p. 33. Furner also identifies the importance of Hull-House to early quantitative sociology in "Knowing Capitalism," p. 242.

115. Deegan, *Jane Addams and the Men of the Chicago School*, pp. 34–37; Rosenberg, *Beyond Separate Spheres*, p. 33; Hunter, "Why Chicago?" As early as 1894 a University of Chicago Sociology Department brochure called settlement houses "'social observing stations' where students could 'establish scientific conclusions by use of evidence which actual experiment affords.'" Quoted by Fitzpatrick, *Endless Crusade*, p. 41.

116. Bulmer, *The Chicago School of Sociology*, pp. 39, 68; Hunter, "Why Chicago?"; Diner, "Department and Discipline."

117. Dorothy Ross draws a similar conclusion in *The Origins of American Social Science* (Cambridge, England: Cambridge University Press, 1991), p. 226. For example: "Primarily under the stimulus of W. I. Thomas and Robert Park (1864–1944), sociologists at the University

of Chicago formed in 1923 the Local Community Research Committee . . . which began a series of studies of the changing character of urban life and group relations." Young, *Scientific Social Surveys and Research*, p. 44.

118. The important early role of women in developing quantitative social science represents an important amendation to Rosenberg's study, *Beyond Separate Spheres*, which suggests that quantification was among the factors excluding women from academic scholarship, p. 241. A more recent article gets the situation entirely wrong. Howard Goldstein, in "The Knowledge Base of Social Work Practice: Theory, Wisdom, Analogue, or Art?" *Families in Society: The Journal of Contemporary Human Services* 71:1 (Jan. 1990), pp. 32–43, distinguishes the male "scientific pursuit" strategy in early social work from the female "down-to-earth, humanistic," do-gooders. On the language of hard and soft, consider Michael Gordon's rendition of these early sociologists' "point of view that the survey provided the vehicle for the transformation of sociology from a 'soft' to a 'hard' discipline." Gordon, "The Social Survey Movement," p. 294.

119. Gordon, ibid.

120. In the 1929 *Social Work Yearbook*, for example, there were separate entries on social surveys and social research. The latter entry considered that "how nearly such informal contributions and the numerous and popular reports, surveys, and social studies approach research rather than unsupported opinion depends upon the validity of the methods used." But his sixteen examples of good recent social research included only six by academics, ten by nonacademic reformers. H. L. Lurie, "Social Research," in Fred S. Hall and Mabel B. Ellis, eds., *Social Work Yearbook 1929* (New York: Russell Sage, 1930), pp. 415–20.

121. Steven R. Cohen, "The Pittsburgh Survey and the Social Survey Movement: A Sociological Road Not Taken," in Martin Bulmer, Keven Bales, and Kathryn Kish Sklar, eds., *The Social Survey in Historical Perspective 1880–1940* (Cambridge, England: Cambridge University Press, 1991), p. 247.

122. Anderson, "The History of Women and the History of Statistics," p. 23; Furner, "Knowing Capitalism," pp. 255–56.

123. Furner, ibid.

124. Quoted in Anderson, "The History of Women," p. 28.

125. Eaton and Harrison, *Bibliography of Social Surveys*.

126. Residents of Hull-House, *Hull-House Maps and Papers*, p. 14.

127. Muncy, *Creating a Female Dominion*, pp. 76–77.

128. Jane Addams, *My Friend Julia Lathrop* (New York: Macmillan, 1935), p. 161, quoted in Ladd-Taylor, *Mother-Work*, chap. 4, p. 28.

129. Julia Lathrop, "Institutional Records and Industrial Causes of Dependency," NCCC, *Proceedings* (1910), p. 523.
130. As a biographer of Edith Abbott put it, Abbott believed "her data alone would determine 'whether or not the unskilled man has been the victim of the industrial system evolved during the last century.'" Fitzpatrick, *Endless Crusade*, p. 69.
131. Jane Lewis, "The Place of Social Investigation, Social Theory and Social Work in the Approach to Late Victorian and Edwardian Social Problems: The Case of Beatrice Webb and Helen Bosanquet," in Bulmer, Bales, and Sklar, eds., *The Social Survey in Historical Perspective*, p. 155.
132. At the 1909 White House Conference on Children, for example, there was disagreement about objectivity in which the two sides seemed female and male: Lillian Wald spoke for the unity of research and advocacy; Homer Folks and a male group insisted on the separation of the two. Muncy, *Creating a Female Dominion*, pp. 44–45.
133. Mary Furner, a critical scholar of social science, disagrees, considering the shift apparently beneficial: "When some ASSA leaders gradually shifted their attention from the unfortunate victims of social change to processes affecting society as a whole and then embarked upon empirical studies to discover how society worked, they took the first tentative steps toward professionalization as social scientists." Furner, *Advocacy and Objectivity*, p. 2.
134. Furner has observed the political implications of this development well, but, not surprisingly given when her book was written, neglected its gender dimensions. Ellen Fitzpatrick, in her fine study of four women of this group, sees them as representing a transitional phrase between less and more advanced scholarship and takes the victory of the male-model "nonpartisan" scholarship of the universities after the 1920s as unarguable and inevitable progress; Fitzpatrick, *Endless Crusade*, p. 66 and passim. I would argue a less determinist version of this transition.
135. This was particularly characteristic of William Ogburn at the University of Chicago, President of the American Sociology Society, who appears to have had a particular animus against the older, female, nonacademic reform tradition of social research. See Oberschall, "Institutionalization of American Sociology," pp. 242–43. For another gendered analysis of Ogburn's views on objectivity, see Barbara Laslett, "Unfeeling Knowledge: Emotion and Objectivity in the History of Sociology," *Sociological Forum* 5:3 (1990), pp. 413–33, and "Biography as Historical Sociology: The Case of William Fielding Ogburn," *Theory and Society* (forthcoming); Fink, "'Intellectuals' versus 'Workers,'" p. 406; Harrison, *The Social Survey*, pp. 20–21.

Kathryn Sklar reached the same conclusion in her "The Historical Foundations of Women's Power." On the technocratic nature of contemporary discussions of poverty and welfare, see Michael B. Katz, *The Undeserving Poor: From the War on Poverty to the War on Welfare* (New York: Pantheon, 1989).

136. Kathryn Kish Sklar, "Hull House Maps and Papers: Social Science as Women's Work in the 1890s," in Bulmer, Bales, and Sklar, eds., *The Social Survey in Historical Perspective*, p. 115. We cannot know if the lines would have been differently drawn had women been numerous in university faculties, but we must at least raise the question, as Ellen Fitzpatrick has done in her "Rethinking the Intellectual Origins of American Labor History," p. 427.

137. This view drew immediate replies from Robert MacIver in his 1930 presidential address and from Robert Lynd. Oberschall, "The Institutionalization of American Sociology," pp. 242–43.

138. Bulmer, *Chicago School of Sociology*, p. 68.

139. Breckinridge defined "applied research" as that directed at supplying answers to specific problems or at finding "methods of improving social organization or procedures;" S. P. Breckinridge and L. D. White, "Urban Growth and Problems of Social Control," Smith and White, eds., *Chicago*, pp. 194–219.

140. Epstein, *The Challenge of the Aged*, p. ix. As if acting out this conviction, Epstein dedicated the book to New York Governor Franklin Roosevelt and Lieutenant Governor Herbert Lehman.

141. Mary Richmond, quoted in Roy Lubove, *The Professional Altruist: The Emergence of Social Work as a Career, 1880–1930* (Cambridge, Mass.: Harvard University Press, 1965), pp. 47–48.

142. Kathy E. Ferguson, *The Feminist Case Against Bureaucracy* (Philadelphia: Temple University Press, 1984), argues that the female style is inherently antibureaucratic; this argument is similar to that made by Carol Gilligan, *In a Different Voice: Psychological Theory and Women's Development* (Cambridge, Mass.: Harvard University Press, 1982), that women have different moral approaches.

143. Zimbalist, *Historic Themes and Landmarks*, p. 19.

144. Lilian Brandt, "Statistics of Dependent Families," in NCCC, *Proceedings* (1906), p. 436, quoted in ibid., p. 43.

145. Warner, Queen, and Harper, *American Charities and Social Work*, p. 45.

146. For example, Margaret F. Byington, "Fifty Annual Surveys," *Survey* 23 (1910), pp. 972–77; Zimbalist, *Historic Themes and Landmarks*, p. 45.

147. Grace Abbott, 1935 speech to the Council of Social Agencies, Abbott Mss., Box 25, Folder 11.

148. Gertrude Vaile, "Principles and Methods of Outdoor Relief," NCCC,

Proceedings (1915), pp. 479, 483–84. Vaile later became president of the NCCC and ultimately associate director of the University of Minnesota School of Social Work.

149. Vaile, "Public Relief," pp. 26, 29–30; see also Lilian Brandt, *An Impressionistic View of the Winter of 1930–31 in New York City, Based on Statements from Some 900 Social Workers and Public-Health Nurses* (New York: Welfare Council of New York City, 1932), pp. 23–24, 44–48.

150. Gertrude Vaile, "Family Case Work and Public Assistance Policy," *The Family* 21:8 (Dec. 1940), pp. 247–53.

151. Julia Lathrop to Marie Obenauer, Oct. 5, 1915, Children's Bureau Mss., Box 122, Folder 10,481; Grace Abbott to Homer Folks Oct. 3, 1934, in Abbott Mss., Box 54, Folder 15; draft proposals by Abbott, 1937, in ibid., Box 25, Folder 11; Abbott to Perkins, Feb. 23, 1934, in ibid., Box 37.

152. Abbott, "Mothers' Aid and Public Assistance, 1938," in *From Relief to Social Security*, p. 263.

153. Rubinow, *Quest for Security*, pp. 495–96. In fact some in the social work network had, by the New Deal, also given up trying to distinguish mothers' aid from relief; for example, Bogue in *Survey* 49, (Feb. 15, 1923), pp. 634–36, cited by Ladd-Taylor, *Mother-Work.*

154. Lubove, *The Professional Altruist*; see chapter 4.

155. Katharine Coman, "Social Insurance, Pensions, and Poor Relief," *Survey* 32 (May 9, 1914), pp. 187–88; Rubinow, "Old-Age Pensions and Moral Values: A Reply to Miss Coman," *Survey* 31 (Feb. 28, 1914), pp. 671–72; both quoted in Lubove, "Economic Security and Social Conflict in America," pp. 342–43.

156. In this feeling they were reflecting a sensibility widespread throughout the working class as well. Its presence does not imply that only men felt the dole as humiliating; there is ample evidence that poor women hated the infantilization and loss of privacy that came with casework. The gendering of that rejection was a secondary, not a primary, attribute—though this is often misunderstood; one is reminded of the once-widespread view that slavery was somehow more of an assault on masculine than feminine identity. The more intense male rejection of casework may have come from the inability of these middle- and upper-class male reformers to adopt a parental stance toward the poor, and the ease with which their female cohort adopted a maternal one.

157. In 1930 the leading historical text on social work argued that "helpful" relationships came in four types—"friendly, benevolent, commercial and professional." Warner, Queen, and Harper, *American Charities and Social Work*, p. 560.

158. Stuart Alfred Queen, *Social Work in the Light of History* (Philadelphia: J. B. Lippincott, 1922), p. 88.
159. Warner, Queen, and Harper, *American Charities and Social Work,* chap. 2.
160. This had not been the history of private and fraternal insurance, which did not envisage collecting contributions from the pay envelope but often by agents who visited homes. The decision to pay into a benevolent society was made at home, sometimes jointly by men and women or just by wives, who frequently controlled the family budget. For an interesting discussion of friendly societies and their subversion by state programs in the British context, but unfortunately without a gender analysis, see Stephen Yeo, "Working-class Association, Private Capital, Welfare and the State in the Late Nineteenth and Twentieth Centuries," in Noel Parry, Michael Rustin, and Carole Satyamurti, eds., *Social Work, Welfare and the State* (London: E. Arnold, 1979).
161. This was nowhere more carefully and beautifully argued than by Sophonisba Breckinridge, "The Home Responsibilities of Women Workers and the 'Equal Wage'," *Journal of Political Economy* 31 (1928), pp. 521–43.
162. This point is made by Sterett, "Constitutionalism and Social Spending," p. 39.
163. Rubinow, *The Quest for Security,* chap. 32, pp. 477, 479.
164. Epstein, *Insecurity,* p. 639. A notable exception here was Paul Douglas, influenced by his feminist first wife Dorothy Wolf Douglas. In the 1920s he argued for family allowances that should be paid directly to mothers, both to ensure their wisest use and to provide them with a measure of freedom from the "tyranny" of male economic control; Douglas, "Family Allowance System as a Protector of Children."
165. Nancy Fraser and Linda Gordon, "Civil Citizenship Against Social Citizenship? On the Ideology of Contract-versus-Charity," in *The Quality of Citizenship,* Bart van Steenbergen, ed. (London: Sage, 1994), pp. 90–107.

Chapter 7. The Depression Crisis and Relief Politics

1. Josephine Chapin Brown, *Public Relief 1929–39* (New York: Henry Holt and Co., 1940), p. 64.
2. Studs Terkel, *Hard Times* (New York: Pantheon, 1970), p. 349.
3. Brock, *Welfare, Democracy,* pp. 84–85.
4. Elsa Ponselle, teacher, and Mary Owsley, farmer, quoted in Terkel, *Hard Times,* pp. 63, 448.

5. Paul Webbink, "Unemployment in the U.S.," *Papers and Proceedings of the American Economic Association* 30 (Feb. 1941); Don D. Lescohier, "Working Conditions," pp. 92–96, in John R. Commons, et al., *History of Labor in the United States*, vol. 3 (New York: Macmillan, 1946).

6. Gordon, *Heroes*.

7. Barbara Melosh, *Engendering Culture: Manhood and Womanhood in New Deal Public Art and Theater* (Washington, D.C.: Smithsonian Institution, 1991); see also Wendy Kozol, "Madonna of the Fields: Photography, Gender and the 1930s Farm Relief," *Genders* 2 (Summer 1988), pp. 1–22; Elizabeth Faue, *Community of Suffering and Struggle: Women, Men, and the Labor Movement in Minneapolis, 1915–1945* (Chapel Hill: University of North Carolina Press, 1991), pp. 62, 69–99.

8. *Mothers' Aid, 1931* (Washington, D.C.: U.S. Children's Bureau Publication No. 220, 1933).

9. Social Security Board, *Social Security in America* (Washington, D.C., 1937), pp. 233–49.

10. John Lewis Gillin, *Poverty and Dependency: Their Relief and Prevention*, 3rd ed. (New York: D. Appleton-Century, 1937), pp. 419–20.

11. Brock, *Welfare, Democracy*, pp. 90–102, 106–7, 163–66; Helen Hall, *Unfinished Business in Neighborhood and Nation* (New York: Macmillan, 1971), p. 12.

12. Grace Abbott, memo to Committee on Economic Security, July 1934, in Social Security Mss., Committee on Economic Security, Box 20; *Trends in Different Types of Public and Private Relief in Urban Areas, 1929–35* (Washington, D.C.: U.S. Children's Bureau Publication No. 237, 1937); Lundberg, *Unto the Least of These*; Gillin, *Poverty and Dependency*, p. 420.

13. Katz, *In the Shadow of the Poorhouse*, p. 214; Grace Abbott, "What About Mothers' Pensions Now?" *Survey* 70:3 (Mar. 19, 1934), pp. 80–81; Children's Bureau, "Memorandum on Children's Bureau Appropriation, 1934," prepared for Senator Hale for Senate Appropriations Committee, Feb. 9, 19–33, 1933, in Eliot Mss., Box 21, Folder 305.

14. *Trends in Different Types of Public and Private Relief*, pp. 26, 37 ff.

15. Traverso, "The Politics of Welfare."

16. Edith Abbott, "The Fallacy of Local Relief," *New Republic* Nov. 9, 1932, p. 149. La Follette reintroduced his bill in January 1933, and the social work group again organized hearings, but by this time Franklin Roosevelt was in office and preferred his own plans. (Hopkins's testimony at these hearings prefigured what was to become the framework for the FERA: grants, not loans; a new administrative agency; federal dealings directly and only with the states; and part of the money distributed according to population and part according to need. Brock, *Welfare, Democracy*, pp. 129–69.)

17. Katz, *In the Shadow of the Poorhouse*, p. 215; Dawley, *Struggles for Justice*, pp. 349–50.
18. Costin, *Two Sisters for Social Justice*, p. 212.
19. Grace Abbott, memo to CES, July 1934, in Social Security Mss., Committee on Economic Security, Box 20, n.d.
20. Brock, *Welfare, Democracy*, pp. 163–64.
21. Ibid., pp. 94, 165–66
22. "The Reminiscences of Isidore Sydney Falk (1968), pp. 7–8, in the Oral History Collection of Columbia University; Ladd-Taylor, *Mother-Work*, pp. 305 ff; Clara Beyer, *History of Labor Legislation for Women in Three States*, part 1 (Washington, D.C.: Women's Bureau Bulletin No. 66, 1932), pp. 5–8 and chap. 3; Bremer, *Depression Winters*; Hall, *Unfinished Business*, p. 11; Thomas Kessner, *Fiorello H. La Guardia and the Making of Modern New York* (New York: Penguin, 1989).
23. William E. Leuchtenburg, *Franklin D. Roosevelt and the New Deal* (New York: Harper & Row, 1963), p. 121; Harry L. Hopkins, *Spending to Save: The Complete Story of Relief* (New York: W.W. Norton, 1936), pp. 97–107.
24. Traverso, "The Politics of Welfare."
25. Lundberg, *Unto the Least of These*, p. 176.
26. Social Security Board, *Social Security in America*, pp. 240–41. This estimate is conservative because it is based on figures for female-headed families reported to the FERA; as explained in chap. 1, such figures almost certainly underestimated the numbers of both single mothers and children with single parents.
27. Brock, *Welfare, Democracy*, chap. 5.
28. "The Reminiscences of Loula Friend Dunn" (1965), p.12, in the Oral History Collection, Columbia University.
29. Gene D. L. Jones, "The Chicago Catholic Charities, the Great Depression, and Public Monies," *Illinois Historical Journal* 83 (Spring 1990), pp. 13–30.
30. Leuchtenburg, *Franklin D. Roosevelt*, pp. 120–21.
31. Edith Abbott, "The Crisis in Relief," *The Nation,* Oct. 11, 1933, reprinted in Edith Abbott, *Public Assistance: American Principles and Policies* (Chicago: University of Chicago Press, 1940), pp. 752–58.
32. The proportion ranged from a high of 42 percent in Jackson, Miss., to 8 percent in Detroit. Katherine D. Wood, *Urban Workers on Relief, Part II—The Occupation Characteristics of Workers on Relief in 79 Cities, May 1934* WPA Research Research Monograph 4, 1936), pp. 12, 76–77.
33. Katherine D. Wood, *Female Heads of Rural Relief and Non-Relief Households October 1933* (June 7, 1935, Research Bulletin G-6); and House Committee on Ways and Means, Report on the Social Security Bill, 74th Cong., 1st sess., April 5, 1935.

34. Mrs. Mary O. Kelly Abright for the Workers Council for Col. Raleigh, North Carolina, to Hopkins, Oct. 12, 1937, in WPA Mss., Box 119-2, Folder 36, Moorland-Spingarn Collection.

35. Statement of Frances Perkins, U.S. Senate Committee on Finance, 74th Cong., 1st sess. (Washington, D.C., 1935), *Hearings*, S. 1130, quoted in Mink, *Wages of Motherhood*, chap. 6, p. 10.

36. FERA, *An Analysis of the "Unemployable" Families and Non-Family Persons on Urban Relief Rolls, December 1934* (Feb. 5, 1935, Research Bulletin D-6).

37. Gladys L. Palmer and Katherine D. Wood, *Urban Workers on Relief, Part I—the Occupational Characteristics of Workers on Relief in Urban Areas, May 1934* (WPA Research Monograph 4, 1936), pp. 24–25.

38. P. G. Beck and M. C. Forster, *Six Rural Problem Areas: Relief—Resources—Rehabilitation, An Analysis of the Human and Material Resources in Six Rural Areas with High Relief Rates* (FERA Research Monograph 1, 1935), pp. 59–60; FERA Division of Research, Statistics, and Finance, *Workers and Dependent Age Groups in Rural and Town Relief Cases in October 1934* (Research Bulletin F-6, Apr. 8, 1934), p. 2; FERA Division of Research, Statistics, and Finance, *Some Types of Unemployability in Rural Relief Cases, February 1935* (Research Bulletin H-2, 1936), pp. 13–15; ibid., *The Ownership of Livestock by Rural Relief and Non-relief Families, October 1933* (Research Bulletin G-1, 1935), p. 2, tables 1–2.

39. Cenci, "Day Care as a Form of Indoor Relief," p. 49.

40. Social Security Board, *Social Security in America*, p. 241.

41. Hickok Report, Sept. 30, 1933, in Harry Hopkins papers, quoted in James T. Patterson, *The New Deal and the States: Federalism in Transition* (Princeton, N.J.: Princeton University Press, 1969), p. 64.

42. Brenda Clegg Gray, *Black Female Domestics During the Depression in New York City, 1930–1940* (New York: Garland, 1993), p. 103.

43. Ethel Martin to Hopkins, n.d., prob. early 1935, in WPA Mss., Box 119-2, Folder 36, Moorland-Spingarn Collection.

44. Joan M. Crouse, *The Homeless Transient in the Great Depression: New York State 1929–1941* (Albany: State University of New York Press, 1986), pp. 9, 83–85, 108–17.

45. Ruth Durant, "Home Rule in the WPA," *Survey Midmonthly* 75:9 (Sept. 1939), p. 273.

46. Schackel, *Social Housekeepers*, p. 145.

47. One Gallup poll of 1936 found that 82 percent believed wives with husbands "capable of supporting" them should not work; by 1939, 90 percent of men believed women should not hold jobs after marriage. George R. Gallup, *The Gallup Poll: Public Opinion, 1935–1971* (New York: Random House, 1972), I, p. 39; Susan Ware, *Holding Their*

Own: American Women in the 1930s (Boston: Twayne, 1982), pp. 27–29.

48. Ware, *Holding Their Own*, pp. 39–41; Donald S. Howard, *The WPA and Federal Relief Policy* (New York: Russell Sage Foundation, 1943), pp. 279–85.

49. Jo Ann E. Argersinger, *Toward a New Deal in Baltimore: People and Government in the Great Depression* (Chapel Hill: University of North Carolina, 1988), p. 67.

50. Howard, *The WPA and Federal Relief Policy*, p. 279.

51. Argersinger, *New Deal in Baltimore*, p. 73.

52. Thurgood Marshall for the NAACP to Hopkins, Jan. 11, 1938, in WPA Papers, Box 119-2, Folder 36, Moorland-Spingarn Collection.

53. Schackel, *Social Housekeepers*, p. 151.

54. The best discussion of federal women's agitation in the New Deal is Ware, *Beyond Suffrage*.

55. Ellen Woodward, press statements June 18, 1935, Folder 13, and Oct. 15, 1938, Folder 16, for examples, in Woodward Mss., Schlesinger Library.

56. Landon Storrs, "Civilizing Capitalism: The National Consumers League and the Politics of 'Fair' Labor Standards in the New Deal Era" (Ph.D. Dissertation, University of Wisconsin-Madison, 1994).

57. Proposal in Beyer Mss., Box 3, Folder 45, Schlesinger Library.

58. Mink, *Wages of Motherhood*, chap. 6, p. 6.

59. Grace Abbott, "Mothers' Aid and Public Assistance," in *From Relief to Social Security*, pp. 275–76.

60. Mink, *Wages of Motherhood*, chap. 6, p. 2.

61. For example, in *Crisis* (1934): Robert C. Weaver, "A Wage Differential Based on Race," 41:8 (Aug.), pp. 236–38; Gustav Peck, "The Negro Worker and the NRA," 41:9 (Sept.), pp. 262–63, 279; John P. Davis, "NRA Codifies Wage Slavery," 41:10 (Oct.), pp. 298–99, 304; Charles H. Houston and John P. Davis, "TVA: A Lily-White Reconstruction," 41:10 (Oct.), pp. 290–91, 311. In *Crisis* (1935): George Edmund Haynes, 42:3 (Mar.), pp. 85–86 and editorial, p. 80; Luther C. Wandall, "A Negro in the CCC," 42:8 (Aug.), pp. 244 ff.; John P. Davis, "The Plight of the Negro in the Tennessee Valley," 10 (Oct.), pp. 294 ff.; Abraham Epstein, "The Social Security Act," 11 (Nov.), pp. 333 ff. In *Opportunity*: for example, Cranston Clayton, "The TVA and the Race Problem," 12:4 (Apr. 1934), pp. 111–12; "The Surrender of the FERA," 12:12 (Dec. 1934), p. 360; E. E. Lewis, "Black Cotton Farmers and the AAA," 13:3 (Mar. 1935), pp. 72–74; Lester B. Granger, "That Work-Relief Bill," 13:3 (Mar. 1935), p. 86; Bonita Golda Harrison, "Social Security: What Does It Mean for the Negro," 14:6 (June 1936), pp. 171–73.

62. Lenroot memo to Perkins July 5, 1933 in Children's Bureau Mss., Box 367, 0-2-9.

63. Howard, *The WPA and Federal Relief Policy*, p. 297.

64. The move included a senate bill introduced in 1937 by Senator Hayden from Arizona and twenty-two others. Miscellaneous correspondence on this conflict between Altmeyer, chairman of the Social Security Board, and Jane Hoey, director, Bureau of Public Assistance of the Social Security Board, and others, 1937–1940, all in Social Security Mss., E, Box 273.

65. Harvard Sitkoff, *A New Deal for Blacks: The Emergence of Civil Rights as a National Issue, The Depression Decade* (New York: Oxford University Press, 1978), p. 67.

66. Schackel, *Social Housekeepers*, pp. 149–50, 161.

67. Christopher G. Wye, "The New Deal and the Negro Community: Toward a Broader Reconceptualization," *Journal of American History* 59:3 (Dec. 1972), pp. 625–26.

68. Alfred E. Smith, "The Negro and Relief," typescript report, n.d., some time after 1935, WPA Mss., Box 119-12, Folder 179, Moorland-Spingarn Collection. Weiss, *Farewell to the Party of Lincoln*; Sitkoff, *A New Deal for Blacks*; John B. Kirby, *Black Americans in the Roosevelt Era* (Knoxville: University of Tennessee Press, 1980); Charles S. Brown, "The Rural Negro on Relief," *Opportunity* 15 (1937), pp. 147–48.

69. Durant, "Home Rule in the WPA."

70. Robin D. G. Kelley, *Hammer and Hoe: Alabama Communists During the Great Depression* (Chapel Hill: University of North Carolina Press, 1990), p. 20.

71. Donald Zelman, "Mexican Migrants and Relief in Depression California," *Mexican American History* 5 (1975), pp. 1–23.

72. Kelley, *Hammer and Hoe*, pp. 21, 157.

73. Howard, *The WPA and Federal Relief Policy*, p. 452, 285–96. State and local project administrators were able to avoid reporting on racial categories in hiring, and as a result there are few data available. A few black federal officials worked at collecting what information they could, but with limited results. WPA reports on Negroes, for example, never give comparative black/white figures, so that claims that some sixty-four thousand Negro youths were employed in the Student Work Program of the National Youth Administration, 1930–1941, cannot be expressed as a percentage of the whole or in comparison to whites. One sample study showed that while Negroes constituted 26 percent of the relief load, they got only 15 percent of the jobs. Alfred E. Smith, "A Summary of the Negro in Federal Government Agencies 1930–1941," WPA Mss., Box 119–12, Folder 176, Moorland-Spingarn Collection.

74. Katharine Lenroot to Paul Kellogg, Oct. 28, 1935, and Mary Irene Atkinson to T. Arnold Hill of Urban League, Oct. 24, 1935, in Children's Bureau Mss., Box 476, 0-2-9-1-0.

75. Children's Bureau Papers Mss., Box 476, 0-2-9-1-0; Box 162, 0-2-8-1-1, for examples, various correspondence to and from Lenroot.

76. Katharine Lenroot to Frances Perkins, July 3, 1933, in Children's Bureau Mss., Box 367, 0-2-9.

77. Smith, "The WPA and the American Negro," p. 4.

78. A tiny selection from these many letters, chosen from one folder in WPA Mss., Box 119-1, Folder 1, Moorland-Spingarn Collection.

79. Schackel, *Social Housekeepers*, p. 161.

80. Among the variety of references on this, see Linda Gordon and Sara McLanahan, "Single Parenthood in 1900," *Journal of Family History* 16 (1991), pp. 97–116; Kenneth L. Kusmer, *A Ghetto Takes Shape: Black Cleveland, 1870–1930* (Urbana: University of Illinois Press, 1976), p. 226.

81. Blacks often got relief in proportion more than their numbers, but always less than their share in the nation's poverty.

82. E. N. Bocanegro Lopez, et al., memo, Nov. 20, 1933, in Children's Bureau Mss., Box 476.

83. This was a very large campaign indeed, widely covered in the national press. A collection of clippings about it is in Clara Beyer Mss., Schlesinger Library, Box 9, Folders 120–24; Lela Costin interview with Beyer, quoted in Costin, *Two Sisters for Social Justice*, p. 177.

84. Haven Emerson to Dr. Edwards A. Park, Nov. 21, 1930; Park to Emerson, Dec. 1, 1930; Emerson to Park Dec. 1930; and Park to Martha Eliot, n.d.; Grace Abbott, "Minority Report," all in Eliot Mss., Box 18, Folder 250.

85. "The Reminiscences of Martha May Eliot," pp. 29–30; "The Reminiscences of Katharine Fredrica Lenroot," p. 100.

86. Abbott Mss., Addenda 2, Box 3, 4, quoted in Covotsos, "Child Welfare," p. 159.

87. Grace Abbott to Josephine Goldmark, June 10, 1932, in Eliot Mss., Schlesinger Library, Box 18, Folder 251; Interdepartmental Committee to Coordinate Health and Welfare, Papers of Josephine Roche, chair, in Social Security Mss., B, Box 11, 025; Children's Bureau Mss., Box 613, Folders 13-0 and 13-0-1; "The Children's Bureau and Reorganization," Eliot Mss., Box 18, Folder 253; Abbott memos to Secretary Perkins, Sept. 18, 1933, Jan. 16, 1934, and Feb. 25, 1934, and miscellaneous other correspondence in Eliot Mss. Box 21, Folder 305.

88. These alternatives are discussed in chap. 6.

89. The bill failed mainly because Roosevelt was lukewarm about it,

instructing his Committee on Economic Security to write something more ambitious, which ultimately became the Social Security unemployment system. Nelson, *Unemployment Insurance*, pp. 192–201.

90. Elizabeth Brandeis Raushenbush to Clara Beyer, Mar. 28, 1933, in Beyer Mss., Box 3, Folder 42; Raushenbush to Beyer, Feb. 14, 1934, and Beyer to Raushenbush Feb. 19, 1934, in Beyer Mss., Box 3, Folder 44, Schlesinger Library; Isabel La Follette to Edwin Witte, Oct. 3, 1935, in Witte Mss, Box 33. As a married woman and a midwesterner after 1923, she was a bit remote from the Children's Bureau's crowd, a distance that may have helped her negotiate between different groups. It is also the reason there is so much documentation on this: She kept up a voluminous correspondence.

91. Perkins shared the expectation that the Children's Bureau would direct welfare. "The Reminiscences of Eveline Mabel Burns" (1965), pp. 21–22, in the Oral History Collection of Columbia University; Costin, *Two Sisters for Social Justice*, pp. 213–15.

92. For example, Molly Dewson to Grace Abbott, Jan. 24, 1934 and reply, Feb. 3, 1934, in Abbott Mss, Box 36, Folder 15.

93. Abbott resigned in June 1933 but hesitated in naming a successor until November. Abbott thought Katharine Lenroot a better potential leader but was aware of the problems Lenroot's Republican background might present to the administration; she thought Martha Eliot (a closer personal friend anyway) more than acceptable. She left the decision to Perkins. Lenroot got the job. Unfortunately the delay allowed both Lenroot and Eliot to campaign among outside pressure groups for support, which created a temporary division within Children's Bureau circles. However, Eliot and Lenroot remained good friends throughout, and permanently. Costin, *Two Sisters for Social Justice*, pp. 216–18.

94. Two examples: When Arthur Altmeyer first came to Washington, as chief of the Labor Compliance Division of the NRA, he turned to the Children's Bureau for help. See correspondence in Altmeyer Mss., Box 1, for example, Altmeyer to Lucy Mason, Jan. 3, 1934, and Swett to Altmeyer Sept. 18, 1933 and Jan. 15, 1934. Perkins asked the bureau for a response to plans for a moratorium on home mortgage foreclosures; M. L. Obenauer to Perkins, Mar. 27, 1933, Abbott Mss., Box 36, Folder 13.

95. "Memorandum on Children's Bureau Appropriation, 1934," Eliot Mss., Box 21, Folder 305.

96. Grace Abbott, memo to Frances Perkins, Mar. 23, 1933, Abbott Mss., Box 36, Folder 13.

97. Murray, "The Work Got Done." That Beyer really ran things is corroborated by a statement of staff member Jean Flexner, interviewed by Murray, "The Work Got Done," p. 205.

98. Clara Beyer to Elizabeth Brandeis Raushenbush, Nov. 10, 1931, and to Grace Abbott, Nov. 30, 1931, in Beyer Mss., Box 2, Folder 40; Beyer to Molly Dewson, in ibid., Nov. 22, 1933, Box 3, Folder 42; General Federation of Women's Clubs to Beyer and LaDame, in ibid., Feb. 20, 1934, Box 3, Folder 44.

99. Children's Bureau Mss., Box 478, Folder 0-3-7-1, 1933–36; Box 598, Folder 0-2-3-1, 1930s and 1940s.

100. Abbott to Kellogg, several letters May 1934, Abbott Mss., Box 36, Folder 15.

101. Hopkins, *Spending to Save*, p. 181; "The Reminiscences of Loula Friend Dunn," pp. 11–12, 14–17.

102. Abbott to Perkins, Feb. 26, 1935 and Feb. 3, 1936, for example, in Abbott Mss., Box 68, Folder 7.

103. Perkins to Abbott, 13, 1936, in Abbott Mss., Box 68, Folder 7.

104. Covotsos, "Child Welfare," p. 274.

105. Costin, *Two Sisters for Social Justice*, p. 220.

106. "The Reminiscences of Eveline Mabel Burns," p. 28.

Chapter 8. New Deal Social Movements

1. Reynolds, *Uncharted Journey*, pp. 159–60.

2. From an elite background—her father a minister, her mother the daughter of a railroad owner—she was one of the most influential women in the white social work network, from her first research on child labor in factories and tenements in 1905–6, through her directorship of the Department of Industrial Studies of the Russell Sage Foundation and of the embryonic U.S. Women's Bureau, to her advocacy of Left positions in the New Deal and 1940s and her subpoena by a McCarthy committee in 1953. In 1933 Frances Perkins appointed her adviser to the U.S. Employment Service, but she resigned after one day in objection to what she considered its antilabor policies. In other words, she moved to the Left from a powerful position in mainstream social work. The most interesting question her biography brings to mind is not so much why Van Kleeck became a leftist as why so few others did, considering the high levels of respect the Communist party commanded among middle-class liberals in the 1930s.

3. Mary Van Kleeck, "Our Illusions Regarding Government," NCSW, *Proceedings* 61 (1934), pp. 473–85, also published in *Survey* 70:6 (June 1934), pp. 190–93.

4. Reynolds, *Uncharted Journey*, p. 161.

5. Gertrude Springer, "Rising to a New Challenge," *Survey* 70:6 (June 1934), pp. 179–80.

Notes to page 211   391

6. Welfare historians have paid little attention to it. Katz, in his *In the Shadow of the Poorhouse*, spends two paragraphs on unemployed organizing, p. 223. Bruce S. Jansson, *The Reluctant Welfare State: A History of American Social Welfare Policies* (Belmont, Calif.: Wadsworth Publishing, 1988), sees the poor almost exclusively as victims, for example, pp. 113–22. Trattner, *From Poor Law to Welfare State*, mentions "disorder" and "talk of revolution" in a sentence but does not elaborate on any protests. Patterson, in *America's Struggle Against Poverty 1900–1980*, makes poor people far more visible and substantial than any of the other welfare historians but still presents them almost exclusively as victims, not as social activists; pp. 37–55. Alan Dawley's *Struggles for Justice: Social Responsibility and the Liberal State* (Cambridge, Mass.: Harvard University Press, 1991) is an exception; he credits popular movements for the "second New Deal," pp. 378 ff. By contrast, historical sociologists have recently engaged in a lively debate about the forces that shaped New Deal welfare legislation, in which interpretations emphasizing state or polity factors have been answered by reassertions of the influence of social movements. The most articulate and learned spokesperson for the state-centered (now called "polity-centered") perspective is Theda Skocpol; see her *Protecting Soldiers and Mothers* and Linda Gordon and Theda Skocpol, "Gender, State and Society: A Debate," *Contention* 2:3 (Spring 1993). In response a few sociologists and political scientists have argued for the impact of depression social movements on specific pieces of legislation. Steve Vallocchi, "The Unemployed Workers Movement of the 1930s: A Reexamination of the Piven and Cloward Thesis," *Social Forces* 37:2 (May 1990), pp. 191–205; J. Craig Jenkins and Barbara G. Brents, "Social Protest, Hegemonic Competition, and Social Reform: A Political Struggle Interpretation of the Origins of the American Welfare State," *American Sociological Review* 54 (1989), pp. 891–909; Michael Goldfield, "Worker Insurgency, Radical Organization and New Deal Labor Legislation," *American Political Science Review* 83:4 (Dec. 1989), pp. 1257–82; John B. Williamson and Joseph W. Weiss, "Egalitarian Political Movements, Social Welfare Effort and Convergence Theory: A Cross-National Analysis," *Comparative Social Research* 2 (1979), pp. 289–302.

7. These two levels of influence are not mutually exclusive but more often telescoped, one inside the other. Richard Cloward and Frances Fox Piven, notably, have shown how disruptive activity in the depression interacted with voting behavior, threatening standing electoral coalitions and forcing politicians to shift their programs and priorities to meet anticipated electoral challenges. Welfare-related disruptive activism, they suggested, was important in building Franklin Roosevelt's

durable new Democratic coalition. Frances Fox Piven and Richard A. Cloward, *Why Americans Don't Vote* (New York: Pantheon, 1988), esp. chap. 5.

8. Such sudden and massive shifts have occurred at other times as well. For example, many participants in the women's liberation movement report that they discovered overnight, as it were, an oppression that they had not "noticed" for a lifetime. Within a decade a majority of Americans came to recognize an entirely new word, "sexism," and to know that it was pejorative, whether or not they agreed.

9. Gordon, *Heroes.*

10. This absence is one of the mysteries of twentieth-century America, one not yet satisfactorily explained by historians. Time after time, and in many places, radical male-dominated activism produced feminist upsurges as a kind of byproduct—the French Revolution, abolitionism, the revolutions of 1848, the civil rights movement. This was true of black as well as white women's movements. The rise of a Left in the early twentieth-century United States was accompanied by a peak of women's activism, but not in the 1930s.

11. On the 1930s see Susan Ware, *Holding Their Own*; Paula Giddings, *When and Where I Enter: The Impact of Black Women on Race and Sex in America* (New York: Morrow, 1984); William H. Chafe, *The American Woman: Her Changing Social, Economic, and Political Roles, 1920–1970* (New York: Oxford University Press, 1972); Susan M. Hartmann, *From Margin to Mainstream: American Women and Politics since 1960* (New York: Knopf, 1989), chap. 1.

12. Gwendolyn Mink, *Old Labor and New Immigrants in American Political Development: Union, Party, and State, 1875–1920* (Ithaca: Cornell University Press, 1986).

13. Altmeyer, "Public Assistance Steps Ahead," written for *The American Federationist* 43:11 (Nov. 1936), typescript in Altmeyer Mss., Box 15, Folder 1.

14. Mink, *Old Labor and New Immigrants*, pp. 182 ff., 250–54.

15. Quoted in Kenneth Casebeer, "The Workers' Unemployment Insurance Bill: American Social Wage, Labor Organization, and Legal Ideology," in Christopher J. Tomlins and Andrew J. King, eds., *Labor Law in America: Historical and Critical Essays* (Baltimore: Johns Hopkins University Press, 1992), p. 239.

16. Gosta Esping-Andersen, *The Three Worlds of Welfare Capitalism* (Princeton: Princeton University Press, 1990).

17. Quoted by Casebeer, "The Workers' Unemployment Insurance Bill," pp. 235–36.

18. Edwin E. Witte, "Organized Labor and Social Security," in Milton Derber and Edwin Young, eds., *Labor and the New Deal* (Madison:

University of Wisconsin Press, 1961), pp. 245–46; Skocpol, *Protecting Soldiers and Mothers*, esp. p. 236; Brandeis, *Labor Legislation*, pp. 555–57.

19. John R. Commons and A. J. Altmeyer, "The Health Insurance Movement of the United States," pp. 15–17.

20. Casebeer, "The Workers' Unemployment Insurance Bill," pp. 236–46; Elizabeth Faue, *Community of Suffering and Struggle: Women, Men, and the Labor Movement in Minneapolis* (Chapel Hill: University of North Carolina Press, 1991), pp. 13, 64, 73, 119–20, 133, 136.

21. Arthur J. Altmeyer, *The Formative Years of Social Security* (Madison: University of Wisconsin Press, 1966), pp. 32–33. Unions weighed in more heavily only after the passage of Social Security, when the AFL *and* the CIO campaigned for extension of UI and OAI coverage. Conservative unions retained their opposition to government provision, while other unions—such as the United Mine Workers—joined the Left opposition to the New Deal, demanding far more than the Administration was willing to propose.

22. The only scholar who addressed explicitly the question of social movement influence on Social Security, Daniel Sanders, concluded that labor's influence was minimal. Daniel S. Sanders, *The Impact of Reform Movements on Social Policy Change: The Case of Social Insurance* (Fair Lawn, N. J.: R. E. Burdick, 1973), pp. 131–35. In Europe, by contrast, labor played a more influential role in the development of welfare programs, but primarily through labor or social-democratic parties in electoral politics, which, of course, did not exist in the United States. Arthur Marwick, "The Labour Party and the Welfare in Britain, 1900–1948," *American Historical Review* 73 (1967), pp. 380–403; Kenneth D. Brown, "Conflict in Early British Welfare Policy: The Case of the Unemployed Workmen's Bill of 1905," *Journal of Modern History* 43 (1971), pp. 615–29. Only Ian Gough in *The Political Economy of the Welfare State* (London: Macmillan, 1975) refers to nonelectoral pressure from labor for welfare programs.

23. Rexford Tugwell, *The Democratic Roosevelt* (New York: Doubleday, 1957), p. 336.

24. Robert Bremner, *From the Depths: The Discovery of Poverty in the United States* (New York: New York University Press, 1956), p. 263; Richard Hofstadter, *The Age of Reform: From Bryan to F.D.R.* (New York: Knopf, 1955), p. 308; Jenkins and Brents, "Social Protest," 1989. This does not negate the fact that there was substantial and growing middle-class support for radical alternatives; Casebeer, "The Workers' Unemployment Insurance Bill," p. 248.

25. Altmeyer, "Public Assistance Steps Ahead."

26. James R. Green, *The World of the Worker: Labor in Twentieth-Century America* (New York: Hill & Wang, 1980), p. 146; George E. Barnett,

"American Trade Unionism and Social Insurance," *American Economic Review* 23:1 (Mar. 1933), pp. 1–8; Casebeer, "The Workers' Unemployment Insurance Bill"; Goldfield, "Worker Insurgency."

27. In fact, one scholar argues that competition among Left groups helped expand the movement: Valocchi, "Unemployed Workers Movement."

28. Max R. Naiman quoted in Studs Terkel, *Hard Times* (New York: Pantheon, 1970), p. 468.

29. Green, *The World of the Worker*, p. 138; Roy Rosenzweig, "Organizing the Unemployed: The Early Years of the Great Depression, 1929-1933," in James Green, ed., *Workers' Struggles, Past and Present: A 'Radical America' Reader* (Philadelphia: Temple University Press, 1983), 168–89, esp. p. 169; Annelise Orleck, "'We Are That Mythical Thing Called the Public': Militant Housewives during the Great Depression," *Feminist Studies* 19:1 (Spring 1993), pp. 147–72.

30. Faue, *Community of Suffering*, p. 65.

31. Argersinger, *New Deal in Baltimore*, p. 45.

32. Quoted in Rosenzweig, "Organizing the Unemployed," p. 174.

33. Ibid.

34. Ibid., pp. 169, 182.

35. Casebeer, "The Workers' Unemployment Insurance Bill," pp. 245–46.

36. Jo Ann E. Argersinger, "Assisting the 'Loafers': Transient Relief in Baltimore, 1933–37," *Labor History* 23 (Spring 1982), pp. 226–45; Bruce Nelson, *Workers on the Waterfront: Seamen, Longshoremen, and Unionism in the 1930s* (Urbana: University of Illinois Press, 1990), pp. 96–97.

37. As historian James T. Patterson said, "Activist social workers in the . . . 1930s probably came closer to poor people than did any other middle-class groups." Patterson, *America's Struggle Against Poverty*, p. 37.

38. This narrative based on Reinders, *American Social Workers in the Years of the Locust*; Ehrenreich, *The Altruistic Imagination*; Fisher, *The Response of Social Work to the Depression*.

39. Edith Abbott, "Don't Do It, Mr. Hopkins!" *The Nation*, Jan. 9, 1935.

40. Fisher, *The Response of Social Work to the Depression*, chap. 4 and 6 and pp. 57–62, 145–150.

41. Grace Coyle, "Social Workers and Social Action," *Survey* 73:5 (May 1937), pp. 138–39.

42. Ralph G. Hurlin, "The Number and Distribution of Social Workers in the United States," NCSW, *Proceedings* (1933), pp. 608–18; Fisher, *The Response of Social Work to the Depression*, pp. 234–35; Posner, "Charlotte Towle," pp. 162–63.

43. Wenocur and Reisch, *From Charity to Enterprise*, p. 56.

44. Ibid., p. 129.

45. In 1929 private sources still provided 25 percent of relief funds and the

majority of all nonrelief social services; by 1939 less than 1 percent of relief funds were nongovernmental.

46. Wenocur and Reisch, *From Charity to Enterprise*, pp. 72–73.

47. Dorothy Kahn, president of the NCSW, 1935; Stanley Davies, AASW president, 1934; and Helen Clark, University of Wisconsin Social Work professor, 1932, quoted by Ehrenreich, *Altruistic Imagination*, pp. 108–9.

48. Quoted by Ehrenreich, *Altruistic Imagination*, p. 141, from Leroy A. Ramsdell, "The New Deal in Social Work," *Family* 14 (Oct. 1930), pp. 191–92. On the general movement of the profession to the Left, see, for example, Antoinette Cannon, "Recent Changes in the Philosophy of Social Workers," NCSW, *Proceedings* (1933), pp. 597–607.

49. Frank J. Bruno, "Social-Work Objectives in the New Era," in ibid., p. 9.

50. Ehrenreich, *Altruistic Imagination*, p. 111.

51. Gertrude Springer, "When a Client Has a Car," *Survey* 69 (Mar. 1933), pp. 103–4; G.S., "Are Relief Workers Policemen?" *Survey* 69 (Apr. 1933), pp. 156–57. The column was signed with a pseudonym, "Miss Bailey."

52. "The Case of Sidonia Dawson," *Survey* 71:1 (Jan. 1935), pp. 8–10, and various letters to the editor, *Survey* 71:3 (Mar. 1935), p. 93. See also Reynolds, *Uncharted Journey*, pp. 154–64; "Rank and File: The Fight for Relief Standards," *Social Work Today* 3:3 (Dec. 1935), p. 25; Mary Siegel, "Worker and Client Join Hands," *Social Work Today* 3:4 (Jan. 1936), p. 18.

53. Helen Hall, "The Consequences of Social Action for the Group-Work Agency," NCSW, *Proceedings* 63 (1936), pp. 234–41.

54. As Alan Brinkley put it, "their messages resonated" with the populist legacy. Alan Brinkley, *Voices of Protest: Huey Long, Father Coughlin, and the Great Depression* (New York: Alfred A. Knopf, 1982), p. 163.

55. Abraham Holtzman, historian of the Townsend movement, called this combination the conservatism of American radicalism. Abraham Holtzman, *The Townsend Movement: A Political Study* (New York: Bookman Associates, 1963), esp. pp. 29–30; Upton Sinclair, "Epic Answers," in *The EPIC Plan for California* (Los Angeles: End Poverty League, 1934), for example, pp. 2, 10–11.

56. Brinkley, *Voices of Protest*, p. 164.

57. Richard M. Valelly, *Radicalism in the States: The Minnesota Farmer-Labor Party and the American Political Economy* (Chicago: University of Chicago, 1989), pp. 72–77.

58. Jess Gilbert and Carolyn Howe, "Beyond 'State and Society': Theories of the State and New Deal Agricultural Policies," *American Sociological Review* 56 (Apr. 1991), p. 209.

59. Mary Heaton Vorse, "Rebellion in the Cornbelt: American Farmers Beat Their Plowshares into Swords," *Harper's* 166 (Dec. 1932), reprinted in David A. Shannon, ed., *The Great Depression* (Englewood Cliffs, N.J.: Prentice-Hall, 1960), pp. 123–27.

60. But not only populism; for example, one of them, Richard Bosch of Minnesota, had done graduate work at the University of Wisconsin with John Commons.

61. Valelly, *Radicalism in the States*, chap. 6.

62. Gilbert and Howe, "Beyond 'State and Society,'" p. 210.

63. Van L. Perkins, *Crisis in Agriculture: The Agricultural Adjustment Administration and the New Deal, 1933* (Berkeley: University of California, 1969), pp. 177–79, quoted in Valelly, *Radicalism in the States*, p. 97; Donald R. McCoy, *Angry Voices: Left-of-Center Politics in the New Deal Era* (Lawrence: University of Kansas Press, 1958), chap. 2. Poor farm laborers got little from all this—many sharecroppers and tenants were hurt by the programs taking land out of cultivation.

64. Many plans are in Witte's files, Social Security Mss., Committee on Economic Security, Boxes 44 and 45.

65. In general the Left and the Right made very similar criticisms of these proposals; see, for example, Harry W. Laidler, "The Townsend Plan: A Critical Analysis," *American Socialist Monthly* 5:1 (Mar. 1935), pp. 12–16; David Lasser, *The $60 at 60 Pension Plan: Minimum Security for Our Senior Citizens* (Washington, D.C.: Workers' Alliance of America, n.d.); historian Arthur M. Schlesinger, Jr., referred to Townsend's supporters as "pathetic old people," *The Age of Roosevelt*, vol. 3: *The Politics of Upheaval* (Cambridge, Mass.: Riverside Press, 1960), p. 33; Jackson K. Putnam, in *Old-Age Politics in California from Richardson to Reagan* (Stanford: Stanford University Press, 1970), referred to the California director of the Social Welfare Department as "histrionic and radical," p. 30, and identifies the sources of EPIC as "boredom probably intensified Californians' inclinations toward fantasy," p. 32; David H. Bennett refers to "bizarre panaceas" and "fanatics," *Demagogues in the Depression: American Radicals and the Union Party, 1932–1936* (New Brunswick, N.J.: Rutgers University Press, 1969), p. 3. There was some more careful criticism, such as that of Norman Thomas who in a speech at a Townsend convention in 1936 insisted that "capitalism can pay a much bigger old age pension than the President's 'insecurity' Bill proposes," but opposed Townsend because you cannot "make the capitalist system pay you twice as much for not working when you are sixty as you got on the average for working before you were sixty," in Richard Polenberg, ed., *Radicalism and Reform in the New Deal* (Reading, Mass.: Addison-Wesley, 1972), p. 127; or that of Lenore K. Bartlett, "The Attack on the Townsend Plan," *Social Work Today* 3:8 (May 1936), pp. 11–12.

66. Gaston V. Rimlinger, *Welfare Policy and Industrialization in Europe, America, and Russia* (New York: John Wiley and Sons, 1971), p. 208.
67. Only in the United States did campaigns for old-age pensions become a social movement, one that was not only to change the federal response to the depression but also to affect the politics of welfare for the rest of the twentieth century, the elderly remaining organized as one of the country's most powerful interest groups.
68. Sinclair, *The EPIC Plan for California*.
69. Greg Mitchell, *The Campaign of the Century: Upton Sinclair's Race for Governor of California and the Birth of Media Politics* (New York: Random House, 1992).
70. One might note that this decision was a sign of a perhaps foolish integrity, not radicalism or craziness.
71. Putnam, *Old Age Politics in California*, pp. 34–41; Laidler, "The Townsend Plan"; Sinclair, "The Lie Factory Starts," in his *The Epic Plan for California*.
72. The plan was probably not original. Many such Keynesian proposals were in the air. Putnam, *Old-Age Politics in California*, p. 50.
73. Holtzman, *The Townsend Movement*, pp. 40–46; Bliven, "Introduction," in Richard L. Neuberger and Kelley Loe, *An Army of the Aged: A History and Analysis of the Townsend Old Age Pension Plan* (Caldwell, Idaho: Caxton Printers, 1936), p. 13; Rimlinger, *Welfare Policy*, p. 203; Norman Thomas in Polenberg, ed., *Radicalism and Reform*, p. 127; Raymond Gram Swing, "Dr. Townsend Solves It All," *The Nation*, Mar. 6, 1935, p. 269.
74. Steven Burg, "Women, Gender, and Social Action: The Townsend Movement and Ideologies of the Welfare State, 1938–1941," 1993 typescript, author's possession.
75. Twentieth Century Fund, Committee on Old Age Security, *The Townsend Crusade: An Impartial Review of the Townsend Movement and the Probable Effects of the Townsend Plan* (New York: 20th Century Fund, 1936), pp. 9–10; *Newsweek*, Nov. 2, 1935, p. 13; Swing, "Dr. Townsend Solves It All," p. 268; Laidler "The Townsend Plan," p. 12; Witte to James A. Farley, Sept. 7, 1934, in Social Security Mss., Committee on Economic Security, Box 56.
76. Leaflet in Witte Mss., State Historical Society of Wisconsin, Box 70, sometime in Oct. 1934.
77. Quoted by Holtzman, *The Townsend Movement*, p. 92.
78. Witte to Marianne Sakmann, Dec. 7, 1935, in Witte Mss., State Historical Society of Wisconsin, Box 33.
79. Witte to James A. Farley, Postmaster General, Sept. 7, 1934, in Social Security Mss., Committee on Economic Security, Box 56; Witte to Lundeen, Sept. 17, 1934, in ibid., Box 44; clippings, in ibid., Box 9.
80. Witte kept up a large correspondence and voluminous files on the various old-age pension movements, not just Townsend. He made a chart for himself on probable votes in Congress for the various alternative

pension plans. Witte Mss., State Historical Society of Wisconsin, Boxes 70 and 234.

81. While mine is the consensus of historians, sociologists Edwin Amenta and Kathleen Dunleavy, of the Skocpol "state-centered" school, deny that Townsend had any significant impact on the grounds that the movement opposed the administration bill and failed to defeat or change it; see their "All the King's Menace: Protest Movement Theories, Huey Long's Share Our Wealth, and Neo-populism in the Depression," typescript, Sept. 1991. In another paper, Edwin Amenta has modified this denial, claiming that Townsend improved Old Age Assistance benefits; Amenta, Bruce G. Carruthers, and Yvonne Zyland, "A Hero for the Aged? The Townsend Movement, the Political Mediation Model, and U.S. Old-Age Policy, 1934–1950," *American Journal of Sociology* 98:2 (Sept. 1992), pp. 308–39. Of course Amenta et al. are right that Townsend's impact, just as Piven and Cloward have always maintained, was mediated by the political system and the political climate.

82. Hadley Cantril, ed., *Public Opinion 1935–1946* (Princeton, N.J.: Princeton University Press, 1951), p. 542; poll dated Mar. 14, 1936.

83. Neuberger and Loe, *An Army of the Aged*, pp. 79–80; Edwin Witte, "Organized Labor and Social Security," in Derber and Young, eds., *Labor and the New Deal*, p. 253; Tugwell, *The Democratic Roosevelt*, p. 339; Paul H. Douglas, *Social Security in the United States* (New York: McGraw-Hill, 1936), pp. 69–74; Norman Furniss and Timothy Tilton, *The Case for the Welfare State: From Social Security to Social Equality* (Bloomington: Indiana University Press, 1977), p. 159; James MacGregor Burns, *Roosevelt: The Lion and the Fox* (New York: Harcourt Brace, 1956), pp. 213, 224; Dexter Perkins, *The New Age of Franklin Roosevelt 1932–45* (Chicago: University of Chicago, 1957), pp. 26–27; Henry J. Pratt, *The Gray Lobby* (Chicago: University of Chicago Press, 1976); Holtzman, *The Townsend Movement*, p. 207; William Graebner, "From Pensions to Social Security: Social Insurance and the Rise of Dependency," in John N. Schacht, ed. *The Quest for Security: Papers on the Origins and the Future of the American Social Insurance System* (University of Iowa: Center for the Study of the Recent History of the United States, 1982), pp. 19–33; Rimlinger, *Welfare Policy*, pp. 202–4; William Graebner, "The Golden Age Clubs," *Social Service Review* (Sept. 1983), pp. 416–28; Schlesinger, *The Politics of Upheaval*, pp. 34 ff.; George Murray, journalist for Chicago's *American*, quoted in Terkel, *Hard Times*, p. 363.

84. "The Reminiscences of Frank Bane," p. 24.

85. Long and his followers offered many different versions of the Share Our Wealth plan. I take this early version from a personal letter of Long to Forrest Davis in Davis, *Huey Long: A Candid Biography* (New York: Dodge Publishing, 1935), pp. 299-307; and additions from Glen Jeansonne, *Messiah of the Masses: Huey P. Long and the Great Depression* (New York: Harper Collins, 1993).

86. Senator Russell Long, quoted in Terkel, *Hard Times*, p. 365.
87. T. Harry Williams, *Huey Long* (New York: Knopf, 1969), p. 694.
88. Edward F. Haas, "Huey Long and the Communists," *Louisiana History* 32:1 (Winter 1991), pp. 29–46.
89. Williams, *Huey Long*, pp. 700–701; Brinkley, *Voices of Protest*, pp. 169–70; Bennett, *Demagogues in the Depression*, pp. 125–26. The 7.5 million estimate and stories about the volume of mail are from Jeansonne, *Messiah of the Masses*, p. 115.
90. For example, Estellas Thomas to Long, Apr. 27, 1935, in WPA Mss., Box 119-1, Folder 7, Moorland-Springarn Collection.
91. Jeansonne, *Messiah of the Masses*, pp. 126–29.
92. Bennett, *Demagogues in the Depression*, p. 127; Amenta and Dunleavy, "All the King's Menace."
93. Williams, *Huey Long*, pp. 828–32; Tugwell, *The Democratic Roosevelt*, p. 348.
94. Douglas, *In the Fullness of Time*, p. 74. Also arguing for the influence of Long were Richard Hofstadter, *The American Political Tradition, and the Men Who Made It* (New York: Knopf, 1962), p. 337, and Leuchtenberg, *Franklin D. Roosevelt*, pp. 146, 153n., 163, and 180 ff.
95. Williams, *Huey Long*, p. 836.
96. Bennett, *Demagogues in the Depression*, p. 55.
97. Ibid., pp. 43–53; Brinkley, *Voices of Protest*, pp. 140–41, 199–200; Charles J. Tull, *Father Coughlin and the New Deal* (Syracuse, N.Y.: Syracuse University Press, 1965), pp. 61–70; Raymond Gram Swing, *Forerunners of American Fascism* (1935; reprint ed., Freeport, New York: Books for Libraries Press, 1962), pp. 34–61.
98. Bennett, *Demagogues in the Depression*, p. 54.
99. Tull, *Father Coughlin and the New Deal*, p. 106.
100. Long was shot by Dr. Carl Austin Weiss, an Austrian immigrant who feared Long's authoritarianism.
101. For example, *Newsweek*, Jan. 26, 1935, cover and pp. 5–7.
102. Raymond Moley, *After Seven Years* (New York: Harper & Brothers, 1939), pp. 301–5. See also Douglas, *In the Fullness of Time*, p. 74, on Long's influence.
103. Some historians and contemporaries tried the word "fascism" against these three groupings (and a few other leaders who sometimes also included welfare proposals, such as anti-Semite William Dudley Pelley). Although Long was a U.S. senator, his methods were distinctly undemocratic. Still, the three were not by any means identical, and only Coughlin mobilized racism (in this case anti-Semitism). Coughlin's base soon took on a political identity to the right of the New Deal, while Long and Townsend were ambiguous in alignment. Whether or not there was an opening to fascism in the United States, and whether or not Long and Coughlin would have supplied the leadership for

such a transition, they were surely impatient with democratic and Democratic politics. Alan Dawley has suggested that, given Coughlin's ability to develop a conservative working-class following through uniting anticommunism, anti-Semitism, antifeminism, and anticonservatism with antiliberalism, and his call for greater state control of economy, had he begun to make deals with big business he would have become a significant right-wing threat to democracy. But Long was shot dead in 1935, and Coughlin, suffering from the loss of a more disciplined ally, declined precipitously in popularity. One year later Roosevelt regretted not having Long as a counterbalance to pressure from the Right, which had dominated in the previous year. Either Tugwell or Roosevelt or both seemed unambivalent in labeling Long as Left. See Dawley, *Struggles for Justice*, pp. 403–4; Swing, *Forerunners*; Norman Thomas, "Roosevelt Faces Re-Election," *American Socialist Monthly* 5:1 (Mar. 1936), pp. 4–7; Brinkley, *Voices of Protest*; on Pelley see Leo P. Ribuffo, *The Old Christian Right: The Protestant Far Right from the Great Depression to the Cold War* (Philadelphia: Temple University Press, 1983), p. 69; Tugwell, *The Democratic Roosevelt*, p. 348.

104. Many other factors, of course, influenced that decline, including most importantly the fact that in 1932 there was little apparent difference between the major-party candidates, and progressive voters felt free to "waste" their votes, while in 1936 FDR had a record proving him by far the more progressive candidate and voters were fearful that a vote for Thomas was effectively a vote for Landon.

105. Theodore Draper, *American Communism and Soviet Russia* (New York: Viking, 1960), p. 188. Needless to say, membership information about the Communist party cannot be confirmed.

106. Irving Howe and Lewis Coser, *The American Communist Party: A Critical History* (New York: Praeger, 1962), pp. 225, 327; Harvey Klehr, *The Heyday of American Communism: The Depression Decade* (New York: Basic Books, 1984), pp. 91–92, 153–54, 161–64, 365–85. Of course there are many different claims as to Communist party size; I have given conservative ones. All agree that a factor keeping the Communist party small was turnover: most of those who joined also left.

107. Rosenzweig, "Organizing the Unemployed," pp. 170–71.

108. David J. O'Brien, *American Catholicism and Social Reform: The New Deal Years* (New York: Oxford University Press, 1968).

109. Kelley, *Hammer and Hoe*, pp. 20–22.

110. For example, Harry W. Laidler, *Unemployment and Its Remedies* (Chicago: Socialist Party, n.d. but 1932); David Berenberg, "Roosevelt," in *American Socialist Quarterly* 2:3 (Summer 1933), pp. 45–52; Henry J. Rosner, "The Economic Policies of Roosevelt," ibid.

(Autumn 1933), pp. 3–121; David Berenberg, "Circuses and a Little Bread," ibid. (Spring 1934), pp. 12–19; Benjamin Stolberg and Warren Jay Winton, *The Economic Consequences of the New Deal* (New York: Harcourt, Brace & Co., 1935); Alex Bittelman, "The New Deal and the Old Deal," *The Communist* 13 (Jan. 1934), pp. 81–98;

111. Witte typed out excerpts from this review, from the *New York Times*, sometime in Mar. 1934; Witte Mss., Box 209.

112. *A Plan for America: Official 1932 Campaign Handbook of the Socialist Party* (Chicago, 1932); Harry W. Laidler, ed., *Socialist Planning and a Socialist Program: A Symposium* (New York, 1932); idem, *Unemployment and Its Remedies*.

113. This language, considering wife and children "dependents," was just beginning to be used in this context; see Nancy Fraser and Linda Gordon, "A Genealogy of *Dependency*: Tracing a Keyword of the U.S. Welfare State," *Signs* 19:2 (Winter 1994): 309–36.

114. Herbert Benjamin, in effect the Communist party lobbyist in Washington as leader of its Unemployed Council, and Earl Browder, head of the party, both claimed to have written it. Franklin Folsom, *Impatient Armies of the Poor: The Story of Collective Action of the Unemployed* (Niwot: University Press of Colorado, 1991), p. 391.

115. Quoted in Casebeer, "The Workers' Unemployment Insurance Bill," p. 239.

116. Maxwell S. Stewart, *Security or the Dole* (Washington, D.C.: Public Affairs Committee, 1936); idem, *Social Security*, p. 280; Folsom, *Impatient Armies*, p. 394.

117. Casebeer, "The Workers' Unemployment Insurance Bill," p. 246.

118. *The Nation*, Apr. 17, 1935, p. 433; A six-part series, "Security for Americans," featured as its fourth installment Mary Van Kleeck's, "The Workers' Bill for Unemployment and Social Insurance," in *The New Republic*, Dec. 12, 1934, pp. 121–24 (other parts written by Epstein, Rubinow, Douglas, and Elizabeth Brandeis Raushenbush). Douglas' ex-wife Dorothy Wolf Douglas, also an economist, promoted Lundeen, as did Johns Hopkins economist Broadus Mitchell. See Dorothy Douglas quoted in *AALL Review* 24:2 (June 1934), p. 67.

119. T. Arnold Hill, "The Negro's Need for Unemployment Insurance," in *Unemployment Insurance Review*, published for the National Congress for Unemployment and Social Insurance, in Social Security Mss., Committee on Economic Security, Box 9.

120. Edwin Witte, *The Development of the Social Security Act* (Madison: University of Wisconsin Press, 1963), p. 86; Altmeyer, *The Formative Years of Social Security*, p. 31.

121. House Committee on Labor, Subcommittee on Unemployment, Old Age, and Social Insurance, *Hearings*, Feb. 1935, pp. 129–35.

122. For example, Rubinow took it to task for its lack of specificity in

defining whether salaried employees, professionals, farmers, and so on, were to be included; in a debate on the Lundeen Bill, untitled, *Survey* 70:12 (Dec. 1934), p. 377.

123. For example, Ewen Clague, "The Lundeen Bill in Action," *Survey* 71:5 (May 1935), pp. 134–35; Witte, "The Lundeen Bill," Social Security Mss., Committee on Economic Security, Box 9.

124. A. G. Nordholm, "Some Pertinent Questions Regarding the Lundeen Bill," n.d., probably early 1935, in Social Security Mss., Committee on Economic Security, Box 20.

125. The closest to objectivity might have been Paul Douglas. He was a partisan of Epstein's views on social insurance, and regarded Lundeen as the opposition, but he was also vaguely to the left of the administration; he criticized Lundeen but did not dismiss its costs as crazy.

126. An ex-Communist turned stool pigeon, Benjamin Gitlow, later said that Lundeen was a "paid under-cover" Communist party agent. Arthur M. Schlesinger, *The Age of Roosevelt*, Vol. 2: *The Coming of the New Deal* (Boston: Houghton Mifflin, 1958), p. 296; Klehr, *The Heyday of American Communism*, p. 289; Benjamin Gitlow, *The Whole of Their Lives* (New York: Charles Scribner's Sons, 1948), p. 260. The historical evidence would seem to make this charge absurd: Congressman, later Senator, Ernest Lundeen was a longtime Farmer-Labor party loyalist; his own positions intersected with those of the Communist party during part of the New Deal, and when they did he looked favorably on tactical alliances with it; but as soon as the Communist party started promoting collective security against Nazi Germany, it began denouncing Lundeen, who was a persistent isolationist. Klehr, *The Heyday of American Communism*, p. 264. Witte claimed that Earl Browder had "described this measure as the principal method of propaganda . . . to gain the support of the working people." Witte, *Development of Social Security*, p. 86. This statement in Witte's memoir was an exaggeration of something he had expressed more cautiously in a report written for his signature, "The Lundeen (Workers' Unemployment and Social Insurance Bill)" [sic], perhaps by Wilbur Cohen or Alex Nordholm, in April 1935, in Social Security Mss., Committee on Economic Security, Box 9. In that earlier report he has Browder saying only that the party regards efforts for the bill as "the front line trench in the fight for life, liberty and the pursuit of happiness."

127. Lizabeth Cohen, *Making a New Deal: Industrial Workers in Chicago, 1919–1939* (Cambridge: Cambridge University Press, 1990), pp. 311 ff., 355.

128. Theron F. Schlabach, *Edwin E. Witte: Cautious Reformer* (Madison: State Historical Society of Wisconsin, 1969), p. 137.

129. Penny Ciancanelli, private communication, Sept. 30, 1992; Van Kleeck, "The Workers' Bill," p. 124.

130. Van Kleeck, "The Workers' Bill," pp. 122–23.

131. Two hundred twelve votes were needed for a discharge petition and Lundeen only collected 166. (Among the signature gatherers was the young Illinois Representative Everett Dirksen.) Casebeer, "The Workers' Unemployment Insurance Bill," p. 250.

132. Douglas, *Social Security*, p. 82; Valelly, *Radicalism in the States*, pp. 168–69.

133. I get at this political culture from a variety of evidence, none of it adequate, most of it anecedotal. It includes a little public opinion poll data; thousands of public letters to various government officials; the writings of commentators, primarily middle-class and primarily intellectuals; the records of some public officials who were particularly attentive to the movement and speech of citizens. I have sampled only small, nonrandom bits of this evidence, though I have done so in an attempt to give a fair representation of what can be seen. This interpretive reading of a variety of evidence is at least as "true" as statistical study of public opinion only, but its truth is about different matters. It is not a report on the strength or weakness of prowelfare sentiment, or an argument that the public or any particular sector of it was to the left or the right of the administration.

134. The major exception to this pattern was on certain administrative questions; for example, the support for a federal Department of Public Welfare, averaging 57 percent in 1938, was higher among those with college degrees. Cantril, ed., *Public Opinion*, pp. 360–61, 439–41, 541–42, 893–97.

135. Leila A. Sussman, *Dear FDR: A Study of Political Letter Writing* (Totowa, N.J.: Bedminster Press, 1963), p. 88–99.

136. Argersinger, *New Deal in Baltimore*, pp. 45, 55.

137. Mrs. Willye Jeffries, in Terkel, *Hard Times*, pp. 456–62. The Workers' Alliance included Communist, Socialist, and independent groups.

138. Searle F. Charles, *Minister of Relief: Harry Hopkins and the Depression* (Syracuse, N.Y.: Syracuse University Press, 1963), p. 61.

139. Howard, *The WPA and Federal Relief Policy*, p. 434.

140. This and much other evidence of such protests are in Mark Naison, *Communists in Harlem during the Depression* (Urbana: University of Illinois Press, 1983), p. 205 and passim.

141. Judith Ann Trolander, *Settlement Houses and the Great Depression* (Detroit: Wayne State University Press, 1975), pp. 64–73.

142. Faue, *Community of Suffering*, pp. 64, 112, 136.

143. Mrs. A.S., Mar. 15, 1940, in Children's Bureau Mss. quoted in "Seeking Health Care for Children," anon. mss., author's possession.

144. Brock, *Welfare, Democracy*, p. 263.

145. Letters to Alfred E. Smith, WPA Mss.; passim, Moorland-Spingarn Collection.

146. Mamie Garvin Fields with Karen Fields, *Lemon Swamp and Other Places: A Carolina Memoir* (New York: Free Press, 1983), p. 239.

147. Gabriel Almond and Harold D. Lasswell, "Aggressive Behavior by Clients toward Public Relief Administrators: A Configurative Analysis," *American Political Science Review* 28 (Aug. 1934), 643–55.

148. Eyewitness account quoted in Rosenzweig, "Organizing the Unemployed," p. 175.

149. Robert Fisher, *Let the People Decide: Neighborhood Organizing in America* (Boston: Twayne, 1984), pp. 35–42; Folsom, *Impatient Armies*; Kelley, *Hammer and Hoe*.

150. Story told by Argersinger, *New Deal in Baltimore*, p. 115.

151. Quoted in Robin D. G. Kelley, "The Black Poor and the Politics of Opposition in a New South City, 1929–1970," in Katz, ed., *The "Underclass" Debate*, pp. 293–333, quote on pp. 298–99.

152. Mick Shufro, quoted in Terkel, *Hard Times*, p. 444.

153. Almond and Lasswell, "Aggressive Behavior."

154. Mrs. C. A. VerNooy, chairman, to FDR and to Perkins, Mar. 2, 1933, Children's Bureau Mss., Box 462.

155. J. E. Perkins to Alfred E. Smith, Apr. 1, 1935, Box 119-7, Folder 94; I. H. Smith to Hopkins, Feb. 3, 1934, Box 119-1, Folder 1; all in WPA Mss., Moorland-Spingarn Collection.

156. Gribov to Harry Hopkins, Dec. 12, 1934, Box 119-1, Folder 1, in ibid.

157. Wye, "The New Deal and the Negro Community."

158. Joel Schwartz, "The Consolidate Tenants League of Harlem: Black Self-Help vs. White, Liberal Intervention in Ghetto Housing, 1934–1944," *Afro-Americans in New York Life and History* 10 (Jan. 1986), pp. 31–51, and William Muraskin, "Black Nationalism and the Rise of Labor-Union Consciousness: The Harlem Boycott of 1934," *Labor History* (Summer 1972), pp. 361–73, both reprinted in Melvyn Dubofsky and Stephen Burwood, eds., *Women and Minorities During the Great Depression* (New York: Garland, 1990); Naison *Communists in Harlem*, p. 143.

159. Kelley, "The Black Poor," pp. 299–300, quoting from Nell Irvin Painter, *The Narrative of Hosea Hudson: His Life as a Negro Communist in the South* (Cambridge, Mass.: Harvard University Press, 1979), p. 161.

160. Brock, *America's Welfare, Democracy*, pp. 263–66; Patterson, *America's Struggle Against Poverty*, p. 51.

161. Reynolds, *Uncharted Journey*, p. 140.

162. E. Wight Bakke, *The Unemployed Worker: A Study of Making a Living Without a Job* (New Haven, Conn.: Institute of Human Relations, Yale University Press, 1940), pp. 369–71 and ff.

163. Almond and Lasswell, "Aggressive Behavior." As was typical for research of that period, there was no gender analysis—we do not even know the sex of the relief recipients surveyed.

164. Barbara J. Nelson, "Help-Seeking from Public Authorities: Who Arrives at the Agency Door?" *Policy Sciences* 12 (1980), pp. 175–92.

165. Patterson, *America's Struggle Against Poverty*, p. 53; Bakke, *The Unemployed Worker*, p. 29 and chap. 1 passim.

166. Jessie A. Bloodworth and Elizabeth J. Greenwood, *The Personal Side* (WPA Division of Research, 1939; reprint ed., New York: Arno Press, 1971), p. 305.

167. Clifford Burke in Terkel, *Hard Times*, p. 105.

168. Lorena Hickok, *One Third of a Nation: Lorena Hickok Reports on the Great Depression*, Richard Lowitt and Maurine Beasley, eds. (Urbana: University of Illinois Press, 1981), p. 323.

169. Terkel, *Hard Times*, pp. 454–503; Katz, *In the Shadow of the Poorhouse*, p. 220.

170. E. Wight Bakke, *Citizens Without Work* (New Haven, Conn.: Institute of Human Relations, Yale University Press, 1940), passim.

171. R. Sam Jones to FDR, July 17, 1934, WPA Mss., Box 119-1, Folder 6, Moorland-Spingarn Collection.

172. J. S. Hayes to Mr. McIntyre, Nov. 19, 1936, Box 119-1, Folder 6, in ibid.

173. June 28, 1934 to Alfred E. Smith, Box 119-7, Folder 94, in ibid.

174. P. I. Kelly Shelton to Eleanor Roosevelt, Aug. 10, 1935, Box 119-1, Folder 6, in ibid.

175. Marguerite Porter to FDR, Aug. 12, 1935, Box 119-1, Folder 6, in ibid.

176. R. C. Morris to FDR, Dec. 10, 1934, Box 119-1, Folder 9, in ibid.

177. Mrs. C. A. VerNooy to Roosevelt, Mar. 2, 1933, Children's Bureau Mss., Box 462.

178. Dawley, *Struggles for Justice*, p. 375.

179. *Newsweek*, Nov. 24, 1934, p. 7.

180. Dean E. McHenry, proposal and letter, Dec. 29, 1934 in Witte Mss., Box 232.

181. Frank D. Graham, "The B Line to Recovery," in *Survey* 70:11 (Nov. 1934), pp. 339–41, summarizing his book *The Abolition of Unemployment* (Princeton, N.J.: Princeton University Press, 1932). See also Albert L. Deane, "The Deane Plan," in Witte Mss., Box 234; Wilbur J. Cohen, "The Dean Plan," Oct. 10, 1934, in Social Security Mss., Committee on Economic Security, Box 12; Witte, "Social Insurance," in Witte Mss., Box 70; A. L. Dean and H. K. Norton, *Investing in Wages* (New York: Macmillan, 1932).

182. Sidney Verba and Kay Lehman Schlozman, "Unemployment, Class Consciousness, and Radical Politics: What Didn't Happen in the Thirties," in Dubofsky and Burwood, *The New Deal*, pp. 291–323; Cohen, *Making a New Deal*.

Chapter 9. The Legislative Process

1. Schlesinger, *Politics of Upheaval*, p. 5.
2. For example, it was the only piece of legislation Wagner ever sponsored without control over its drafting. Casebeer, "The Workers' Unemployment Insurance Bill," p. 57.
3. Of those who spoke against Social Security in Congress, most protected themselves by supporting ADC—it was unemployment and old-age insurance they opposed. In the House debate, see statements by Congressmen Massachusetts Republican Allen Treadway, Apr. 12, 1935, p. 5535; Ohio Republican Thomas Jenkins, Apr. 15, p. 5679; Kentucky Republican John Robison, Apr. 15, p. 5693; Michigan Republican Fred Crawford, Apr. 15, p. 5710; Massachusetts Democrat William Granfield, Apr. 15, p. 5714; Pennsylvania Democrat Charles Haines, Apr. 16, p. 5825; Washington Democrat Marion Zioncheck, Apr. 17, p. 5910; in 74th Cong., 1st sess., *Congressional Record*, vol. 79, pts. 5–6.
4. Rep. Claude Fuller, Apr. 17, 1935, p. 5862, 74th Cong., 1st sess., *Congressional Record*, vol. 79, pt. 6.
5. Wilbur Cohen, "Legislative History of the Social Security Act," speech at American University, Apr. 26, 1937, in Social Security Mss., Chairman of the Board correspondence, Box 39, 062.2, p. 9.
6. Daniel S. Hirshfield, *The Lost Reform: The Campaign for Compulsory Health Insurance in the United States from 1932 to 1943* (Cambridge, Mass.: Harvard University Press, 1970).
7. Witte, as executive director of the CES, organized and coordinated several groups: a small, hand-picked staff that he then kept quite subordinate, to the resentment of many of these experts; a "technical board," consisting of twenty administration officials and advisers, with Arthur Altmeyer as chair and Witte as secretary; and several advisory committees, including an influential business committee and a main advisory council, to which Witte also acted as secretary.
8. Lenroot to Witte, Sept. 6, 1934 and enclosed memorandum; Lenroot to Abbott, Sept. 13, 1934 and enclosed memorandum; both in Abbott Mss., Box 61, Folder 3.
9. "The Reminiscences of Martha May Eliot," p. 48.
10. In the first memo sent to Witte, written by Katharine Ward Fisher of the Children's Bureau network, ADC was the last of five suggestions: Katharine Ward Fisher, "Suggestions for Child Security," n.d., Witte Mss., State Historical Society of Wisconsin, Box 200; Witte, *The Development of the Social Security Act*, p. 165. "The Reminiscences of Katharine Fredrica Lenroot" referred to her expectation of getting a new Sheppard-Towner from the Social Security Act, pp. 50–53, 91–92.
11. Grace Abbott to Martha Eliot, Apr. 17, 1934, in Eliot Mss., Box

18, Folder 253; Children's Bureau Mss., Box 613, Folders 13-0 and 13-0-1.

12. "Security for Children," Outline by Witte of CB Recommendations, n.d. but probably December 1934, in Social Security Mss., Committee on Economic Security, Box 29.

13. Children's Bureau Mss., Box 613, Folders 13-0 and 13-0-1, passim; Social Security Mss., Chairman of the Board, papers of the Interdepartmental Committee to Coordinate Health and Welfare, Box 11, Folder 025; Eliot Mss., Box 18, Folders 250, 253, 305. Both Katharine Lenroot, Abbott's successor, and Martha Eliot, a physician at the Children's Bureau, attributed this timidity to Abbott. Eliot thought that her own background in the Yale Medical School made her think bigger than Abbott, accustomed by now to the difficulty of getting any federal welfare spending. "The Reminiscences of Martha May Eliot," pp. 46–47; "The Reminiscences of Katharine Fredrica Lenroot," pp. 50 ff.

14. For example, Memorandum on Children's Bureau Appropriation, 1934, Feb. 9, 1933, in Eliot Mss., Box 21, Folder 305.

15. See for example Grace Abbott to Josephine Goldmark, June 10, 1932; memo from Abbott to Perkins, "The Children's Bureau and Reorganization," Sept. 18, 1933; "Memorandum on Relationships between the U.S. Public Health Service and the Children's Bureau," July 20, 1935; Lenroot to Perkins, memo Sept. 21, 1936; Lenroot, "Memorandum Re Reorganization," Dec. 26, 1939, all in Eliot Mss.

16. Coll, "Public Assistance," pp. 230–31.

17. For example, Abbott to Perkins, Feb. 23, 1934, supporting a proposal from Joan A. Kingsbury of the Milbank Memorial Fund, in Eliot Mss., Box 21, Folder 305. In this long and detailed memo, Abbott even recommends the composition of a proposed committee on a national health program.

18. Gordon, "Putting Children First."

19. "The Reminiscences of Martha May Eliot," pp. 46–48.

20. Witte, *The Development of the Social Security Act*, p. 171.

21. "The Reminiscences of Katharine Fredrica Lenroot," pp. 91–92.

22. Clara Beyer claimed that the Social Security bill was thrashed out in her living room at Springhill Farm in McLean, Virginia, among Perkins, Armstrong, Altmeyer, and others. Murray, "The Work Got Done," p. 204.

23. Thomas Eliot to Witte, May, 3, 1935, Social Security Mss., Committee on Economic Security, Box 56.

24. Interview with Wilbur Cohen by Schlabach, *Edwin E. Witte*, p. 102.

25. The closest to a Children's Bureau representative on the inner group was Frances Perkins, who disagreed with the bureau on several major points. "The Reminiscences of Katharine Fredrica Lenroot," p. 54.

26. Abbott complains about these exclusions in various documents in Abbott Mss., Box 54, Folder 1. A fifth woman, Josephine Roche, owner of Rocky Mountain Fuel Corporation, was originally appointed, but she soon became assistant secretary of the treasury and was therefore transferred to the Technical Board, which consisted of federal officials. These various CES committees had an exclusively political function, of course, but the social work group was also excluded from final revisions to the bill.

27. "The Reminiscences of Katharine Fredrica Lenroot," pp. 115–18.

28. For example, calling for a report on foreign maternity benefit provisions; Ann Kalet Smith of Children's Bureau to Violet Libby of Social Security Board, Feb. 1, 1935, in Social Security Mss., Committee on Economic Security, Box 19, Folder Libby; correspondence in Wilbur Cohen Mss., Box 1.

29. Their birth dates: Brown, 1887; Armstrong, 1890; Hoey, 1892; Burns, 1900; Merriam, 1904.

30. "The Reminiscences of Eveline Mabel Burns," p. 21.

31. Ibid., p. 89.

32. Proceedings of the December 1936 meeting of the 20th Century Fund Commission on Old Age Security, in Abbott Mss., Box 72, Folders 1–6.

33. Folks to Grace Abbott, Sept. 28, 1934, in ibid., Box 54, Folder 15.

34. Schlabach, *Edwin E. Witte*, p. 106.

35. Edith Abbott, "Abolish the Pauper Laws," *Social Service Review* 8:1 (Mar. 1934), pp. 1–16.

36. Grace Abbott to Perkins, Feb. 3, 1938 in Abbott Mss., Box 68, Folder 7; Abbott, "The Social Security Act and Relief" (1936), in her *From Relief to Social Security*, p. 261; correspondence in and out of Children's Bureau on relief, in Children's Bureau Mss., Box 367 and 613, Folders 12-8-5; Costin, *Two Sisters for Social Justice*, chap. 9; Archie Hanlan, "From Social Reform to Social Security: The Separation of ADC and Child Welfare," *Child Welfare* 45:11 (Nov. 1966), pp. 493–500.

37. 1934 statement, Abbott Mss., Box 25, Folder 11.

38. Abbott to Perkins, to Feb. 23, 1934, in Eliot Mss., Box 21, Folder 305, and in Abbott Mss., Box 36, Folder 15; Abbott to Martha Eliot, Apr. 17, 1934, in ibid., Box 18, Folder 253.

39. Andrews to Abbott, Apr. 17, 1935, in ibid., Box 54, Folder 5.

40. Draft proposals in ibid., Box 25, Folder 11.

41. For example, letter to members of Congress, Mar. 20, 1935, from Abbott, Andrews, and others, in Altmeyer Mss., Box 1.

42. Abbott to Kellogg, Dec. 28, 1934, in Abbott Mss., Box 54, Folder 2.

43. For example, Grace Abbott to Mary Dewson, June 13, 1938, in ibid., Box 68, Folder 8.

44. Witte to Abbott, Jan. 21, 1935, in ibid., Box 54, Folder 2; Abbott to Lenroot, in ibid., Box 54, Folder 3; Witte to Edith Abbott, Oct. 18, 1939, in ibid., Box 54, Folder 11; the statements of support Abbott collected are in ibid., Box 54, Folders 2 and 3.

45. Abbott to Steelman, assistant secretary of labor, Jan. 19, 1935, in ibid., Box 37, Folder 4.

46. Abbott to Mary Dewson, June 5, 1936, in ibid., Box 68, Folder 8.

47. Marie L. Obenauer, memo to Perkins, Mar. 27, 1933, in ibid., Box 36. Folder 13.

48. Ibid., Addenda II, Box 4; Covotsos, "Child Welfare," pp. 275–77.

49. Ware, *Beyond Suffrage*, p. 103; Muncy, *Creating a Female Dominion*, p. 153.

50. Quoted by Susan Ware, *Partner and I: Molly Dewson, Feminism, and New Deal Politics* (New Haven, Conn.: Yale University Press, 1987), p. 210.

51. Abbott to Homer Folks, Oct. 3, 1934, in Abbott Mss., Box 54, Folder 15.

52. The male members of the CES committees and Advisory Council included no social insurance or economic planners; these men influenced the bill through the CES staff and through the executive branch.

53. Graebner, "From Pensions to Social Security," pp. 19–33.

54. Brock, *Welfare, Democracy*, pp. 269–79.

55. Brown, *Public Relief*, pp. 309–10.

56. Howard M. Vollmer and Donald L. Mills, eds., *Professionalization* (Englewood Cliffs, N.J.: Prentice-Hall, 1966), p. 340.

57. Kathleen D. McCarthy, *Noblesse Oblige: Charity and Cultural Philanthropy in Chicago, 1849–1929* (Chicago: University of Chicago Press, 1982), pp. 142–44, for vivid examples. The depression pushed more men into social work since other jobs were so scarce. In 1930 women were 80 percent of social workers; in 1940, 65 percent. Cott, *Grounding of Modern Feminism*, p. 218.

58. And a change of governing party lost them their jobs. Muncy cites the replacement of Jane Hoey with a political appointment by Eisenhower; *Creating a Female Dominion*, p. 156.

59. Cott, *Grounding of Modern Feminism*, table p. 219.

60. Julia Lathrop to Grace Abbott, Nov. 3, 1929, Box 58, Folder 3, Abbott Mss.; also quoted by Muncy, *Creating a Female Dominion*, p. 148.

61. While there is no contesting the long-term decline of women's political influence in the welfare system between, say, 1920 and 1950, there is room for disagreement about when the peak of their power occurred and when the downward slide began. Robyn Muncy believes the white women's dominion over welfare to have been weakening before the New Deal. Susan Ware, New Deal historian, considers 1936 the acme,

and Mary Dewson's retirement that year to mark the beginning of the decline. Ware attributes a large share of credit for New Deal welfare programs to Perkins who proposed six reforms to FDR in 1933, and by 1940 all but health insurance had passed. Muncy, *Creating a Female Dominion*, pp. 124–25; Ware, *Beyond Suffrage*, pp. 119–28; Ware, *Partner and I*.

62. For example: Joseph Harris to Hopkins, and Harris to Altmeyer, both Feb. 28, 1935, and Witte to Wisconsin Congressmen, "Possible Constructive Amendments to the Social Security Act, April 1935," in Social Security Mss., Committee on Economic Security, Box 9; "Statement Concerning Amendments to the Social Security Bill Supplementary to the Memorandum by Mr. Witte," n.d., and CES to Perkins, "Amendments to the Social Security Act which are Absolutely Essential," Apr. 28, 1935, both in ibid., Box 11; Altmeyer, handwritten notes, n.d., probably April 1935, in ibid., Box 56; Lenroot to Grace Abbott, Apr. 25, 1935, in Abbott Mss., Box 61, Folder 4.

63. Martha H. Swain, *Pat Harrison: The New Deal Years* (Jackson: University of Mississippi Press, 1978).

64. Some critics blamed the CES for the delays, arguing that the original bill was poorly drafted, and it is true that the bill rewritten by the Congressional drafting service was more logically and lucidly laid out. But a close examination of the Congressional process reveals that the delays were political. Douglas, *Social Security*, p. 86.

65. Abbott, memo to Perkins, "The Children's Bureau and Reorganization," Sept. 18, 1933, in Eliot Mss., Box 18, Folder 253; Abbott to Perkins, Feb. 23, 1934, in Box 21, Folder 305; "The Reminiscences of Martha May Eliot," pp. 49–51. In 1935 the president appointed an Interdepartmental Committee for the Coordination of Health and Welfare Activities, which included Lenroot, Surgeon-General Parran, and seven other high-level officials (usually assistant secretaries of departments) to mediate this and related disputes. Correspondence and memos in Social Security Mss., Committee on Economic Security, Box 11, 025. See also June 10, 1932 Abbott to Josephine Goldmark, Eliot Mss., Schlesinger Library, Box 18, folder 251; Sept. 18, 1933 memo from Abbott to Perkins, "The Children's Bureau and Reorganization," and "Memorandum on Relationships between the U.S. Public Health Service and the Children's Bureau," July 20, 1935, in ibid., Box 18, Folder 253; Lenroot to Perkins, memo, Sept. 21, 1936, and Lenroot, "Memorandum Re Reorganization, Dec. 26, 1939, in ibid., Box 19, Folder 254.

66. "The Reminiscences of Martha May Eliot," pp. 49–51.

67. The CES Preliminary Report (Sept. 1934), did not specify who was to administer ADC and mentioned the Children's Bureau in regard to the

health program. I interpret this silence as taking the Children's Bureau for granted; Altmeyer Mss., CES, Folder 3, p. 66 of report.

68. Witte described this blandly in his memoir—"In the final stage of the preparation ... the F.E.R.A. people, particularly Mr. Aubrey J. Williams and Miss Josephine Brown, took the position that aid to dependent children was public assistance and should be administered by the Federal Emergency Relief Administration"—but he must have understood the implications for the Children's Bureau; clearly he was trying to avoid this discussion or didn't think it important. Just as clearly the FERA people could only have been acting out of hostility to the Children's Bureau because they knew how much it counted on this program. Witte, *The Development of the Social Security Act*, p. 162. In a panic, Lenroot wrote about this change to Abbott on Jan. 10, 1935, in Abbott Mss., Box 61, Folder 4.
69. For example, Homer Folks to Grace Abbott, Sept. 28, 1934, in ibid., Box 54, Folder 15.
70. There were three factions, outlined in chap. 7.
71. Even the mainstream social work professional organization sent a letter of protest. Hopkins's views about public jobs and public assistance were contradictory. A proponent of the idea that jobs were always better than relief—more dignified, more effective—he nevertheless designed a program to provide jobs only for a minority. See Lester M. Salamon, *Welfare: The Elusive Consensus* (New York: Praeger, 1978), p. 73.
72. Jacob Fisher, *The Response of Social Work*, chap. 4 and p. 62.
73. "The Reminiscences of Katharine Fredrica Lenroot," pp. 50–53; Eveline Burns, *Toward Social Security: An Explanation of the Social Security Act* (New York: McGraw-Hill, 1936), p. 107; Grace Abbott, "What About Mothers' Pensions Now?" *Survey* 70:3 (Mar. 19, 1934), pp. 80–81; Grace Abbott, "Mothers' Aid and Public Assistance," in *From Relief to Social Security*, pp. 286–89.
74. Brown, *Public Relief*, pp. 311–12.
75. Ibid., p. 48; Coll, "Public Assistance," p. 224.
76. Emilia Martinez-Brawley, "From Countrywoman to Federal Emergency Relief Administrator: Josephine Chapin Brown, A Biographical Study," *Journal of Sociology and Social Welfare* 14:2 (June 1987), pp. 129–85.
77. Folks to Stanley P. Davies, president, AASW, Mar. 7, 1934, and Abbott to Martha Eliot, n.d. [spring 1934], both in Eliot Mss., Box 18, Folder 253; Lenroot to Abbott, Apr. 25, 1935, in Abbott Mss., Box 61, Folder 4; Lenroot to Perkins, Sept. 21, 1936, and Lenroot to Abbott, Oct. 22, 1936, in ibid., Box 61, Folder 6; E. Wight Bakke of Social Security to John Winant of Brookings Institution, Nov. 27, 1936, in Social Security Mss., Chairman of the Board, Box 41, 062.2.

78. Lenroot to Perkins, Sept. 21, 1936, in Eliot Mss., Box 19, Folder 254, and in Abbott Mss., Box 61, Folder 6.
79. Lenroot to Perkins, Sept. 21, 1936, in Eliot Mss., Box 19, Folder 254; Abbott to Lenroot, Dec. 17, 1936, in Abbott Mss., Box 61, Folder 6.
80. Grace Abbott to Lillian Wald, Feb. 25, 1937, in ibid., Box 72, Folder 7.
81. Ibid.
82. Abbott to Lenroot, Feb. 21, 1935, in ibid., Box 61, Folder 4.
83. It could be argued, with some truth, that the Women's Bureau, focused as it was on employed women, was more representative of the interests of nonelite women. The civic organizational base of the Women's Bureau was unions, which were heavily male dominated and unusually insensitive to the interests of women. The Children's Bureau, by contrast, had as its base the women's organizations descended from the women's rights movement—the League of Women Voters, the YWCA, the NCL. Neither bureau represented minority women in any way; both had all-white staffs, and both condoned the exclusion of blacks from white organizations and/or segregation.
84. Richard Ely, for example, was a champion of public works; Benjamin G. Rader, *The Academic Mind and Reform: The Influence of Richard T. Ely in American Life* (Lexington: University of Kentucky Press, 1966), pp. 230–32.
85. Witte, *The Development of the Social Security Act*, p. 163.
86. Witte's memoir denies that the Senate Finance Committee ever made this change; ibid. He is mistaken, however, according to the actual text of the bill as reported out of the Finance Committee, H.R. 7260, Calendar No. 661. Witte is also corrected by Altmeyer, *The Formative Years of Social Security*, p. 41; Altmeyer writes that this change came at the specific request of the president; I have seen no corroborating evidence for this claim.
87. Witte to Perkins, "Amendments to the Social Security Act which are *Absolutely Essential*," Apr. 28, 1935, Social Security Mss., Committee on Economic Security, Box 11; Witte to Wisconsin congressmen, "Possible Constructive Amendments," Apr. 1935, in ibid., Box 9; Lenroot to Perkins, Sept. 21, 1936, in Eliot Mss., Box 19, Folder 254.
88. Altmeyer, *The Formative Years of Social Security*, pp. 36–37.
89. "The Reminiscences of Katharine Fredrica Lenroot," pp. 103 ff. Mildred Rein argued that had ADC gone to FERA, there would have been a broader definition of eligibility, since employable but employed parents could have received it for their kids; had it gone to the Children's Bureau, there would have been more selectivity and "rehabilitative counseling toward the goal of self-maintenance." Mildred Rein, *Work or Welfare? Factors in the Choice for AFDC Mothers* (New York: Praeger, 1974), p. 6). The last seems dubious given the bureau's commitment to women's domesticity.

90. Proceedings of an April 4, 1938, conference on the participation of African American women in federal welfare programs, also known as the White House Conference of the National Council of Negro Women, Bethune Archives, NCNW, Series 4, Box 1.

91. Grace Abbott argued strongly for the "budget system" against the FERA's preference for flat grants; see her "What About Mothers' Pensions Now?" *Survey* 70:3 (Mar. 19, 1934), pp. 80–81.

92. For a critique of the "children-first" strategy, see Gordon, "Putting Children First."

93. This explanation is offered by Archie Hanlan, "From Social Reform to Social Security," *Child Welfare* 45:11 (Nov. 1966), pp. 493–500.

94. On changes in federalism see Richard K. Caputo, *Welfare and Freedom American Style: The Role of the Federal Government, 1900–1940* (Lanham, Md.: University Press of America, 1991).

95. Joseph P. Harris, "Suggested Provisions in a Federal Bill Proving Grant-in-Aid to the States of [*sic*] Public Welfare Purposes and for Unemployment Insurance," n.d., Social Security Mss., Committee on Economic Security, Box 18.

96. Salamon, *Welfare*, p. 76; Jill Quadagno, "From Old Age Assistance to Supplemental Security Income: The Political Economy of Relief in the South, 1935–1972," in Margaret Weir, Ann Shola Orloff, and Theda Skocpol, eds., *The Politics of Social Policy in the United States* (Princeton, N.J.: Princeton University Press, 1988), pp. 235–63; Lee J. Alston and Joseph P. Ferrie, "Labor Costs, Paternalism, and Loyalty in Southern Agriculture: A Constraint on the Growth of the Welfare State," *Journal of Economic History* 45:1 (Mar. 1985), pp. 95–117; Schlabach, *Edwin E. Witte*, chap. 7; Altmeyer, *The Formative Years of Social Security*; Witte, *The Development of the Social Security Act*; Weiss, *Farewell to the Party of Lincoln*. For a contemporary recognition of this political reality at the state level, see Paul H. Douglas, "Social Security for Today," *The Christian Century*, Nov. 28, 1934, pp. 1515–17. Although it has frequently been argued that including farm workers and domestics in Social Security was impossible because of administrative difficulties, there are good reasons to question these arguments. First, as discussed in chap. 5, one should not take the "contributory" nature of old-age insurance as inevitable, since it could have been funded through taxes. Second, there were proposals to include these workers in contributory plans: for example, to collect workers' payments through the use of stamp books with stamps purchased from post offices; see Clegg Gray, *Black Female Domestics*, p. 99.

97. Orloff, "Gender and Early U.S. Social Policy," p. 20.

98. Bell, *Aid to Dependent Children*, pp. 29 ff.

99. "Tentative Redraft of Bill for Aid to Dependent Children," Dec. 17, 1936, in Social Security Mss., E, Box 273.

100. Salamon, *Welfare*, p. 77.

101. In February 1935 Lenroot had already drafted, at Altmeyer's request, a new version of ADC with fewer requirements of the states; Lenroot to Altmeyer, Social Security Mss., Committee on Economic Security, Box 29. By June 1, 1935, Joseph Harris, assistant director of the CES, wrote to Aubrey Williams, "We have long since given up the hope to get any strong supervisory power [over ADC programs] granted to the federal administrative agency"; Harris to Williams, June 1, 1935, in ibid., Box 60.

102. Bremer, *Depression Winters*, p. 89.

103. Bell, *Aid to Dependent Children*, pp. 33–35, 46, 107, 141. Bell found that the "farm policy" was responsible for 39–57 percent of the ejections of mothers from ADC rolls in Arkansas between 1953 and 1960.

104. Robert T. Lansdale, "The Impact of the Federal Social Security Act on Public Welfare Programs in the South," Research Reports in Social Science 4:1 (Feb. 1961), p. 37.

105. Some historians, and some contemporaries, viewed the Children's Bureau establishment, and, indeed, the whole Department of Labor, as opposed to federal programs and favoring state autonomy above all. This is an erroneous characterization. Abstracted from the experience and particular context of the Children's Bureau's work, it fails to capture their particular mixture of practical politics, leadership style, and welfarist vision. The Children's Bureau view was rather that federal control was not feasible, that the support of state welfare proponents and bureaucrats was needed to make Titles IV and V work, and that state programs could actually provide a useful base for the combination of casework and assistance which they proposed. They believed that a federal-state joint system could become increasingly coherent in part because it would rest on the national professional standards of social work. See Schlabach, *Edwin E. Witte*, pp. 114 ff.; "The Reminiscences of Eveline Mabel Burns."

106. For example, the Children's Bureau was pressed throughout the New Deal to hire a black person, without success. See correspondence in Children's Bureau Mss., Box 476, 0-2-9-1-0.

107. The 1935 CES study uncovered thirty-one other programs of federal aid to the states and the standards they imposed. It concluded that there had been a fairly consistent policy of setting forth federal standards, in such programs as the Morrill Acts of 1862 and 1890, establishing state agricultural colleges, the Highways Acts of 1916 and 1921, the forest fire prevention law of 1924, and the establishment of public employment offices by the Wagner-Peyser Act of 1933. "The Reminiscences of Katharine Fredrica Lenroot," p. 20; Mar. 14, 1935 Memo in Social Security Mss., Committee on Economic Security, Box 9.

108. Witte, "Statement Concerning Amendments To The Social Security Bill," n.d., in ibid., Box 11.

109. Brown, *Public Relief*, p. 309.
110. Harris to Williams, June 1, 1935, Social Security Mss., Committee on Economic Security, Box 60; misc. correspondence and memos in ibid., Box 9.
111. Witte to Wisconsin congressmen, "Possible Constructive Amendments," Apr. 1935, in ibid., Box 9. Witte was disregarded and in his memoir, published thirty years later, he said no change was made because "there was so little interest." This is an implausible diagnosis; more likely the penuriousness was deliberate, since what Witte preferred to call a "lack of interest" continued even after Perkins argued to the Finance Committee personally that the maximum on ADC should be eliminated. In fact Witte contradicted this analysis in the same paragraph: admitting that it was a mistake not to insist on the same federal matching share for ADC as in OAA, he justified the misjudgment by saying that the refusal to remove the maximum on ADC showed that there was reason to fear that Congress might cut out ADC altogether. Witte, *The Development of the Social Security Act*, pp. 164–65.
112. Their proposal was based on the precedent of the 1917 Smith-Hughes Act authorizing federal grant to state agricultural extension programs. Harris to Altmeyer, Feb. 28, 1935, and Harris to Hopkins, Feb. 28, 1935, Social Security Mss., Committee on Economic Security, Box 9.
113. Ibid.
114. For example, before the depression all but three states had mothers' aid laws but they operated in only 55 percent of counties. Brown, *Public Relief*, p. 27.
115. Bell, *Aid to Dependent Children*, pp. 21–22.
116. The depression deepened these contradictions: while high unemployment led many to condemn employed married women for stealing men's jobs, in fact women's employment grew in proportion to men's, because women's earnings were increasingly needed to support families. In the first three years of the Depression women's unemployment was higher than men's, but after 1932 this began to shift. By 1937 U.S. Women's Bureau reports showed decisively that unemployment was greater among men.
117. Kessler-Harris, *Out to Work*, chap. 9, summarizes these trends.
118. The greater the emphasis on casework, the more such jobs would have been professional; the greater the emphasis on preventing cheating, the more they would have been unskilled; the more universal benefits, the less administrative labor would have been necessary proportional to the caseload.
119. Several scholars who have argued for the impact of big business,

particularly of liberal and welfare capitalist orientation, on Social Security have suggested that this influence was responsible for the separate funding including a further tax on workers. See, for example, Edward D. Berkowitz and Kim McQuaid, *Creating the Welfare State: The Political Economy of 20th-Century Reform*, 2nd ed. (Lawrence: University Press of Kansas, 1992), pp. 132–33. Ann Orloff disputes this in *The Politics of Pensions: A Comparative Analysis of Britain, Canada, and the United States, 1880–1940* (Madison: University of Wisconsin Press, 1993), p. 292. Mark H. Leff, "Taxing the 'Forgotten Man': The Politics of Social Security Finance in the New Deal," *Journal of American History* 70 (Sept. 1983), pp. 359–81, argues that the separate tax for old-age insurance was developed because federal income tax was undeveloped: 95 percent of Americans paid no income tax in 1935. Berkowitz endorses this view in his *America's Welfare State from Roosevelt to Reagan*, p. 21.

120. Orloff, *Politics of Pensions*, p. 290.
121. *Second Annual Report of the Social Security Board* (Washington, D.C., 1937), p. 43.
122. Theda Skocpol, "The Narrow Vision of Today's Experts on Social Policy," *Chronicle of Higher Education*, Apr. 15, 1992, p. B1.
123. This campaign was so dramatic that it has been studied by several historians: Jerry R. Cates, *Insuring Inequality: Administrative Leadership in Social Security, 1935–54* (Ann Arbor: University of Michigan Press, 1983); Martha Derthick, *Policymaking for Social Security* (Washington, D.C.: Brookings Institution, 1979); Brian Balogh, "Security Support: The Emergence of the Social Security Board as a Political Actor, 1935–1939," in Donald T. Critchlow and Ellis Hawley, eds., *Federal Social Policy: The Historical Dimension* (University Park: Pennsylvania State University Press, 1988).
124. For a discerning understanding of this strategy, see Eveline Burns, "Amending the Social Security Act," *Independent Woman* 16:4 (Apr. 1937), pp. 108, 118.

Chapter 10. Welfare and Citizenship

1. Preexisting differences between the terms of mothers' aid and workman's compensation, for example, had already created two welfare tracks, as did differential treatment of various groups receiving relief; Barbara J. Nelson, "The Origins of the Two-Channel Welfare State: Workmen's Compensation and Mothers' Aid," in Linda Gordon, ed., *Women, the State, and Welfare* (Madison: University of Wisconsin Press, 1990), pp. 123–51.

2. They do not, however, all define its criteria identically: Michael Katz follows James Patterson in emphasizing that this stratification is a fundamental and unique characteristic of the U.S. welfare system. Patterson, *America's Struggle Against Poverty*, p. 76 Katz, *In the Shadow of the Poorhouse*, pp. 238–39. James Leiby characterizes the distinction thus: "Social insurance was the norm; public assistance—the heir of poor relief or public charity—was a supplement for cases that would fall outside the norm." James Leiby, *A History of Social Welfare and Social Work in the U.S.* (New York: Columbia University Press, 1978), p. 247. Samuel Mencher interprets the two tracks in terms of the classic status/contract distinction in political theory: The automatic entitlements, such as OAI, come from status while public assistance went only to those who qualified on an individual basis and were a privilege in exchange for which the recipient had responsibilities. Samuel Mencher, "Status and Contract in Assistance Policy, *Social Service Review* 25:1 (Mar. 1961), p. 18. This conceptualization does not, in fact, describe very well the distinction between, say, OAI and OAA. But it was then reformulated more helpfully by Mildred Rein: "Status assistance is group oriented, impersonal, requiring few ground rules and few mutual obligations. Contract assistance is individual, personal, complicated, and demanding." Mildred Rein, "Continuities in Assistance Policy," *Poverty and Human Resources Abstracts* 4:5 (Sept./Oct. 1969), p. 6. For a British view of the American two tracks, see David Willets, "Theories and Explanations of the Underclass," in David J. Smith, ed., *Understanding the Underclass* (London: Policy Studies Institute, 1992), p. 50. For a critique of the two-track analysis, see Ann Shola Orloff, "Gender and the Social Rights of Citizenship: The Comparative Analysis of Gender Relations and Welfare States," *American Sociological Review* 58:3 (June 1993), pp. 303–28.
3. In 1930 the figure was 6 percent of 2.7 million; in 1940, 5.1 percent of 1.9 million. See 15th Census, *Reports on Population*, vol. 5, "General Report on Occupations (1933), p. 40, table 3; and 16th Census, *Population*, vol. 3, "The Labor Force: Occupation, Industry, Employment and Income" (1943), part 1, p. 69, table 58. These figures are almost certainly *substantial* underestimates, because women who worked in agriculture were so likely to be not counted or categorized as housewives.
4. Diana Pearce, "Welfare Is Not *for* Women," in Linda Gordon, ed., *Women, the State, and Welfare* (Madison: University of Wisconsin Press, 1990), pp. 265–79.
5. The original federal contribution to the states was less for ADC than for the other assistance programs; the maximum ADC stipend was eighteen dollars per month for the first child—that is, for two people—while the OAA maximum was thirty dollars; ADC programs were put

into operation later than OAA; and only ADC recipients were subject to scrutiny of their "moral" lives in determining eligibility. By 1939 states were spending about four times as much for OAA as for ADC.

6. On the connections between the meanings of "welfare dependency" and women's status as dependents of husbands, see Nancy Fraser and Linda Gordon, "A Genealogy of *Dependency*: Tracing a Keyword of the U.S. Welfare State," *Signs* 19:2 (Winter 1994), pp. 309–36.

7. Eveline Burns, "Childhood Poverty and the Children's Allowance," in *Children's Allowances and the Economic Welfare of Children: The Report of a Conference* (New York: Citizens' Committee for Children of New York, Inc., 1968), p. 5.

8. Eveline M. Burns, *The American Social Security System* (Boston: Houghton Mifflin, 1949), pp. 34–35.

9. "Tentative Redraft of Bill for Aid to Dependent Children," Dec. 17, 1936, in Social Security Mss., E, Box 273.

10. Reynolds, *Uncharted Journey*, p. 140.

11. Charlotte Towle, *Common Human Needs: An Interpretation for Staff in Public Assistance Agencies* (Washington, D.C.: Social Security Board, Bureau of Public Assistance, 1945), pp. 11–26.

12. This requirement was extended to Old Age Assistance in 1939, another result of the campaign to make Old Age Insurance more advantageous.

13. Bell, *Aid to Dependent Children*, p. 88 and passim.

14. Ibid, chap. 7; Joel F. Handler and Yeheskel Hasenfeld, *The Moral Construction of Poverty: Welfare Reform in America* (Newbury Park, Calif.: Sage, 1991), esp. pp. 126–67.

15. Coll, "Public Assistance," pp. 230–31.

16. This interpretation is influenced by that of Piven and Cloward in *Why Americans Don't Vote*, esp. pp. 124–40, and Frances Fox Piven, "Structural Constraints and Political Development: The Case of the American Democratic Party," in Piven, ed., *Labor Parties in Postindustrial Societies* (N.Y.: Oxford University Press, 1992), pp. 235–64.

17. Crowning the South's power in the party were indirect elections through the electoral college, disproportional representation expressed in the power of the Senate, and the seniority system of Congress.

18. Southern voter turnout, by contrast, increased from 24 to 26 percent.

19. Patterson, *America's Struggle Against Poverty* pp. 76, 92–94; Sheldon Danziger, Robert Haveman, and Robert Plotnick, "Antipoverty Policy: Effects on the Poor and the Nonpoor," in Sheldon H. Danziger and Daniel H. Weinberg, eds., *Fighting Poverty: What Works and What Doesn't* (Cambridge, Mass.: Harvard University Press, 1986), pp. 66–67; Marcus D. Pohlman, "Profits, Welfare, and Class Position: 1965–1984," *Journal of Sociology and Social Welfare* 15:3 (Sept. 1988), pp. 3–28; Bernadetta Chachere, "Welfare and Poverty as Road-

blocks to the Civil Rights Goals of the 1980s," *Rutgers Law Review* 37:4 (Summer 1985), pp. 789–99.

20. Thomas F. Jackson, "The State, the Movement, and the Urban Poor: The War on Poverty and Political Mobilization in the 1960s," in Michael B. Katz, ed., *The "Underclass" Debate: Views from History* (Princeton, N.J.: Princeton University Press, 1993), pp. 403–39.
21. Michael R. Sosin, "Legal Rights and Welfare Change," in Danziger and Weinberg, eds., *Fighting Poverty*, p. 276.
22. Ralf Dahrendorf, *Law and Order* (London: Stevens & Sons, 1985), p. 98; Michael Walzer, "Exclusion, Injustice, and the Democratic State," *Dissent* (Winter 1993), pp. 55–64; Michael Walzer, *Spheres of Justice: A Defense of Pluralism and Equality* (New York: Basic Books, 1983).
23. Nancy Fraser and Linda Gordon, "Contract Versus Charity: Why Is There No Social Citizenship in the United States?" *Socialist Review* 22:3 (July–Sep. 1992), pp. 45–67.

Index

Leiserson, William Morris, 155, 156, 313
Lemke, William, 233
Lenroot, Katharine Fredrica, 78, 81, 83, 101, 103, 197, 206, 256, 259, 260, 268–270, 272, 308
Lesbianism, 79, 80
Liberals, 47
Life insurance, 28
Lincoln, Abraham, 242
Lindsay, Inabel Burns, 136, 310
Lindsay, Samuel McCune, 313
Lindsey, Benjamin, 313
Living wage, 53
Lobbying, 98, 138, 212
Loeb, Sophie Irene Simon, 86–87, 308
Long, Huey, 229–234, 236, 238, 239
Long, Russell, 230
Los Angeles, California, 49, 50, 186
Lothropp, John, 68
Lovejoy, Owen, 313
Lowenstein, Solomon, 219
Lundberg, Emma Octavia, 308
Lundeen, Ernest, 236, 240
Lundeen Bill (Workers' Bill), 236–241, 251, 268, 282
Lurie, Harry, 313
Lyle, Ethel Hedgman, 310
Lynching, 116–118, 132, 213, 251, 293

Macy, Valentine, 313
Maggard, Curtis, 244
Maher, Amy, 73, 308
Malkiel, Theresa, 56
Mallory, Arenia Cornelia, 124, 310
Malone, Annie M. Turnbo, 137, 310
Marine Workers Industrial Union, 218
Marsh, Vivian Osborne, 311
Marshall, T. H., 181
Martin, Anna, 57
Mason, Lucy Randolph, 308
Maternal and infant health services, 253, 254, 256–258, 267
Maternalism, 38, 55–56, 103, 104, 126–127, 130, 135, 136, 141, 161, 195, 196, 260, 273, 280, 290, 306

Maternal mortality, 94
Matthews, Victoria Earle, 122, 311
Mays, Sadie Gray, 311
McCormick, Medill, 83
McCormick, Ruth Hanna, 83
McDougald, G. Elsie Johnson (Ayer), 130, 311
McDowell, Mary Eliza, 164, 308
McGroaty, John, 228
McGorey, Mary Jackson, 311
McKane, Alice Woodby, 311
McKelway, Alexander Jeffrey, 313
McKinley, William, 242
McLain movement, 225
McMain, Eleanor Laura, 309
Mead, George Herbert, 171
Means-testing, 128, 129, 141, 149, 166, 192, 222, 273, 281, 282, 297, 305
Merriam, Frank, 226
Merriam, Ida, 169, 259
Merritt, Emma Frances Grayson, 311
Mexican Americans, 48, 88, 196
Midwives, 125
Milbank Fund, 104, 250
Miller, Frieda Segelke, 77, 309
Miller, Lucy, 140
Minimum wage 75, 100, 106, 138
Mink, Gwendolyn, 48–49, 195
Mississippi Health Project, 125, 139
Mitchell, Joseph, 140
Moley, Raymond, 234
Moralistic interpretations of single motherhood, 16–17, 28–29
Morality/respectability, 28, 29, 33, 130–132, 298–299
Morals-testing, 51, 129, 141, 149, 192, 273, 282, 298–299
Morris, R. C., 249
Mortality rates, 19, 30, 69, 77, 94, 104
Moskowitz, Belle Israels, 74, 97, 309
Mossell, Gertrude, 132
Mothers' aid (pensions), 28, 37–43, 45–57, 59–64, 67, 68, 96, 104, 114, 159, 165, 166, 177, 185–186, 189, 193, 257, 268
Mumford, Lewis, 250

Murphy, J. Prentice, 313
Muscle Shoals, 98
Mutual benefit societies, 115–116

National Annuity League, 225
National Association for the Advance-
    ment of Colored People
    (NAACP), 87, 117, 137, 138
National Association of Colored
    Women (NACW), 112, 118, 119,
    126, 133, 138
National Association of Wage Earners,
    136, 137
National Child Labor Committee, 89,
    90
National Christian Mission, 133
National Conference of Charities and
    Corrections (NCCC), 39–41,
    154, 168
National Conference of Social Work
    (NCSW), 106, 187, 209, 218, 270
National Congress of Mothers
    (NCM), 61–63, 90
National Consumers' League (NCL),
    61, 75, 77, 90, 99, 101, 104,
    159, 212, 259
National Council of Negro Women
    (NCNW), 138, 139
National Economic and Social Plan-
    ning Association, 250
National Federation of Settlements,
    87, 259
National Industrial Recovery Act
    (NIRA) of 1933, 190, 217
National Recovery Administration
    (NRA), 77, 190, 195
National Retail Dry Goods Associa-
    tion, 250
National Training School for Girls,
    Washington, D.C., 124, 133, 137
National Union for Social Justice, 232,
    233
National Welfare Rights Organization
    (NWRO), 212, 303
National Woman's Party (NWP), 54,
    55, 70, 77, 99, 213
National Youth Administration
    (NYA), 190

Nativism, 47
Needs, as basis for welfare, 10–11,
    160–167
Negro Elks, 121
Negro Health Movement, 130
Neighborhood Union, Atlanta, 125
Nelson, Alice Ruth Dunbar, 311
Neuberger, Richard, 228
Neustadt, Richard, 150
New Deal, 3, 4, 28, 63, 77 88, 93, 96,
    101, 102, 104, 107, 112, 114,
    117, 139, 155, 162, 188–207,
    209–251, 299–301
Newman, Pauline, 54, 309
New Negro Manhood Movement, 112
New York City, influence of, 73–74,
    188–189
New York Department of Public Wel-
    fare, 186
New York State Commission on
    Relief for Widowed Mothers,
    27–28, 41
Night work, 22, 23, 50
Nordholm, Alex, 238

Ogburn, W. F., 171, 174
"Ohio plan," 155–156
Old-Age Assistance (OAA), 44, 256, 283
Old-Age Insurance (OAI), or old-age
    pensions, 4, 5, 7, 225–230, 234,
    242, 253, 256, 274, 282–284,
    293–295, 298, 302
Old people's homes, 124
Orphanages, 23, 52
"Our Illusions Concerning Govern-
    ment" (Van Kleeck), 210, 221
Ovington, Mary White, 87

Paine, Thomas, 160
Park, Robert, 171, 174
Paternalism, 55, 161–162
Patriarchy, 6–7, 13, 19, 21, 85, 179
Pauperization, 175, 177, 246
Pennsylvania School of Social and
    Health Work, 250
Perkins, Frances, 54, 73, 74, 88, 93,
    106, 191, 200, 203–207, 228,
    258, 266, 270, 271, 309